Originally published in 1798
by J. Mundell & Co., London

Reprinted 1969 by
Negro Universities Press
A DIVISION OF GREENWOOD PUBLISHING CORP.
NEW YORK

Library of Congress Catalogue Card Number 69-18996

SBN 8371-1554-X

PRINTED IN UNITED STATES OF AMERICA

CONTENTS.

VOL. IV.

BOOK XI.

BOOK XII.

BOOK XIII.

CONTENTS.

A
PHILOSOPHICAL AND POLITICAL
HISTORY
OF THE
SETTLEMENTS AND TRADE
OF THE
EUROPEANS
IN THE
EAST AND WEST INDIES.

BOOK XI.

The Europeans go into Africa to purchase Slaves to culti-
vate the Caribbee Islands. The manner of conduct-
ing this species of Commerce. Produce arising from
the labour of the Slaves.

WE have seen immense countries invaded and laid
waste; their innocent and peaceable inhabitants either
massacred or loaded with chains; a dreadful solitude
established upon the ruins of a numerous population;
ferocious usurpers destroying one another, and heap-
ing their dead bodies upon those of their victims.
What is to be the result of so many enormities? They
will still be repeated, and they will be followed by
one, which, though it may not produce so much
bloodshed, will nevertheless be more shocking to humanity : this is the traffic of man, sold and purchased by his fellow-creature. The islands of America

BOOK
XI.

The Euro-
peans set-
tled in the
American
islands pro-
cure culti-
vators from
Africa.

B O O K have firſt ſuggeſted the idea of this abominable trade,
    XI.   and we ſhall now ſee in what manner this misfortune
hath been brought about.

Certain reſtleſs fugitives, the greateſt part of whom
had either been diſgraced by the laws of their country, or ruined by their exceſſes, in this ſtate of deſpe-
ration, formed a deſign of attacking Spaniſh or Portugueſe ſhips that were richly laden with the ſpoils
of the New World. Some deſert iſlands, whoſe ſituation enſured ſucceſs to theſe piracies, ſerved at firſt
for a place of rendezvous to theſe robbers, and ſoon
became their country. Habituated to murder, they
meditated the maſſacre of a plain and unſuſpecting
people, who had received and treated them with humanity ; and the civilized nations, of which theſe
free-booters were the refuſe, adopted this infamous
ſcheme without heſitation ; which was immediately
put in execution. It then became neceſſary to conſider what advantages might accrue from ſo many
enormities. Gold and ſilver, which were ſtill looked
upon as the ſole valuable productions to be derived
from America, had either never exiſted in ſeveral of
theſe new acquiſitions, or were no longer to be found
there in ſufficient quantities to expect any conſiderable emoluments from working the mines. Certain
ſpeculative men, leſs blinded by their prejudices than
the multitude generally are, imagined, that a ſoil and
climate, ſo totally different from ours, might either
furniſh us with commodities to which we were ſtrangers, or which we were obliged to purchaſe at an exorbitant price : they therefore determined to apply
themſelves to the culture of them. There were ſome
obſtacles, apparently inſurmountable, to the execution of this plan. The ancient inhabitants of the
country were now entirely deſtroyed ; and had they
not been ſo, the weakneſs of their conſtitutions, their
habit of eaſe and indolence, and their invincible averſion for labour, would ſcarce have rendered them fit
inſtruments to execute the deſigns of their oppreſſors.
Theſe barbarians too, born in a temperate clime,

could not fupport the laborious works of agriculture B O O K
under a burning and unwholefome fky. Self-inte- XI.
reft, ever fruitful in expedients, fuggefted the plan of
feeking cultivators in Africa, a country in which the
abominable and inhuman cuftom of felling its inhabitants hath ever prevailed.

Africa is an immenfe region, connected to Afia only
by a narrow neck of land of twenty leagues, called
the Ifthmus of Suez. This natural and political boundary muft fooner or later be broken down by the
ocean, from that tendency it is obferved to have of
forming gulfs and ftraits eaftward. This peninfula,
cut by the equator into two unequal parts, forms an
irregular triangle, one of the fides of which fronts
the eaft, the other the north, and the third the weft.

The eaftern fide, which extends from Suez nearly Opinions
as far as the Cape of Good Hope, is wafhed by the concerning
Red Sea and the ocean. The inland parts of the coaft of
country are but little known, and what has been dif- Africa.
covered of them can neither excite the mercenary
views of the trader, the curiofity of the traveller, nor
the humanity of the philofopher. Even the miffion-
aries, after having made fome progrefs in thefe countries, efpecially in Abyffinia, totally difcouraged by
the treatment they met with, have abandoned thefe
people to their inconftancy and perfidy. The coafts
are in general only dreadful rocks, or a wafte of dry
and burning fand. Thofe portions which are fit for
cultivation, are parcelled out among the natives of
the country, the Arabs, the Portuguefe, and the
Dutch. Their commerce, which confifts only in a
little ivory or gold, and fome flaves, is connected with
that of the Eaft Indies.

The northern fide, which extends from the Ifthmus of Suez to the Straits of Gibraltar, is bounded
by the Mediterranean. On this fide, nine hundred
leagues of coaft are occupied by a country, which
hath for feveral centuries been known by the name
of Barbary ; and by Egypt, which is under the yoke
of the Ottoman empire.

B O O K
XI.

Opinions
concerning
the nor-
thern coaft
of Africa,
and of
Egypt in
particular.

This great province is bounded by the Red Sea on the eaft, by Nubia on the fouth, by the deferts of Barca, or by Lybia on the weft, and on the north by the Mediterranean. It is about two hundred and twelve leagues long from north to fouth. A break of rocks, and a chain of mountains, running almoft in the fame direction, prevent it from being more than fix or feven leagues broad as far as Cairo. From that capital to the fea the country defcribes a triangle, the bafis of which is one hundred leagues. This triangle includes another, known by the name of Delta, and formed by two branches of the Nile, which empty themfelves into the Mediterranean, one of them at the diftance of a league from Rofetto, and the other of two from Damietta.

Although this be a burning region, yet the climate is in general healthy ; the only infirmity peculiar to Egypt is, the two frequent lofs of fight. This calamity is thought to be occafioned by a fine kind of fand, which is fcattered about in May and June by the fouth winds. Would it not be more reafonable to attribute it to the cuftom thofe people have of fleeping in the open air nine months in the year? This opinion will be readily admitted, fince it is obferved, that thofe who pafs the night in their houfes, or under tents, feldom experience fo great a misfortune.

There are few countries on the face of the globe fo fruitful as Egypt. The foil yields annually three crops, which require but one tillage. Vegetables fucceed corn, and thefe are followed by pot-herbs ; this happy fertility is owing to the Nile.

That river, the fource of which is in Ethiopia, owes its increafe to clouds, which falling down in rain, occafion its periodical fwell. It begins in the month of June, and augments till the end of September, at which time it gradually decreafes. Its waters, after having traverfed an immenfe fpace without dividing, are feparated five leagues above Cairo, into two branches, which meet no more.

A country, however, where nothing is fo feldom

met with as a fpring, and where rain is an extraordi- B O O K XI.
nary phenomenon, could only have been fertilized
by the Nile. Accordingly, from times of the moft
remote antiquity, fourfcore confiderable canals were
digged at the entrance of the kingdom, befide a great
number of fmall ones, which diftributed thefe waters
all over Egypt. Except five or fix of the deepeft,
they are all dry at the beginning, or towards the middle of winter; but then the foil no longer requires
watering. If it fhould happen, that the river hath
not fwelled to the height of four hundred inches, the
lower grounds are only watered. The others, to
which their wells, conftructed with fwing-gates, or
with wheels, become ufelefs, are confidered as barren, and freed for that year of all impofts.

The grounds are divided into three claffes. That
which is confidered as the firft of them, is the one
which forms the Vakoups, or domain allotted to the
mofques, or other religious eftablifhments. It is the
worft cultivated of any of the grounds, and that which
is more fpared in the taxes by an ignorant and fuperftitious government.

The principal civil and military officers of the ftate
enjoy the profits of the fecond clafs. They leave
very little to the bondfmen, who till the grounds with
the fweat of their brows; and they feldom pay into
the treafury the taxes they are indebted to it.

The third clafs is divided between a greater number of plain citizens, whofe poffeffions, more or lefs
extenfive, are cultivated by active and intelligent
farmers. Thefe grounds compofe the wealth of Egypt,
and become the refource of the public treafury.

Though one third of the grounds be left untilled,
yet the country is not depopulated. It is reckoned
to contain five or fix millions of inhabitants, the moft
numerous of which are the Cophts, who derive their
origin from the ancient Egyptians, to whom they have
no fmall fhare of refemblance. Some of them have
fubmitted to the yoke of the Koran, the reft have remained fubject to the Gofpel. They occupy, almoft

exclufively, all the Upper Egypt, and are very numerous in the Lower ; feveral of them are cultivators,
but more of them profefs the arts. The moft intelligent among them fuperintend the affairs of rich
families, or ferve as fecretaries to men in office. When
they have obtained thefe pofts, which are deemed
honourable, they foon acquire an abfolute fway over
mafters enervated by the climate and by luxury. This
kind of power foon leads them to the poffeffion of
wealth, which they generally fquander in the moft
infamous exceffes. If motives of avarice fhould have
made them abftain from the purfuit of pleafure, they
are deprived of their riches before the clofe of a turbulent life, by the tyrants whom thy had deceived.
Children are fcarce ever known to inherit the fortune
of their fathers.

The moft numerous race after the Cophts, is that
of the Arabs. Thefe defcendants of a people, who
were formerly a conquering nation, all live in a ftate
of the utmoft ignominy. In this abject condition,
their actions are never animated with fpirit, and they
have never been known to take any part in the revolutions with which this country is fo frequently agitated. Their mafters confider them only in the light
of animals that are neceffary for cultivation. Their
lives and their fortunes are arbitrarily difpofed of,
while thefe acts of injuftice and cruelty have never
brought down the vengeance of government upon
the offenders. Thefe unfortunate people have a particular drefs, they dwell in the fields, intermarry with
one another, and fcarce live upon any thing but vegetables and milk. If there be any among them who
are able to indulge in a few conveniencies, they would
not dare to do it, from the apprehenfion of expofing
themfelves to the rifk of being taken notice of, which
might, fooner or later, become fatal to them.

The remainder of the population is compofed of
Turks, Jews, and Armenians, and of men of divers
countries and fects, who have fucceffively fettled in
Egypt. Thefe foreigners, whatever be the reafon of

it, feldom leave a numerous pofterity, and their de- BOOK
fcendants are not more fortunate. This humiliating XI.
fterility, however, is chiefly obferved among the Mamelucs.

In vain have thefe Circaffians, or Georgians, been
chofen in their youth from among the moft healthy men
in their provinces. In vain have the moft beautiful
wives of their country been beftowed upon them.
In vain have they been all kept in a ftate of plenty,
freed from the apprehenfions of want, and from every
anxiety. Scarce any children iffue from thefe well-
adapted connections, and the few that are born die
within the year. Only two families are known to be
the defcendants of this race, and they have yet reached no further than to the fecond generation.

The government of Egypt differs from every other.
Before the invafion of the Turks, this region was
under the fway of a chief, who was chofen by foldiers,
all born in flavery, and who fhared his authority with
him. Selim would undoubtedly have been defirous
to fubmit this new conqueft to the fame defpotifm as
his other provinces; but circumftances were not favourable to this ambitious defign. He was obliged
to content himfelf with the rights of the dethroned
Soldan, and to leave his haughty lieutenants in poffeffion of the prerogatives they had for fo long a time
enjoyed. The Sultan fent into Egypt fourteen thoufand of his beft troops, in order to counterbalance
this formidable militia. Far from attending to the
interefts of the Port, this corps employed themfelves
only about their own. They foon acquired fufficient
influence to have every thing determined by their
caprice; and they maintained the afcendant they
had gained, till growing effeminate by the climate,
they were no longer able to maintain a power which
was not fixed on any kind of bafis. It paffed again
into the hands of the Mamelucs, and that in a more
extenfive manner than ever.

This fingular dynafty is compofed of ten or twelve
thoufand flaves, brought from Georgia and Circaffia

B O O K when they were very young. They enter into the
XI.   fervice of the great men of their nation, who have,
like them, been all in a ftate of flavery, and who,
fooner or later, give them their freedom. Thefe
freedmen are obferved to rife from one poft to another,
till they attain to the rank of Bey, which is the higheft of all.

Thefe Beys govern the twenty-four provinces of
the kingdom. Their number feldom exceeds fixteen
or feventeen, becaufe the moft refolute among them
are in poffeffion of more than one government, and
becaufe fome feeble diftricts of Upper Egypt have
been intrufted to Arabian Chieks from time immemorial. Although they ought all to be of equal rank,
the Bey who governs the capital moft commonly affumes an authority over the reft, unlefs he be fup-
planted by fome one of his colleagues, richer, more
powerful, or more artful than himfelf. But whether
the equilibrium be maintained or not, the free Turks
never obtain any but civil or ecclefiaftical employments. The military dignities, the offices of government, and all the higheft honours, are deftined only
for thofe who have lived in fervitude. The Divan,
which is compofed of the Beys and of their creatures,
is the real fovereign. The Pacha, who reprefents the
Sultan, receives homage, and orders are even given
in his name ; but they are dictated to him by infolent
flaves. If he fhould refufe to do what is required of
him, he is depofed, and leads a retired life, till the
feraglio hath either fentenced him to death or recalled
him.

The Mamelucs conftitute the real force of Egypt.
As they are all born in either a rough or a temperate
climate, and as they have received an auftere education, they form different troops of cavalry, which are
divided among the Beys, in proportion to the degree
of influence, or the ambition of thofe chiefs, and the
greater or lefs eftimation they are holden in. Thefe
powerful men difpofe of the Turkifh infantry in a
manner almoft as abfolute. This infantry is effemi-

nate, and hath entirely loft its military fpirit. It is fcarce compofed of any but peaceable tradefmen, who caufe their names to be regiftered, in order to enjoy the prerogatives attached to the name of a fol-dier. But whatever it may be, its officers are en-tirely dependent upon the Beys, without whofe pro-tection they would not be able to obtain promotion.

Befide the contributions in kind, which are fent as an offering from the Grand Signior to Mecca and Medina, which he caufes to be diftributed among the troops, feveral impofts are raifed in coin. The lands pay a tribute, and the Chriftians a poll-tax. The monopoly of caffia, fenna, and fal-ammoniac, is fold very dear. The cuftoms produce a great deal. Thefe objects united amount at leaft to ten millions of livres [416,666l. 13s. 4d.], of which there is feldom more than a fourth part conveyed to Conftantinople. The chief Bey retains the remainder, or divides it with colleagues, if he be not able to keep it all.

The intereft of the Pacha is not more attended to than that of the Sultan. Even the militia feldom receive their entire pay; and citizens of all ranks are habitually plundered.

Such numerous vexations could not have been fup-ported, had it not been for the refources derived from a very advantageous foreign trade, to which feveral ports are laid open. There are two in Alexandria, which formerly, it is faid, communicated with each other, and are at prefent feparated by a very narrow flip of land: The eaftern, or New Port, is of eafier accefs than the other; but is almoft filled up by the ballaft of the fhips, which it is cuftomary to fling into it. It is not a century fince the veffels were faf-tened to the quay; but they are now at the diftance of more than two hundred toifes from it. The fpace which they can occupy is fo narrow, that it is ne-ceffary to fix them with feveral anchors, to prevent their fhocking each other; and even this precaution is not always fufficient. It happens very often in ftormy weather, that thefe veffels run foul of thofe that are near them, and drag them along with them into flats, where they are miferably foundered together.

The weftern, or Old Harbour, is large and commodious. Men of war and merchantmen are equally fecure in it ; but the Europeans are excluded from it. Jealoufy hath induced the Turkifh navigators to invent a prophecy, which announces, that the city will fall into the hands of the Chriftians, whenever their fhips are admitted into that fine harbour.

Bequees is four leagues diftant from this place. It carries on no trade ; and is never frequented except when the winds prevent the fhips from getting to Alexandria, or from entering the Nile. Its harbour is very fmall, but exceedingly good ; men of war would be fheltered from all danger there even in winter.

The merchandifes which are carried down the river upon boats, that are called *macks*, and brought up again as far as the laft cataract, or the fouthern extremity of Egypt, are landed at Rozetto, one league diftant from the weftern mouth of the Nile. The provifions are conveyed from the town itfelf to the fhips, which are at no great diftance, upon larger boats, known in that country by the name of *germes*.

A fimilar ftaple, but infinitely more confiderable, hath been formed near the eaftern mouth of the river at Damietta. This, perhaps, was formerly a harbour ; but at prefent the veffels are obliged to anchor in the open fea, at two leagues from the coaft, upon a good bottom. If they are driven from thence by ftormy weather, which is rather frequent in thefe latitudes in the winter, they take refuge in the harbours of Cyprus, from whence they return to their poft when the danger is over.

Seven or eight hundred Turkifh, Barbary, or Chriftian fhips, or fuch as belong to the Chriftians, which trade for thefe people, arrive annually in Egypt. One hundred and forty, or one hundred and fifty of them, come from Syria, feventy or fourfcore from Conftantinople, fifty or fixty from Smyrna, thir-

ty or forty from Salonica, twenty-five or thirty from
Candia, and all the reft from fome iflands, or from
fome parts of the continent, which are lefs opulent
and lefs fruitful. Their cargoes are valued, one with
another, at 30,000 livres [1250l]. If we fuppofe
there are feven hundred and fifty veffels, the country
confumes to the amount of 22,500,000 livres [937,500l.]
of the productions brought by thefe traders. But it
delivers above double that fum, in rice, coffee, flax,
cloths, corn, vegetables, and in other articles. It
muft therefore receive 22,500,000 livres [937,500l.]
in money.

The connections of the Europeans with Egypt are
not fo lucrative. The people among them by whom
they are carried on, fell woollen cloths, gildings, filk
ftuffs, iron, lead, tin, paper, cochineal, hardware,
and glafs; and receive in exchange rice, coffee, faf-
fron, ivory, gums, cotton, fenna, caffia, fpun thread,
and fal-ammoniac.

In 1776, the importations of the Venetians were
reduced to 755,035 livres [31,459l. 15s. 10d.], and
their exports to 820,062 livres [34,169l. 5s.]. The
importations of the Tufcans and the Englifh, who
trade to Leghorn, did not exceed 2,143,660 livres
[89,319l. 3s. 4d.], nor their exports 2,099,635 livres
[87,484l. 15s.]. The importations of the French did
not exceed 3,997,615 livres [166,567l. 5s. 10d.], nor
their exports 3,075,450 livres [128,143l. 15s.]. The
total importation did not therefore amount to more
than 6,896,310 livres [287,346l. 5s.], and the exportation to more than 5,995,147 livres [249,797l. 16s.
10d.].

All the merchandife either bought or fold by the
Europeans pay a duty of three per cent. This tax
amounts to fix per cent. for coffee, and to ten per
cent. for rice, the exportation of which is prohibited.
This impofition is for the profit of two fhips fent every year from the Dardanelles to guard the coafts of
Egypt from the depredations of the pirates, and which

are of no other ufe but to opprefs the traders, and to
encourage fmuggling.

Europe employs one hundred veffels in this trade ;
but only fifty or fixty of them return immediately to
the ports from whence they were difpatched. The
others enter into the fervice of any people who choofe
to employ them in the Levant.

Summer is the moft favourable feafon for failing
from Europe to Egypt ; the voyages are fhortened
by the weft or north winds which blow almoft continually at that time. Spring and autumn are the
moft proper feafons for returning. The navigation is
very dangerous during winter upon thefe coafts, which
are fo low, that land is not difcovered at two leagues
diftance, if the day be in the leaft dark, or the fky
cloudy.

If Egypt fhould ever emerge from the ftate of
anarchy in which it is plunged ; if an independent
government fhould be formed there ; and if the new
conftitution fhould be founded upon wife laws, that
region will again become what it formerly was, one
of the moft induftrious and fertile countries of the
earth. It would be abfurd to foretel the fame profperity to Lybia, which is inhabited at prefent by the
people of Barbary.

Revolu-
tions in
Lybia.
The early periods of this extenfive country are in-
volved in the greateft obfcurity ; nor was any light
thrown upon their hiftory till the arrival of the Car-
thaginians. Thefe merchants, originally of Phœni-
cian extraction, about a hundred and thirty-feven
years before the foundation of Rome, built a city, the
territory of which, at firft very limited, in procefs of
time extended to all that country known by the name
of the kingdom of Tunis, and afterwards much further. Spain, and the greateft part of the iflands in
the Mediterranean, fell under its dominion. Many
other kingdoms muft apparently have ferved to aggrandize this enormous power, when her ambitious
views interfered with thofe of Rome. At the time of

this dreadful collifion, a war between thefe two nations was inftantly kindled, and carried on with fuch
obftinacy and fury, that it was eafy to forefee it would
not terminate but in the utter deftruction of the one
or the other. Rome, which was now in the height
of its republican and patriotic principles, after many
ftubborn engagements, in which the greateft military fkill was difplayed, obtained a decifive fuperiority
over that which was corrupted by its riches. The
commercial people became the flaves of the warlike
power.

The conquerors maintained themfelves in the poffeffion of their conquefts, till about the middle of the
fifth century. The Vandals, then hurried on by
their original impetuofity beyond the limits of Spain,
of which they were mafters, paffed the Pillars of Her-
cules, and, like an inundation, diffufed themfelves
over the country of Lybia. Thefe conquerors would
certainly have preferved the advantages they had acquired by their irruptions, had they kept up that military fpirit which their king Genferic had infpired
them with. But with this barbarian, who was not
deftitute of genius, this fpirit became extinct; military difcipline was relaxed, and the government,
which refted only on this bafis, was overthrown. Be-
lifarius furprifed thefe people in this confufion, extir-
pated them, and re-eftablifhed the empire in its ancient privileges. But this revolution was only momentary. Great men, who can form and bring to
maturity a rifing nation, cannot impart youth and vigour to an ancient and decayed people.

This is accounted for from a variety of reafons, all
of them equally ftriking. The founder of an empire
addreffes himfelf to an inexperienced man, who is
fenfible of his misfortune, and difpofed, by the continuance of it, to docility. He hath only to difplay
the appearance of, and the character of benevolence,
to be attended to, obeyed, and cherifhed. Daily experience adds to the perfonal confidence he infpires,
and gives influence to his counfel. The fuperiority

B O O K of his judgment is foon neceffarily acknowledged.
XI. His precepts of virtue muft ever acquire a greater degree of force, in proportion to the fimplicity of his
difcipline. It is not difficult for him to depreciate
vice, of which the guilty perfon is the firft victim. He
attacks openly fuch prejudices only as he expects to
eradicate. He trufts to time for the fubverfion of the
reft ; and the fuccefs of his projects is enfured by the
impoffibility of difcovering their tendency. His policy fuggefts to his imagination a variety of meafures,
calculated to excite aftonifhment and to procure him
veneration. He then gives his orders, and his commands are occafionly fanctified by the authority of
Heaven. He is high-prieft and legiflator during his
life, and at his death altars are erected to him ; he is
invoked ; he is a god. The fituation of the reftorer
of a corrupted nation is very different. He is an
architect, who propofes to build upon a fpace covered
with ruins ; he is a phyfician, who attempts to cure a
mortified carcafe ; he is a wife man, who preaches
reformation to a hardened people. He can expect
nothing but hatred and perfecution from the prefent,
and will not live to fee the future generation. He
will reap few advantages, with a great deal of labour,
during his life, and will obtain nothing but fruitlefs
regret after his death. A nation is only regenerated
in a fea of blood. It is the image of old Efon, whofe
youth Medea could renew by no other mode, except
that of cutting him to pieces and boiling him. It is
not in the power of one man to raife a fallen nation.
It appears that this muft be the refult of a long feries
of revolutions. The man of genius doth not live long
enough, and leaves no fucceffors.

In the feventh century, the Saracens, formidable in
their inftitutions and their fuccefs, armed with the
fword and with the Koran, obliged the Romans,
weakened by their divifions, to repafs the feas, and
augmented with the acceffion of the northern part of
Africa, that vaft dominion Mohammed had juft founded with fo much glory. The lieutenants of the Ca-

liphs afterwards deprived their masters of these rich spoils, and erected the provinces intrusted to their care into independent states.

This division, with respect to strength and power, inspired the Turks with the ambition of making themselves masters of this territory. Their success was perhaps more rapid than they had expected ; but a new revolution soon reduced these considerable conquests to very trifling advantages.

The Pachas, or Viceroys, intrusted with the care of the conquered countries, carried along with them that spirit of rapine, of which their nation had left such indelible traces. They were not the people alone who were exposed to perpetual pillage ; the oppression was also extended to the troops, although they were all Ottoman. These soldiers, who were more inclined to commit acts of injustice than to put up with them, represented to the Port, that the Moors and Arabs, irritated by repeated acts of tyranny, were ripe for a rebellion ; that Spain, on her part, was preparing for an immediate invasion ; and that the army, being incomplete and ill paid, had it neither in their inclination nor in their power to prevent these troublesome events. There was but one effectual method discovered to escape so many calamities ; this was the founding of a particular government, which, under the protection of the seraglio, and paying a tribute to it, would itself provide for its maintenance and for its defence. Algiers, Tunis, and Tripoli, were put under a similar legislation, which is a species of aristocracy. The chief, who, under the title of Dey, governs the republic, is elected by the soldiers, who are always Turkish, and constitute the only nobility of the country. These elections are seldom made without bloodshed ; and it is no unusual thing for a man, who hath been elected in the midst of riot and slaughter, to be afterwards assassinated by a restless faction, who design either to secure that distinction for themselves, or to sell it for their advancement. The empire of Morocco, though hereditary,

B O O K is fubjected to the fame revolutions. We are going
XI.   to fee to what ftate of degradation this anarchy hath
reduced a great part of the globe.

Prefent   The ftate of Tripoli is bounded by Egypt on one
condition
of Tripoli. fide, and by Tunis on the other, and extends two
hundred aud thirty leagues along the coaft. Though
the territory be not very fertile, yet the population
might be eafily increafed ten fold, becaufe the abundance of fifh might fupply the deficiency of crops,
and thefe might alfo be improved by additional labour. The inland part of the country is nothing but
a defert. We meet only, at a diftance from each
other, fome Moorifh and Arabian families, fettled in
the few places where they difcovered land enough to
furnifh them with a moderate fubfiftence. At thirty
days journey from the capital, is fituated the miferable and tributary kingdom of Fez, the inhabitants of
which are black. The little intercourfe the countries
maintain with each other, can only be kept up through
dry and moveable fands, where water is feldom to be
met with. The republic may enjoy a revenue of
2,000,000 livres [83,333l. 6s. 8d.], from the palm-
trees, the wells that are in the country, the cuftoms,
and the mint.

The caravans of the Gadamies, and of Tombuto,
formerly carried a great deal of gold to Tripoli ; but
they have not lately been fo rich or fo conftant. The
caravan of Morocco ftill continues to call there in its
way to and from Mecca, that place which is fo much
revered by the Muffulmen ; but, as the number of
pilgrims hath evidently decreafed, this paffage is no
longer fo ufeful. For thefe reafons, the trade which
is carried on by land is reduced to nothing, or to very
little.

That which is carried on by fea is rather more confiderable. The navigators of the Levant fometimes take
in their cargoes from fome of the indifferent harbours
fcattered along that immenfe coaft, but moft of them
make their purchafes and fales in the harbour of the
capital, which is much better than the reft, and in

which are collected all the foreign merchandise, as well as thofe of the country. Although thefe operations be not very important, yet the connections of the republic with Europe are ftill more infignificant.

No people, except the Tufcans and Venetians, maintain any conftant intercourfe with Tripoli; and yet the mercantile articles of the former are not fold for more than 140,000 livres [5833l. 6s. 8d.], and thofe of the latter do not amount to 200,000 livres [8333l. 6s. 8d.]. The former have remained fubject to all the formalities of the cuftoms; 'the fecond have freed themfelves from them, by paying annually 55,500 livres [2312l. 10s.] to the treafury. The French have difdained to have any fhare in this bargain, though their fovereign hath not difcontinued to fend an agent to Tripoli.

Of all the Barbary ftates, Tripoli was for a long time the one which had the moft numerous and the beft armed privateers. They always failed from the capital, which bears the fame name as the kingdom.

This town, which hath long been fufpected of being the ancient Orea, on account of its magnificent ruins, and of a beautiful aqueduct in great prefervation, and which muft at leaft have been a Greek or Roman colony, is fituated on the borders of the fea, in a plain which only produces dates, and where neither fprings nor rivers are to be found. It was one of the firft pofts occupied by the Arabians, who entered into Lybia through Egypt. The Spaniards took it in 1510, and eighteen years after, it was given by the Emperor Charles V. to the Knights of Malta, in whofe hands it remained only till the year 1551. It hath fince been twice bombarded by the French; but the boldnefs of thefe pirates hath not been in the leaft reftrained by thefe chaftifements. The decline, and fubfequent ruin of its maritime forces, have been entirely brought about by the civil commotions by which this unfortunate country hath been inceffantly fubverted.

Tunis hath likewife neglected its military navy, fince the time that the regency hath concluded treaties with the northern powers, and fince Corfica hath fallen under the dominion of the French. It was found that the value of the prizes was hardly fufficient to reimburfe the expences of fitting out, and fcarce any other veffels have been preferved, except fuch as were thought neceffary to protect the coafts from the invafions of the Maltefe.

The land forces have experienced no diminution. Five or fix thoufand Turks, or Chriftian renegadoes, conftitute the firmeft fupport of the republic.

Their children, under the name of Couloris, form a fecond troop; they are put upon pay as foon as they are born, and the firft payment they receive is two afpres, or one fol [about a halfpenny.] This increafes with their age, and with their rank, as far as twenty-nine afpres, or fourteen fols fix deniers [rather more than 8d.]; and it is reduced to half that fum, when thefe foldiers are obliged by their infirmities, or by the wounds they have received, to retire.

The cavalry of the ftate confifts of feven thoufand Moors; their pay is very trifling, and, moft frequently, given to them in provifions. Their moft common occupation is to collect the duties impofed upon the Arabs.

Thefe troops are all armed with firelocks without bayonets, and with two piftols at their girdle. Befide thefe, the Turks have a dagger, and the Moors a ftiletto. In all of them, courage and impetuofity muft both fupply the deficiency of regular manœuvres and difcipline.

No country in the northern part of Africa hath fo confiderable a revenue as Tunis. It confifts of 18,000,000 of livres [750,000l.]. This profperity, which is entirely of a very modern date, hath been the confequence of a very fortunate revolution in the government. The Dey, who, in conjunction with his Turks, held the reins of government, hath been

deprived of the greateft part of his authority, and
hath been fucceeded by a Moorifh prince, who, under the title of Bey, at prefent conducts the affairs
of government, and is affifted by a more wife and
more moderate council. Oppreffions have, in fome
degree, been alleviated; the foil hath been lefs ill-
cultivated, and the manufactures have acquired fome
extenfion. It was fcarce poffible that the connections
with the inland parts of Africa could increafe; they
will always be confined to the barter of a fmall number of articles, for gold duft, conveyed acrofs immenfe
fands and deferts : but the maritime connections have
been extended. The Levant hath received a greater
quantity of productions, and the trade with Europe
hath likewife improved.

Though England, Holland, Denmark, Sweden,
Venice, Ragufa, and fometimes Tufcany, fend con-
fuls to Tunis, the trade carried on with thofe nations
is very trifling; and, indeed, the Englifh have no
concern in it. They only keep an agent there for
the greater fecurity of their flag in the Mediterranean, and to procure an additional mart to the inhabitants of Minorca. The French carry off the
greateft part of the trade from their united rivals;
and yet they do not introduce goods annually into
the dominions of the republic, to the amount of more
than 2,000,000 of livres [83,333l. 6s. 8d.]. To the
profit which thefe people derive from their exports
and imports, which become every day more confiderable, muft be added, the benefits which accrue to
their navigators, by employing their veffels to carry
the provifions of the republic to every fea-port of the
Levant, and by bringing back what the republic receives from thofe places for its fubfiftence. Every
one of the numerous veffels employed in this coafting
trade, pays thirty-one livres ten fols [1l. 6s. 3d.] for
the privilege of anchoring, and an equal fum when
they land their cargoes.

Every commodity that enters the ftate is not obliged
to pay more than three per cent. if it comes directly

BOOK
XI.

B O O K from the country which furnishes it. But the pro-
XI. ductions of the north, or of other parts, which have
been deposited at Leghorn, pay eight per cent. as
well as those which come immediately from that celebrated port, and even eleven per cent. when directed to Jews. Formerly government had kept in
their own hands the exclusive trade of the oils, which
are required by some parts of Europe for their soap
manufactories, and by Egypt, Algiers, and Tripoli,
for other purposes ; they have given up this monopoly ; but this sacrifice hath been purchased by very
considerable duties.

Though Tunis hath concentrated within its own
walls a great part of the trade, the other harbours of
the republic, scattered along a coast of fourscore
leagues in extent, receive likewise some vessels.

The one which is the nearest to Tripoli, is called
Sfax. It hath a clayish bottom, and hath so little
water, that the smallest vessels are obliged to anchor
at a distance, and to fatigue their crews to excess, or
to ruin themselves in expences for boats. The soil
doth not produce any provisions proper for exportation, but some important manufactures have been formed in the town, which is mostly inhabited by Arabs.

The harbour of Susa is defended by three castles,
even the most modern of which is falling into ruin,
though it be not yet finished. This harbour is very
unsafe, the ships in it being constantly agitated by
the east and by the north-west winds, which sometimes occasion the loss of those that have not had
time to shelter themselves in the bay of Monoster.
Notwithstanding this inconvenience, this city is the
second in the republic ; and this is owing to the abundance of its oils and of its wool.

Tunis is situated in the midst of infectious morasses,
at the foot, or upon the declivity of a hill. Though
the air be not pure, and though the waters be so bad,
that the inhabitants are obliged to go two or three
miles before they can find any that is fit to drink,
yet one hundred and fifty thousand of the least bar-

barous people of Africa are collected within its walls.
This town hath a communication with the sea, by
means of a lake, which can admit none but very flat
boats, that are called *Sandals*. At the extremity of
this lake is found a narrow canal leading to the Gou-
lette, which muſt be conſidered as the harbour of the
capital. This harbour is immenſe, ſafe, and moſt
uncommonly even in its bottom and on its ſurface:
it is only open to the north-eaſt winds, and is cloſed
by two chains of mountains, which are terminated
on the north by Cape Bona and by Cape Zebib.

Biſerta was very famous at the time that the republic kept up a great number of galleys; it was
from that port they were fitted out, and they brought
back to it the profits they reaped from their perpetual piracies. The canal which led from the harbour to the town hath been gradually filled up with
mud, and it is at preſent acceſſible to no other veſſels
than Sandals; even merchantmen can no longer enter it, and are obliged to caſt anchor rather in a dangerous ſituation.

Port-Farine, ſituated on the ruins, or in the neighbourhood of the ancient Utica, was formerly one of
the moſt extenſive, ſafe, and commodious harbours
of the Mediterranean, and would ſtill be ſo under
any other government except that of the Moors. It
is defended by four forts, and cloſed by a narrow
paſs, which at this time is ſcarce acceſſible to the
ſmalleſt veſſels, and if it be ſtill neglected, will be
quite filled up in a ſhort time, by the ſands continually thrown in by the ſea. It is, however, the ar-
ſenal, and the only aſylum for the naval military
forces, which are at preſent reduced to three half-
galleys and five xebecs. The place where Carthage
formerly ſtood, is a few miles diſtant from this town;
there are no other remains of this renowned city, beſide the ruins of a great aqueduct, and ſome ciſterns
in tolerable preſervation. The traces even of its harbour are ſo much effaced, that the ſea is at the diſtance of a league from it.

BOOK
X   The ifland of Galite is fituated almoft at the mouth
of the Zaine, which feparates Tunis from Algiers.
This ifland is covered with flocks, and more efpecially with mules, which are in great requeft throughout
the whole of the Levant. Its numerous inhabitants
are all weavers of wool, or employed in gathering
fponge. Not far from this ifland is that of Tabarco,
which the family of the Lomellini had been in poffeffion of for two centuries, when they were deprived
of it in 1741. The Genoefe drew from this barren
rock a great quantity of very fine coral.

Prefent
ftate of Al-
giers.   To the weft of Tunis is the republic of Algiers, the
inland parts of which are bounded by the defert of
Sahara, as are all the interior parts in Barbary; they
are more extenfive, more populous, and better cultivated than is generally fuppofed. There are not
many towns in them, and moft of thefe are built upon
the coafts, the extent of which is one hundred and
twenty leagues.

The public revenue is not proportionate to the
number of inhabitants and to the quantity of productions. The duties are commonly loft in the hands
of difhoneft perfons who are appointed to collect them.
The three Beys, or governors of the eaft, of the fouth,
and of the weft, do not deliver into the treafury more
than 1,250,000 livres [52,083l. 6s. 8d.], and give only 117,000 livres [4875l.] to the troops; whatever
more is required for the expences of the ftate, is fupplied by the cuftoms, by the domain, by the annual
levies in provifions, and in cattle, by the more precarious profit arifing from prizes taken at fea, and
from the fale of flaves.

The principal militia of the country confifts entirely of Turks; their number ought to be twelve thoufand, but they are never complete. The Dey, his
lieutenants, and the members of the divan, are chofen out of this powerful body.

The defcendants of thefe privileged men are called Couloris; their number is fixty thoufand, they

are all in the fervice of the regency, and paid in the fame manner as at Tunis.

The cavalry, which confifts of about twenty thoufand men, is compofed entirely of Moors ; whether they make war againft the Arabs, or are employed by government for the defence of the provinces, or in collecting the taxes, their pay is very trifling.

Befide this numerous army, which is always kept up, the government can difpofe at pleafure of the Moors who dwell in the plains, or among the mountains, if they fhould be in want of them ; they all of them join their ftandards without reluctance, and attack the enemy with great intrepidity.

The naval forces are not near fo numerous as thofe of the land ; at prefent they are reduced to feventeen veffels ; one fhip of fifty guns, two frigates of forty-two and thirty-four guns, five large barks, two xebecs, four half-galleys, and three galliots ; feveral of thefe veffels, which are all deftined for piracy, belong to the ftate, others to the officers of the regency, and fome even to private individuals. Every proprietor bears the expence of his armament, and divides the profits with the treafury and with the crew. The Dey commonly requires the prizes which confift of timber for fhip-building, and of military ftores. He ought to pay the value of them, but the indemnity is never proportioned to the facrifice.

The navigators, to whom the ports of Algiers are opened, can land in feven or eight places.

The port of Callaa, at a fmall diftance from the frontiers of Tunis, is tolerably good, but it cannot hold more than five or fix fhips. Thofe that are admitted into it are all French : fome individuals of that nation have obtained, ever fince the year 1560, from the Moorifh prince who governed the diftrict at that time, the liberty of forming a fettlement to carry on the coral fifhery. They were driven away eight years after by the Turks, and re-eftablifhed in 1597, but they were again expelled : they were recalled in 1637, and permitted to rebuild a fmall fortification formerly erected there, under the name of the Baſtion of France. Being ſoon diſguſted with ſo inconvenient a ſituation, the perſons concerned tranſferred their ſettlement to Chale, which the Engliſh had been compelled to abandon ; they themſelves were expelled ſoon after, and they were not allowed to return to their poſt, till after the bombardment of Algiers, executed in 1682 and 1684, by command of Lewis XIV.

In 1694, a more powerful aſſociation than any of the preceding obtained the excluſive trade upon a conſiderable extent of coaſt, by a treaty which hath often been renewed, and which will in all probability be maintained, becauſe the conditions of it are favourable to the militia, to whom the tribute upon which it is founded belongs. Several companies have ſucceſſively excerciſed this monopoly with more or leſs advantage. Since 1741, it is in the hands of a company, which hath formed at Marſeilles a capital of 1,200,000 livres [50,000l.], divided into twelve hundred ſhares, three hundred of which belong to the chamber of commerce of this celebrated city.

The firſt tranſactions of the ſociety were unfortunate. The depredations made by pirates and by the natives, by the competition of ſmugglers, and by a corrupt adminiſtration, reduced their capital, in 1766, to 570,000 livres [23,750l.] ; ſince that period, their affairs have been ſo proſperous, that in the latter part of December 1773, they were in poſſeſſion of 4,512,445 livres 3 ſols 4 deniers [about 188,018l. 11s.], beſide the doubtful debts, the value of their buildings, and ſome merchandiſe which remained unſold in the warehouſes.

Their exports are trifling, and it is chiefly with money that they purchaſe coral, wax, wool, tallow, hides, and eſpecially corn. In 1773, they brought into the kingdom eighty-four thouſand three hundred and ſix loads of wheat, and ſixteen thouſand one hundred and ſeventy-three loads of barley, beans, and millet ſeed. One hundred, or one hundred and twenty veffels, the fitting out of which cofts about one hundred thoufand crowns [12,500l.], are annually employed in this bufinefs.

Though the company hath agents at Bona and at Callaa, all the tranfactions are carried on at the laft place. They are even permitted to have a few batteries and fome foldiers in this fortified factory, in order to fecure themfelves from the plunders of the pirates and from the infults of the neighbouring Moors.

The court of Verfailles hath been often cenfured, for having fhackled thefe connections in the bonds of a monopoly. It hath not been obferved, that it was neceffary to enfure the fubfiftence of Provence ; and there was no other method of doing this, becaufe the exportation of corn from the ftates of Barbary is feldom permitted.

Bona appears to have been the ancient Hippona. A few beautiful ruins are difcovered amidft the boldnefs of the Moorifh tafte. It would be an eafy matter to make a commodious harbour to the town, as it hath already an exceeding good road. This new afylum would be fufficiently protected by the works which have exifted for a long while, under the name of the Fort of Genoa.

Bugia is a tolerably large ftaple for oil, and for the wax, which is found in the neighbouring plains ; and efpecially for iron, which is brought from more diftant mountains, that abound in mines. Though its harbour be too much expofed to the north winds, the fquadrons of the republic ufed to anchor in it, before they were deftroyed there by the Englifh in the laft century.

The antiquities which are found in Tedelez prove that it was formerly a confiderable place. The veftiges of a great pier are even difcerned upon the fhore, which probably advanced into the fea, and formed a port to the town. It is at prefent a very indifferent harbour, where fhips which go to take in their lading are too often deftroyed.

Algiers, the capital of the ftate, forms an amphi-

theatre, upon the declivity of a hill, which is crowned by the citadel. Its territory is well cultivated by
flaves, and is covered with wheat, rice, hemp, fruits,
vegetables, and even with vines, planted by the
Moors who were expelled from Grenada. The entering into, and the going out of the port, are very difficult ; it is exceedingly narrow, and doth not contain fufficient water to hold men of war : and in
ftormy weather even the merchantmen are not fafe ;
they often run foul of each other, and are fometimes
fhattered, when the north or north-eaft winds blow
with violence. The harbour forms a femicircle ; it
hath a good botom ; but as it is expofed to the fame
winds as the port, the fhips are in equal danger in the
ftormy feafons.

Sereelli is five or fix leagues diftant from Algiers.
This town hath a creek, or fmall bay, where feveral
veffels caft anchor. Its foil is very low, its fhore beautiful, and it is the part of the coaft the moft favourable for a defcent.

Arfew, the environs of which are delightful, muft
be the Arfenaria of the ancients. Some tolerably
fine remains of feveral monuments are found in it.
Its port is fafe, commodious, and well frequented. A
harbour might be formed in it, at a trifling expence,
capable of receiving the largeft fhips. This is the
Moorifh town neareft to Oran, which the Spaniards
took poffeffion of in 1509 ; which was taken from
them in 1708 ; and which they retook in 1732, and
have kept ever fince.

The numbers of European fhips which land annually at the ftates of Algiers, vary according to circumftances ; but they are never confiderable ; the
moft plentiful harveft doth not attract above one hundred. A French veffel, whether great or fmall, lad-
en or empty, pays for its anchorage 143 livres 8 fols
[5l. 19s. 6d.] ; and this tax is ftill higher for other
nations. They ought all, without diftinction, to pay
three per cent. for all the merchandife they bring in ;
but this duty is reduced to two per cent. by the ar-

rangements made with the farmers of the cuftoms. B O O K
The provifions that are exported from the country are XI.
fubjected to no tax, becaufe government are the only
dealers in them.

Though the Englifh, the Danes, the Dutch, the
Swedes, and the Venetians, are perfectly free in the
ports of Algiers, they neverthelefs carry on no great
trade there. Three fourths of the trade are fallen
into the hands of the French; and yet their annual
fales do not amount to more 200,000 livres [8333l.
6s. 8d.], nor their purchafes to above 600,000 livres
[25,000l.]. Two thoufand fix hundred and fifty quintals of wool, five thoufand of oil, fixteen thoufand of
wheat, and thirty thoufand hides, are the amount of
all their exports. The tranfactions of the African
Company are not included in thefe calculations.

Morocco hath been as often and as dreadfully fub-   Prefent
verted as the reft of the northern coafts of Africa;   ftate of
                                                        Morocco.
but hath not fubmitted to the Turkifh yoke. Even
thofe provinces which had been difmembered from it,
under the name of Fez, of Sus, and of Tafilet, have
been fucceffively united to the empire. One fingle
defpot governs this immenfe country, according to
his caprices, which are almoft always extravagant or
fanguinary. The deftructive authority which he hath
been fuffered to ufurp, is perpetuated without any
other regular troops, except a feeble guard of timid
negroes. It is only with fome of thefe flaves, whom
he choofes occafionally to affemble under his banners,
that he makes war. His maritime forces are fcarce
more formidable. They confift of three frigates, two
half-galleys, three xebecs, and fifteen galliots. Piracy hath been hitherto their only occupation. It
might be expected that thefe depredations would foon
be put an end to, if it were reafonable to rely upon
the faith of a tyrant, or to hope that his fucceffors
would at laft adopt fome more humane fentiments.
The public revenue muft be very trifling, in a region
which is for ever ruined by vexations and maffacres.
The expences, however, are ftill lefs. Whatever can

be spared is added to increase an immense treasure, anciently formed out of the spoils of Spain, and always augmented by a long series of sovereigns, more or less cruel, who looked upon money as the only good, and thought nothing of the happiness of their subjects.

This ardent thirst of wealth hath descended from the throne to individuals. A caravan sets out annually from the town of Morocco, which was the capital of the state, before Mequinez was preferred by the sovereigns. This caravan, which goes in search of gold from Upper Guinea, must have travelled over a space of five hundred leagues before its arrival in in the kingdom, two hundred in the empire itself, two hundred in the desert of Sahara, and one hundred after having quitted it. In the midst of the desert, surrounded with barren and accumulated sands, where it is not possible to travel but in the night, where the march must necessarily be slow, where one must be guided by a compass, and by observing the stars, in the same manner as on the ocean; in this desert nature hath placed a less savage district, abounding in springs and in salt mines. The camels are laden with this necessary fossil, and it is carried to Tombuto, where gold is received in exchange.

This precious metal, when arrived at Morocco, is very seldom circulated there. It is buried, as in all governments where the fortunes of individuals are not secure. A similar destiny attends the money which is introduced by the Europeans in the empire, in the nine harbours which are always open to them.

Tetuan is the nearest port to the state of Algiers. It is safe, unless the easterly winds blow with violence, which seldom happens. The river of Bourfega, which empties itself into it, serves for an asylum to some pirates during the winter. The garrison of Gibraltar formerly sent to purchase there the cattle, fruit, and vegetables, necessary for its consumption; but this connection hath ceased, since the sovereign of the country hath required that the Englifh conful fhould refide at Tangier.

This town, conquered by Portugal in 1471, was given to the Englifh in 1662. Thefe forfook it, after keeping it two-and-twenty years. When they re- tired, they blew up a pier, which they had conftruct- ed for the fecurity of the largeft fhips. The ruins of this beautiful work have rendered the approach of the bay very difficult. Accordingly, it would be of no importance, if the mouth of the river, which is difcovered at the end, did not afford a fhelter to moft of the galliots of the empire. Tangier hath fucceed- ed Tetuan in fupplying Gibraltar with provifions. The communication between thefe two Moorifh towns is interrupted by the fortrefs of Ceuta, which is part- ed from Spain, to which it belongs, only by a ftrait of five leagues.

Arrach is the natural vent for the productions of Afgar, one of the largeft and the moft fertile pro- vinces of the empire. This advantage, a fortunate pofition, and the goodnefs of its port, muft fooner or later impart to it fome degree of activity. At prefent it is inhabited only by foldiers. Since the expedition which the French attempted againft it in 1765, the fortifications raifed by the Spaniards, when they were mafters of the place, have been reftored.

Sallee was, not long ago, almoft an independent republic, under a chief elected by itfelf. Its fituation, in the midft of the country fubject to Morocco, ena- bled it to collect a great many provifions. Its inhabi- tants were at once both merchants and pirates. They have almoft ceafed to exercife either of thefe pro- feffions, after having been fubdued, and fpoiled of their riches by the prefent monarch, at the time that his father was upon the throne. A fand-bank, which feems to be perpetually increafing, prevents all fhips from entering the river, except thofe which do not carry more than fix or feven feet of water ; but the harbour is fafe from the end of April till the end of September.

Muley Mehemet was defirous of building a commercial town in the peninfula of Fedale, and moft of
the buildings were begun. A harbour, which is fafe
in all feafons, though the fea be conftantly agitated,
had fuggefted this idea to him. He hath given it up,
fince he hath been made to underftand that the expence would be thrown away, upon a coaft which
was acceffible almoft in all parts.

In 1769, the Portuguefe forfook Mazagan, after
having deftroyed the works. Since this period, the
place is almoft deferted. Its harbour is convenient
in fummer for fmall veffels ; but even in that feafon
the men of war are obliged to anchor at a diftance.

Saffi hath a large harbour, which is very fafe part
of the year, but too much expofed in winter to the
violence of the fouth and fouth-eaft winds. Its fituation, in the midft of a fertile, rich, and populous
country, had rendered this great town almoft the general market of the productions of the empire. It
hath been lately ftripped of this advantage by Mo-
gador, which is built on the moft weftern part of
Africa.

The port of this new ftaple is only a canal formed
by an ifland, at the diftance of five hundred toifes
from the land. One may fail in and out of it with
every wind ; but it hath not fufficient depth to harbour large fhips, and the anchorage is not fafe in bad
weather. No man of war can anchor on the coaft,
on account of the great rapidity of the currents.
Though the territory furrounding this place be not
very fit for cultivation, the caprice of the defpot, who
ftill governs the country, hath rendered it the moft
important mart of his dominions, more confiderable
even than all the others collectively.

Santa Cruz, fituated in the kingdom of Sus, in the
thirtieth degree of latitude, is the laft maritime place
of the empire. Its harbour is convenient, and very
fafe even for fhips of the line, but during fummer
only. It was formerly a tolerably great market,
where the navigators found collected together all the

productions of an extenfive and well cultivated coun- try, and where all the gold which Tarodant drew from Tombuto was brought. The town was taken out of the hands of the Portuguefe, and returned under the dominion of the Moors, without entirely lofing its importance. An earthquake, which deftroyed part of it in 1731, was more fatal than this revolution. It might perhaps have recovered from this calamity, had not Muley Muhammet, in a fit of paffion, the caufe of which was never known, driven the inhabitants out of it fome years after, and fubftituted to them a colony of Negroes.

Morocco receives but few European veffels. Its ports are fhut againft feveral nations, and England, Holland, and Tufcany, who have formed treaties with that power, reap no great advantage from them. In order to give fome fpirit to this trade, which was perhaps too much neglected, a capital of 1,323,958 livres 6 fols 6 deniers [about 55,164l. 18s. 8d.], was formed at Copenhagen in 1755, which was divided into five hundred fhares, of 2647 livres 18 fols 4 deniers each [about 110l. 6s. 8d.]. This affociation was to laft forty years; but, for what reafon is not known, it hath not continued half the time. Though the connections of France with that empire have not fubfifted beyond the year 1767, the tranfactions of this crown are of much more importance, and yet its annual fales do not exceed 400,000 livres [16,666l. 13s. 4d.], nor its purchafes 1,200,000 livres [50,000l.].

Every thing that enters, or comes out of the ftates of Morocco, pays ten per cent. Each veffel is alfo obliged to deliver five hundred pounds of gunpowder, and ten bullets from ten to twelve inches in diameter, or 577 livres ten fols [24l. 1s. 3d.] in fpecie. The Spanifh coin is moft commonly ufed; but all the others are admitted according to their weight and their denomination.

The picture that hath juft been traced of the coun- Origin of tries of Barbary, muft have appeared very horrid. the piracies committed The ftate of defolation in which we have feen them upon the

B O O K
XI.

eastern
coasts of
Africa.
Means of
putting a
stop to
them.
plunged, hath been the unavoidable confequence of the propenfity of thefe people to piracy. This tafte, which is very ancient in thefe regions, increafed confiderably after they had fhaken off a foreign yoke. It became a paffion, upon occafion of an event which greatly increafed their maritime forces.

Spain, which, for feveral centuries, had been fubject to the difciples of the Koran, had, at laft, broken its chains, and fubdued the Mohammedans in its turn. It was defirous of compelling them to turn Chriftians; and its zeal was irritated by unfurmountable refiftance. Its blindnefs went fo far as to depopulate the ftate, in order to purge it of fufpicious fubjects, and fuch as were of an inimical religion. Moft of thefe exiles fought a refuge among the people of Barbary. Their new country was too ignorant of trade and induftry, to enable them to put forth their talents, and to avail themfelves of their riches. The fpirit of revenge made them pirates. At firft they contented themfelves with ravaging the vaft and fertile plains of their oppreffors. They furprifed, in their beds, the lazy inhabitants of the rich countries of Valencia, Grenada, and Andalufia, and reduced them to flavery. But, at length, difdaining the fpoils they acquired upon a foil which they had formerly cultivated with their own hands, they conftructed large veffels, infulted the flag of the other nations, and reduced the greateft powers of Europe to the fhameful neceffity of fending them annual prefents, which, under whatever denomination we may difguife them, are, in fact, a tribute. Thefe pirates have been fometimes punifhed, fometimes humbled; but their depredations have never been totally fuppreffed, although this might be done with the greateft eafe.

The Arabs, wandering in the deferts; the ancient inhabitants of the country, who cultivate the fields; the Moors come out of Spain, moft of whom are fettled upon the coafts; the Jews, who are defpifed, oppreffed, and outraged: all the people, in a word, of that continent, deteft the yoke which oppreffes

them, and would not make the leaft exertion to con- B O O K
tinue under it. XI.

No foreign fuccour would retard for a moment the
fall of this authority. The only power that might
be fufpected of wifhing its prefervation, the fultan of
Conftantinople, is not fo highly gratified with the
vain title of protector, which it confers on him, nor
fo jealous of that of the chief of the religion which
is afcribed to him, to intereft himfelf warmly in its
prefervation. All endeavours to excite the Turks to
interfere, by fubmiffions, which particular circumftances might probably extort from thefe plunderers,
would certainly be ineffectual. Their intreaties would
not impart ftrength. For thefe two centuries paft,
the Porte has no navy, and its military power is continually decaying.

But to what people is referved the glory of break-
ing thofe fetters which Africa is thus infenfibly preparing for us, and of removing thofe terrors, which
are fo formidable to our navigators? No nation can
attempt it alone ; and, perhaps, if it did, the jealoufy
of the reft would throw fecret obftacles in its way.
This muft, therefore, be the work of a general combination. All the maritime powers muft concur in
the execution of a defign, in which all are equally
interefted. Thefe ftates, which every thing invites
to mutual alliance, to mutual good-will, to mutual
defence, ought to be weary of the calamities which
they reciprocally bring upon each other. After having fo frequently united for their mutual deftruction,
let them at length take up arms for their prefervá-
tion. War, for once at leaft, will then become ufeful
and juft.

One may venture to affert, that fuch a war would
be of no long continuance, if it were conducted with
fkill and unanimity. Each member of the confederacy, attacking at the fame time the enemy it had
to reduce, would experience but a weak refiftance,
or, perhaps, none. Perhaps, this nobleft and greateft
of enterprifes would coft Europe lefs blood and trea-

fure, than the moft trivial of thofe quarrels with which it is continually agitated.

No man would do the politicians who fhould form this plan the injuftice to fuppofe, that they would confine their ambition to the filling up of roads, the demolifhing of forts, and the ravaging of coafts. Such narrow notions would be inconfiftent with the prefent improvements of reafon. The countries fub-dued would remain to the conquerors, and each of the allies would acquire poffeffions proportionate to the affiftance they had given to the common caufe. Thefe conquefts would become fo much the more fe-cure, as the happinefs of the vanquifhed would be the confequence of them. This race of pirates, thefe fea-monfters, would be changed into men by falutary laws and examples of humanity. The progrefs they would gradually make, by the knowledge we fhould impart to them, would, in time, difpel that fanaticifm which ignorance and mifery have kept up in their minds. They would ever recollect, with gratitude, the memorable era which had brought us to their fhores.

We fhould no longer fee them leave a country un-cultivated, which was formerly fo fertile. Corn and various fruits would foon cover this immenfe track of land. Thefe productions would be bartered for the works of our induftry and of our manufactures. Eu-ropean traders, fettled in Africa, would become the factors of this trade, which would prove of mutual advantage to both countries. A communication fo natural, between oppofite coafts, and between people who have a neceffary intercourfe with each other, would, as it were, extend the boundaries of the world. This new kind of conqueft which prefents itfelf to us, would amply compenfate for thofe which, during fo many centuries, have contributed to the diftrefs of mankind.

The jealoufy of the great maritime powers, who have obftinately rejected all expedients to re-eftablifh tranquillity on our feas, hath been the chief impedi-ment to fo important a revolution. The hope of

checking the induſtry of every weak ſtate, hath ac-
cuſtomed them to wiſh that theſe piracies of Barbary
ſhould continue, and hath even induced them to encourage theſe plunders. This is an enormity, the ignominy of which they would never have incurred, if
their underſtanding had equalled their mercenary
views. All nations would certainly profit from this
happy change ; but the greateſt advantages would
infallibly redound to the maritime ſtates, in proportion to their power. Their ſituation, the ſafety of
their navigation, the greatneſs of their capital, and
various other means, would ſecure them this ſuperiority. They are conſtantly complaining of the ſhackles which national envy, the folly of reſtraints and
prohibitions, and the confined idea of excluſive traffic, have impoſed upon their activity. The people
gradually become as much ſtrangers to one another,
as they were in the barbarous ages. The void, which
this want of communication neceſſarily occaſions would
be filled up, if Africa were brought to have wants
and reſources to ſatisfy them. The ſpirit of commerce
would have a new career opened to its exertion.

Neverthelefs, if the reduction and ſubjection of
Barbary would not become a ſource of happineſs for
them as well as for ourſelves ; if we are reſolved not
to treat them as brethren ; if we wiſh not to conſider them as our friends ; if we muſt keep up and
perpetuate ſlavery and poverty among them ; if fa-
naticiſm can ſtill renew thoſe deteſtable cruſades,
which philoſophy, too late, hath conſigned to the indignation of all ages; if Africa muſt at length become
the ſcene of our cruelties, as Aſia and America have
been, and ſtill are ; may the project which humanity
hath now dictated to us, for the good of our fellow-
creatures, be buried in perpetual oblivion ! Let us remain in our ports. It is indifferent, whether they be
Chriſtians or Muſſelmen who ſuffer. Man is the only
object worthy to intereſt man.

Men ! you are all brethren. How long will you
defer to acknowledge each other ? How long will it

B o o k be before you perceive that Nature, your common
XI. mother, offers nourifhment equally to all her children? Why muft you deftroy each other; and why
muft the hand that feeds you be continually ftained
with your blood? The acts that would· excite your
abhorence in animals, you have been committing almoft ever fince you exift. Are you apprehenfive of
becoming too numerous? And do you not think that
you will be exterminated faft enough by peftilential
difeafes, by the inclemency of the elements, by your
labours, by your paffions, by your vices, by your prejudices, by the weaknefs of your organs, and by the
natural fhortnefs of your life? The wifdom of the
Being to whom you owe your exiftence hath prefcribed limits to your population, and to that of all living
creatures, which will never be broken through. Have
you not, in your wants, which are inceffantly renewed, a fufficient number of enemies confpiring againft
you, without entering into a league with them? Man
boafts of his fuperior excellence to all natural beings;
and yet with a fpirit of ferocioufnefs, which is not
obferved even in the race of tigers, man is the moft
terrible fcourge of man. If his wifhes were to be
accomplifhed, there would foon remain no more than
one fingle being of the fame fpecies upon the whole
face of the globe.

Colour of   This being, fo cruel and fo compaffionate, fo odious
the inha-   and fo interefting, unhappy in the northern part of
bitants of
the weft-   Africa, experiences a deftiny infinitely more dread-
ern coaft of ful in the weftern part of this vaft region.
Africa,
known by   Upon this coaft, which extends from the Strait
the name   of Gibraltar to the Cape of Good Hope, the inhabi-
of Guinea.
Inquiry   tants have all, beyond the Niger, an oblong head;
into the   the nofe large, flattened, and fpread out; thick lips;
caufe of
this phe-   and curled hair, like the wool of our fheep. They
nomenon.   are born white; and the only brown colour they at
firft exhibit, is round the nails and the eyes, with a
fmall fpot formed at the extremity of the genitals.
Towards the eighth day after their birth the children
begin to change colour, their fkin darkens, and at

length grows black, but of a dirty fallow, and almoſt livid black ; which, in proceſs of time, becomes gloſ-ſy and ſhining.

The fleſh however, the bones, the viſcera, and all the internal parts, are of the ſame colour in Ne-groes as in white people. The lymph is equally white and limpid ; and the milk of the nurſes is every where the ſame.

The moſt palpable difference betwen them is, that the Negroes have the ſkin much hotter, and, as it were, oily, the blood of a blackiſh hue, the bile very deep coloured, the pulſe quicker, a ſweat which yields a ſtrong and diſagreeable ſmell, and a perſpir-ation which often blackens the ſubſtance it comes in contact with. One of the inconveniences of this black colour, the image of night, which confounds all objects, is, that it hath, in ſome meaſure, obliged theſe people to ſcar their face and breaſt, and to ſtain their ſkin with various colours, in order that they may know each other at a diſtance. There are ſome tribes in which this practice is univerſal ; among others, it appears to be a diſtinction reſerved to ſu-perior rank. But as we ſee this cuſtom eſtabliſhed among the people of Tartary, of Canada, and of other ſavage nations, it may be doubted, whether it be not rather the effect of their wandering way of life, than of their complexion.

This colour proceeds from a mucous ſubſtance, which forms a kind of network between the epider-mis and the ſkin. This ſubſtance, which is white in Europeans, brown in people of an olive complexion, and ſprinkled over with reddiſh ſpots 'among light-haired or carotty people, is blackiſh among the Ne-groes.

The deſire of diſcovering the cauſes of this colour, hath given riſe to a variety of ſyſtems.

Theology, which hath taken poſſeſſion of the hu-man mind by opinion ; which hath availed itſelf of the firſt fears of infancy, to inſpire reaſon with eter-nal apprehenſions ; which hath altered every thing, geography, aftronomy, philofophy, and hiftory; which hath introduced the marvellous and the myfterious in every thing, in order to arrogate to itfelf the right of explaining every thing : theology, after having made a race of men guilty and unfortunate from the fault of Adam, hath made a race of black men, in order to punifh the fratricide of his fon. The Negroes are the defcendants of Cain. If their father was an affaffin, it muft be allowed, that his pofterity, have made a fevere atonement for his crime ; and that the defcendants of the pacific Abel have thoroughly avanged the innocent blood of their father.

Reafon hath attempted to explain the colour of the Negroes, from confequences deduced from the phenomena of chemiftry. According to fome naturalifts, it is a vitriolic fluid contained in the lymph of the Negroes, and being too grofs to pafs through the pores of the fkin, it ferments and unites with the mucous body, which it colours. It is then urged, why is the hair curled, and why are the eyes and teeth of Negroes fo white ? for the authors of this fyftem do not confider, that a vitriolic falt of fuch power and activity would at length deftroy all organization. This, however, is as perfect in Negroes, as in the whiteft of the human race.

Anatomy hath thought to have difcovered the origin of the blacknefs of Negroes in the principles of generation. Nothing more, it fhould feem, would be neceffary to prove, that Negroes are a particular fpecies of men. For if any thing difcriminates the fpecies, or the claffes in each fpecies, it is certainly the difference of the femen. But upon confidering the matter more attentively, this hath been found to be a miftake, fo that this explanation of the colour of Negroes hath been given up. Neither have the confequences, pretended to be deduced from the difference between their figure and that of other people, appeared more convincing. Some of thefe forms are owing to the climate, moft of them to ancient cuftoms. It hath been conceived, that thefe

barbarians might poffibly have formed fome extravagant ideas of beauty, according to which they had
endeavoured to form their children ; that this habit,
in procefs of time, had been turned into nature, fo
that it was very feldom neceffary to have recourfe to
art, in order to obtain thefe fingular forms.

There are other caufes of the colour of Negroes, more fatisfactory than thefe : the feat of it, as
we have obferved, is in the *Rete Mucofum*, under the
epidermis, or cuticle. The fubftanc of this network, which is mucous in the firft inftance, is afterwards changed into a web of veffels, the diameter of which is confiderable enough to admit, either
a portion of the colouring part of the blood, or of
the bile, which is faid to have a peculiar tendency
towards the fkin. From hence proceeds among white
people, in whom this *Rete Mucofum* is more lax, the
more vivid complexion of the cheeks. From hence
alfo, that yellow or copper colour, which diftinguifhes
whole nations ; while under another climate, it
is confined to one perfon, and produced by difeafe.
The exiftence of one or of the other of thefe fluids,
is fufficient to colour the Negroes, efpecially if we
add, that the epidermis, and the *Rete Mucofum*, is
thicker in them ; that the blood is blackifh, and the
bile deeper coloured, and that their fweat, which is
more plentiful and lefs fluid, muft neceffarily thicken
under the epidermis, and increafe the darknefs of
the colour.

This fyftem is alfo fupported by natural philofophy,
which obferves, that the parts of the body expofed
to the fun are moft deeply coloured, and that travellers, and people who dwell in the country, and who
lead a wandering life ; all thofe, in a word, who live
continually in the open air, and under a more burning fky, have darker complexions. Philofophy thinks,
from thefe obfervations, that the primitive caufe of
the colour of the Negroes may be attributed to the
climate and to the ardour of the fun. There are
no Negroes, it is faid, except in hot climates ; their

B O O K colour becomes darker in proportion as they ap-
XI.   proach the equator. It grows lighter at the extremities of the torrid zone, All the human fpecies, in
general, whitens in the fnow, and is tanned in the
fun. We perceive the different fhades from white
to black, and thofe from black to white, marked,
as it were, by the parallel degrees which cut the
earth in the direction from the equator to the poles.
If the zones, contrived by the inventors of the fphere,
were reprefented by real bands, we fhould fee the
black ebony colour infenfibly changing to the right
and left as far as the tropics, and from thence the
brown colur would be feen to grow paler and lighter
as far as the polar circles, by fhades of white continually increafing in clearnefs.

As the fhades of black are, however, deeper upon
the weftern coafts of Africa, than in other regions
perhaps as much heated, the ardour of the fun muft
certainly be combined with other caufes, which have
an equal influence upon organization. Such of the
Europeans as have made the longeft refidence in thofe
countries, attribute this greater degree of blacknefs
to the nitrous, fulphureous, or metallic particles, that
are continually exhaling from the furface or from the
bowels of the earth, to the cuftom of going naked, to
the proximity of burning fands, and to other particulars which do not occur elfewhere in the fame degree.

The circumftance that feems to confirm the opinion, that the colour of the Negroes is the effect of
the climate, of the air, of the water, and of the food
of Guinea, is, that this colour changes when the inhabitants are removed into other countries. The
children they procreate in America are not fo black
as their parents were. After each generation, the
difference becomes more palpable. It is poffible, that
after a numerous fucceffion of generations, the men
come from Africa would not be diftinguifhed from
thofe of the country into which they may have been
tranfplanted,

Although the opinion, which afcribes to the climate the firft caufe of the colour of the inhabitants
of Guinea, be almoft generally adopted, all the objec-
tions that may be urged againft this fyftem have not
yet been anfwered. This is one proof added to a
multitude of others, of the uncertainty of our knowledge.

And, indeed, how is it poffible that our knowledge
fhould not be uncertain and circumfcribed ? Our organs are fo feeble, and our means fo infufficient, our
ftudies fo much interrupted, our life fo much agitated, and the object of our inquiries is of fo immenfe
an extent ! Let naturalifts, philofophers, chemifts,
and accurate obfervers of nature in all her works, perfevere in their labours inceffantly ; and, after ages of
united and continual efforts, the fecrets of nature
which they will have difcovered, when compared to
her immenfe treafures, will be no more than as a drop
of water to the vaft ocean. The rich man fleeps, and
the learned man is watchful, but he is poor. His
difcoveries are matters of too little concern to government, to encourage him to folicit affiftance or to hope
for reward. More than one Ariftotle would be found
among us, but where is the monarch who would fay
to him, My power is at thy difpofal, make a free ufe
of my riches, and perfevere in thy labours ? Tell us,
thou celebrated Buffon, tell us to what height of perfection thou wouldft have carried thine immortal work,
hadft thou lived under an Alexander?

The contemplative man is fedentary, and the traveller is either ignorant or deceitful. The man on
whom genius hath been beftowed, defpifes minute
details and experiments ; and the man who makes
experiments is almoft always deftitute of genius.
Among the multitude of agents which nature employs, we are only acquainted with fome, and even
thefe we have but an imperfect knowledge of. Who
fhall determine, whether the others are not of fuch
a nature as to elude for ever our fenfes, as not to be
wrought upon by our inftruments, and not to be fub-

mitted to our obfervations and experiments ? The nature of thofe two principles that compofe the univerfe,
fpirit and matter, will be ever a myftery.

Among the natural qualities of bodies, there is not
a fingle one, upon which multitudes of experiments
are not yet remaining to be tried ; and it is even
a matter of doubt, whether all thefe experiments are
feafible. How long fhall we be reduced to the neceffity of forming conjectures, which are one day
brought forth, and the next refuted ? Who fhall reftrain that almoft invincible propenfity to analogy, a
mode of judging fo feducing, fo convenient, and fo
fallacious ? No fooner have we collected a few facts,
than we haften to build up a fyftem, which leads the
multitude, and fufpends our refearches after truth.
The time employed in forming an hypothefis, and
the time employed in refuting it, are both equally
loft. The fciences of calculation, that are fo fatisfactory to felf-love, which delights in overcoming difficulties, and to the accurate man, who is fond of exact inferences, will continue, but with little advantage, in the common ufages of life. Religion, which
looks with difdain upon the labours of a being in a
chryfalis, and which is fecretly alarmed at the progrefs of reafon, will multiply idle perfons, and retard
the labours of the induftrious by fear or by fcruples.
In proportion as a fcience advances, the improvement
of it becomes more difficult, the greater number become difgufted, and the fcience is no longer cultivated, unlefs by a few perfevering men, who ftill attend
to it, either from habit, or from the expectation, well
or ill founded, of acquiring fame ; till at length ridi-
cule interferes, and the man is pointed at as a fool
or a madman, who flatters himfelf that he fhall overcome a difficulty, which fome celebrated perfons may
not have been able to folve. Thus it is, that his co-
temporaries endeavour to conceal their apprehenfion
of his being really fuccefsful.

In all ages, and among all nations, we have feen
fome ftudies prevailing, which were afterwards ne-

glected, and succeeded by others in a kind of regu- B O O K
lar order. This ficklenefs and difguft are not the de- XI.
fects of one man alone ; they are the vice of the moft
numerous and moft enlightened focieties. It fhould
feem as if the arts and fciences had their periods of
fafhion.

We have begun by having erudite men. After
thefe came the poets and orators. To the poets and
orators fucceeded metaphyficians, who gave way to
geometricians, and thefe again to natural philofophers, which in their turn have been replaced by
naturalifts and chemifts. The turn for natural hiftory feems to be upon the decline. We are now entirely abforbed in queftions of government, of legiflation, of morality, of politics, and of commerce. If
I might be allowed to hazard a prophefy, I fhould pre-
dict, that the minds of men will inceffantly be turned
towards hiftory, an immenfe career, in which philofophy hath not yet made any advances.

For, in fact, if from that infinite multitude of vo-
lumes, we were to tear out the pages beftowed upon
great affaffins, who are called conquerors, or reduce
the accounts of them to a few pages, which even
they fcarce deferve, what would there be remaining?
Who is it that hath fpoken to us of the climate, of the
foil, of productions, of quadrupeds, of birds, of fifh, of
plants, of fruits, of minerals, of manners, of cuftoms,
of fuperftitions, of prejudices, of fciences, of arts, of
commerce, of government, and of laws? What do
we know of a multitude of ancient nations, that can
be of the leaft ufe to modern ones? Both their wifdom and their folly are equally loft to us. Their annals never give us any information upon thofe points
which it moft concerns us to know ; upon the true
glory of a fovereign, upon the bafis of the ftrength of
nations, upon the felicity of the people, upon the
duration of empires. Let thofe beautiful addreffes
of a general to his foldiers upon the point of action,
ferve as models of eloquence to the rhetorician ; there
can be no objection to this ; but were I to get them

B O O K by heart, I fhould neither become more equitable,
XI.   nor more firm, nor more informed, nor a better man.
The time draws near, when reafon, juftice, and truth,
fhall fnatch out of the hands of ignorance and flattery, the pen which they have holden but for too
long a time. Tremble, you who delude men with
falfehoods, or who make them groan under the yoke
of oppreffion. Sentence is going to be paffed upon
you.

There are but two feafons known in Guinea. The
moft wholefome, and the moft agreeable one, begins
in April and ends in October. Then it never rains;
but thick vapours, which cover the horizon, intercept
the rays of the fun, and moderate the ardour of them;
and every night there are dews that fall in fufficient
quantities to keep up the vegetation of plants. During the reft of the year the heats are exceffive, and
would perhaps be infupportable, were it not for the
rains, which fucceed each other with great rapidity.
Unfortunately, nature hath feldom difpofed the territory fo as to favour the running off of thefe waters
when too plentiful; and art hath never interfered to
affift nature. Hence the origin of fo many moraffes
in this part of the globe. They are moft commonly
fatal to ftrangers, whom their avidity leads into the
vicinity of them. The natives of the country, by
kindling fires every night near their dwellings, purify the corrupt air, to which they are moreover accuftomed from their infancy. The little varieties
which the north and fouth of the line may exhibit,
do not invalidate the accuracy of thefe obfervations.

Nature of   From the frontiers of the empire of Morocco, as
the foil and far as Senegal, the land is entirely barren. A long
coafts of   band of the deferts of Sahara, which extends from
Guinea.   the Atlantic Ocean as far as Egypt, to the fouth of
all the ftates of Barbary, occupies this immenfe fpace.
Some Moorifh families live in the midft of thefe burning fands, in a few places where fprings, which are
very fcarce, have been found, and where it hath been

possible to plant palm-trees and gather dates. Their chief employment confists in collecting the gums which have attracted the attention of all Europe upon that country. Thefe Moors carry to Upper Guinea, and principally to Bambouk, a great quantity of falt, in exchange for which they receive gold, and fometimes flaves.

The banks of the Niger, Gambia, and Sierra Leone, and thofe of fome lefs confiderable rivers, which flow in that long fpace that intervenes between thefe principal rivers, would prove extremely fertile if they were cultivated. The care of flocks conftitutes almoft the fole employment of the inhabitants. They are fond of mare's milk, which is their principal nourifh-ment; and travel but little, becaufe they have no wants to induce them to leave their country.

The inhabitants of Cape Monte, environed on every fide by fands, form a nation entirely feparated from the reft of Africa. In the rice of their marfhes confifts all their nourifhment and their fole riches. Of this they fell a fmall quantity to the Europeans, for which they receive in exchange brandy and hardware.

From the Cape of Palmas to the river Volta, the inhabitants are traders and hufbandmen. They are hufbandmen, becaufe their land, though ftony, abundantly requites the neceffary labour and expence of clearing it. They are traders, becaufe they have behind them nations which furnifh them with gold, copper, ivory, and flaves; and becaufe nothing ob-ftructs a continued communication between the people of the inland country and thofe of the coaft. It is the fole country in Africa, where, throughout a long fpace, there are no deferts or deep rivers to ob-ftruct the traveller, and where water and the means of fubfiftence may be found.

Between the river of Volta and that of Calbary, the coaft is flat, fertile, populous and cultivated. The country which extends from Calbary to Gabon is very different. Almoft totally covered with thick

B O O K forefts, producing little fruit and no corn, it may be
XI.   faid to be rather inhabited by wild beafts than by
men.   Though the rains be there very frequent and
copious, as they muft be under the Equator, the land
is fo fandy, that immediately after the fhowers are
fallen, there remains not the leaft appearance of moifture.

To the fouth of the line, and as far as Zara, the
coaft prefents an agreeable profpect.   Low at its beginning, it gradually rifes, and exhibits a fcene of
cultivated fields, intermixed with woods always ver-
dant, and of meadows covered with palm-trees.

From Zara to Coanza, and ftill further, the coaft
is in general high and craggy.   In the interior parts
of this country is an elevated plain, the foil of which
is compofed of a large, thick, and fertile fand.

Beyond Coanza and the Portuguefe fettlements, a
barren region intervenes, of above two hundred
leagues in extent, which is terminated by the country of the Hottentots.   In this long fpace there are
no inhabitants known except the Cimbebes, with
whom no intercourfe is kept up.

The varieties obfervable on the fhores of the weft
of Africa do not prevent them from enjoying a very
extraordinary, and perhaps a fingular advantage.
On this immenfe coaft, thofe tremendous rocks are
nowhere feen which are fo alarming to the navigator.   The fea is univerfally calm, and the anchorage
fecure.   Were it not for thefe advantages, it would
be difficult to remain there, becaufe there are very
few harbours, and becaufe the fhips are obliged to
anchor out at fea on account of the fand banks, which
are almoft contiguous to each other.

The winds and currents, during fix months of the
year, from April to November, have nearly the fame
direction.   To the fouth of the line, the fouth-eaft
wind predominates, and the direction of the currents
is towards the north; and to the north of the line
the eaft wind prevails, and the direction of the currents is towards the north-eaft.   During the fix other

months, ſtorms, by intervals, change the direction of the wind, but it no longer blows with the ſame vio-lence : the ſpring of the air ſeems to be relaxed. The cauſe of this variation appears to influence the direction of the currents : to the north of the line they tend to the ſouth-weſt, beyond the line to the ſouth.

BOOK XI.

The revolutions which muſt have happened in the north of Africa, as well as in the other parts of the globe, are entirely unknown, and it was impoſſible it ſhould be otherwiſe, in a region where the art of writing hath never penetrated. No tradition hath even been preſerved, which might ſerve as a baſis to conjectures well or ill founded. When the people of theſe regions are aſked, why they have ſuffered the remembrance of their father's actions to be buried in oblivion ? they anſwer, that it is of little conſequence to be informed in what manner the dead have lived ; that the material thing is, that the living ſhould be virtuous. So indifferent are they about the paſt time, that they neglect even to keep an account of their annual revolutions. This would be, ſay they, to load one's memory with a uſeleſs calculation, ſince it would not preſerve us from death, and could not inform us how long we have to live. In ſpeaking, therefore, of this part of the world, we are obliged to count from the epochas of the arrival of the Euro-peans upon theſe ſhores. We muſt even confine ourſelves to the coaſts, ſince no traveller of any cre-dit hath ever penetrated into the inland parts of the country ; and ſince our navigators have ſcarce ex-tended their inquiries beyond the harbours where they took in their cargoes.

Idea of the ſeveral go-vernments eſtabliſhed in Guinea.

All their accounts affirm, that the known parts of this region are ſubject to an arbitrary government. Whether the deſpotic ſovereign aſcend the throne by right of birth or by election, the people have no other law but his will.

But what will ſeem extraordinary to the inhabi-tants of Europe, where the great number of heredi-

BOOK
XI.

tary monarchies obftructs the tranquillity of elective
governments and the profperity of all free ftates, is,
that in Africa, the countries which are the leaft liable
to revolutions are thofe which have preferved the
right of electing their chiefs. This is ufually an old
man, whofe wifdom is generally known. The manner in which this choice is made is very fimple ; but
it is only fuited to very fmall ftates. In three days
time, the people, by mutual confent, meet at the houfe
of that citizen who appears to them the moft proper
perfon to be their fovereign. If the fuffrages be divided, he who hath obtained the greateft number of
them, names on the fourth day one of thofe who have
had fewer voices than himfelf. Every freeman hath
a right to vote. There are even fome tribes where
the women enjoy this privilege.

Such is, excepting the hereditary kingdoms of Benin and Juda, the manner in which that little group
of ftates, that are to the north of the line, is formed.
To the fouth we meet with Mayumba and Cilingo,
where chiefs are elected from among the minifters of
religion ; and with the empires of Loango and Congo,
where the crown is perpetual in the male line, by the
female fide ; that is, the eldeft fon of the king's eldeft fifter inherits the throne when it becomes va-
cant. Thefe people believe, that a child is much
more certainly the fon of his mother than of the man
whom fhe marries : they truft rather to the time of
delivery, which they fee, than to that of conception,
of which they are not witneffes.

Thefe nations live in a total ignorance of that art
fo revered among us, under the name of politics.
They do not, however, neglect to obferve fome of its
formalities. The cuftom of fending embaffies is familiar to them, whether to folicit aid againft a powerful enemy, or to requeft a mediator in their differences, or to congratulate others upon their fucceffes,
upon the birth of a child, or upon the falling of a
fhower after a great drought. The envoy muft never
ftay longer than a day at the place of his miffion ;

nor travel during the night in the states of a foreign prince. He is preceded by a drum, which announces from afar his dignity, and he is accompanied by five or fix friends. In those places where he stops to refresh himself, he is received with respect; but he cannot depart before the sun rises, and without the ceremony of his host assembling some persons, to witness that no accident hath happened to him. In other respects, these people are strangers to any negotiations that are in the least complicated. They never enter into any stipulations for the past nor for the future, but confine themselves wholly to the present. Hence we may conclude, that these nations cannot have any regular or settled connections with the other parts of the globe.

Their system of war is as little complicated as that of their politics. None of these governments retain troops in pay. Every freeman is by condition a soldier. All take up arms to guard their frontiers, or to make excursions in quest of booty. The officers are chosen by the soldiers, and the choice is confirmed by the prince. The army marches, and most frequently the hostilities, which are begun in the morning, are terminated in the evening. At least, the incursion never continues for any length of time; for as they have no magazines, the want of subsistence obliges them to retire. It would prove a great misfortune to these people if they were taught the art of keeping the field for a fortnight together.

The desire of extending their territories is not the cause of the disturbances which frequently throw these countries into confusion. An insult committed in a ceremony, a clandestine or violent robbery, the rape of a daughter, these are the ordinary occasions of a war. The day after the battle, each side redeems their respective prisoners. They are exchanged for merchandise or for slaves. No portion of the territory is ever ceded, the whole belongs to the community, whose chief fixes the extent which eve-

Manner of making war in Guinea.

BOOK ry perfon is to cultivate, in order to reap the fruits
XI. of it.

This manner of terminating differences is not merely that of little ftates, whofe chiefs are too wife to
afpire after enlarging their dominions, and too much
advanced in years not to be fond of peace. Great
empires are obliged to conform to thefe principles
with neighbours much weaker than themfelves. The
fovereign hath never any ftanding army ; and though
he difpofes at pleafure of the lives of the governors
of his provinces, he prefcribes them no rules of adminiftration. Thefe are petty princes, who, for fear
of being fufpected of ambition and punifhed with
death, live in concord with the elective colonies which
furround them. Unanimity between the more confiderable powers and the fmaller ftates, is preferved
as much by the great authority the prince hath over
his fubjects, as by the impoffibility there is of his exerting it at pleafure. He can only ftrike a fingle
blow, or caufe a fingle head to be cut off. He may,
indeed, command that his lieutenant fhould be affaf-
finated, and the whole province will obey his orders ;
but were he to command all the inhabitants of a province to be put to death, he would find no one ready
to execute his orders ; nor would he be able to excite
any other province to take up arms againft that which
difobeyed him. His power againft individuals is unlimited ; but he can do very little againft the collec-
tive body.

Another reafon which prevents the fmall ftates
from being enflaved by the great ones, is, that thefe
people annex no idea to the glory of conquefts. The
only perfon who appears to have been animated with
it, was a flave broker, who from his infancy had frequented the European veffels, and who in his riper
years had made a voyage to Portugal. Every thing
he faw and heard fired his imagination, and taught
him that a great name was frequently acquired by
being the caufe of great calamities. At his return
into his country, he felt himfelf greatly humiliated

at being obliged to obey people lefs enlightened than himfelf. His intrigues raifed him to the dignity of chief of the Acanis, and he prevailed on them to take up arms againft their neighbours. Nothing could oppofe his valour, and his dominion extended over more than an hundred leagues of coaft, of which Anamabou was the centre. At his death no one dared to fucceed him : and all the fupports of his authority failing at once, every thing returned to its former fituation.

The Chriftian and Mohammedan religions feem to Modes of worfhip eftablifhed in Guinea. have taken poffeffion of the two extremities of that part of the weft of Africa which is frequented by the Europeans. The Muffulmen of Barbary have carried their religious fyftem to the people of the Cape de Verd Iflands, who have extended it ftill further. In proportion as thefe religious opinions have been diftant from their fource, they have undergone fo great an alteration, that each kingdom, each village, each family, have maintained a different fyftem. Excepting circumcifion, which is univerfal, it would fcarcely be imagined that thefe people profeffed the fame worfhip. This religion does not penetrate beyond the Cape of Monte, the inhabitants of which have no communication with their neighbours.

What the Arabs had done to the north of the line for the Koran, the Portuguefe afterwards did to the fouth for the Gofpel. Towards the end of the fifteenth century, they eftablifhed it from the country of Benguela to Zara. A mode of worfhip, which offered fure and eafy means for the expiation of all crimes, was perfectly agreeable to the tafte of nations whofe religion did not afford them fuch comfortable profpects. If it was afterwards profcribed in feveral ftates, it was owing to the exceffes of thofe who propagated it, which drew upon it this difgrace. It hath even been totally difguifed in the countries where it hath been preferved ; a few trifling ceremonies are the only remains of it.

The coafts which are in the centre have preferved
fome local fuperftitions, the origin of which muft be
very ancient. They confift in the worfhip of that
innumerable multitude of divinities or Fetiches, which
every perfon makes after his own fancy, and for his
own ufe ; in the belief of auguries, trials by fire and
boiling water, and in the power of Gris-Gris. There
are fome fuperftitions more dangerous ; I mean that
blind confidence which they repofe in the priefts,
who are the minifters and promoters of them. The
correfpondence which they are fuppofed to hold with
the evil fpirit, makes them confidered as the arbiters
of the barrennefs and fertility of the country. On
this account the firft fruits are always offered to them.
All their other errors have a focial tendency, and
confpire to render men more humane and peaceable.

Manners,
cuftoms,
and occupa-
tions of the
people of
Guinea.
The country is generally ill peopled. Habitations
are feldom found any where but near rivers, lakes,
and fountains. In thofe countries, men are induced
to live in a focial ftate, rather from the ties of con-
fanguinity than from any reciprocal wants. Accordingly, fmall hamlets are found in the fame town,
and fometimes in the fame village, which are fo many
families, over which a patriarch prefides.

There are no traces to be found in thefe fettlements of any great progrefs in civilization. The
houfes are conftructed with branches of trees, or with
rufhes faftened to ftakes, which are driven far enough
into the ground to refift the winds. Windows are
feldom feen in them. The covering of the houfe
confifts only of leaves, and, if they can be obtained,
of the leaves of the palm-tree, which are more proper than others to bear the inclemency of the feafons. The huts of the capital, thofe even of the defpot, are fcarce diftinguifhed from the reft, except by
their extent. Thefe people are not prevented from
forming other conftructions, by a want of the beft
and the fineft wood, which they poffefs in abundance,
nor of earth proper to make bricks ; but they have

never had an idea that it was neceſſary to take ſo
much trouble to lodge themſelves.

The furniture is conſiſtent with the dwelling. In the towns, in the country, in the habitation of the prince, as well as that of the meaneſt citizens, it conſiſts only of baſkets, a few earthen pots, and ſome utenſils made out of gourds. The only difference is, that the poor ſleep upon mats, and the rich upon European carpets.

Their food is likewiſe the ſame. Rice, caſſava, maize, yams, or potatoes, according to the nature of the ſoil; wild fruits, palm-wine, game, and fiſh, which all perſons get according to their inclination: ſuch is the food which they all live upon, the ſlaves not excepted.

A girdle tied acroſs their loins, and which we call a *pagne*, is the only clothing of both ſexes. Glaſs beads, which are brought to them, and ſold very dear, compoſe the ornaments of moſt of the women, and of the few men who wiſh to make themſelves remarkable.

The arts are very trifling in theſe regions. None are known but thoſe which are commonly found in a riſing ſociety, and even thoſe are in their infancy. The ingenuity of a carpenter conſiſts only in building huts. The blackſmith hath no other tools than a ſmall hammer and a wooden anvil, to work the iron which is ſent from Europe. The potter makes ſome clumſy veſſels, and ſome pipes of clay, without the aſſiſtance of a mould. The *pagnes* are made only of a plant which grows naturally, and requires no preparation: the length of it conſtitutes the breadth of the piece. The weaver works it upon his lap, without either loom or ſhuttle, by paſſing the tram with his fingers between each of the threads of the chain, in the ſame manner as our baſket-makers make their hurdles. The inhabitants of the country carry ſalt to the moſt diſtant places; and ſeparate it from the ſea water by means of a great fire. The ſlaves, and a ſmall number of free men, are employed

in thefe fedentary labours; the reft live in a ftate of
habitual indolence.   If they fhould be roufed from
this lethargy by fome caprice, or by wearifome-
nefs, it is only to go a-hunting or a-fifhing.   They
never demean themfelves fo far as to cultivate the
ground.   Agriculture, confidered as the meaneft of
occupations, is left to the women, to whom they allow no greater comfort than the liberty of refting one
day after three days of exceffive fatigue.

The people of Guinea have manners very fimilar
to each other.   Polygamy is authorifed throughout
the whole extent of this vaft region.   It muft, however, be very uncommonly practifed, fince all the
free men, and moft of the flaves, find companions
for themfelves.   The young men confult nothing but
their own inclination in their marriage; but their
fifters muft have the confent of their mothers.   The
marriage tie is generally refpected; nothing but adul-
tery can diffolve it, and this is very uncommon.   On
the coaft of Angola only, the daughters of the chiefs
of the ftate are allowed to choofe the hufband they
like beft, even if he fhould be engaged; they may
prevent him from taking another wife; they may be
divorced from him when he difpleafes them; and
may even caufe his head to be ftricken off if he be
inconftant.   Thefe princeffes, if they may be fo called, enjoy their privileges with a difdainful haughtinefs, and a great deal of feverity, as if they meant
to be revenged upon the unfortunate man who is under their authority, for the fpecies of flavery to which
their fex is condemned.

Their fate is indeed deplorable.   Befides being
employed in the labours of the field, the women are
alfo obliged to attend to the domeftic employments.
It refts upon them alone to provide for the fubfiftence, and to fupply all the wants of their families.
They never appear before their hufbands but in a
humiliating pofture; they always wait upon him at
table, and retire afterwards to feed upon what he either could not or would not eat.   This ftate of la-

bour and humiliation is not confined to the common people; the women in the towns, the wives of the rich, of the great, and even of the fovereigns, are in the fame condition; they derive neither comfort nor prerogative from the rank or the opulence of their hufbands.

While they wafte in the fervice of their tyrants the fmall proportion of ftrength beftowed upon them by nature, thefe barbarians fpend their ufelefs days in a ftate of total inaction. Affembled under thick foliages, they pafs their time in fmoking, finging, or dancing. The fame amufements are repeated every day; and their pleafures are never interrupted by difputes. A decency and propriety prevail in them, which could not reafonably be expected from a people fo little enlightened.

Their difintereftednefs is a no lefs furprifing circumftance. If we except the coafts, where the example of our robberies hath made them robbers, a great indifference for riches is obferved in all parts. Even the wifeft among them feldom think of the morrow; and accordingly, hofpitality is the virtue univerfally practifed. The man who fhould not divide the game or the fifh he had caught with his neighbours, his relations, and his friends, would draw upon himfelf the public contempt. With them, the reproach of avarice is beyond any other. It is beftowed upon the Europeans, who give nothing without a compenfation; which induces thefe Africans to call them *clofe-fifted*.

Such is the general character of the people of Guinea. It now remains to fpeak of the cuftoms which diftinguifh the inhabitants of one country from thofe of another.

On the banks of the Niger, the women are generally handfome, if beauty may be faid to confift in fymmetry of proportion, and not in colour. Modeft, affable, and faithful, an air of innocence appears in their looks, and their language is an indication of their bafhfulnefs. The names of Zilia, Calypfo, Fanny, Zama, which feem to be names of voluptuoufnefs, are pronounced with an inflection of voice, of the foftnefs and fweetnefs of which our organs are not fufceptible. The men are of a proper fize, their fkin is as black as ebony, and their features and countenances pleafing. The habit of taming horfes, and hunting wild beafts, gives them an air of dignity. They do not eafily put up with an affront ; but the example of thofe animals they have reared, infpires them with boundlefs gratitude for a mafter who treats them with indulgence. It is impoffible to find fervants more attentive, more fober, and who have ftronger attachments ; but they do not make good hufbandmen ; becaufe their body is not habituated to ftoop and bend towards the ground, in order to clear it.

The complexion of the Africans degenerates towards the Eaft. The people of this climate are ftrong, but fhort. They have an air of ftrength, which is denoted by firm mufcles ; and the features of their faces are fpread out, but have no expreffion. The figures impreffed on their foreheads and on their cheeks increafe their natural deformity. An ungrateful foil, which is not improveable by culture, hath forced them to have recourfe to fifhing, though the fea, which they can fcarce venture upon, on account of a bar that runs along the coaft, feems to divert them from it. Thus repulfed, as it were, by thefe two elements, they have fought for aid among adjacent nations more favoured by nature ; from whom they have derived their fubfiftence by felling them falt. A fpirit of traffic hath been diffufed among them fince the arrival of the Europeans ; becaufe ideas are unfolded in all men in proportion to the variety of objects that are prefented to them ; and becaufe more combinations are neceffary to barter a flave for feveral forts of merchandife, than to fell a bufhel of falt. Though they be well adapted to all employments where ftrength only is required, yet they are unfit for the internal duties of domeftic life. This condition of life is repugnant to their cuftoms,

according to which they are paid separately for every B O O K
thing they do. And, indeed, the reciprocation of
daily labour and daily recompense is, perhaps, one of
the best incentives to industry among all men. The
wives of these mercantile Negroes have neither the
amiableness, modesty, discretion, nor beauty of the
women of the Niger, and they appear to have less
sensibility. On comparing the two nations, it might,
perhaps, be imagined, that the one consisted of the
lowest class of people in a polished and civilized city,
and that the other had enjoyed the advantages of su-
perior education. Their language is a strong indication of their character. The accents of the one have
an extreme sweetness, those of the other are harsh
and dry, like the soil they inhabit. Their vivacity,
even in pleasures, resembles the furious transports of
anger.

Beyond the river Volta, in Benin, and in the other
countries known under the general name of the Gold
Coast, the people have a smooth skin, and are of a
dark black colour; their teeth are beautiful; they
are of a middling stature, but well shaped, and have a
haughty countenance. Their faces, though agreeable enough, would be much more so, if the women
were not used to scar them, and the men to burn
their foreheads. The basis of their creed is a me-
tempsychosis of a peculiar kind : they believe, that
in whatever place they remove to, or wherever they
are transported, they shall return after their death,
whether caused by the laws of nature, or by their
own hands, to their native country. This conviction
constitutes their happiness ; because they consider
their country as the most delightful abode in the
universe. This pleasing error conduces to humanize
them. Foreigners, who reside in this climate, are
treated with respectful civility, from a persuasion that
they are come there to receive the recompense due
to their good conduct. These people have a disposition to cheerfulness not observable in the neighbouring nations ; they are inclined to labour, have prin-

BOOK ciples of equity feldom altered by circumftances, and
XI. a great facility of adapting themfelves to foreign
manners. They are tenacious of their commercial
cuftoms, even when they are not advantageous to
them. The method of trafficking with them was,
for a long time, the fame that had been at firft practifed among them. The firft veffel that arrived difpofed of its cargo before another was permitted to
trade. Each had its turn. The commodities were
fold at the fame fixed price to all. It is but very
lately that the nation had refolved to avail itfelf of
the advantages it might derive from the competition
between the European nations frequenting its ports.

The people fituated between the line and Zara
have all a great refemblance to each other. They
are well made. Their bodies are lefs robuft than thofe
of the inhabitants to the north of the equator; and
though there be fome marks on their faces, none of
thofe fcars are to be perceived which are fo fhocking
at firft fight. Their feafts are accompanied with military fports, which revive the idea of our ancient
tournaments; with this difference, that in Europe
they conftituted the exercifes of a warlike nation,
whereas in Africa they are the amufements of a timid people. The women are not admitted to thefe
public diverfions. Affembled together in certain
houfes, they fpend their day in private; and no men
are ever admitted into their fociety. The pride of
rank is the ftrongeft paffion of thefe people, who are
naturally peaceable. A certain degree of ceremony
obtains both at the court of princes and in private
life. Upon the moft trivial occurrences, they haften
to their friends, either to congratulate them or to con-
dole with them. A marriage occafions vifiting for
three months. The funeral obfequies of a perfon of
diftinction continue fometimes two years. Thofe who
are related to him in any degree, carry his remains
through feveral provinces. The crowd gathers as
they proceed, and no perfon departs till the corpfe
is depofited in the tomb, with all the demonftrations'

of the deepeſt ſorrow. So determined a taſte for ce-remony hath proved favourable to ſuperſtition, and ſuperſtition hath promoted a ſpirit of indolence.

From Zara to the river of Coanza, the ancient cuſtoms ſtill remain ; but they are blended with a confuſed mixture of European manners, which are not to be found elſewhere. It is probable that the Portugueſe, who have large ſettlements in this country, and who were deſirous of introducing the Chriſtian religion among them, had a greater intercourſe with them than other nations, who having only factories to the north of the line, have been entirely engaged in carrying on their commerce.

The reader need not be told, that all we have related concerning the people of Guinea, ought only to be applied to that claſs which, in all countries, ſtamps the character of a nation. The inferior orders and ſlaves are further removed from this reſemblance, in proportion as they are debaſed or degraded by their occupations or their conditions. The moſt diſcerning inquirers have, however, imagined that the difference of conditions did not produce in this people varieties ſo diſtinguiſhable as we find in the ſtates which are ſituated between the Elbe and the Tiber, which exhibit nearly the ſame extent of coaſt as the diſtance between the Niger and the Coanza. The further men depart from nature, the leſs muſt they reſemble one another. Nature is a ſtraight line, from which there are various ways of deviating. The counſels of nature are ſpeedy and tolerably uniform ; but the ſuggeſtions ariſing from taſte, from fancy, from caprice, from perſonal intereſt, from circumſtances, from paſſions, from the accidental events of health or ſickneſs, and even from dreams, are ſo numerous and ſo various, that they are not, neither can they ever be exhauſted. One violent man is ſufficient to lead a thouſand more aſtray, from motives of condeſcenſion, flattery, or imitation. If a woman of rank be deſirous of concealing ſome natural defect, ſhe immediately contrives ſomething for that purpoſe.

B O O K This is foon adopted by her companions, though they
   XI.   have not the fame reafon for it. Thus it is, that from
          one eccentric circle to another, a fafhion is extended,
          and becomes national. This inftance is fufficient to
          explain an infinite number of fingularities, which our
          fagacity would in vain be tortured in finding out the
          reafons of, in the wants, the pains, or pleafures of
          mankind. The diverfity of civil and moral inftitu-
          tions, which often are neither more combined, nor
          lefs cafual, alfo neceffarily occafions a difference in
          the moral character and in the natural cuftoms of
          men, which is unknown to focieties lefs complicated.
          Befides, nature being more powerful under the torrid
          than under the temperate zone, does not permit the
          influence of manners to exert itfelf fo ftrongly. Men
          in thefe countries bear a greater fimilitude to one
          another, becaufe they owe every thing to nature, and
          very little to art. In Europe, an extenfive and di-
          verfified commerce, varying and multiplying the
          enjoyments, the fortunes, and feveral conditions of
          men, adds likewife to the differences which the cli-
          mate, the laws, and the common prejudices, have
          eftablifhed among active and laborious nations.

Ancient   In Guinea, trade hath never been able to caufe a
flate of the material alteration in the manners of its inhabitants.
trade of
Guinea. It formerly confifted only of certain exchanges of falt
          and dried fifh, which were confumed by the nations
          remote from the coaft. Thefe gave in return ftuffs
          made of a kind of thread, which was only a woody
          fubftance, clofely adhering to the inner fide of the
          bark of a tree peculiar to thefe climates. The air
          hardens it, and renders it fit for every kind of weav-
          ing. Bonnets, fcarfs, and aprons to ferve for girdles,
          are made of it, which vary in fhape according to the
          particular mode of each nation. The natural colour
          of the thread is a pale grey. The dew, which bleaches
          our flax, gives it a citron colour, which rich people pre-
          fer. The black dye, generally ufed 'mong the people, is
          extracted from the bark of the tree of which this
          thread is made, by fimple infufion in water,

The firſt Europeans who frequented the weſtern B O O K coaſts of Africa fixed a price on wax, ivory, gum, and XI. wood for dying, which, before that time, had been thought of little value. A ſmall quantity of gold, which had been formerly carried off by caravans from the ſtates of Barbary, was likewiſe given in exchange to their navigators. This gold came from the inland parts, and chiefly from Bambouk, an ariſtocratic ſtate, under the twelfth and thirteenth degrees of north latitude, and where each village was governed by a chief called Farim. This rich metal is ſo common in this country, that it is found almoſt indiſcriminately every where, merely by ſcraping the ſurface of the earth, which is clayiſh, light, and mixed with ſand. When the mine is very rich, it is digged only to the depth of a few feet, and never deeper; though it hath been obſerved, that the lower it was digged, the more gold it afforded. The people are too indolent to purſue a toil which conſtantly becomes more fatiguing, and too ignorant to prevent the inconveniences it would be attended with. Their negligence and their folly are ſo extraordinary, that in waſhing the gold, in order to ſeparate it from the earth, they only preſerve the larger pieces: the light parts paſs away with the water, which flows down an inclined plain.

The inhabitants of Bambouk do not work theſe mines at all times, nor are they at liberty to do it when they chooſe. They are obliged to wait till private or public wants determine the Farims to grant this permiſſion. When it is proclaimed, all who are able to avail themſelves of this advantage meet at the appointed place. When their work is finiſhed, a diviſion is made. Half of the gold goes to the lord, and the remainder is equally diſtributed among the labourers. Thoſe who want gold at any other time than that of the general digging, ſearch for it in the beds of the torrents, where it is very common.

Several Europeans have endeavoured to penetrate into a region which contains ſo many treaſures. Two

or three of them, who had fucceeded in approaching the coaft, were unmercifully repulfed. M. David
governor of the French in Senegal, in 1740, thought
of fending a prince of that country, in order to lay
wafte the borders of the Felemé, from whence Bambouk received all its provifions. This unfortunate
country was upon the point of being deftroyed, in the
midft of its piles of gold, when the author of this
calamity propofed to them, that he would fend them
provifions from Fort Galam, which was only at forty
leagues diftance, if they would confent to receive
him, and permit his people to work the mines. Thefe
conditions were accepted, and the obfervance of
them was again fworn to the author of the propofal,
who went himfelf to thofe provinces four years after;
but the treaty produced no effect. Only the remembrance of the hardfhips that had been endured, and
of thofe thas had been apprehended, determined the
people to cultivate a foil, which had produced, till
then, nothing but metals. It feems that the gold
hath been abandoned, and that the attention of all
men hath been turned to the flave trade

The com-
merce of
Guinea
hath been
extended
by the fale
of flaves.
The property which fome men have acquired over
others in Guinea, is of very high antiquity. It is generally eftablifhed there, excepting in fome fmall diftricts, where liberty hath, as it were, retired, and is
ftill maintained. No proprietor, however, hath a right
to fell a man who is born in a ftate of fervitude. He
can only difpofe of thofe flaves whom he gets either
by war, in which every prifoner is a flave unlefs
exchanged, or in lieu of compenfation for fome injury ; or if he hath received them as a teftimony of
acknowledgment. This law, which feems to be made
in favour of one who is born a flave, to indulge him
in the enjoyment of his family, and of his country,
is yet ineffectual, fince the Europeans have eftablifhed luxury on the coafts of Africa. It is every day
eluded by concerted quarrels, which two proprietors
mutually diffemble, in order to be reciprocally condemned, each in his turn, to a fine, which is paid in

BOOK XI.

perfons born flaves, the difpofal of whom is allowed by the fanction of the fame law.

Corruption, contrary to its ordinary progrefs, hath advanced from private perfons to princes. The procuring of flaves hath given frequent occafion to wars, as they are excited in Europe, in order to obtain foldiers. The cuftom has been eftablifhed of punifhing with flavery, not only thofe who have attempted the lives or properties of citizens, but thofe alfo who were incapable of paying their debts, and thofe who have violated conjugal faith. This punifhment, in procefs of time, has been inflicted for the moft trivial offences, after having been at firft referved only for the greateft crimes. Prohibitions, even of things indifferent, have been conftantly multiplied, in order to increafe the revenues raifed from the fines, by increafing the number of offences. Injuftice hath known no bounds or reftraints. At a great diftance from the coaft there are chiefs, who give orders for every thing they meet with in the villages around them to be carried off. The children are thrown into facks; the men and women are gagged to ftifle their cries. If the ravagers fhould be ftopped by a fuperior force, they are conducted before the prince, who always difowns the commiffion he hath given, and, under pretence of doing juftice, inftantly fells his agents to the fhips he hath treated with.

Notwithftanding thefe infamous arts, the people of the coaft have found it impoffible to fupply the demands of the merchants. They have experienced what every nation muft, that can trade only with its fpecies. Slaves are to the commerce of the Europeans in Africa, what gold is in the commerce we carry on in the New World. The heads of the Negroes reprefent the fpecie of the ftate of Guinea. Every day this fpecie is carried off, and nothing is left them but articles of confumption. Their capital gradually vanifhes, becaufe it cannot be renewed, by reafon of the fpeedy confumptions. Thus the trade for blacks would long fince have been entirely loft, if the in-

habitants of the coafts had not imparted their luxury
to the people of the inland countries, from whence
they now draw the greateft part of the flaves that are
put into our hands. Thus the trade of the Europeans, by gradual advances, hath almoft exhaufted the
only vendible commodities of this nation.

In the fpace of twenty years this circumftance hath
raifed the price of flaves almoft to four times above
the former coft. The reafon is this : the flaves are
chiefly paid for in merchandife from the Eaft Indies,
which hath doubled its value in Europe. A double
quantity of thefe goods muft be given in Africa.
Thus the colonies of America, where the fale for
blacks is concluded, are obliged to fupport thefe feveral augmentations, and confequently to pay four
times more than they formerly did.

Notwithftanding this, the diftant proprietor who
fells his flave, receives a lefs quantity of merchandife
than the perfon received fifty years ago, who fold his
flave in the neighbourhood of the coaft. The profits
intercepted by paffing through different hands, the
expences of tranfport, the impofts, fometimes of three
per cent. that muft be paid to thofe princes through
whofe territories they pafs, fink the difference betwixt
the fum which the firft proprietor receives, and that
which the European trader pays. Thefe expences
continually increafe on account of the great diftances
of the places where there are ftill flaves to be fold.
The further off the firft fale is, the greater will be
the difficulties attending the journey. They will become fuch, that of the fum which the European
merchant will be able to pay, there will remain fo
little to offer to the firft feller, that he will rather
choofe to keep his flave. All trade of this kind will
then be at an end. In order, therefore, to fupport
it effectually, our traders muft furnifh at an exorbitant price, and fell in proportion to the colonies ;
which, on their part, not being able to difpofe of their
produce but at a very advanced price, will no longer
find a confumption for it. But till that time comes,

which is, perhaps, not fo diftant as the colonifts may
imagine, they will, without the leaft remorfe, continue to make the lives and labours of the Negroes
fubfervient to their interefts. They will find navigators who will hazard the purchafing of them, and
thefe will meet with tyrants who will fell them.

Slave merchants collect themfelves into companies,
and forming a fpecies of caravans, in the fpace of
two or three hundred leagues they conduct feveral
files of thirty or forty flaves, all laden with water and
corn, which are neceffary to their fubfiftence in thofe
barren deferts through which they pafs. The manner of fecuring them without much incommoding
their march, is ingeniously contrived. A fork of
wood, from eight to nine feet long, is put round the
neck of each flave. A pin of iron, rivetted, fecures
the fork at the back part in fuch a manner that the
head cannot difengage itfelf. The handle of the fork,
the wood of which is very heavy, falls before, and fo
embarraffes the perfon who is tied to it, that though
he hath his arms and legs at liberty, he can neither
walk, nor lift up the fork. When they get ready for
their march, they range the flaves on the fame line,
and fupport and tie the extremity of each fork on the
fhoulder of the foremoft flave, and proceed in this
manner from one to another, till they come to the
firft, the extremity of whofe fork is carried by one of
the guides. Few reftraints are impofed that are not
felt by the perfons who impofe them. In order that
thefe traders may enjoy the refrefhment of fleep without uneafinefs, they tie the arms of every flave to the
tail of the fork which he carries. In this condition
he can neither run away, nor make any attempt to
recover his liberty. Thefe precautions have been
found indifpenfable, becaufe if the flave can but break
his chain, he becomes free. The public faith, which
fecures to the proprietor the poffeffion of his flave,
and which at all times delivers him up into his hands,
is filent with regard to a flave and a trader who exercifes the moft contemptible of all profeffions.

Reader, while thou art perufing this horrid account, is not thy foul filled with the fame indignation as I experience in writing it? Doft thou not, in imagination, rufh with fury upon thofe infamous conductors? Doft thou not break thofe forks with which thefe unfortunate people are confined? and doft thou not reftore them to their liberty?

Great numbers of flaves arrive together, efpecially when they come from diftant countries. This arrangement is neceffary, in order to diminifh the expence which is unavoidable in conducting them. The interval between one journey and another, which by this fyftem of economy is already made too diftant, may become ftill greater by particular circumftances. The moft ufual are the rains, which caufe the rivers to overflow, and put a ftop to this trade. The feafon moft favourable for travelling in the interior parts of Africa, is from February to September; and it is from September to March that the return of thefe flave traders produces the greateft plenty of this traffic on the coafts.

Account of the coafts where foreign navigators land in fearch of flaves.
The trade of the Europeans is carried on to the fouth and north of the line. The firft coaft begins at Cape Blanco: very near this are Arguin and Portendic. The Portuguefe difcovered them in 1444, and fettled there the next year. They were deprived of them in 1638 by the Dutch, who, in their turn, ceded them to the Englifh in 1666, from whom they recovered them fome months after. Lewis XIV. again drove them away in the beginning of 1678, and contented himfelf with having the works deftroyed.

At this period, Frederic William, that great elector of Brandenburg, was meditating upon the means of improving his dominions, which till then had been inceffantly ruined by wars, which were feldom interrupted. Some Dutch merchants, difcontented with the monopoly which excluded them from the weftern parts of Africa, perfuaded him to build forts in this immenfe diftrict, and to have flaves purchafed there, which would be fold to advantage in the New

World. This fcheme was thought to be ufeful, and B O O K
the company formed to carry it on obtained, in XI.
1682, three fettlements on the Gold Coaft, and one
in the ifland of Arguin three years afterwards. This
new body was fucceffively ruined by the oppofitions
of the rival nations, by the unfaithfulnefs or the inexperience of its agents, and by the depredations of
the pirates. As nothing but the name of them was
remaining, the King of Pruffia fold, in 1717, to the
Dutch Company, poffeffions which had been long
ufelefs to him. Thefe republicans had not yet taken
poffeffion of Arguin, when it was again attacked in
1721, and taken, by the orders of the court of Verfailles, who had been maintained in that conqueft by
the treaty of Nimeguen. The Dutch foon after planted their flag there, but were obliged to take it down
again in 1724.

From that period to 1763, France remained in
quiet poffeffion of thefe forts. The Britifh miniftry,
who had required the facrifice of the Niger, infifted,
befid s, that they fhould be dependent upon it. This
pretenfion does not appear to us to be well founded.
It is only neceffary to fee the grants made to the focieties which have fucceffively exercifed the monopoly in Senegal, to be convinced that Arguin and
Portendic were never comprehended in their charter.
England, however, doth not permit the French, nor
other navigators, to approach thefe latitudes ; even
its own fubjects go there no more, fince thofe precious gums, from which they have acquired fome importance, have been conveyed by the Niger.

This river, which is more commonly called Senegal, is very confiderable, is reckoned by fome geographers to have more than eight hundred leagues
of extent. It hath been proved, that from June to
November, it is navigable throughout a fpace of
three hundred and twenty leagues. The bar which
runs acrofs the mouth of the river prohibits the entrance of it to all fhips which draw more than eight

BOOK or nine feet of water. The other ships are obliged
XI. to cast anchor very near this spot, in an exceeding
good bottom. Their cargoes are brought to them in
light vessels from Fort St. Lewis, which is built in a
small island near the sea. They consist only of the
gums which have been collected during the year,
and of twelve or fifteen hundred slaves. The gums
are sent from the left shore, and the slaves from the
right, which is the only one that can be said to be
peopled, since the tyrants of Morocco have extended
their ferocious sway to these regions.

Since the peace of 1763 hath assured to Great Britain the possession of Senegal, the conquest of which
was made by its navy during the course of the war,
the French are confined to the coast which begins at
Cape Blanco, and terminates at the river Gambia.
Although they have not been disturbed in the claim
they have to the right of an exclusive trade through
that immense space, yet they have scarcely received
annually from their factories of Zoal, Portudal, and
Albreda, three or four hundred slaves. Goree, which
is only a league distant from the continent, and
which is no more than four hundred toises in length,
and one hundred in breadth, is the chief of these
wretched settlements. During the hostilities begun
in 1756, this island, which hath a good harbour, and
which may be easily defended, fell into the hands of
the English; but the subsequent treaties restored it
to its ancient masters.

Till the year 1772, this country had been open to
all the traders of the nation. At this period, a restless and turbulent man persuaded some credulous
citizens, that it would be an easy matter to get to
Bambouk, and to other mines of equal wealth. An
ignorant administration encouraged the illusion, by
granting an exclusive privilege; and considerable
sums were expended in pursuit of this chimerical
prospect. The direction of this monopoly, two years
after, passed into the hands of more prudent men,

who confined themfelves to the purchafe of the flaves that are to be brought to Cayenne, where the Company have obtained an immenfe territory.

The river Gambia would be navigable for the fpace of two hundred leagues for veffels of a confiderable fize; but they all ftop at the diftance of eight or ten leagues from the mouth of that river at Fort James. This fettlement, which hath been conquered, ranfomed, and pillaged, feven or eight times in the courfe of a century, is fituated in an ifland, which is not a mile in circumference. The Englifh trade annually there for three thoufand flaves, which come moftly, as at Senegal, from very diftant and inland countries.

The ten Cape de Verd Iflands, at no great diftance from the fhores, and of which Sant Yago is the principal, were difcovered by the Portuguefe about the year 1449. This fmall Archipelago, which, though much divided, hilly, and not well watered, would be able to furnifh all the productions of the New World, fcarce fupplies fufficient fubfiftence to the few Negroes, moft of them free, who have efcaped from a fyftem of tyranny continued for four centuries. The weight of the fetters which opprefs them was rendered ftill more burdenfome, when they were put under the power of a company which had the exclufive right both of fupplying all their wants, and of purchafing the commodities they had to fell. Accordingly, the exports of that foil, though of tolerable extent, were reduced for Europe to the plant known by the name of Perella, which is made ufe of in dying fcarlet; to a few oxen and mules for America, and for that part of Africa which is fubject to the court of Lifbon; to a fmall quantity of fugar, and to feveral pagnes of cotton. The fate of this unfortunate country was not to be altered. No one could appeal in its favour, while, from the general to the foldier, from the bifhop to the curate, every man was in the pay of the Company, which was at length abolifhed.

Several Portuguefe, who had gone to the Cape de

Verd Iflands, foon arrived upon the banks of the river of Cafamane and Cacheo, and upon the largeft
of the Biffagos iflands. Their defcendants degenerated fo much in procefs of time, that they fcarce
differed from the natives. They have always preferved, however, the ambition of confidering themfelves as fovereigns of the country, where they had
built three villages and two fmall forts. The rival
nations have paid very little refpect to this pretenfion, and have difcontinued to trade in competition
with the veffels arrived from the Cape de Verd
Iflands, from the Brazils, and from Lifbon.

Serre-Leone is not under the Britifh dominion, although the fubjects of that power have concentrated
almoft all the commercial tranfactions in two private
factories, very anciently eftablifhed. Exclufive of
the wax, ivory and gold, which are found there, they
receive annually four or five thoufand flaves either
from this or from the neighbouring rivers.

Next to this mart we meet with the Grain Coaft,
and the Ivory Coaft, which occupy the fpace of one
hundred and fifty leagues. Rice, ivory, and flaves,
are purchafed there. The navigators, from temporary factories upon fome of thefe coafts, moft frequently wait at anchor till the blacks come of their own
accord, upon their canoes, to propofe the things they
mean to barter. It is faid, that this cuftom hath been
eftablifhed, fince repeated acts of ferocioufnefs have
evinced the danger of difembarking.

The Englifh fince formed a fettlement at the Cape
of Apolonia, where the flave trade is confiderable ;
but they have not yet obtained an exclufive commerce, which they wifhed for, and which, perhaps,
they flattered themfelves they fhould obtain.

After Cape Apolonia begins the Gold Coaft, which
terminates at the river Volta. It is one hundred and
thirty leagues in extent. As the country is divided
into a great many fmall ftates, and as the inhabitants
are the moft robuft men of Guinea, the factories of
the commercial nations of Europe have been exceed-

ingly multiplied here. Five of them belong to the B O O K Danes; twelve or thirteen, of which St. George de XI. la Mina is the capital, belong to the Dutch ; and the Englifh have conquered, or formed, nine or ten of them, the chief of which is Cape Corfo. The French, who faw themfelves, with regret, excluded from a region abounding in flaves, attempted, in 1749, to appropriate Anamabou to themfelves. They were fortifying themfelves in it, with the confent of the natives of the country, when their workmen were driven away by the cannon of the fhips of Great Britain. An able merchant, who was then at London, upon the news of this outrage, exprefled his aftonifhment at a conduct fo imprudent. *Sir*, faid a minifter to him, who was in great favour with this enlightened people, *if we were to be juft to the French, we fhould not exift thirty years longer.* At this period the Englifh formed a firm eftablifhment at Anamabou, and fince that time they have never fuffered any competitor in this important market.

At the diftance of eight leagues from the river Volta is Kela, which abounds in articles of fubfiftence. There it is that the navigators go to fupply themfelves with provifions ; and from thence it is that they fend their canoes, or boats, in fearch of proper places to eftablifh their trade in.

The Little Popo often attracts them. The Englifh and the French frequent this latitude ; but the Portuguefe refort there in ftill greater numbers, for the following reafon :

The people who formerly held the fway in Africa, were reduced, in procefs of time, to fuch a ftate of weaknefs, that, in order to preferve the liberty of trading on the Gold Coaft, they agreed to pay the tenth of their cargoes to the Dutch. This fhameful tribute, which hath always been paid regularly, was fo difadvantageous to the privateers of Bahia and of Fernambucca, the only ones that frequent that coaft, that they agreed among themfelves, that no more than one veffel of each of thefe two provinces fhould

BOOK ever be in any port.   The reft remain at Little Popo,
XI. till their turn for trading comes about.

Juida, at fourteen leagues diftance from the Little
Popo, is famous for the number and the quality of
the flaves which come from thence.   It is open only
to the Englifh, the French, and the Portuguefe.
Each of thefe nations hath a fort there, built in the
ifland of Gregoi, two miles from the fhore.   The
chiefs of thefe factories undertake, every year, a journey of thirty leagues, in order to carry to the fovereign of the country prefents, which he receives,
and requires as an homage.

At the diftance of eight leagues from Juida, is Epée;
where there are fometimes a great many flaves, but
moft commonly none.   Accordingly, this harbour is
frequently void of fhips.

A little beyond this is Porto Novo.   The trade,
which in other places is fettled on the fea-coaft, is
carried on here in the inland parts, at feven leagues
from the fhore.   This inconvenience made it languid
for a long time, but it is now very confiderable.   The
paffion for the tobacco of Brazil, which is ftill more
prevailing at this place than in any other part of the
coaft, gives a confiderable fuperiority to the Portuguefe.   The Englifh and French are obliged to form
their cargoes from the refufe of theirs.

Badagry is only at three leagues diftance from Porto Novo.   A great many flaves are brought there.
At the time when all nations were admitted, the navigators could only make their purchafes, and difpofe
of their cargoes, one after the other ; but fince the
Englifh and the Dutch are fecluded, the French
and the Portuguefe are allowed to trade in competition, becaufe their merchandifes are very different.
This is the part of the coaft the moft frequented by
French privateers.

Ahoni, which is feparated from Badagry by an interval of fourteen or fifteen leagues, is fituated in the
iflands of Curamo, in a difficult, marfhy, and unhealthy port.   This mart is principally, almoft ex-

clufively indeed, frequented by the Englifh, who
come there in large floops, and carry on their trade
between the iflands and the neighbouring continent.

From the river Volta to this Archipelago, the coaft
is inacceffible. A fand-bank, againft which the waves
of the fea break with great violence, obliges the navigators, who are attracted to thefe latitudes by the
hopes of gain, to make ufe of Indian boats, and of
the natives of the country, to land their cargoes, and
to bring back the goods they receive in exchange.
Their veffels are fafely anchored upon an exceeding
good bottom, at the diftance of three or four leagues
from the coaft.

The river of Benin, which abounds in ivory and
in flaves, receives fome fhips. Its trade is fallen almoft entirely into the hands of the Englifh. The
French and the Dutch have been difgufted with the
character of the natives, who are indeed lefs favage
than thofe of the neighbouring countries, but fo extremely capricious, that it is never known what kind
of merchandife they will choofe to accept in exchange.

After Cape Formofa, are the Old and the New
Calbary. The coaft is low, under water for fix months
in the year, and very unwholefome. All the water
is tainted ; fhipwrecks are frequent there, and whole
crews are fometimes the victims of the intemperance
of the climate. Thefe various calamities have not
been able to prevent the navigators of Great Britain
from frequenting thefe dangerous latitudes. They
purchafe there, every year, feven or eight thoufand
blacks, but at a very low price. The French, who
formerly feldom reforted to thefe marts, now begin
to land there in greater numbers. The fhips, which
draw above twelve feet water, are obliged to caft anchor near the ifland of Panis, where the chief of thefe
barbarous countries refides, and where he hath drawn
a confiderable trade.

Trade is much more brifk on the Gabon. This is

BOOK a large river, which waters an immenfe plain, and
XI. which, together with feveral other lefs confiderable
rivers, forms a multitude of iflands, more or lefs extenfive, which are each of them governed by a feparate chief. There is fcarce any country more plentiful, more funk under water, or more unwholefome.
The French, more volatile than enterprifing, feldom
go there, notwithftanding their wants. The Portuguefe of Prince's and St. Thomas's Iflands fend only
a few floops. The Dutch export from thence ivory,
wax, and woods for dyeing. The Englifh buy up almoft all the flaves which the petty nations, that are
perpetually intent upon each other's deftruction, make
of the prifoners taken on both fides, in the wars carried on between them. There is no confiderable ftaple where the exchanges are made. The Europeans
are obliged to penetrate, with their boats, to the extent of fifty or fixty leagues, in thefe infectious moraffes. This cuftom prolongs the trade exceffively,
it is deftructive to an infinite number of failors, and
occafions fome murders. Thefe calamities would
ceafe, if a general mart were eftablifhed in Parrot
Ifland, fituated at the diftance of ten leagues from
the mouth of the Gabon, and where fhips of a tolerable fize can land. The Englifh attempted it, undoubtedly with a view of fortifying themfelves there,
and in hopes of obtaining an exclufive trade. Their
agent was murdered in 1769, and matters have remained as they were before.

It muft be obferved, that the flaves which come
from Benin, from Calbary, and from Gabon, are very
inferior to thofe which are bought elfewhere. They
are therefore fold as much as poffible to the foreign
colonies by the Englifh, who frequent thefe indifferent markets more than any other nation. Such is
the ftate of things to the north of the line.

On the fouth, the markets are much lefs numerous,
but generally more confiderable. The firft that prefents itfelf, after Cape de Lopo, is Mayumba. Till
the fhips arrive at this harbour, the fea is too rough

to admit approaching the land. A bay, which is two leagues over at its mouth, and one league in depth, affords a fafe afylum to the veffels that are impeded by the calms and the currents, which are frequent in thofe latitudes. The landing is eafy near a river. It may be imagined, that the deferts of a climate, too full of moraffes, hath been the only reafon that hath kept the Europeans, and confequently the Africans, away. If from time to time a few captives are fold there, they are purchafed by the Englifh and by the Dutch, who go there regularly to take in cargoes of a kind of red wood, that is employed in dyeing.

At Cape Segundo is found another bay, which is very healthy, more fpacious, and more commodious, than even that of Mayumba, and in which water and wood may be obtained with eafe and fecurity. All thefe advantages muft undoubtedly have drawn a confiderable trade there, if the time and the expences which are requifite to reach to the extremity of a long flip of land, had not difgufted the flave merchants of it.

They have preferred Loango, where they anchor at eight or nine toifes diftance from the river, in three or four fathom water, upon a muddy bottom. Such is the agitation of the fea, that it is impoffible to land on the coaft, except upon Indian boats. The European factories are at a league's diftance from the town, upon an eminence, which is confidered as very unwholefome. This is the reafon why, notwithftanding the blacks are cheaper there than any where elfe, and the natives are lefs difficult about the quality of the merchandife, yet the navigators feldom land at Loango, except when the competition is too great in the other ports.

At Molembo, the veffels are obliged to ftop at one league's diftance from the fhore; and the boats, in order to land, muft clear a bar that is rather dangerous. The tranfactions are carried on upon a very agreeable mountain, but very difficult of accefs. The flaves are here in greater number, and of fuperior quality to thofe upon the reft of the coaft.

The bay of Gabinda is fafe and commodious. The fea is fmooth enough to admit of refitting the veffels in cafe of neceffity. Anchor is caft at the foot of the houfes, and the bufinefs is tranfacted at the diftance of one hundred and fifty paces from the fhore.

It hath long been faid, and it cannot be too often repeated, that the climate is exceedingly deftructive in thefe three ports, and efpecially at Loango. Let us endeavour to find out the reafons of this calamity, and let us fee whether it may not be remedied.

The grafs which grows on the coaft is almoft always four or five feet high, and receives abundant dews during the night. The Europeans who crofs thefe fields in the morning, are feized with violent, and frequently fatal colics, unlefs the natural heat of the inteftines, which are probably chilled by the impreffion of this dew, be reftored without delay by brandy. Would not this danger be avoided, by keeping away from this grafs till the fun fhould have diffipated the kind of venom that had fallen upon it?

The fea is unwholefome in thefe latitudes. Its waves, of a yellowifh caft, and which are covered with whales blubber, muft obftruct the pores of the fkin in thofe who bathe in it, and check their perfpiration. This is probably the caufe of the burning fevers which carry off fuch a prodigious number of failors. In order to prevent thefe deftructive maladies, it would perhaps be fufficient to employ the natives of the country in all the fervices that cannot be done without entering into the water.

In that country, the days are exceffively hot, the nights damp and cold, which is a dangerous alternative. The inconveniences of it might be avoided by lighting fires in the bedchambers. This precaution would make the two extremes lefs fenfible, and would produce the neceffary degree of temperature for a man who is afleep, and who cannot put on additional

coverings in proportion as the cold of the night in-
creases.

Inaction and wearisomeness are fatal to the crews
of ships that are commonly detained four or five
months on the coast. This double inconvenience
would be removed, if a third of them were constantly
employed alternately on land, in those trifling labours
which are improperly thrown upon the Negroes, and
which would occupy without fatiguing them.

It will perhaps be said, that we are for ever attending to the preservation of man. But what object is
there which ought more seriously to engage our
thoughts? Is it gold, or silver, or precious stones?
Some person of an atrocious disposition might imagine it. Should he dare to avow such a sentiment in
my presence, I would say to him, I know not who
thou art; but nature had formed thee to be a despot,
a conqueror, or an executioner; for she hath divested
thee of all kind of benevolence towards thy fellow
creature. If we should happen to mistake with regard to the means we propose for their preservation,
we shall be happy to find them censured, and to have
some more effectual means suggested.

Our confidence, however, in the advice we have
just been giving, is the more confirmed, as it is founded upon experiments made by one of the most intelligent seamen we have ever known. This able
man lost only one sailor during a twelvemonth's stay
at Loango itself; and even that sailor had infringed
the orders that were given.

A very singular custom is generally observed in the
country of Angola; and the people are equally ignorant of its origin and of its tendency. The kings
of those provinces are not allowed to have in their
possession, nor even to touch, any European goods,
except metals, arms, and carved wood or ivory. It
is probable that some of their predecessors have submitted to this self-denial, in order to diminish the inordinate desire of their subjects for foreign merchandise. If this was the motive of that institution, the

succefs hath not anfwered the expectation. The loweft claffes of men intoxicate themfelves with our liquors whenever they have the means of purchafing
them ; and the wealthy, the great, and even the
minifters, generally clothe themfelves with our linens
and our ftuffs. They take care only to quit thefe
dreffes when they go to court, where it is not allowed
to difplay a luxury prohibited to the defpot alone.

There is no other landing place from the laft port
we have mentioned till we come to the Zaire. The
river Ambris is at no great diftance from this ; it receives a few fmall veffels fent from Europe itfelf.
More confiderable fhips, which arrive at Loango, at
Molembo, and at Gabinda, likewife fend fome boats
there occafionally to trade for Negroes, and to fhort-
en their ftay on the coaft ; but the traders who are
fettled there do not always allow this competition.

Thefe difficulties are not to be apprehended at
Moffula, where no fhips can enter. The Englifh,
the French, and the Dutch, who carry on their trade
in the moft important harbours, fend their floops freely there, which feldom return without a few flaves,
purchafed at a more reafonable price than in the
larger markets.

After Moffula, the Portuguefe poffeffions begin,
which extend along the coaft from the eighth to the
eighteenth degree of fouth latitude, and fometimes
as far as a hundred leagues in the inland parts. This
great fpace is divided into many provinces, the feveral diftricts of which are governed by chiefs, who
are all tributary to Lifbon. Seven or eight feeble
corps, of ten or twelve foldiers each, are fufficient to
keep thefe people in fubjection. Thefe Negroes are
fuppofed to be free, but the flighteft mifdemeanour
plunges them into fervitude. Plentiful mines of iron,
fuperior in quality to any that has been found in any
other part of the globe, have been difcovered a few
years fince in the midft of thefe forefts, in a place
which hath been called the New Oeiras. The Count
de Souza, at that time governor of this diftrict, and

at prefent ambaffador at the court of Spain, caufed BOOK
them to be worked ; but they have been forfaken XI.
fince the mother country hath paffed from the yoke
of tyranny under that of fuperftition. This active
commandant likewife extended the frontiers of the
empire under his command. His ambition was, to
reach as far as the rich mines of Monomotapa, and
to pave the way for his fucceffors to purfue their conquefts as far as the territory which his nation is in
poffeffion of in the Mozambique.

We leave it to others to judge of the poffibility or
the fancifulnefs, the inutility or the importance, of
this communication. We will only obferve, that the
firft Portuguefe fettlement, near the ocean, is Bamba,
the chief bufinefs of which confifts in furnifhing the
woods which may be wanted at St. Paul de Loanda.

This capital of the Portuguefe fettlements in Africa
hath a tolerably good harbour. It is formed by a
fandy ifland, and protected at its entrance, which is
very narrow, by regular fortifications, and defended
by a garrifon, which would be fufficient, did it not
confift of officers and foldiers, moft of whom are branded by the laws, or are at leaft exiles. The population of the town confifts of feven or eight hundred
white men, and of about three thoufand Negroes, or
free Mulattoes.

St. Philip de Benguela, which belongs to the fame
nation, hath but one harbour, where the fea is often
very rough. The town, much lefs confiderable than
St. Paul, is covered by an indifferent fort, which
would eafily be reduced to afhes by the guns of the
fhips. No very obftinate refiftance would be made
by two or three hundred Africans who guard, and
who, even at St. Paul's, are moft of them diftributed
in pofts, at fome diftance from one another.

At ten leagues beyond St. Philips, we find another
Portuguefe fettlement, where numerous flocks are
bred, and where the falt is gathered that is neceffary
for the people fubject to that crown. The fettle-

B O O K ments and the trade of the Europeans do not extend
   XI. upon the weſtern coaſt of Africa.

The Portugueſe veſſels which frequent theſe latitudes all repair to St. Paul's or to St. Philip's. They
purchaſe a greater number of ſlaves in the firſt of
theſe markets, and in the latter, ſlaves that are more
robuſt. Theſe ſhips are not in general diſpatched
from the mother-country, but from the Brazils, and
almoſt ſolely from Rio de Janeiro. As the Portugueſe
have an excluſive privilege, they pay leſs for theſe
unfortunate blacks than they are ſold for any where
elſe. It is with tobacco, and with cowries, which
they get upon the ſpot itſelf, as well as the tobacco,
that they pay upon the Gold Coaſt ; and upon the
coaſt of Angola they give in exchange ſome tobacco,
rums, and coarſe linens.

In what
number, at
what price,
and with
what mer
chandiſe,
the ſlaves
are pur-
chaſed.
In the early times, after the diſcovery of the
weſtern Africa, the population of that immenſe portion of the globe did not ſenſibly decreaſe. Its inhabitants were not at that time employed ; but, in
proportion as the conqueſts and the cultivations were
increaſed in America, more ſlaves were required :
this want hath gradually increaſed ; and ſince the
peace of 1763, eighty thouſand of theſe wretched inhabitants have been carried off from Guinea every
year : theſe unfortunate men have not all arrived in
the New World. According to the natural courſe of
things, about one eighth part of them muſt have pe-
riſhed in the paſſage. Two thirds of theſe deplorable
victims of our avarice have come from the north, and
the remainder from the ſouth of the line.

They were originally purchaſed every where at a
very cheap rate. Their value hath gradually increaſed, and in a more remarkable manner, during
the courſe of the laſt fifteen years. In 1777, a French
merchant ſent to purchaſe one hundred and fifty of
them at Molembo, which coſt him, one with another, 583 livres 18 ſols 10 deniers [about 24l. 6s.
5½d.], beſide the expences of fitting out. At the

same period he sent for 521 at Porto Novo, which he obtained for 460 livres 10 deniers [about 19l. 3s. 4½d.].
This difference in the price, which may be confidered as habitual, is not to be attributed to the infe-
riority of the slaves from the north; they are, on the
contrary, stronger, more laborious, and more intelligent, than those from the south; but the coast from
which they are brought is less convenient and more
dangerous; they are not always to be found there,
and the privateer runs the risk of losing the profits of
the voyage; it is necessary to put in at Prince's, and
St. Thomas's Islands, in order to procure water for
them; besides, that several of them perish in the
passage, which is delayed by contrary winds, calms,
and currents; and that their disposition inclines them
to despair and to rebellion. All these reasons must
render them cheaper in Africa, though they be sold
for something more in the New World.

Supposing that fourscore thousand blacks have been
purchased in 1777, and all of them at the prices we
have mentioned, the amount of the whole will be
41,759,333 livres 6 sols 8 deniers [about 1,739,970l.
4s. 5½d.], which the African coasts will have obtained for the most horrid of all sacrifices.

The slave merchant doth not receive this entire
sum. Part of it is absorbed by the taxes required by
the sovereigns of the ports in which the trade is carried on. An agent of the government, whose business it is to maintain order, hath likewise his demands. Intermediate persons are employed between
the buyer and the seller, whose interposition is become dearer, in proportion to the increase of the competition between the European navigators, and to
the diminution of the number of the blacks. These
expences, foreign to the trade, are not exactly the
same in all the markets; but they do not experience
any important variations, and are too considerable
every where.

These slaves are not paid for with metals, but with
our productions, and with our merchandise. All na-

B O O K tions, except the Portuguefe, give nearly things of
XI. the fame value. They confift of broad fwords, firelocks, gunpowder, iron, brandy, toys, carpets, glafs,
woollen ftuffs, and efpecially Eaft India linens, or fuch
as are manufactured and printed in imitation of them
in Europe. The people to the north of the line have
adopted for their coin a fmall white fhell, which we
bring to them from the Maldives. The trade of the
Europeans, on the fouth of the line, hath not this
object of exchange. The coin is reprefented there
by a fmall piece of ftraw ftuff, eighteen inches in
length, and twelve in breadth, which is current for
5 fols [2¼d.] of France.

Who are   The European nations have thought that it would
the people   be of ufe to their trade to have fettlements in the
who pur-
chafe flaves. weftern part of Africa. The Portuguefe, who, according to the generally received opinion, arrived
there the firft, carried on the flave trade for a long
while without any competitors, becaufe they alone
had eftablifhed cultures in America. From a concurrence of unfortunate circumftances, they were fubdued by Spain, and attacked in every part of the
world by the Dutch, who had difengaged themfelves
from the fetters under which they were oppreffed.
The new republicans triumphed, without any extraordinary exertions, over an enflaved people, and more
efpecially on the coaft of Guinea, where no means of
defence had been prepared. But no fooner had the
court of Lifbon recovered their independency, than
they were defirous of reconquering thofe poffeffions,
of which they had been deprived during their ftate
of flavery. Their navigators were encouraged by
their fucceffes in the Brazils to fail towards Africa.
Though they did not fucceed in reftoring to their
country all its ancient rights, they recovered at leaft,
in 1648, the country of Angola, which hath remained ever fince under its dominion. A few iflands,
more or lefs confiderable, in thefe immenfe feas, belong likewife to Portugal. Such are the remains of

the empire which the court of Lifbon had eftablifhed, and which extended from Ceuta to the Red Sea.

The Dutch gave up their fhare of thefe rich fpoils to the Weft India Company, who had feized upon them. This monopolizing company built forts, levied taxes, took upon themfelves the fettling of all dif-putes, ventured to punifh any perfon with death whom they judged to act contrary to their intereft ; and even went fo far as to confider as enemies all the European navigators whom they found in thefe lati-tudes, the exclufive trade of which they claimed to themfelves. This conduct fo totally ruined this char-tered body, that, in 1730, they were obliged to give up the expeditions which they had hitherto carried on without competition. They only referved to them-felves the property of the forts, the defence and the maintenance of which cofts them annually 280,000 florins, or 616,000 livres [25,666l. 13s. 4d.]. They fend a fhip every year to victual thefe forts, unlefs they can prevail upon the merchantmen, who fre-quent thofe latitudes, to convey provifions to them at a moderate freight. They fometimes even make ufe of the right they have referved to themfelves of fend-ing twelve foldiers upon every fhip, by paying feven-ty-nine livres four fols [3l. 6d.] for the paffage, and for the fubfiftence of each.

The directors of the feveral factories are allowed to purchafe flaves, upon giving forty-four livres [1l. 16s. 8d.] a head to the companies on which they depend ; but they are obliged to fell them in Africa itfelf, and are forbidden by the laws to fend them on their own account to the New World.

Thefe regions are open at prefent to all the fub-jects of the republic. Their obligations to the Com-pany confift only in paying 46 livres 14 fols [2l. 10s. 7d.] to it, for every ton which is contained in the veffel, and three per cent. for all the provifions which they bring back from America to Europe.

In the firft beginning of their liberty, the trade of gold, ivory, wax, red wood, and of that fpecies of

pepper known by the name of *Malaguette*, employed
feveral veffels.   None are fitted out at prefent for
thefe objects. portions of which are put upon the
fhips that are fent to purchafe Negroes.

The number of thefe veffels, which are moftly of
two hundred tons burden, and the crews of which
confifted of twenty-eight, and as far as thirty-fix
men, formerly amounted annually to twenty-five or
thirty, which traded for fix or feven thoufand flaves.
This number is confiderably diminifhed, fince the
lowering of the coffee hath difabled the colonies from
paying for thofe cargoes.   The province of Holland
hath fome fhare in this fhameful traffic, but it is
chiefly carried on by the province of Zeeland.

The deplorable victims of this barbarous avidity
are difperfed in the feveral fettlements which the
United Provinces have formed in the iflands, or on
the American continent.   They ought to be expofed
to public view, and fold feparately, but this rule is
not always adhered to; it even frequently happens,
that a privateer, at the time of the fale, agrees for
the price for which he will fell the flaves at the next
voyage.

In 1552, the Englifh flag appeared, for the firft
time, on the weftern coafts of Africa.   The merchants who traded there formed an affociation thirty-
eight years after, to which, according to the general
cuftom of thofe times, an exclufive charter was granted.   This fociety, and thofe that followed it, had
their veffels often confifcated by the Portuguefe, and
afterwards by the Dutch, who pretended that they
were the fovereigns of thofe countries; but the peace
of Breda at length put a perpetual ftop to thefe
tyrannical perfecutions.

The Englifh iflands in the New World began, at
that time, to require a great number of flaves for the
cultivation of their lands.   This was an infallible
fource of profperity for the companies whofe bufinefs
it was to furnifh thefe planters; and yet thefe companies, which fucceeded each other with great rapi-

dity, were all ruined ; and retarded, by their indolence, or by their difhonefty, the improvement of the
colonies, from which the nation had expected to reap
fuch confiderable advantages.

Public indignation againft fuch mifconduct mani-
fefted itfelf, in 1697, in fo violent a manner, as to
compel government to allow individuals to frequent
the weftern part of Africa ; but upon condition that
they fhould give ten per cent. to the monopoly for
the maintenance of the forts built in thofe regions.
The privilege itfelf was afterwards abolifhed. This
trade hath been open fince 1749 to all the Englifh
navigators without any expence, and the treafury
hath taken upon itfelf the expences of fovereignty.

Since the peace of 1763, Great Britain hath fent
annually to the coaft of Guinea 195 veffels, confifting, collectively, of twenty-three thoufand tons, and
feven or eight thoufand men. Rather more than
half this number have been difpatched from Liverpool ; and the remainder from London, Briftol, and
Lancafter. They have traded for forty thoufand
flaves ; the greateft part of which have been fold in
the Englifh Weft India iflands, and in North America. Thofe that were not difpofed of in thefe markets, have been either fraudulently or publicly introduced in the colonies belonging to other nations.

This confiderable trade hath not been conducted
upon uniform principles. The part of the coaft which
begins at Cape Blanco, and ends at Cape Rouge, was
put under the immediate infpection of the miniftry
in 1765. From that period to 1778, the civil and
military expences of this fettlement have amounted
to 4,050,000 livres [168,750l.] : a fum which the nation have confidered as inadequate to the advantages
they have acquired from it.

A committee, chofen by the merchants themfelves,
and confifting of nine deputies, three from Liverpool,
three from London, and three from Briftol, are to take
care of the fettlements which are formed between
Cape Rouge and the line. Though parliament have

BOOK annually granted four or five hundred thoufand livres
XI. [from 16,666l. 13s. 4d. to 20,833l. 6s. 8d.] for the
maintenance of thefe fmall forts, moft of them are in
a ruinous condition ; but they are protected by the
difficulty of landing.

The Englifh have no factory upon the remaining
part of the weft of Africa. Every trader reforts to
them in the manner he thinks the moft fuitable to his
intereft, without reftraint, and without any particular
protection. As the competition is greater in thefe
ports than in the others, the navigators of the nation
have gradually forfaken them, and they fcarce deal
annually for two thoufand flaves, in markets where
they formerly purchafed twelve or fifteen thoufand.

It can fcarce be doubted that the French appeared
on thofe favage coafts before their rivals ; but they
entirely loft fight of them till the year 1621, when
their flag began again to appear there. The fettlement which they formed at that period in Senegal,
acquired, in 1678, fome increafe from the terror
which the victorious arms of Lewis XIV. had infpired. This rifing power became the prey of a formidable enemy under the reign of his fucceffor.
Other factories, fucceffively formed, and become ufelefs in the hands of a monopoly, had already been
forfaken. Accordingly, for want of fettlements, the
trade of that country hath always been infufficient
for its rich colonies. In its greateft profperity, it hath
never furnifhed them more than thirteen or fourteen
thoufand flaves annually.

The Danes fettled above a century ago in thofe
countries. An exclufive company exercifed its privileges there with that degree of barbarity, of which
the more polifhed countries of Europe have fo often
fet the example in thofe unfortunate climates. Only
one of its agents had the courage to forego thefe
atrocious proceedings, which, from habit, they had
confidered as legal. Such was his reputation for his
goodnefs, and fuch the confidence repofed in his in-
tegrity, that the Negroes ufed to come from the

diftance of a hundred leagues to fee him. The fovereign of a diftant country fent his daughter to him
with gold and flaves, to obtain a grandfon of Schil-
derop's, which was the name of this European fo
much revered upon all the coafts of Nigritia. O
Virtue! thou doft ftill exift in the hearts of thofe miferable people, who are condemned to live among
tigers, or to groan under the tyranny of man! They
are then capable of feeling the delightful attractions
of benevolent humanity! Juft and magnanimous
Dane! What monarch ever received an homage fo
pure and fo glorious as that which thy nation hath
feen thee enjoy! And in what countries? On a fea,
and on a land, which hath been contaminated for
three centuries paft with an infamous traffic, of crimes
and misfortunes, of men exchanged for arms, of children fold by their fathers! We have not tears fufficient to deplore fuch horrors, and thofe tears would
be unavailing!

In 1754, the trade of Guinea was opened to all citizens, upon condition of paying twelve livres [10s.]
to the treafury for every Negro which they fhould
introduce into the Danifh iflands in the New World.
This liberty did not extend, *communibus annis*, beyond
the purchafe of five hundred flaves. Such a degree
of indolence determined government to liften, in
1765, to the propofals of a foreigner, who offered to
give a proper degree of extenfion to this vile commerce, and the tax impofed upon it was taken off.
This new experiment was entirely unfuccefsful, becaufe the author of the project was never able to collect more than 170,000 crowns [21,250l.] for the execution of his enterprifes; and in 1776, the fyftem
which had been given up eleven years before, was
reaffumed.

Chriftianfbourg and Fredericfbourg are the only
factories which are in fome degree fortified; the
others are only plain lodges. The crown maintains,
in the five fettlements, fixty-two men, fome of whom
are Negroes, for the fum of 53,160 livres [2215l.].

If the magazines were properly fupplied, it would be eafy to treat every year for two thoufand flaves; only two hundred are purchafed in the prefent ftate of things, moft of which are given up to foreign nations, becaufe no Danifh navigators appear to carry them off.

It cannot be eafily forefeen what maxims Spain will adopt in the connections fhe is going to form in Africa. This crown hath fucceffively received flaves, fometimes openly, and fometimes fraudulently, from the Genoefe, from the Portuguefe, from the French, and from the Englifh. In order to emerge from this ftate of dependence, it hath caufed to be ceded, by the treaties of 1777 and of 1778, by the court of Lifbon, the iflands of Annabona, and of Fernando del Po, both fituated very near the line, the one to the fouth, and the other to the north. The former hath only one very dangerous harbour, too little water to contain fhips, and is fix miles in circumference. The greateft part of this fpace is occupied by two high mountains. The thick clouds with which they are almoft conftantly covered, keep the valleys in that ftate of moifture which would render them fufceptible of cultivation. A few hundred Negroes are feen here, whofe labours furnifh a fmall number of white men with a great abundance of hogs, goats, and poultry. The fale of a fmall quantity of cotton fupplies them with their other wants, which are enclofed in a very narrow compafs. The fecond acquifition is of lefs intrinfic value, as it hath no kind of harbour, and as its inhabitants are very ferocious ! but its proximity to Calbari and to Gabon, renders it more proper for the purpofe which hath dictated the acquiring of it.

Let not, however, the Spanifh miniftry imagine, that it is fufficient to have fome poffeffions in Guinea, in order to procure flaves. Such was, indeed, the origin of this infamous traffic. At that time, every European nation had only to fortify its factories, in order to drive away ftrangers, and to oblige the natives to fell to no other traders except their own. But when thefe fmall diftricts have had no more flaves to deliver, the trade hath languifhed, becaufe the people of the inland countries have preferred the free ports, where they might choofe their purchafers. The advantage of thefe eftablifhments, formed at fo much expence, was loft, when the object of their commerce was exhaufted.

The difficulty of procuring flaves naturally points out the neceffity of employing fmall fhips for carrying them off. At a time when a fmall territory, adjacent to the coaft, furnifhed in a fortnight or three weeks a whole cargo, it was prudent to employ large veffels, becaufe there was a poffibility of underftanding, looking after, and encouraging the flaves, who all fpoke the fame language. At prefent, when each fhip can fcarce procure fixty or eighty flaves a month, brought from the diftance of two or three hundred leagues, exhaufted by the fatigues of a long journey, obliged to remain on board the veffels they are embarked upon, five or fix months, in fight of their country, having all different idioms, uncertain of the deftiny that awaits them, ftruck with the prepoffeffion that the Europeans eat them and drink their blood ; their extreme uneafinefs alone deftroys them, or occafions diforders which become contagious, by the impoffibility of feparating the fick from the healthy. A fmall fhip deftined to carry two or three hundred Negroes, by means of the fhort ftay it makes on the coaft, avoids half the accidents and loffes to which a fhip, capable of holding five or fix hundred flaves, is expofed.

There are other abufes, and thofe of the utmoft confequence, to be reformed in this voyage, which is naturally unhealthy. Thofe who engage in it commonly fall into two great miftakes. Dupes to a mercenary difpofition, the privateers pay more regard to the quantity of ftowage than to the difpatch of their veffels ; a circumftance that neceffarily prolongs the voyage, which every thing fhould induce them to fhorten. Another inconvenience ftill more dangerous

BOOK
XI.

Methods
made ufe of
in the pur-
chafe, in
the treat-
ment, and
in the fale
of flaves.
Reflections
upon this
fubject.

B O O K is, the cuftom they have of failing from Europe at all
XI. times ; though the regularity of the winds and the
currents hath determined the moft proper feafon for
arriving in thefe latitudes.

This bad practice hath given rife to the diftinction
of the great and little voyage. The little voyage is
the ftraighteft and the fhorteft. It is no more than
eighteen hundred leagues to the moft diftant ports
where there are flaves. It may be performed in thirty-
five or forty days, from the beginning of September
to the end of November ; becaufe, from the time of
fetting out to the time of arrival, the winds and the
currents are favourable. It is even poffible to attempt
it in December, January, and February, but with
lefs fecurity and fuccefs.

Sailing is no longer practicable in thefe latitudes,
from the beginning of March to the end of Auguft.
The fhips would have continually to ftruggle againft
the violent currents which run northward, and againft
the fouth-eaft wind, which conftantly blows. Experience hath taught navigators, that during this feafon, they muft keep at a diftance from the fhore, get
into the open fea, fail towards the fouth as far as
twenty-fix or twenty-eight degrees betwixt Africa
and Brazil, and afterwards draw gradually nearer and
nearer to Guinea, in order to land at a hundred and
fifty or two hundred leagues to windward of the port
where they are to difembark. This route is two thoufand five hundred leagues, and requires ninety or a
hundred days fail.

This great route, independent of its length, deprives them of the moft favourable time for trade,
and for returning. The fhips meet with calms, are
thwarted by winds, and carried away by currents ;
water fails them, the provifions are fpoiled, and the
flaves are feized with the fcurvy. Other calamities, not
lefs fatal, often increafe the danger of this fituation.
The Negroes to the north of the line are fubject to
the fmall-pox, which, by a fingularity very diftreffing,
feldom breaks out among this people till after the age

of fourteen. If this contagious diftemper fhould af- fect a fhip which is at her moorings, there are feveral known methods to leffen its violence. But a fhip at-- tacked by it, while on its paffage to America, often lofes the whole cargo of flaves. Thofe who are born to the fouth of the line efcape this difeafe by another, which is a kind of virulent ulcer, the malignity of which is more violent and more irritable on the fea, and which is never radically cured. Phyficians ought, perhaps, to obferve this double effect of the fmall-pox among the Negroes, which is, that it favours thofe who are born beyond the equator, and never attacks the others in their infancy. The number and variety of effects fometimes afford occafion for the inveftiga- tion of the caufes of diforders, and for the difcovery of remedies proper for them.

Though all the nations concerned in the African trade be equally interefted in preferving the flaves in their paffage, they do not all attend to this with the fame care. They all feed them with beans mixed with a fmall quantity of rice ; but they differ in other refpects in their manner of treating them. The En- glifh, Dutch, and Danes, keep the men conftantly in irons, and frequently hand-cuff the women : the fmall number of hands they have on board their fhips obliges them to this feverity. The French, who have great numbers, allow them more liberty ; three or four days after their departure they take off all their fetters. All thefe nations, efpecially the Englifh, are too negligent with regard to the intercourfe be- tween the failors with the women flaves. This irre- gularity occafions the death of three-fourths of thofe whom the Guinea voyage deftroys every year. None but the Portuguefe, during their paffage, are fecured againft revolts and other calamities. This advantage is a confequence of the care they take, to man their veffels only with the Negroes to whom they have given their freedom. The flaves, encouraged by the converfation and condition of their countrymen, form a tolerably favourable idea of the deftiny that awaits

B o o k them. The quietnefs of their behaviour induces the
XI. Portuguefe to grant the two fexes the happinefs of
living together; an indulgence which, if allowed in
other veffels, would be productive of the greateft inconveniences.

The fale of flaves is not carried on in the fame manner throughout all America. The Englifh, who have
promifcuoufly bought up whatever prefented itfelf in
the general market, fell their cargo by wholefale.
A fingle merchant buys it entire; and the planters
parcel it out. What they reject is fent into foreign
colonies, either by fmuggling, or with permiffion.
The cheapnefs of a Negro is a greater object to the
buyer to induce him to purchafe, than the badnefs
of his conftitution is to deter him from it. Thefe
traders will one day be convinced of the abfurdity
of fuch a conduct.

The Portuguefe, Dutch, French, and Danes, who
have no way of difpofing of the infirm and weakly
flaves, never take charge of any of them in Guinea.
They all divide their cargoes, according to the demands of the proprietors of plantations. The bargain is made for ready money, or for credit, according as circumftances vary.

Wretched   In America it is generally believed and afferted,
condition   that the Africans are equally incapable of reafon and
of the flaves
in America. of virtue. The following well-authenticated fact will
enable us to judge of this opinion.

An Englifh fhip, that traded in Guinea in 1752,
was obliged to leave the furgeon behind, whofe bad
ftate of health did not permit him to continue at fea.
Murray, for that was his name, was there, endeavouring to recover his health, when a Dutch veffel
drew near the coaft, put the blacks in irons, whom
curiofity had brought to the fhore, and inftantly failed off with the booty.

Thofe who interefted themfelves for thefe unhappy people, incenfed at fo bafe a treachery, inftantly
ran to Cudjoc, who ftopped them at his door, and
afked them what they were in fearch of? *The white*

man who is with you, replied they, *who should be put to*
death, because his brethren have carried off ours. The
Europeans, anfwered the generous hoft, *who have car-*
ried off our countrymen, are barbarians ; kill them when-
ever you can find them. But he who lodges with me is
a good man, he is my friend ; my houfe is his fortrefs ; I
am his foldier, and I will defend him. Before you can
get at him, you shall pafs over me. O my friends, what
juft man would ever enter my doors, if I had fuffered my
habitation to be ftained with the blood of an innocent man?
This difcourfe appeafed the rage of the blacks : they
retired, afhamed of the defign that had brought them
there ; and fome days after acknowledged to Murray
himfelf, how happy they were that they had not committed a crime which would have occafioned them
perpetual remorfe.

This event renders it probable, that the firft impreffions which the Africans receive in the New
World, determine them either to good or bad actions.
Repeated experience confirms the truth of this obfervation : thofe who fall to the fhare of a humane
mafter willingly efpoufe his interefts. They infenfibly
adopt the fpirit and manners of the place where they
are fixed. This attachment is fometimes exalted even
into heroifm. A Portuguefe flave who had fled into
the woods, having learnt that his old mafter had been
taken up for an affaffination, came into the court of
juftice, and acknowledged himfelf guilty of the fact,
let himfelf be put in prifon in lieu of his mafter ;
brought falfe, though judicial proofs of his pretended
crime, and fuffered death inftead of the guilty perfon.
Actions of fo fublime a nature muft be uncommon.
We will mention one, which, though lefs heroic, is
neverthelefs very praife-worthy.

A planter of St. Domingo had a confidential flave,
whom he was perpetually flattering with the hope of
fpeedy freedom, which, however, he never granted
him. The more pains this kind of favourite took to
render himfelf ufeful, the more firmly rivetted were
his fetters, becaufe he became more and more ne-

B O O K ceſſary.   Hope, however, did not forſake him, but
   XI.   he reſolved to attain the deſired end by a different
mode.

In ſome parts of the iſland, the Negroes are obliged to provide themſelves with clothes and nouriſh-
ment ; and for this purpoſe they are allowed a ſmall
portion of territory, and two hours every day to cultivate it.   Thoſe among them who are active and intelligent, do not merely gain their ſubſiſtence from
theſe little plantations, but they likewiſe acquire a
ſuperfluity, which enſures a fortune to them more or
leſs conſiderable.

Lewis Deſrouleaux, whoſe ſchemes rendered him
very economical and very laborious, had ſoon amaſſed
funds more than ſufficient to purchaſe his liberty.
He offered them with tranſport for the purchaſe of
his independence, which had been ſo often promiſ-
ed him.   *I have too long traded with the blood of my
fellow-creatures*, ſaid his maſter to him in a tone of
humiliation ; *be free, you reſtore me to myſelf.*   Immediately the maſter, whoſe heart had been rather
led aſtray, than corrupted, ſold all his effects, and
embarked for France.

He was obliged to go through Paris, in order to
reach his province.   His intention was to make but
a ſhort ſtay in that metropolis ; but the various plea-
ſures he met with in that ſuperb and delightful capital, detained him till he had fooliſhly diſſipated the
riches which he had acquired by long and fortunate
labours.   In his deſpair, he thought it leſs humiliating
to ſolicit, in America, aſſiſtance from thoſe who were
obliged to him for their advancement, than to aſk it
in Europe of thoſe who had ruined him.

His arrival at Cape François cauſed a general ſur-
priſe.   No ſooner was his ſituation known, than he
was generally forſaken ; all doors were ſhut againſt
him, no heart was moved by compaſſion.   He found
himſelf reduced to the neceſſity of paſſing the remainder of his days in that retirement and obſcurity
which is the conſequence of indigence, and eſpecially

when merited, when Lewis Defrouleaux came to B O O K throw himfelf at his feet. " Condefcend," faid that XI. virtuous freeman, " condefcend to accept the houfe " of your flave ; you fhall be ferved, obeyed, and be- " loved in it." But foon perceiving that the refpect which is owing to the unfortunate, and the attention which is due to benefactors, did not render his old mafter happy, he preffed him to retire to France. " My gratitude will follow you," faid he, embracing his knees. " Here is a contract for an annual in- " come of 1500 livres [62l.], which I conjure you to " accept. This frefh inftance of your goodnefs will " be the comfort of my future days."

The annuity hath always been paid beforehand fince that period. Some prefents, as tokens of friend-fhip, conftantly accompanied it from St. Domingo to France. The giver, and the receiver, were both alive in 1774. May they both ferve for a long time as a model to this proud, ungrateful, and unnatural age !

Several acts refembling this of Lewis Defrouleaux, have affected fome of the planters. Several of them would readily fay, as Sir William Gooch, governor of Virginia, when he was blamed for returning the falu-tation of a Negro, *I fhould be very forry that a flave fhould be more mannerly than myfelf.*

But there are barbarians, who confidering pity as a weaknefs, delight in making their dependents per-petually fenfible of their tyranny. They juftly, how-ever, receive their punifhment in the negligence, in-fidelity, defertion, and fuicide of the deplorable vic-tims of their infatiable avarice. Some of thefe un-fortunate men, efpecially thofe of Mina, courageoufly put an end to their lives, under the firm perfuafion that they fhall, immediately after death, rife again in their own country, which they look upon as the fineft in the world. A vindictive fpirit furnifhes others with refources ftill more fatal. Inftructed from their infancy in the arts of poifons, which grow, as it were, under their hands, they employ them in the deftruction of the cattle, the horfes, the mules, the

B O O K companions of their flavery, and of every living thing
  XI.   employed in the cultivation of the lands of their oppreffors. In order to remove from themfelves all
fufpicion, they firft exercife their cruelties on their
wives, their children, their miftreffes, and on every
thing that is deareft to them. In this dreadful project, that can only be the refult of defpair, they have
the double pleafure of delivering their fpecies from
a yoke more dreadful than death, and of leaving
their tyrant in a wretched ftate of mifery, that is an
image of their own condition. The fear of punifhment
doth not check them. They are fcarce ever known
to have any kind of forefight ; and they are, moreover, certain of concealing their crimes, being proof
againft tortures. By one of thofe inexplicable con-
tradictions of the human heart, though common to
all people whether civilized or not, Negroes, though
naturally cowards, give many inftances of an un-
fhaken firmnefs of foul. The fame organization which
fubjects them to fervitude, from the indolence of their
mind, and the relaxation of their fibres, infpires them
with vigour and unparalleled refolution for extraordinary actions. They are cowards all their lifetime,
and heroes only for an inftant. One of thefe miferable men hath been known to cut his wrift off with
a ftroke of a hatchet, rather than purchafe his liberty
by fubmitting to the vile office of an executioner.
Another flave had been flightly tortured for a trifling
fault, which he was not even guilty of. Stung by
refentment, he determined to feize upon the whole
family of his oppreffor, and to carry them up to the
roof of the houfe. When the tyrant was preparing
to enter his dwelling, he beheld his youngeft fon
thrown down at his feet ; he lifted up his head and
faw the fecond fall likewife. Seized with defpair, he
fell on his knees, to implore, in great agitation, the
life of the third. But the fall of this laft of his off-
fpring, together with that of the Negro, convinced
him, that he was no longer a father, nor worthy to
be one.

Nothing, however, is more miferable than the con-B O O K dition of the Negro, throughout the whole American ^{XI.} Archipelago. The firft thing done, is to difgrace him with the indelible mark of flavery, by ftamping with a hot iron, upon his arms, or upon his breaft, the name or the mark of his oppreffor. A narrow, un-wholefome hut, without any conveniences, ferves him for a dwelling. His bed is a hurdle, fitter to put the body to torture than to afford it any eafe. Some earthen pots, and a few wooden difhes, are his furni-ture. The coarfe linen which covers part of his body, neither fecures him from the infupportable heats of the day, nor the dangerous dews of the night. The food he is fupplied with, is caffava, falt beef, falt cod, fruits, and roots, which are fcarce able to fupport his miferable exiftence. Deprived of every enjoyment, he is condemned to a perpetual drudgery in a burn-ing climate, conftantly under the rod of an unfeeling mafter.

All Europe hath, for this century paft, been filled with the moft fublime and the foundeft fentiments of morality. Writings, which will be immortal, have eftablifhed in the moft affecting manner, that all men are brethren. We are filled with indignation at the cruelties, either civil or religious, of our ferocious an-ceftors, and we turn away our eyes from thofe ages of horror and blood. Thofe among our neighbours, whom the inhabitants of Barbary have loaden with irons, obtain our pity and affiftance. Even imaginary diftreffes draw tears from our eyes, both in the filent retirement of the clofet, and efpecially at the theatre. It is only the fatal deftiny of the Negroes which doth not concern us. They are tyrannized, mutilated, burnt, and put to death, and yet we liften to thefe accounts coolly and without emotion. The torments of a people to whom we owe our luxuries, can never reach our hearts.

The condition of thefe flaves, though every where deplorable, is fomething different in the colonies. In thofe where there are very extenfive territories, a portion of land is generally given them, to fupply them with the neceffaries of life. They are allowed to employ a part of the Sunday in cultivating it, and the few moments that on other days they fpare from the time allotted for their meals. In the more confined iflands, the colonift himfelf furnifhes their food, the greateft part of which hath been imported by fea from other countries. Ignorance, avarice, or poverty, have introduced into fome colonies a method of providing for the fubfiftence of Negroes, equally deftructive both to the men and the plantation. They are allowed on Saturday, or fome other day, to work in the neighbouring plantations, or to plunder them, in order to procure a maintenance for the reft of the week.

Befide thefe differences arifing from the particular fituation of the fettlements in the American iflands, each European nation hath a manner of treating flaves peculiar to itfelf. The Spaniards make them the companions of their indolence ; the Portuguefe, the inftruments of their debauchery ; the Dutch, the victims of their avarice. By the Englifh, they are confidered merely as natural productions, which ought neither to be ufed nor deftroyed without neceffity ; but they never treat them with familiarity ; they never fmile upon them, nor fpeak to them. One would think they were afraid of letting them fufpect, that nature could have given any one mark of refemblance betwixt them and their flaves. This makes them hate the Englifh. The French, lefs haughty, lefs difdainful, confider the Africans as a fpecies of moral beings ; and thefe unhappy men, fenfible of the honour of feeing themfelves almoft treated like rational creatures, feem to forget that their mafter is impatient of making his fortune, that he always exacts labours from them above their ftrength, and frequently lets them want fubfiftence.

The opinions of the Europeans have alfo fome influence on the condition of the Negroes of America. The Proteftants, who are not actuated by a defire of

making profelytes, fuffer them to live in Moham- BOOK
medifm, or in that idolatry in which they were born, XI.
under a pretence, that it would be injurious to keep
their *brethren in Chrift* in a ftate of flavery. The Ca-
tholics think themfelves obliged to give them fome
inftruction, and to baptife them ; but their charity
extends no further than the bare ceremonies of a
baptifm, which is wholly ufelefs and unneceffary to
men who dread not the pains of hell, to which, they
fay, they are accuftomed in this life.

The torments they experience in their flavery, and
the diforders to which they are liable in America,
both contribute to render them infenfible to the
dread of future punifhment. They are particularly
fubject to two difeafes, the yaws, and a complaint
that affects their ftomach. The firft effect of this
laft diforder is, to turn their fkin and complexion to
an olive colour. Their tongue becomes white, and
they are overpowered by fuch a defire of fleeping
that they cannot refift : they grow faint, and are incapable of the leaft exercife. It is a languor, and a
general relaxation of the whole machine. In this
fituation they are in fuch a ftate of defpondency,
that they fuffer themfelves to be knocked down rather than walk. The loathing which they have of
mild and wholefome food, is attended with a kind of
rage for every thing that is falted or fpiced. Their
legs fwell, their breath is obftructed, and few of them
furvive this diforder. The greateft part die of fuffo-
cation, after having fuffered and languifhed for feveral months.

The thicknefs of their blood, which appears to be
the fource of thefe diforders, may proceed from feveral caufes. One of the principal is, undoubtedly,
the melancholy which muft feize thefe men who are
violently torn away from their country, are fettered
like criminals, who find themfelves all on a fudden
on the fea, where they continue for two months or
fix weeks, and who, from the midft of a beloved family, pafs under the yoke of an unknown people,

BOOK from whom they expect the most dreadful punish-
XI. ments. A species of food, new to them, and difagreeable in itself, difgufts them in their paffage. At
their arrival in the iflands, the provifions that are diftributed to them, are neither good in quality, nor
fufficient to fupport them. The caffava, which is
particularly allotted to them, is very dangerous in
itself. The animals who eat of it are rapidly deftroyed, though, by a contradiction which is often
found in nature, they are very fond of it. If this
root doth not produce fuch fatal effects among mankind, it is becaufe they do not make ufe of it till
all its poifon hath been extracted by preparation.
But with what negligence muft not thefe preparations be made, when flaves only are the object of
them ?

Art hath for a long time been employed in endeavouring to find out fome remedy againft this diforder in the ftomach. It has been found, after feveral experiments, that nothing was more falutary
than to give the blacks who were attacked with it
three ounces of the juice of a fpecies of colocynth,
with almoft a fimilar dofe of a kind of oracte, known
in the iflands by the name of *jargon*. This drink is
preceded by a purgative, which confifts of half a
drachm of gumbooge diluted in milk, or in honey-
water.

The yaws, which is the fecond diforder peculiar
to Negroes, and which accompanies them from Africa
to America, is contracted in the birth, or by communication between the fexes. No age is free from it ;
but it more particularly attacks at the periods of infancy and youth. Old people have feldom ftrength
fufficient to fupport the long and violent treatment
which it requires.

There are faid to be four fpecies of yaws. The
yaws with puftules, large and fmall, as in the fmall-
pox ; that which refembles lentils ; and laftly the red
yaws, which is the moft dangerous of all.

The yaws attack every part of the body, but more

especially the face. It manifests itself by granulated red spots, resembling a raspberry. These spots degenerate into sordid ulcers, and the disorder at length affects the bones. It is not in general attended with much sensibility.

Fevers seldom attack the persons who are afflicted with the yaws; they eat and drink as usual, but they have an almost insuperable aversion for every kind of motion, without which, however, no cure can be expected.

The eruption lasts about three months; the patients are fed, during this long space of time, with the Catalou, or *Retmia Brafilienfis*, with rice dressed without either grease or butter, and the only drink which is allowed them is water, in which one or other of these vegetables hath been boiled. They must also be kept very warm, and made to use every sort of exercise that can most powerfully promote perspiration.

At length the period comes, when it is necessary to purge and bathe the patient, and to administer mercury to him, both internally and by friction, in such a manner as to bring on a gentle salivation. The effect of this remedy, which is the only specific against the disease, is to be assisted by a diet drink made with herbs, or with the sudorific woods. This process must even be continued for a long time after the cure is considered as complete.

The ulcer, which hath served as a drain during the treatment, is not always closed at the termination even of the disorder. It is then cured with red precipitate, and a digestive ointment.

The Negroes have a peculiar method of drying up their pustules; they apply to them the black of the saucepans, mixed with the juice of lemon or citron.

All the Negroes, as well male as female, who come from Guinea, or are born in the islands, have the yaws once in their lives: it is a disease they must necessarily pass through; but there is no instance of any of them

B O O K being attacked with it a fecond time, after having
   XI.   been radically cured. The Europeans feldom or never catch this diforder, notwithstanding the frequent
and daily connection which they have with the Negro women. Thefe women fuckle the children of the
white people, but do not give them the yaws. How
is it poffible to reconcile thefe facts, which are inconteftible, with the fyftem which phyficians feem to
have adopted with regard to the nature of the yaws?
Can it not be allowed, that the femen, the blood, and
fkin of the Negroes, are fufceptible of a virus peculiar to their fpecies? The caufe of this diforder, perhaps, is the fame as that which occafions their colour:
one difference is naturally productive of another: and
there is no being or quality that exifts abfolutely detached from others in nature.

But whatever this diforder may be, it is demonftrated, that fourteen or fifteen hundred thoufand
blacks, who are now difperfed over the European
colonies of the New World, are the unfortunate remains of eight or nine millions of flaves that have
been conveyed there. This dreadful deftruction cannot be the effect of the climate, which is nearly the
fame as that of Africa, much lefs of the diforders, to
which, in the opinion of all obfervers, but few fall a
facrifice. It muft therefore originate from the manner in which thefe flaves are governed : and might
not an error of this nature be corrected?

In what   The firft ftep neceffary in this reformation would
manner the   be, to attend minutely to the natural and moral ftate
condition of
flavesmight of man. Thofe who go to purchafe blacks on the
be rendered
more fup-   coafts of favage nations; thofe who convey them to
portable.   America, and efpecially thofe who direct their labours, often think themfelves obliged, from their fituation, and frequently too for the fake of their own
fafety, to opprefs thefe wretched men. The heart
of thofe who conduct the flaves is loft to all fenfe of
compaffion, is ignorant of every motive to enforce
obedience, except thofe of fear or feverity, and thefe
are exercifed with all the ferocious fpirit of a tem-

porary authority. If the proprietors of plantations
would ceafe to regard the care of their flaves as an
occupation below them, and confider it as an office
to which it is their duty to attend, they would foon
difcard thefe errors that arife from a fpirit of cruelty
The hiftory of all mankind would fhow them, that,
in order to render flavery ufeful, it is at leaft neceffary to make it eafy ; that force doth not prevent the
rebellion of the mind ; that it is the mafter's intereft
that the flave fhould be attached to life, and that nothing is to be expected from him the moment that he
no longer fears to die.

This principle of enlightened reafon, derived from
the fentiments of humanity, would contribute to
the reformation of feveral abufes. Men would acknowledge the neceffity of lodging, clothing, and
giving proper food to beings condemned to the moft
painful bondage that hath ever exifted fince the infamous origin of flavery. They would be fenfible,
that it is naturally impoffible that thofe who reap no
advantage from their own labours, can have the fame
underftanding, the fame economy, the fame activity,
the fame ftrength, as the man who enjoys the produce
of his induftry. That political moderation would gradually take place, which confifts in leffening labour,
alleviating punifhment, and rendering to man part of
his rights, in order to reap, with greater certainty,
the benefit of thofe duties that are impofed upon him.
The prefervation of a great number of flaves, whom
diforders occafioned by vexation or regret deprive the
colonies of, would be the natural confequence of fo
wife a regulation. Far from aggravating the yoke
that oppreffes them, every kind of attention fhould
be given to make it eafy, and to diffipate even the
idea of it, by favouring a natural propenfity that
feems peculiar to the Negroes.

Their organs are extremely fenfible of the powers
of mufic. Their ear is fo true, that in their dances,
the time of a fong makes them fpring up a hundred
at once, ftriking the earth at the fame inftant. En-

chanted, as it were, with the voice of a finger, or
the tone of a ftringed inftrument, a vibration of the
air is the fpirit that actuates all the bodies of thefe
men : a found agitates, tranfports, and throws them
into extafies. In their common labours, the motion
of their arms, or of their feet, is always in cadence.
At all their employments they fing, and feem always
as if they were dancing. Mufic animates their courage, and roufes them from their indolence. The
marks of this extreme fenfibility to harmony are vifible in all the mufcles of their bodies, which are always naked. Poets and muficians by nature, they
make the words fubfervient to the mufic, by a licence
they arbitrarily affume of lengthening or fhortening
them, in order to accommodate them to any air that
pleafes them. Whenever any object or incident ftrikes
a Negro, he inftantly makes it the fubject of a fong.
In all ages this hath been the origin of poetry. Three
or four words, which are alternately repeated by the
finger and the general chorus, fometimes conftitute
the whole poem. Five or fix bars of mufic compofe
the whole length of the fong. A circumftance that
appears fingular is, that the fame air, though merely
a continual repetition of the fame tones, takes entire
poffeffion of them, makes them work or dance for
feveral hours : neither they, nor even the white men,
are difgufted with that tedious uniformity which thefe
repetitions might naturally occafion. This particular
attachment is owing to the warmth and expreffion
which they introduce into their fongs. Their airs
are generally double time. None of them tend to
infpire them with pride. Thofe intended to excite
tendernefs promote rather a kind of languor. Even
thofe which are moft lively carry in them a certain
expreffion of melancholy. This is the higheft enter-
tainment to minds of great fenfibility.

So ftrong an inclination for mufic might become a
powerful motive of action under the direction of fkil-
ful hands. Feftivals, games, and rewards, might on
this account be eftablifhed among them. Thefe a-

mufements, conducted with judgment, would prevent that ftupidity fo common among flaves, eafe their labours, and preferve them from that conftant melancholy which confumes them, and fhortens their days. After having provided for the prefervation of the blacks exported from Africa, the welfare of thofe who were born in the iflands themfelves would then be confidered.

The Negroes are not averfe from the propagation of their fpecies, even in the chains of flavery. But it is the cruelty of the mafters which hath effectually prevented them from complying with this great end of nature. Such hard labour is required from Negro women, both before and after their pregnancy, that their children are either abortive, or live but a fhort time after delivery. Mothers, rendered defperate by the punifhments which the weaknefs of their condition occafions them, fometimes fnatch their children from the cradle, in order to ftrangle them in their arms, and facrifice them with a fury mingled with a fpirit of revenge and compaffion, that they may not become the property of their cruel mafters. This barbarity, the horror of which muft be wholly imputed to the Europeans, will perhaps convince them of their error. Their fenfibility will be roufed, and engage them to pay a greater attention to their true interefts. They will find, that by committing fuch outrages againft humanity, they injure themfelves; and if they do not become the benefactors of their flaves, they will at leaft ceafe to be their executioners.

They will, perhaps, refolve to fet free thofe mothers who fhall have brought up a confiderable number of children to the age of fix years. The allurements of liberty are the moft powerful that can influence the human heart. The Negro women, animated by the hope of fo great a bleffing, to which all would afpire, and few would be able to obtain, would make neglect and infamy be fucceeded by a virtuous emulation to bring up children, whofe num-

ber and prefervation would fecure to them freedom
and tranquillity.

After having taken wife meafures not to deprive
their plantations of thofe fuccours arifing from the
extraordinary fruitfulnefs of the Negro women, they
will attend to the care of conducting and extending
cultivation by means of population, and without foreign expedients. Every thing invites them to eftablifh this eafy and natural fyftem.

There are fome powers, whofe fettlements in the
American ifles every day acquire extent, and there
are none whofe manual labour doth not continually
increafe. Thefe lands, therefore, conftantly require
a greater number of hands to clear them. Africa,
where all Europeans go to recruit the population of
the colonies, gradually furnifhes them with fewer
men, and fupplies them at the fame time with worfe
flaves, and at a higher price. This fource for the obtaining flaves will be gradually more and more exhaufted.
But were this change in trade as chimerical; as it
feems to be not far diftant, it is neverthelefs certain,
that a great number of flaves, drawn out of a remote
region, perifh in their paffage, or in the New World ;
and that when they come to America they are fold
at a very advanced price ; that there are few of them
whofe natural term of life is not fhortened ; and that
the greater part of thofe who attain a wretched old
age, are extremely ignorant, and being accuftomed
from their infancy to idlenefs, are frequently very
unfit for the employments to which they are deftined,
and are in a continual ftate of defpondency, on account of their being feparated from their country. If
we do not miftake in our opinion, cultivators born in the
American iflands themfelves, always breathing their
native air, brought up without any other expence
than what confifts in a cheap food, habituated in early
life to labour by their own parents, endowed with a
fufficient fhare of underftanding, or a fingular apti-

tude for all the ufeful arts; fuch cultivators cannot BOOK
but be preferable to flaves that have been fold, and XI.
live in a ftate of perpetual exile and reftraint.

The method of fubftituting in the place of foreign
Negroes, thofe of the colonies themfelves, is very obvious. It wholly confifts in fuperintending the black
children that are born in the iflands, in confining to
their workhoufes that multitude of flaves who carry
about with them their worthleffnefs, their licentiouf-
nefs, and the luxury and infolence of their matters,
in all the towns and ports of Europe; but above all,
in requiring of navigators who frequent the African
coafts, that they fhould form their cargo of an equal
number of men and women, or even of a majority of
women, during fome years, in order to reduce that
difproportion which prevails between the two fexes.

This laft precaution, by putting the pleafures of
love within the reach of all the blacks, would contribute to their eafe and multiplication. Thefe unhappy men, forgetting the weight of their chains,
would with tranfport fee themfelves live again in their
children. The majority of them are faithful, even
to death, to thofe Negro women whom love and flavery hath affigned to them for their companions; they
treat them with that compaffion which the wretched
mutually derive from one another, even in the rigour
of their condition; they comfort them under the load
of their employments; they fympathize, at leaft, with
them, when, through excefs of labour, or want of
food, the mother can only offer her child a breaft that
is dry, or bathed in her tears. The women, on their
part, though tied down to no reftrictions of chaftity,
are fixed in their attachments; provided that the
vanity of being beloved by white people does not
render them inconftant. Unhappily this is a temptation to infidelity, to which they have too often opportunities to yield.

Thofe who have inquired into the caufes of this
tafte for black women, which appears to be fo depraved in the Europeans, have found it to arife from the

BOOK nature of the climate, which, under the torrid zone,
XI. irresistibly excites men to the pleasures of love; the
facility of gratifying this insurmountable inclination
without restraint, and without the trouble of a long
pursuit; from a certain captivating attraction of beauty, discoverable in black women, as soon as custom
hath once reconciled the eye to their colour; but principally from a warmth of constitution, which gives
them the power of inspiring and returning the most
ardent transports. Thus they revenge themselves, as
it were, for the humiliating despondency of their condition, by the violent and inordinate passion which
they excite in their masters; nor do our ladies in Europe possess, in a more exalted degree, the art of
wasting and running out large fortunes than the Negro women. But those of Africa have the superiority over those of Europe, in the real passion they
have for the men who purchase them. The happy
discovery and prevention of conspiracies that would
have destroyed all their oppressors by-the hands of
their slaves, hath been often owing to the faithful attachment of these Negro women. The double tyranny of these unworthy usurpers of the estates and liberty of such a number of people, deserved, doubtless,
such a punishment.

Origin and   We will not here so far debase ourselves as to en-
progress of   large the ignominious list of those writers who devote
slavery.
Arguments their abilities, to justify by policy what is reprobated
made use of by morality. In an age where so many errors are
to justify it.
Refutation boldly exposed, it would be unpardonable to conceal
of them.   any truth that is interesting to humanity. If whatever we have hitherto advanced hath seemingly tended only to alleviate the burden of slavery, the reason
is, that it was first necessary to give some comfort to
those unhappy beings, whom we cannot set free; and
convince their oppressors that they are cruel to the
prejudice of their real interests. But, in the mean
time, until some considerable revolution shall make
the evidence of this great truth felt, it may not be
improper to pursue this subject further. We shall

then firft prove, that there is no reafon of ftate that B O O K
XI.
can authorife flavery. We fhall not be afraid to cite
to the tribunal of reafon and juftice thofe governments
which tolerate this cruelty, or which even are not
afhamed to make it the bafis of their power.

Slavery is a ftate in which a man hath loft, either
by force or by convention, the property of his own
perfon, and of whom a mafter can difpofe as of his
own effects.

This odious ftate was unknown in the firft ages.
Men were all equals; but that natural equality did
not laft long. As there was not yet any regular form
of government eftablifhed to maintain focial order;
as none of the lucrative profeffions exifted, which the
progrefs of civilization hath fince introduced among
the nations, the ftrongeft, or the moft artful, foon
feized upon the beft territories; and the weakeft, and
lefs cunning, were obliged to fubmit to thofe who
were able to feed and to defend them. This ftate of
dependence was tolerable. In the fimplicity of ancient
manners, there was no great difference between a mafter and his fervants. Their drefs, their food, their
lodging, were almoft alike. If, at any time, the fuperior, impetuous and violent, as favages generally
are, gave way to the ferocioufnefs of his character,
this was a tranfitory act, which made no alteration in
the habitual ftate of things. But this arrangement
did not long fubfift. Thofe who commanded, readily
accuftomed themfelves to believe that they were of a
fuperior nature to thofe who obeyed. They kept
them at a diftance, and debafed them. This contempt was attended with fatal confequences; the idea
of confidering thefe unfortunate people as flaves,
grew familiar; and they became really fo. Each mafter difpofed of them in the manner which was the
moft favourable to his intereft and to his paffions. A
mafter who had no further ufe for their labour, fold
or exchanged them : and he who was defirous of increafing the number of them, encouraged them to
multiply.

When societies, become more strong and more numerous, acquired a knowledge of the arts and of commerce ; the weak found a support in the magistrate,
and the poor found resources in the several branches
of industry. They both emerged, by degrees, from
the kind of necessity they had experienced of sub-
mitting to slavery, in order to procure subsistence.
The custom of putting one's self in the power of another, became every day less frequent, and liberty was
at length considered as a precious and unalienable
property.

In themean while, the laws, which were imperfect
and ferocious, still continued, for some time, to impose the penalty of servitude. As in the times of
profound ignorance, the satisfaction of the offended
person was the only aim which an ill-contrived authority proposed, those who had infringed the principles
of justice, with regard to the person who accused
them, were given up to him. The tribunals were
afterwards determined by more extensive and more
useful views. Every crime appeared to them, and
with reason, an offence against society ; and the criminal became the slave of the state, which disposed of
him in the manner most advantageous for the public
good. At that period there were no other captives,
except those acquired in war.

Before a power was established to maintain order,
the contests between individuals were very frequent,
and the conqueror never failed to reduce the van-
quished to a state of servitude. This custom continued for a long time, in the disputes between nations, because, as each combatant took the field at
his own expence, he remained master of the prisoners he had taken himself, or of those which, in the
division of the spoil, were given to him as a reward
for his actions. But when the armies became mercenary, the government, who were at the expence
of the war, and who ran the risk of the event, appropriated to themselves the spoils of the enemy, of
which the prisoners were always the most important.

part. It was then neceſſary to purchaſe ſlaves from the ſtate, or from the neighbouring ſavage nations. Such was the practice of the Greeks and of the Romans, and of all people who choſe to increaſe their enjoyments by this inhuman and barbarous cuſtom.

Europe relapſed again into the chaos of the primary ages, when the people of the North ſubverted the coloſſal empire, which had been raiſed, with ſo much glory, by a warlike and politic republic. Theſe barbarians, who had had ſlaves in the midſt of their foreſts, multiplied them prodigiouſly in the provinces which they invaded. Not only thoſe who were taken in arms were reduced to ſervitude, this humiliating ſtate became alſo the portion of citizens, who cultivated quietly at home the arts which flouriſh in times of peace. However, the number of freemen was more conſiderable in the ſubdued countries, during the time that the conquerors remained faithful to the form of government which they had thought proper to eſtabliſh, in order to contain their new ſubjects, and to protect them from foreign invaſions. But, no ſooner had this ſingular inſtitution, which collected a nation, commonly diſperſed, into a conſtantly ſtanding army, loſt its influence; no ſooner had the fortunate affinities which united the meaneſt ſoldier of this powerful body to their king, or to their general, ceaſed to exiſt, than a ſyſtem of univerſal oppreſſion was eſtabliſhed. There was no longer any remarkable diſtinction between thoſe who had preſerved their independence, and thoſe who had for a long time groaned under the yoke of ſlavery.

The men who were free, whether they were inhabitants of the towns or of the country, reſided upon the king's domains, or upon the territories of ſome baron. All thoſe who were in poſſeſſion of fiefs, pretended, in thoſe times of anarchy, that a man who enjoyed no diſtinction from birth, whoever he might be, could only poſſeſs a precarious kind of property, which had originally proceeded from their liberality. This prejudice, perhaps the moſt extravagant that

B O O K
XI.
hath ever afflicted the human species, persuaded the nobles that they could never be guilty of injustice, whatever were the obligations they might impose upon so base an order of beings.

According to these principles, they were not allowed to absent themselves, without leave, from their native country. They were not allowed to dispose of their property, either by will or by any other act made in their life-time ; and their lord was their undoubted heir, when they died without leaving any posterity, or when this posterity were fixed in another part of the country. They were not allowed to appoint guardians to their children ; and the liberty of marrying was granted to those only who had purchased it. So much was it apprehended that the people should acquire an insight on their rights and interests, that the liberty of learning to read was one of the favours granted with the most reluctance. They were compelled to the most humiliating vassalages. The taxes which were imposed upon them were arbitrary, unjust, oppressive, and destructive of the spirit of activity and industry. They were obliged to bear the tyrant's expences when he arrived ; their provisions, their furniture, their flocks, were all abandoned to pillage. If a law-suit was begun, it was not possible to end it in an amicable manner, because this method would have deprived the lord of the rights that would accrue to him from the sentence. Every kind of exchange between individuals was prohibited, at the period when the lord of the manor chose himself to sell the provisions which they had collected, or which they had even purchased. Such was the state of oppression under which the class of people groaned who were the least ill treated. If any of the vexations we have just given an account of, were unknown in certain places, others were substituted to them which were often more intolerable.

Some towns in Italy, which by fortunate chance had acquired the possession of some branches of commerce, were the first to be ashamed of such a situation ; and their riches furnifhed them with the means B O O K of fhaking off the yoke of their feeble defpots. Others XI. purchafed their liberty of the emperors, who, in the courfe of the bloody and lafting difputes which they had with the popes, and with their vaffals, thought themfelves exceedingly fortunate to fell privileges, which the ftate of their affairs did not permit them to refufe. Some princes were even prudent enough to facrifice that part of their authority, which the ferment excited in men's minds made them forefee that they fhould foon be deprived of. Several of thefe towns remained infulated : but the majority united their interefts. All of them formed political focieties, governed by laws which had been dictated by the citizens themfelves.

The fuccefs with which this revolution in government was attended, furprifed the neighbouring nations. In the meanwhile, as the kings and barons who oppreffed them, were not compelled by circumftances to give up their fovereignty, they contented themfelves with granting to the towns in their dependence valuable and confiderable immunities. They were authorifed to furround themfelves with walls, to bear arms, and to pay no more than a regular and moderate tribute. Liberty was fo effential a point of their conftitution, that whenever a bondfman took refuge among them, he became a citizen, if he was not claimed during the courfe of the year. Thefe communities, or municipal bodies, profpered in proportion to their pofition, their population, and their induftry.

While the condition of men, reputed free, was fo fortunately improved, that of the flaves remained the fame ; that is to fay, the moft deplorable which it is poffible to conceive. Thefe wretched people belonged fo entirely to their mafters, that they fold or exchanged them at pleafure. They were not allowed any kind of property, even out of their favings, whenever a fixed fum was affigned them for their fubfiftence. They were put to the torture for the fmall-

B O O K eft mifdemeanour. They might be punifhed with
 ___XI.___ death, without the interference of the magiftrate.
Marriage was for a long time forbidden to them; the
connections between the two fexes were illegal; they
were tolerated, and even encouraged, but they were
not honoured with the nuptial benediction. The condition of the children was the fame as that of their
fathers; they were born, they lived, and they died
in flavery. In moft of the courts of judicature, their
teftimony was not admitted againft a free man.
They were obliged to wear a particular drefs; and
this humiliating diftinction recalled every moment to
their minds the ignominy of their exiftence. To
complete thefe misfortunes, the fpirit of the feudal
fyftem oppofed the disfranchifement of this fpecies
of men. A generous mafter might indeed break the
bonds of his domeftic flaves whenever he chofe; but
innumerable formalities were required to change the
fituation of the flaves which belonged to the glebe.
According to a maxim generally received, a vaffal
could not diminifh the value of the fief which he
had received; and the releafing of any of its cultivators was diminifhing it. This obftacle muft neceffarily have retarded, but could not entirely prevent,
the revolution, and for the following reafon:

The Germans, and the other conquerors, had appropriated immenfe domains to themfelves at the
time of their invafion. The nature of thefe eftates
did not allow them to be difmembered. From that
time it became impoffible for the proprietor to retain
all his flaves under his own infpection, and he was
compelled to difperfe them over the foil they were
to cultivate. Their diftance preventing their being
overlooked, it was thought proper to encourage them
by rewards proportioned to their labour. Thus gratifications, which moft commonly confifted of a greater or lefs confiderable part of the produce of the
lands, were added to their ufual maintenance.

By this arrangement the *villains* formed a kind of
affociation with their mafters. The riches which they

acquired in this advantageous market enabled them
to offer a fixed rent for the grounds with which they
were intrusted, upon the condition that the overplus
should belong to them. As the lords acquired by
these means, without risk or uneasiness, from their
possessions, as much, or more income, than they had
formerly obtained, this practice gained credit, and
was soon universally adopted. It was no longer the
interest of the proprietor to attend to slaves who cultivated at their own expence, and who were exact in
their payments. Thus ended this personal slavery.

It sometimes happened, that a bold enterprising
man, who had laid 'out considerable funds on his
farm, was driven from it before he had reaped the
fruits of his advances. This inconvenience occasioned the requisition of leases for several years. They
were extended, in process of time, to the whole life
of the cultivator, and were often settled upon his most
distant posterity. This was the termination of real
slavery.

This great change, brought on in a manner by itself, was hastened by a cause which deserves to be observed. All the European governments were then
aristocratic. The chief of every republic was perpetually at war with his barons. Being for the most
part unable to resist them by force, he was obliged to
have recourse to artifice. That artifice, which was
employed to the greatest advantage, was to protect
the slaves against the tyranny of their masters, and to
undermine the power of the nobles, by diminishing
the dependence of their subjects. It is not improbable but that some kings favoured the spirit of liberty, from the only motive of general utility; but
most of them were visibly induced to adopt this fortunate policy, more on account of their personal interests, than from principles of humanity and benevolence.

However this may be, the revolution was so complete, that liberty became more general throughout
the greatest part of Europe, than it had been in any

climate, or in any age. In all ancient governments,
in thofe even which are always propofed to us as models, moft of the people were condemned to a fhameful and cruel fervitude. The more the focieties acquired knowledge, riches, and power, the more did
the number of flaves increafe, and the more deplorable became their fate. Athens reckoned twenty
vaffals to one citizen. The difproportion was ftill
greater at Rome, become the miftrefs of the univerfe.
In both the republics, flavery was carried to the utmoft excefs of fatigue, of mifery, and of ignominy.
Since it hath been abolifhed among us, the people
are infinitely more happy, even· under the moft defpotic empires, than they were formerly under the
beft-regulated democracies.

But no fooner was domeftic liberty revived in Europe, than it was annihilated in America. The Spaniards, whom the waves firft caft upon thefe fhores of
the New World, did not imagine they owed any duties to a fet of men who were not of their complexion,
and who did not practife their cuftoms or their religion. They confidered them only as the inftruments of their avarice, and loaded them with irons.
Thefe weak men, who had not the habit of labour,
foon expired among the vapours of the mines, or in
other occupations almoft as deftructive. Slaves were
then fent for from Africa. Their number hath increafed in proportion as the cultivations have been
extended. The Portuguefe, the Dutch, the Englifh,
the French, the Danes, all thefe nations, whether
free or enflaved, have fought, without remorfe, an increafe of fortune in the labours, the blood, and the
defpair of thefe unfortunate people. What a horrid
fyftem !

Liberty is the property of one's felf. Three kinds of
it are diftinguifhed : natural liberty, civil liberty, and
political liberty ; that is to fay the liberty of the individual, the liberty of the citizen, and the liberty of a
nation. Natural liberty is the right granted by nature,
to every man to difpofe of himfelf at pleafure. Civil

liberty is the right which is enfured by fociety to eve- B O O K
ry citizen, of doing every thing which is not contra- XI.
ry to the laws. Political liberty is the ftate of a people who have not alienated their fovereignty, and
who either make their own laws, or who conftitute a
part in the fyftem of their legiflation.

The firft of thefe liberties is, after reafon, the di-
ftinguifhing characteriftic of man. Brutes are chained up, and kept in fubjection, becaufe they have no
notion of what is juft or unjuft, no idea of grandeur
or meannefs. But in man, liberty is the principle of
his vices or his virtues. None but a free man can
fay, *I will* or *I will not* ; and confequently none but
a free man can be worthy of praife, or be liable to
cenfure.

Without liberty, or the property of one's own body, and the enjoyment of one's mind, no man
can be either a hufband, a father, a relation, or a
friend ; he hath neither a country, a fellow-citizen,
nor a God. The flave, impelled by the wicked man,
and who is the inftrument of his wickednefs, is inferior even to the dog, let loofe by the Spaniard upon the American ; for confcience which the dog hath
not, ftill remains with the man. He who bafely ab-
dicates his liberty, gives himfelf up to remorfe, and
to the greateft mifery which can be experienced by
a thinking and fenfible being. If there be not any
power under the heavens, which can change my nature and reduce me to the ftate of brutes, there is
none which can difpofe of my liberty. God is my
father, and not my mafter ; I am his child and not
his flave. How is it poffible that I fhould grant
to political power, what I refufe to divine omnipo-
tence?

Will thefe eternal and immutable truths, the foundation of all morality, the bafis of all rational government be contefted? They will, and the audacious argument will be dictated by barbarous and fordid avarice. Behold that proprietor of a veffel, who lean-
ing upon his defk, and with the pen in his hand, re-

gulates the number of enormities he may caufe to be committed on the coafts of Guinea; who confiders at leifure, what number of firelocks he fhall want to obtain one Negro, what fetters will be neceffary to keep him chained on board his fhip, what whips will be required to make him work; who·calculates with coolnefs every drop of blood which the flave muft neceffarily expend in labour for him, and how much it will produce; who confiders whether a Negro woman will be of more advantage to him by her feeble labours, or by going through the dangers of child-birth. You fhudder!—If there exifted any religion which tolerated, or which gave only a tacit fanction to fuch kind of horrors; if, abforbed in fome idle or feditious queftions, it did not inceffantly exclaim againft the authors or the inftruments of this tyranny; if it fhould confider it as a crime in a flave to break his chains; if it fhould fuffer to remain in its community, the iniquitous judge who condemns the fugitive to death; if fuch a religion, I fay, exifted, ought not the minifters of it to be fuffocated under the ruins of their altars?

Men or demons, whichever you are, will you dare to juftify the attempts you make againft my independence, by pleading the right of the ftrongeft? What! is not the man who wants to enflave me guilty? Doth he only make ufe of his rights? Where are thefe rights? Who hath ftamped them with a character facred enough to filence mine? I hold from nature the right of defending myfelf; and it hath not given thee that of attacking me. If thou doft think thyfelf authorifed to opprefs me, becaufe thou art ftronger or more dexterous than I am, complain not if my vigorous arm fhall rip up thy bofom in fearch of thy heart. Complain not, when in thy torn entrails thou fhalt feel that death which I fhall have conveyed into them with thy food. I am ftronger or more dexterous than thou art; be the victim in thy turn, and expiate the crime of having been an oppreffor.

But it is alleged, that in all regions, and in all
ages, flavery hath been more or lefs eftablifhed.

I grant it; but what doth it fignify to me, what
other people in other ages have done? Are we to
appeal to the cuftoms of ancient times, or to our
confcience? Are we to liften to the fuggeftions of
intereft, of infatuation, and of barbarifm, rather than
to thofe of reafon and of juftice? If the univerfality
of a practice were admitted as a proof of its innocence,
we fhould then have a complete apology for ufurpations, conquefts, and for every fpecies of oppreffion.

But the ancients, it is faid, thought themfelves to
be mafters of the lives of their flaves; and we, become more humane, difpofe only of their liberty and
of their labours.

It is true, the progrefs of knowledge hath enlightened the minds of all modern legiflators upon this
important point. All codes of laws, without exception, have exerted themfelves for the prefervation of
man, even of him who languifhes in a ftate of flavery. They have agreed, that his exiftence fhould be
put under the protection of the magiftrates, and
that the tribunals of juftice alone fhould be able to
haften the end of it. But hath this law, the moft
facred of all focial inftitutions, ever been put in force?
Is not America peopled with atrocious colonifts, who
infolently ufurp the rights of the fovereign, and deftroy by the fword, or by fire, the unfortunate victims
of their avarice? Doth not this facrilegious infraction
of the laws, to the difgrace of all Europe, ftill remain unpunifhed? I challenge any defender or panegyrift of our humanity and of our juftice, to ad-
duce an inftance of any one of thefe affaffins having
loft his life upon a fcaffold.

Let us fuppofe, that the regulations which, according to the panegyrift, do fo much honour to our age,
be ftrictly obferved; will the flave be, on that account, much lefs an object of compaffion? What!
does not the mafter, who difpofes of my ftrength at
his pleafure, likewife difpofe of my life, which de-

pends on the voluntary and proper ufe of my facul-
ties? What is exiftence to him who has not the difpofal of it? I cannot kill my flave; but I can make
him bleed under the whip of an executioner; I can
overwhelm him with forrows, drudgery, and want;
I can injure him every way, and fecretly undermine
the principles and fprings of his life; I can fmother,
by flow punifhments, the wretched infant which a
Negro woman carries in her womb. Thus the laws
protect the flave againft a violent death, only to leave
to my cruelty the right of making him die by degrees. The right of flavery is, in fact, that of per-
petrating all forts of crimes: thofe crimes which invade property; for flaves are not fuffered to have
any even in their own perfons: thofe crimes which
deftroy perfonal fafety; for the flave may be facrificed to the caprice of his mafter: thofe crimes which
make modefty fhudder.—My blood rifes at thefe horrid images. I deteft, I abhor the human fpecies compofed only of victims and executioners; and if it is
never to become better, may it be annihilated!

But thefe Negroes, fay they, are a race of men
born for flavery; their difpofitions are narrow, treacherous, and wicked; they themfelves allow the fuperiority of our underftandings, and almoft acknowledge the juftice of our authority.

The minds of the Negroes are contracted; becaufe
flavery deftroys all the fprings of the foul. They are
wicked; but not fufficiently fo with you. They are
treacherous; becaufe they are under no obligation
to fpeak truth to their tyrants. They acknowledge
the fuperiority of our underftandings, becaufe we
have perpetuated their ignorance: they allow the
juftice of our authority, becaufe we have abufed their
weaknefs. As it was impoffible for us to maintain
our fuperiority by force, we have, by a criminal policy, had recourfe to cunning. We have almoft perfuaded them that they were a fingular fpecies, born
only for dependence, for fubjection, for labour, and
for chaftifement. We have neglected nothing that

might tend to degrade thefe unfortunate people, and we have afterwards upbraided them for their mean-nefs.

But thefe Negroes, it is further urged, were born flaves.

Barbarians, will you perfuade me, that a man can be the property of a fovereign, a fon the property of a father, a wife the property of a hufband, a domef-tic the property of a mafter, a Negro the property of a planter?

Proud and difdainful being, who doft difavow thy brethren, wilt thou never perceive that this contempt recoils upon thyfelf? If thou doft wifh that thy pride fhould be ennobled, exert a fufficient elevation of mind, to make it confift in the neceffary affinities which thou haft with thefe unfortunate men whom thou doft debafe.

One common Father, an immortal foul, a future ftate of felicity, fuch is thy true glory, and fuch like-wife is theirs.

But it is government itfelf that fells the flaves.

How did the ftate acquire that right? Let the ma-giftrate be ever fo abfolute, is he proprietor of the fubjects fubmitted to his empire? Hath he any fur-ther authority, but that with which he is intrufted by the citizen? And have any people ever had the privilege of difpofing of their liberty?

But thefe flaves have fold themfelves. If they be-long to themfelves, they have a right to difpofe of themfelves. It is his bufinefs to put a price on his li-berty; and when that is fettled, whoever gives him the money, hath acquired a legal right over him.

No man hath the right of felling himfelf; becaufe he hath no right to accede to every thing which an unjuft, violent, and depraved mafter might require of him. He is the property of God, who is his firft mafter, and from whofe authority he is never releafed. The man who fells him, makes a deceitful bargain with his purchafer, becaufe he lofes his own value. And the money, as foon as it is paid to him, remains,

B O O K with his perfon, in the hands of his mafter. What
XI. property can a man be in poffeffion of, who hath
given up every right of property? Nothing can belong to him who hath agreed to have nothing. He
cannot even have virtue, honefty, nor a will of his
own. The man who hath reduced himfelf to the
condition of a deftructive weapon, is a madman, and
not a flave. A man may fell his life, in the fame
manner as a foldier does, but he cannot as a flave;
and this conftitutes the difference of the two conditions.

But thefe flaves had been taken in war, and would
have been murdered if we had not interfered.

Would there have been any wars without you?
Are not the diffenfions among thofe people owing to
yourfelves? Do you not carry deftructive weapons to
them? Do you not infpire them with the defire of ufing
them? Will your veffels never forfake thofe deplorable
fhores, till after the deftruction of the miferable race
who inhabit them? Why do you not fuffer the victor
to make what ufe he choofes of his victory; and why
do you become his accomplice?

But they were criminals, who deferved death, or
the greateft punifhments, and were condemned in
their own country to flavery. Are you then the executioners of the people of Africa? Befide, who was
it that condemned them? Do you not know, that in
a defpotic ftate there is no criminal but the tyrant?
The fubject of an abfolute prince is the fame as the
flave in a ftate repugnant to nature. Every thing
that contributes to keep a man in fuch a ftate, is an
attempt againft his perfon. Every power which fixes
him to the tyranny of one man, is the power of his
enemies : and all thofe who are about him, are the
authors or abettors of this violence. His mother,
who taught him the firft leffons of obedience; his
neighbour, who fet him the example of it; his fupe-
riors, who compelled him into this ftate; and his equals,
who led him into it by their opinion : all thefe are
the minifters and inftruments of tyranny. The ty-

rant can do nothing of himfelf; he is only the *pri-* B O O K
mum mobile of thofe efforts which all his fubjects exert XI.
to their own mutual oppreffion. He keeps them in
a ftate of perpetual war, which renders robberies,
treafons, affaffinations lawful. Thus, like the blood
which flows in his veins, all crimes originate from
his heart, and return thither as to their primary
fource. Caligula ufed to fay, that if the whole human race had had but one head, he fhould have taken pleafure in cutting it off. Socrates would have
faid, that if all crimes were heaped upon one head,
that fhould be the one which ought to be ftricken off.

But they enjoy more felicity in America, than they
did in Africa.

Wherefore then are thefe flaves conftantly fighing
after their own country? Why do they refume their
liberty as foon as they are able? Why do they prefer
deferts, and the fociety of wild beafts, to a condition
that appears to you fo mild? Why doth defpair induce them to deftroy themfelves, or to poifon you?
Why do their women fo frequently procure abortion,
in order that their children may not partake of their
melancholy deftiny? When you fpeak to us of the
happinefs of your flaves, you are falfe to yourfelves,
and you deceive us. It is the utmoft pitch of extra-
vagance to attempt to transform fo ftrange a barbarity into an act of humanity.

But it is urged, that in Europe, as well as in
America, the people are flaves. The only advantage
we have over the Negroes is, that we can break one
chain to put on another.

It is but too true; moft nations are enflaved. The
multitude is generally facrificed to the paffions of a
few privileged oppreffors. There is fcarce a region
known, where a man can flatter himfelf that he is
mafter of his perfon, that he can difpofe, at pleafure,
of his inheritance; and that he can quietly enjoy the
fruits of his induftry. Even in thofe countries that
are leaft under the yoke of fervitude, the citizen, deprived of the produce of his labour, by the wants in-

B O O K ceſſantly renewed of a rapacious or needy govern-
XI. ment, is continually reſtrained in the moſt lawful
means of acquiring felicity. Liberty is ſtifled in all
parts, by extravagant ſuperſtitions, by barbarous cuſtoms, and by obſolete laws. It will one day certainly
riſe again from its aſhes. In proportion as morality
and policy ſhall be improved, man will recover his
rights. But wherefore, while we are waiting for
theſe fortunate times, and theſe enlightened ages of
proſperity, wherefore muſt there be an unfortunate
race, to whom even the comfortable and honourable
name of freeman is denied, and who, notwithſtanding
the inſtability of events, muſt be deprived of the hope
even of obtaining it ? Whatever, therefore, may be
ſaid, the condition of theſe unfortunate people is very
different from ours.

The laſt argument which hath been uſed in juſti-
fication of ſlavery, hath been to ſay, that it was the
only method which could be found to lead Negroes
to the bleſſings of eternal life, by the great benefit of
baptiſm.

O beneficent Jeſus ! how is it poſſible that thy mild
maxims could have been perverted to juſtify ſuch
an infinite number of horrid acts ? If the Chriſtian
religion did really thus give a ſanction to the avarice
of empires, its ſanguinary tenets ought for ever to
be proſcribed. It ſhould either be aboliſhed, or it
ſhould diſavow, in the face of the whole univerſe, the
enormities that are imputed to it. Let not its miniſters be apprehenſive of diſplaying too much enthuſiaſm upon ſuch a ſubject. The more they ſhall
be inflamed upon it, the better will they ſerve their
cauſe. Tranquillity would be criminal in them, and
wiſdom will break forth in their tranſports.

The man who defends the ſyſtem of ſlavery, will
undoubtedly complain, that we have not allowed to
his arguments all the energy of which they were
ſuſceptible. This may poſſibly be. Who is the man,
who would proſtitute his talents in the defence of the
moſt abominable of all cauſes, or who would employ

his eloquence, if he had any, in the juftification of a
multitude of murders already committed, and of a multitude of others ready to be perpetrated? Execu-tioner of thy brethren, take thyfelf the pen in thy hand if thou dareft, quiet the perturbations of thy con-fcience, and harden thine accomplices in their crimes.

I could have refuted with greater energy, and more at large, the arguments I had to combat ; but the fubject was not worth the pains. Are many ex-ertions due, or muft the utmoft intenfenefs of thought be beftowed upon him who doth not fpeak as he thinks ? Would not the filence of contempt be more fuitable, than difpute with him who pleads for his own intereft againft juftice and againft his own con-viction ?

I have already faid too much for the honeft and feeling man. I fhall never be able to fay enough for the inhuman trader,

Let us, therefore, haften to fubftitute the light of reafon and the fentiments of nature to the blind fe-rocioufnefs of our anceftors. Let us break the bonds of fo many victims to our mercenary principles, fhould we even be obliged to difcard a commerce which is founded only on injuftice, and the object of which is luxury.

But even this is not neceffary. There is no oc-cafion to give up thofe conveniences which cuftom hath fo much endeared to us. We may draw them from Africa itfelf. The moft valuable of them are in-digenous there, and it would be an eafy matter to na-turalize the others. Can there be a doubt, that a people, who fell their children in order to fatisfy fome tranfient caprices, would determine to cultivate their lands, that they might enjoy habitually all the advantages of a virtuous and well-regulated fociety ?

Perhaps it would not even be impoffible to obtain thefe productions from the colonies without peo-pling them with flaves. The provifions might be ga-thered by the hands of free people, and would from that time be confumed without remorfe.

In order to obtain this end, which is generally confidered as chimerical, it would not be neceffary, according to the ideas of an enlightened man, to re-
leafe from their chains thofe unfortunate people, who
are either born, or have grown old in fervitude. Thefe
ftupid men, who would not have been prepared for fuch
a change of fituation, would be incapable of conducting
themfelves, they would fpend their lives in habitual indolence, or in the commiffion of all kinds of crimes. The
great benefit of liberty muft be preferved for their pofterity, and even that with fome modifications. Thefe
children, till they attain their twentieth year, fhould
belong to the mafters of the manufacture or plantation where they were born, in order that he may be
reimburfed the expences which he will have been
obliged to incur for bringing them up. The five following years they fhould ftill be obliged to ferve
him, but for a ftipulated falary fettled by the law.
After this time they fhould be independent, provided
their conduct had not deferved much cenfure. If
they fhould have been guilty of any weighty crime,
they fhould be condemned by the magiftrates to public labour for a more or lefs confiderable time. A hut
fhould be given to the new citizens, with ground
fufficient to make a fmall garden, and the treafury
fhould be at the expence of this eftablifhment. No
regulation fhould deprive thefe men, become free,
of the power of extending the property which fhall
have been gratuitoufly beftowed upon them. To put
fuch reftraints upon their activity and their intelligence, would be to lofe, by abfurd laws, the fruits
of fo laudable an inftitution.

This arrangement, according to all appearances,
would be attended with the happieft effects. The
population of the blacks, which is at prefent checked by the regret of bringing into the world none but
beings who are condemned to misfortune and infamy,
will make a rapid progrefs. This offspring will be
moft tenderly taken care of by thofe very mothers
who often took inexpreffible delight in ftifling them,

or in feeing them perish. Thefe men, accuftomed to B o o K XI. occupation, in expectation of certain liberty, and who will not have an extent of property fufficient for their fubfiftence, will fell their labours to whomfoever would be inclined or able to pay for them. Their work will indeed coft more than that of the flaves, but it will alfo be more profitable. A greater degree of labour will give a greater abundance of productions to the colonies, which will be enabled, by their riches, to acquire a greater quantity of merchandife from the mother-country.

Is it then apprehended, that the facility of acquiring fubfiftence without labour, on a foil naturally fertile, and of difpenfing with the want of clothes, would plunge thefe men in idlenefs? Why then do not the inhabitants of Europe confine themfelves to fuch labours as are of indifpenfable neceffity? Why do they exhauft their powers in laborious employments. which tend only to the gratification of a few momentary fancies? There are amongft us a thoufand profeffions, fome more laborious than others, which owe their origin to our inftitutions. Human laws have given rife to a variety of factitious wants, which otherwife would never have had an exiftence. By difpofing of every fpecies of property according to their capricious. inftitutions, they have fubjected an infinite number of people to the imperious will of their fellow-creatures, fo far as even to make them fing and dance for fubfiftence. We have amongft us beings, formed like ourfelves, who have confented to bury themfelves under mountains, in order to furnifh us with metals, and with copper, which may perhaps poifon us: why do we imagine that the Negroes are lefs dupes and lefs foolifh than the Europeans?

While we are reftoring thefe unhappy beings to liberty, we muft be careful to fubject them to our laws and manners, and to offer them our fuperfluities. We muft give them a country, give them interefts to ftudy, productions to cultivate, and articles of confumption agreeable to their refpective taftes, and our colonies will never want hands, which, being eafed of their chains, will become more active and robuft.

In order to overturn the whole fyftem of flavery, which is fupported by paffions fo univerfal, by laws fo authentic, by the emulation of fuch powerful nations, by prejudices ftill more powerful, to what tribunal fhall we refer the caufe of humanity, which fo many men are in confederacy to betray ? Sovereigns of the earth, you alone can bring about this revolution. If you do not fport with the reft of mortals, if you do not regard the power of kings as the right of a fuccefsful plunder, and the obedience of fubjects as artfully obtained from their ignorance, reflect on your own obligations. Refufe the fanction of your authority to the infamous and criminal traffic of men turned into fo many herds of cattle, and this trade will ceafe. For once unite, for the happinefs of the world, thofe powers and defigns which have been fo often exerted for its ruin. If fome one among you would venture to found the expectation of this opulence and grandeur on the generofity of all the reft, he inftantly becomes an enemy of mankind, who ought to be deftroyed. You may carry fire and fword into his territories. Your armies will foon be infpired with the facred enthufiafm of humanity. You will then perceive what difference virtue makes between men who fuccour the oppreffed, and mercenaries who ferve tyrants

But what am I faying ? Let the ineffectual calls of humanity be no longer pleaded with the people and their mafters : perhaps they have never been attended to in any public tranfactions. If then, ye nations of Europe, intereft alone can exert its influence over you, liften to me once more. Your flaves ftand in no need either of your generofity or your counfels, in order to break the facriligeous yoke of their oppreffion. Nature fpeaks a more powerful language than philofophy or intereft. Already have two colonies of fugitive Negroes been eftablifhed, to whom treaties and power give a perfect fecurity from your attempts.

Thefe are fo many indications of the impending ftorm, B O O K
and the Negroes only want a chief, fufficiently cou- XI.
rageous, to lead them on to vengeance and flaughter.

Where is this great man, whom nature owes to her
afflicted, oppreffed, and tormented children? Where
is he? He will undoubtedly appear, he will fhow
himfelf, he will lift up the facred ftandard of liberty.
This venerable fignal will collect around him the
companions of his misfortunes. They will rufh on with
more impetuofity than torrents; they will leave behind them, in all parts, indelible traces of their juft
refentment. Spaniards, Portuguefe, Englifh, French,
Dutch, all their tyrants will become the victims of
fire and fword. The plains of America will fuck up
with tranfport the blood which they have fo long expected, and the bones of fo many wretches, heaped
upon one another, during the courfe of fo many centuries, will bound for joy. The Old World will join
its plaudits to thofe of the New. In all parts the
name of the hero, who fhall have reftored the rights
of the human fpecies, will be bleft; in all parts trophies will be erected to his glory. Then will the
black code be no more; and the *white code* will be a
dreadful one, if the conqueror only regards the right
of reprifals.

Till this revolution fhall take place, the Negroes
groan under the oppreffion of labours, the defcription
of which cannot but intereft us more and more in
their deftiny.

The foil of the American iflands hath little refem- The culture
blance to ours. It productions are very different, as of the foil
well as the manner of cultivating them. Except ricanArchi-
fome pot-herbs, nothing is fown there; every thing pelago hath
is planted. to neglect-

Tobacco being the firft production that was culti- ed.
vated, as its roots do not ftrike deep, and the leaft
injury deftroys them, a fimple harrow was only employed to prepare the lands which were to receive it,
and to extirpate the noxious weeds which would have
choked it. This cuftom ftill prevails.

BOOK
XI.

When more troublefome cultures began to be attended to, and which were lefs delicate, the hoe was
made ufe of to work and weed ; but it was not employed over the whole extent of ground that was to
be cultivated. It was thought fufficient to dig a hole
for the reception of the plant.

The inequallity of the ground, moft commonly full
of hillocks, probably gave rife to this cuftom. It
might be apprehended, that the rains, which always
fall in torrents, fhould deftroy, by the cavities they
make, the land that had been turned up. Indolence,
and the want of means at the time of the firft fettlements, extended this practice to the moft level plains ;
and cuftom, which no one ever thought of deviating
from, gave a fanction to it. At length fome planters,
who were adventurous enough to difcard former prejudices, thought of ufing the plough ; and it is probable that this method will become general wherever
it fhall be found practicable. It has every circumftance in its favour that can make it defirable.

All the lands of the iflands were virgin lands, when
the Europeans undertook to clear them. The firft
that were occupied, have for a long time yielded lefs
produce than they did in the beginning. Thofe
which have been fucceffively cleared, are likewife
more or lefs exhaufted, in proportion to the period of
their firft cultivation. Whatever their fertility at firft
might have been, they all lofe it in procefs of time,
and they will foon ceafe to requite the labours of thofe
who cultivate them, if art be not exerted to affift
nature.

It is a principle of agriculture generally admitted
by naturalifts, that the earth becomes fertile only in
proportion as it can receive the influence of the air,
and of all thofe meteors which are directed by this
powerful agent, fuch as fogs, dews, and rains. Continual tillage can only procure this advantage to it :
the iflands in particular conftantly require it. The
wet feafon muft be chofen for turning up the ground,
the drynefs of which would be an impediment to fer-

tility. Ploughing cannot be attended with any inconvenience in lands that are level. One might prevent the danger of having fhelving grounds deftroyed by ftorms, by making furrows tranfverfely, on a
line that fhould crofs that of the flope of the hillocks.
If the declivity were fo fteep that the cultivated grounds
could be carried away, notwithftanding the furrows,
fmall drains, fomething deeper, might be added for
the fame purpofe at particular diftances, which would
partly break the force and velocity that the fteepnefs
of the hills adds to the fall of heavy rains.

The utility of the plough would not be merely limited to the producing a greater portion of the vegeta-
ble juice in plants ; it would make their produce the
more certain. The iflands are the regions of infects:
their multiplication there is favoured by a conftant
heat, and one race fucceeds another without interruption. The extenfive ravages they make are well
known. Frequent and fucceffive ploughing would
check the progrefs of this devouring race, difturb
their re-production, kill great numbers of them, and
deftroy greateft part of their eggs. Perhaps this expedient would not be fufficient againft the rats which
fhips have brought from Europe into America, where
they have increafed to that degree, that they often deftroy one-third of the crops. The induftry of flaves
might alfo be called in to affift, and their vigilance
might be encouraged by fome gratification.

The ufe of the plough would probably introduce
the cuftom of manuring : it is already known on the
greateft part of the coaft. The manure there in ufe
is called Varech, a kind of fea-plant, which, when
ripe, is detached from the water, and driven on the
ftrand by the motion of the waves : it is very productive of fertility ; but if employed without previous preparation, it communicates to the fugar a
difagreeable bitternefs, which muft arife from the
falts that are impregnated with oily particles abounding in fea-plants. Perhaps, in order to take off this
bitter tafte, it would only be neceffary to burn the

BOOK plant, and make ufe of the afhes. The falts being
XI. by this operation detached from the oily particles,
and triturated by vegetation, would circulate more
freely in the fugar-cane, and impart to it purer juices.
The interior parts of this country have not till lately been dunged. Neceffity will make this practice
become more general; and in time the foil of America will be affifted by the fame methods of cultivation as the foil of Europe; but with more difficulty. In the iflands, where herds of cattle are not
fo numerous, and where there is feldom the convenience of ftables, it is to have recourfe to other kinds
of manure, and multiply them as much as poffible, in
order to compenfate the quality by the quantity. The
greateft refource will always be found in the weeds,
from which ufeful plants muft be conftantly freed.
Thefe muft be collected together in heaps, and left to
putrify. The colonifts who cultivate coffee have fet
the example of his practice; but with that degree of
indolence which the heat of the climate occafions in
all manual labour. A pile of weeds is heaped up at
the bottom of the coffee-trees, without regarding
whether thefe weeds, which they do not even take
the trouble of covering with earth, heat the tree,
and harbour the infects that prey upon it. They
have been equally negligent in the management of
their cattle.

All the domeftic quadrupeds of Europe were imported into America by the Spaniards; and it is
from their fettlements that the colonies of other nations have been fupplied. Excepting hogs, which are
found to thrive beft in countries abounding with
aquatic productions, infects, and reptiles, and are become larger and better tafted, all thefe animals have
degenerated, and the few that remain in the iflands
are very fmall. Though the badnefs of the climate
may contribute fomething to this degeneracy, the
want of care is perhaps the principal caufe. They
always lie in the open field. They never have either

bran or oats given them, and are at grafs the whole year. The colonifts have not even the attention of dividing the meadows into feparate portions, in order to make their cattle to pafs from one into the other. They always feed on the fame fpot, without allowing the grafs time to fpring up again. Such paftures can only produce weak and watery juices. Too quick a vegetation prevents them from being properly ripen-ed. Hence the animals, deftined for the food of man, afford only flefh that is tough and flabby.

Thofe animals, which are referved for labour, do but very little fervice. The oxen draw but light loads, and that not all day long. They are always four in number. They are not yoked by the head, but by the neck, after the Spanifh cuftom. They are not ftimulated by the goad, but driven by a whip, and are directed by two drivers.

When the roads do not allow the ufe of carriages, mules are employed inftead of oxen. Thefe are fad-dled after a fimpler method than in Europe, but much inferior to it in ftrength. A mat is fixed on their back, to which two hooks are fufpended on each fide, the firft that are cafually met with in the woods. Thus equipped, they carry, at moft, half the weight that European horfes can bear, and go over but half the ground in the fame time.

The pace of their horfes is not fo flow : they have preferved fomething of the fleetnefs, fire, and docility of thofe of Andalufia, from which they derived their pedigree ; but their ftrength is not anfwerable to their fpirit. It is neceffary to breed a great number of them, in order to obtain that fervice which might be had from a fmaller number in Europe. Three or four of them muft be harneffed to very light car-riages ufed by indolent people for making excurfions, which they call journeys ; but which with us would only be an airing.

The degeneracy of the animals in the iflands might have been prevented, retarded, or diminifhed, if care had been taken to renew them by a foreign race.

Stallions brought from colder or warmer countries, would in fome degree have corrected the influence of the climate, feed, and rearing. With the mares of the country they would have produced a new race far fuperior, as they would have come from a climate different from that into which they were imported.

It is very extraordinary, that fo fimple an idea fhould never have occurred to any of the planters ; and that there has been no legiflature attentive enough to its interefts, to fubftitute in its fettlements the bifon to the common ox. Every one who is acquainted with this animal, muft recollect that the bifon has a fofter and brighter fkin, a difpofition lefs dull and ftupid than our bullock, and a quicknefs and docility far fuperior. It is fwift in running, and when mounted can fupply the place of a horfe. It thrives as well in fouthern countries, as the ox that we employ loves cold or temperate climates. This fpecies is known only in the eaftern iflands, and in the greater part of Africa. If cuftom had lefs influence than it commonly has, even over the wifeft governments, they would have been fenfible that this ufeful animal was fingularly well adapted to the great Archipelago of America, and that it would be very eafy to export it, at a very fmall expence, from the Gold Coaft, or the coaft of Angola.

Two rich planters, one in Barbadoes, the other in St. Domingo, equally ftricken with the weaknefs of thofe animals, which, according to eftablifhed cuftom, were employed in drawing and carrying, endeavoured to fubftitute the camel to them. This experiment, formerly tried without fuccefs in Peru by the Spaniards, did not fucceed better here, nor was it poffible it fhould. It is well known, that though a native of hot countries, it dreads exceffive heat, and can as little thrive as propagate under the burning fky of the torrid zone, as in the temperate ones. It would have been better to have tried the buffalo.

The buffalo is a very dirty animal, and of a fierce difpofition. Its caprices are fudden and frequent.

Its skin is firm, light, and almost impenetrable, and its horns serviceable for many purposes. Its flesh is black and hard, and disagreeable to the taste and smell. The milk of the female is not so sweet, but much more copious than that of the cow. Reared like the ox, to which it hath a striking resemblance, it greatly surpasses it in strength and swiftness. Two buffaloes yoked to a waggon by means of a ring passed through their nose, will draw as much as four of the stoutest bullocks, and in less than half the time. They owe this double superiority to the advantage of having longer legs, and a more considerable bulk of body, the whole power of which is employed in drawing, because they naturally carry their head and neck low. As this animal is originally a native of the torrid zone, and is larger, stronger, and more manageable in proportion to the heat of the country it is in, it cannot ever have been doubted that it would have been of great service in the Caribbee Islands, and have propagated happily there. This is highly probable, especially since the successful experiments that have been made of it at Guiana.

Indolence, and old established customs, which have hindered the propagation of domestic animals, have no less impeded the success of transplanting vegetables. Several kinds of fruit trees have been successively carried to the islands. Those that have not died, are some wild stocks, the fruit of which is neither beautiful nor good. The greatest part have degenerated very fast, because they have been exposed to a very strong vegetation, ever lively, and constantly quickened by the copious dews of the night and the strong heats of the day, which are the two grand principles of fertility. Perhaps an intelligent observer would have known how to profit from these circumstances, and have been able to raise tolerable fruit ; but such men are not found in the colonies. If our kitchen herbs have succeeded better ; if they are always springing up again, ever green and ripe ; the reason is that they had not to struggle against

B O O K the climate, where they were aſſiſted by a moiſt and
   XI.   clammy earth, which is proper for them ; and becauſe
        they required no trouble.   The labour of the ſlaves
        is employed in the cultivation of more uſeful pro-
        ductions.

The ſlaves   The principal labours of theſe unhappy men are
are employ- directed towards thoſe objects that are indiſpenſable
ed firſt to
get their   to the preſervation of their wretched exiſtence.   Be-
ſubſiſtence.
Rich pro-   fore their arrival in the iſlands, potatoes and yams
ductions are grew without labour in the midſt of the foreſts.   The
afterwards
expected   potato is a ſpecies of convolvulus, which grows up
from them.   gradually ; the leaves of which are alternate, angu-
        lar, and cordiform ; and its flower reſembles in figure,
        and in the number of its parts, that of the ordinary
        convolvulus.   The ſtem of the yam is climbing, her-
        baceous, furniſhed with oppoſite or alternate leaves,
        cut in the ſhape of a heart, and which ſhoot forth
        from their axillæ cluſters of male flowers on one ſtem,
        and female ones upon another, each provided with
        one calix that hath ſix diviſions.   The male flowers
        have ſix ſtamina.   The piſtil of the female flowers is
        ſurmounted with three ſtyles.   It adheres to the ca-
        lix, and becomes, along with it, a cloſe capſula, with
        three cells filled with two ſeeds.   Theſe plants, which
        are ſufficiently multiplied by nature alone for the
        ſubſiſtence of a ſmall number of ſavages, muſt have
        been cultivated, when it became neceſſary to feed a
        more conſiderable population.   This was accordingly
        reſolved upon, and other plants were joined to them,
        drawn from the country itſelf of the new conſumers.

        Africa hath furniſhed the iſlands with a ſhrub,
        which grows to the height of four feet, lives four
        years, and is uſeful throughout its whole duration.
        Its leaves are. compoſed of three ſmaller elongated
        leaves, united on one common petal.   Its flowers,
        which are yellowiſh, and irregular, as thoſe of legu-
        minous plants, are diſpoſed in cluſters at the extre-
        mity of the branches.   It bears pods, which contain
        a number of a kind of pea, which is very wholeſome
        and very nouriſhing.   This ſhrub is called the Angola

pea. It flourishes equally in lands naturally barren, and in those the salts of which have been exhausted. For this reason, the best managers among the colonists never fail to sow it on all those parts of their estates, which in other hands would remain uncultivated.

The most valuable present, however, which the islands have received from Africa, is the manioc. Most historians have considered this plant as a native of America. It does not appear on what foundation this opinion is supported, though pretty generally received. But were the truth of it demonstrated, the Caribbee Islands would yet stand indebted for the manioc to the Europeans, who imported it thither along with the Africans, who fed upon it. Before our invasions, the intercourse between the continent of America and these isles was so trifling, that a production of the continent might be unknown in the Archipelago of the Antilles. It is certain, however, that the savages who offered our first navigators bananas, yams, and potatoes, offered them no manioc; that the Caribs in Dominica and St. Vincent had it from us; that the character of the savages did not render them fit to conduct a culture requiring so much attention; that this culture can only be carried on in very open fields; and that in the forests, with which these islands were overgrown, there were no clear and unencumbered spaces of ground above five and twenty toises square. In short, it was beyond a doubt, that the use of the manoic was not known till after the arrival of the Negroes; and that from time immemorial it hath constituted the principal food of a great part of Africa.

However this may be, the manioc is a plant which is propagated by slips. It is set in furrows that are five or six inches deep, which are filled with the same earth that has been digged out. These furrows are at the distance of two feet, or two feet and a half from each other, according to the nature of the ground. The shrub rises a little above six feet, and

B O O K its trunk is about the thickneſs of the arm. In pro-
XI. portion as it grows, the lower leaves fall off, leaving
a ſemicircular impreſſion on the ſtem, and only a few
remain towards the top : its wood is tender and brittle.
They are always alternate, and deeply cut into ſeveral
lobes. The extremity of the branches is terminated
by cluſters of male and female flowers blended together. The calix of the firſt is in five diviſions, and
contains ten ſtamina ; that of the ſecond is compoſed
of five pieces. The piſtil which they ſurround is ſur-
mounted with three hairy ſtyles, and becomes a rough
capſula, with three diviſions, filled with three ſeeds.
There is no part of the plant uſeful except the root,
which is tuberoſe, and at the end of eight months, or
more, grows to the ſize of a large radiſh. There are
ſeveral varieties of them diſtinguiſhed, which differ in
their bulk, their colour, and the time they take in
coming to maturity. This is a delicate plant, and
the culture of it is laborious ; it is incommoded by
the vicinity of every kind of herb, and it requires a
dry and light ſoil.

When the roots have acquired their proper ſize and
maturity, they are plucked up, and undergo various
preparations, to render them fit for the food of man.
Their firſt ſkin muſt be ſcraped, they muſt be waſh-
ed, grated, and afterwards put into a preſs to extract
the juice, which is conſidered as a very active poiſon.
Any thing that might remain of the venomous principles they contained, is completely evaporated by
roaſting. When they do not yield any more ſmoke,
they are taken off the iron plate uſed for this operation, and ſuffered to cool.

The root of the manioc, grated and reduced into
little grains by roaſting, is called flour of manioc.
The paſte of manioc is called caſſava, which hath
been converted into a cake by roaſting without ſtir-
ring it. It would be dangerous to eat as much caſſava as flour of manioc, becauſe the former is leſs roaſt-
ed. Both keep a long time, and are very nouriſhing,
but a little difficult of digeſtion. Though this food

feems at firft infipid, there are a great number of white people who have been born in thefe iflands, who prefer it to the beft wheat. Moft of the Spaniards in general ufe it conftantly. The French feed their flaves with it. The other European nations, who have fettlements in the iflands, are little acquainted with the manioc. It is from North America that thefe colonies receive their fubfiftence; fo that if by any accident, which may very poffibly take place, their connections with this fertile country were interrupted but for four months, they would be expofed to perifh by famine. An avidity that hath no bounds, makes the colonifts.of the iflands infenfible of this imminent danger. All, at leaft the greater part, find their advantage in turning the whole induftry of their flaves towards thofe productions which are the objects of commerce. The principal of thefe are indigo, cochineal, cocoa, arnotto, cotton, coffee, and fugar. We have mentioned the three firft in the hiftory of the regions under the dominion of Caftile; and we will now defcribe the reft.

The arnotto is a red dye, called by the Spaniards *achiote*, into which they dip the white wool, whatever colour they intend to give to it. The tree that yields this dye is as high, and more bufhy than the plumtree. It hath a reddifh bark; its leaves are large, alternate, cordiform, and fupplied at their bafe with two ftipulæ or membranes, which fall off early. The flowers, difpofed in clufters, have a calix of five divifions, and ten petals of a flight purple colour, five of which are internal and fmaller. They are found, as well as a great number of ftamina, under the piftil, which is crowned with a fingle ftyle. The fruit is a capfula of a deep red colour, ftuck with foft points, wide at its bafe, and narrowed at the top. It opens longitudinally into two great valves, furnifhed internally with a longitudinal receptacle, covered with feeds. Thefe feeds are done over with a red fubftance, which may be extracted from them, and which is

BOOK
XI.

Of the culture of arnotto.

properly speaking, the arnotto. This tree flowers, and bears fruit twice a year.

As soon as one of the eight or ten pods which each cluster contains opens of itself, the rest may be gathered. All the seeds are then to be taken out, and thrown directly into large troughs full of water. When the fermentation begins, the seeds must be strongly stirred up with wooden spatulas, till the arnotto be entirely taken off. The whole is then poured into sieves made of rushes, which retain all the solid parts, and let out a thick, reddish, and fetid liquor, into iron coppers prepared to receive it. As it boils, the scum is skimmed off, and kept in large pans. When the liquor yields no more scum, it is thrown away as useless, and the scum poured back into the copper.

The scum, which is to be boiled for ten or twelve hours, must be constantly stirred with a wooden spatula, to prevent its sticking to the copper, or turning black. When it is boiled enough, and somewhat hardened, it is spread upon boards to cool. It is then made up into cakes of two or three pounds weight, and the whole process is finished.

Cultivation of cotton.
The cotton shrub, that supplies our manufactures, requires a dry and stony soil, and thrives best in grounds that have already been tilled. Not but that the plant appears to thrive better in fresh lands, than in those which are exhausted; but while it produces more wood, it bears less fruit.

An eastern exposition is fittest for it. The culture of it begins in March and April, and continues during the first spring rains. Holes are made at seven or eight feet distance from each other, and a few seeds thrown in. When they are grown to the height of five or six inches, all the stems are pulled up, except two or three of the strongest. These are cropped twice before the end of August. This precaution is the more necessary, as the wood bears no fruit till after the second pruning; and if the shrub were suffered to grow more than four feet high, the crops would not be greater, nor the fruit so easily gathered.

This ufeful plant will not thrive, if great attention B o o k be not paid to pluck up the weeds which grow about ___XI.___ it. Frequent rains will promote its growth,, but they muft not be inceffant. Dry weather is particularly neceffary in the months of March and April, which is the time of gathering the cotton, to prevent it from being difcoloured and fpotted.

In order to renew this fhrub, it is cut every two or three years down to the root, which produces feveral fprigs. Leaves grow upon them, which from three to five lobes, alternately difpofed upon the ftems, and accompanied with two ftipulæ. At the end of eight or nine months, there appear fome yellow flowers, ftreaked with red, rather large, and refembling the mallow flower in the ftructure and the number of their parts. The piftil, placed in the middle, becomes a pod, of the fize of a pigeon's egg, with three or four cells. Each cell, on burfting, exhibits feveral roundifh feeds, furrounded with a white kind of wadding, which is the cotton, properly fo called. This burfting of the fruit indicates its maturity, and the time proper for gathering it.

When it is all gathered in, the feeds muft be picked out from the wool. This is done by means of a cotton-mill, which is an engine compofed of two rods of hard wood, about eighteen feet long, eighteen lines in circumference, and fluted two lines deep. They are confined at both ends, fo as to leave no more diftance between them than is neceffary for the feed to flip through. At one end is a kind of little millftone, which being put in motion with the foot, turns the rods in contrary directions. They feparate the cotton, and throw out the feed contained in it.

The coffee-tree, originally the produce of Arabia, Cultivation where nature, fcantily fupplying the neceffaries of of coffee. life, fcatters its luxuries with a lavifh hand, was long the favourite plant of that fortunate country. The unfuccefsful attempts made by the Europeans in the cultivation of it, induced them to believe that the inhabitants of that country fteeped the fruit in boiling water, or dried it in the oven, before they fold it, in order to fecure to themfelves a trade from which they derived moft of their wealth. This opinion ftill prevailed, till the tree itfelf had been conveyed to Batavia, and afterwards to the Ifland of Bourbon, and to Surinam,-when it was demonftrated from experience, that the feed of the coffee tree, as well as of many other plants, will never come to any thing, unlefs it be put frefh into the ground.

This tree, which flourifhes only in thofe climates where the winters are extremely mild, hath fmooth, entire, oval leaves, and fharp like thofe of the laurel; they are, moreover, oppofite, and feparate at their bafe by an intermediate fcale. The flowers, difpofed in rings, have a white corolla, refembling that of jeffamine, charged with five ftamina, and bearing themfelves upon the piftil, which being enclofed in a calix of five divifions, becomes along with it a berry, which is at firft green, and afterwards reddifh, of the fize of a fmall cherry, and filled with two kernels, or beans, of a hard, and as it were horny fubftance. Thefe kernels, which are externally convex, and flattened and furrowed on the fide where they touch each other, yield, when they have been roafted and reduced to powder, a very agreeable infufion, fit to keep off fleep, and the ufe of which, anciently adopted in Afia, hath been infenfibly fpread over the greateft part of the globe.

The beft and higheft priced coffee is always that which comes from Arabia; but the iflands of America, and the coafts of this New World, which have cultivated it from the beginning of this century, furnifh a much greater quantity. It is not equally good every where. That which grows in a favourable foil, and in an eaftern expofure, which enjoys the frefhnefs of the dews and of the rains, and which is ripened by a moderate heat, is fuperior to any other.

The coffee plants are to be planted in holes of ten or twelve inches, and at intervals of fix, feven, eight,

or nine feet, according to the nature of the foil. B O O K
They would naturally grow to the height of eighteen XI.
or twenty feet, but they are not allowed to exceed
five, in order that their fruit may be conveniently
gathered. When thus cropped, they fpread their
branches in fuch a manner as to intermix with each
other.

Sometimes this tree rewards the labours of the cultivator as early as the third year, and at other times
only at the fifth or fixth. Sometimes it doth not produce a pound of coffee, and at other times it yields
as much as three or four pounds. In fome places it
does not laft more than twelve or fifteen years, and
in others five-and-twenty or thirty. Thefe variations
depend much upon the foil on which it is planted.

The coffee of America remained for a long time
in a ftate of imperfection, which brought it into difgrace. No care was taken of it ; but this negligence
hath gradually diminifhed. It is only after having
been well wafhed, and deprived of its gum, and after having received all neceffary preparations, that it
is at prefent carried to the mill.

This mill is compofed of two wooden rollers, furnifhed with plates of iron eighteen inches long, and
ten or twelve in diameter. Thefe are moveable,
and are made to approach a third, which is fixed,
and which they call the chops. Above the rollers is
a hopper, in which the coffee is put, from whence it
falls between the rollers and the chops, where it is
ftripped of its fkin, and divided into two parts, as
may be feen by the form of it, after it hath undergone this operation, being flat on one fide, and round
on the other. From this machine it falls into a brafs
fieve, where the fkin drops between the wires, while
the fruit flides over them into bafkets, placed ready
to receive it. It is then thrown into a veffel full
of water, where it foaks for one night, and is afterwards thoroughly wafhed. When the whole is
finifhed, and well dried, it is put into another machine, which is called the peeling mill. This is a

wooden grinder, which is turned vertically upon its trendle by a mule or a horfe. In paffing over the dried coffee, it takes off the parchment, which is nothing more than a thin fkin, that detaches itfelf from the berry as it grows dry. The parchment being removed, it is taken out of the mill, to be winnowed in another, which is called the winnowing mill. This machine is provided with four pieces of tin, fixed upon an axle, which is turned by a flave with confiderable force; and the wind that is made by the motion of thefe plates clears the coffee of all the pellicles that are mixed with it. It is afterwards put upon a table, where the broken berries, and any filth that may happen to remain, are feperated by the Negroes. After thefe operations the coffee is fit for fale.

The price of this berry was at firft very trifling. The exceffive paffion that all Europe took for it raifed its value exceedingly : and for that reafon its cultivation was carried on with great alacrity, after the peace of 1763. The produce foon exceeded the confumption, and for feveral years paft all the planters have been ruined. They will not recover till after a proper equilibrium hath been eftablifhed; and it is not in our power to fix the period of this happy revolution.

Cultivation of fugar. The cane that yields the fugar is a kind of reed, which commonly rifes eight or nine feet, and fometimes higher, according to the nature of the foil. Its moft common diameter is of one inch. It is covered with a rind, which is not very hard, and contains a kind of pulp, more or lefs compact, full of a fweet and vifcid juice. It is interfected at intervals with joints, from which originate leaves, that are long, narrow, fharp at their edges, and fulcated at their bafis. The lower ones fall off as the ftem grows. This is terminated by a filky pannicle, of a confiderable fize, every flower of which hath three ftamina and one fingle feed, covered with a two-leaved calix, with a fhaggy furface.

This plant hath been cultivated from the earlieft antiquity in fome countries of Afia and Africa. About the middle of the twelfth century, it became known in Sicily, from whence it paffed into the fouthern provinces of Spain. It was afterwards tranf-planted into Madeira and the Canaries. From thefe iflands, it was brought into the New World, where it fucceeded as well as if it had been indigenous there.

All foils are not equally proper for it. Such as are rich and ftrong, low and marfhy, environed with woods, or lately cleared, however large and tall the canes may be, produce only a juice that is aqueous, infipid, of a bad quality, difficult to be boiled, puri-fied, and preferved. Canes planted in a ground where they foon meet with foft ftone or rock, have but a very fhort duration, and yield but little fugar. A light, porous, and deep foil, is by nature moft favourable to this production.

The general method of cultivating it, is to pre-pare a large field ; to make at the diftance of three feet from one another, furrows eighteen inches long, twelve broad, and fix deep ; to lay in thefe two, and fometimes three flips of about a foot each, taken from the upper part of the cane and to cover them lightly with earth. From each of the joints in the flips iffues a ftem, which in time becomes a fugar-cane.

Care fhould be taken to clear it conftantly from the weeds, which never fail to grow around it. This labour only continues for fix months. The canes then are fufficiently thick and near one another to deftroy every thing that might be prejudicial to their fertility. They are commonly fuffered to grow eighteen months, and are feldom cut at any other time.

From the ftock of thefe iffue fuckers, which are in their turn cut fifteen months after. This fecond cut-ting yields only half of the produce of the firft. The planters fometimes make a third cutting, and even a fourth, which are always fucceffively lefs, however

good the foil may be. Nothing, therefore, but want
of hands for planting afrefh, can oblige a planter to
expect more than two crops from his cane.

Thefe crops are not made in all the colonies at the
fame time. In the Danifh, Spanifh, and Dutch fettlements, they begin in Jannary and continue till
October. This method doth not imply any fixed feafon for the maturity of the fugar-cane. The plant,
however, like others, muft have its progrefs ; and it
hath been juftly obferved to be in flower in the
months of November and December. It muft neceffarily follow from the cuftom thefe nations have
adopted, of continuing to gather their crops for ten
months without intermiffion, that they cut fome canes
which are not ripe enough, and others that are too
ripe, and then the fruit hath not the requifite qualities. The time of gathering them fhould be at a
fixed feafon, and probably the months of March and
April are the fitteft for it ; becaufe all the fweet
fruits are ripe at that time, while the four ones do
not arrive to a ftate of maturity till the months of
July and Auguft.

The Englifh cut their canes in March and April ;
but they are not induced to do this on account of
their ripenefs. The drought that prevails in their
iflands renders the rains which fall in September neceffary to their planting ; and as the canes are
eighteen months in growing, this period always brings
them to the precife point of maturity.

In order to extract the juice of the canes, when
cut, which ought to be done in four-and-twenty hours,
otherwife it would turn four, they are paffed between
two cylinders of iron, or copper, placed perpendicu-
larly on an immoveable table. The motion of the
cylinders is regulated by an horizontal wheel, turned
by oxen or horfes ; but in water-mills this horizontal
wheel derives its movement from a perpendicular one,
the circumference of which meeting a current of water, receives an impreffion which turns it upon its
axis : this motion is from right to left, if the current

of water strike the upper part of the wheel; from
left to right, if it strike the lower part.

From the reservoir, where the juice of the cane is
received, it falls into a boiler, where those particles
of water are made to evaporate that are most easily
separated. This liquor is poured into another boiler,
where a moderate fire makes it throw up its first scum.
When it has lost its clammy consistence, it is made to
run into a third boiler, where it throws up much more
scum by means of an increased degree of heat. It
then receives the last boiling in a fourth cauldron,
the fire of which is three times stronger than the
first.

This last fire determines the success of the process.
If it hath been well managed, the sugar forms crystals that are larger or smaller, more or less bright, in
proportion to the greater or less quantity of oil they
abound with. If the fire hath been too violent, the
substance is reduced to a black and charcoal extract,
which cannot produce any more essential salt. If the
fire hath been too moderate, there remains a considerable quantity of extraneous oils, which stain the sugar, and render it thick and blackish; so that when
it is to be dried, it becomes always porous, because
the spaces which these oils filled up remain empty.

As soon as the sugar is cool, it is poured into earth-
en vessels of a conic figure; the base of the cone is
open, and its top hath a hole, through which the
water is carried off that hath not formed any crystals.
This is called the syrup. After this water hath flowed
through, the raw sugar remains, which is rich, brown
and salt.

The greatest part of the islands leave to the Europeans the care of giving sugar the other preparations
which are necessary to make it fit for use. This practice spares the expence of large buildings, leaves
them more Negroes to employ in agriculture, allows
them to make their cultures without any interruption
for two or three months together, and employs a
greater number of ships for exportation.

BOOK XI.

BOOK   The French planters alone have thought it their
XI.   intereſt to manage their ſugars in a different manner.
To whatever degree of exactneſs the juice of the ſu-
gar-cane may be boiled, there always remains an infinite number of foreign particles attached to the ſalts
of the ſugar, to which they appear to be what lees
are to wine. Theſe give it a dead colour, and the
taſte of tartar, of which they endeavour to deprive
it, by an operation called earthing. This conſiſts in
putting again the raw ſugars into a new earthen veſſel, in every reſpect ſimilar to that we have mentioned. The ſurface of the ſugar, throughout the whole
extent of the baſis of the cone, is then covered with
a white marl, on which water is poured. In filtering
it through this marl, the water carries with it a portion of a calcareous earth, which it finds upon the
different ſaline particles, when this earth meets with
oily ſubſtances to which it is united. This water is
afterwards drained off through the opening at the
top of the mould, and a ſecond ſyrup is procured,
which they call *Molaſſes*, and which is ſo much the
worſe, in proportion as the ſugar was finer : that is,
contained leſs extraneous oil : for then the calcareous
earth, diſſolved by the water, paſſes alone, and carries with it all its acrid particles.

This earthing is followed by the laſt preparation,
which is effected by fire, and ſerves for the evaporat-
ing of the moiſture with which the ſalts are impregnated during the proceſs of earthing. In order to do
this, the ſugar is taken in its whole form out of the
conical veſſel of earth, and conveyed into a ſtove,
which receives from an iron furnace a gentle and
gradual heat, where it is left till the ſugar is become
very dry, which commonly happens at the end of
three weeks.

Though the expence which this proceſs requires
be in general uſeleſs, ſince the earthed ſugar is commonly refined in Europe in the ſame manner as the
raw ſugar; all the inhabitants of the French iſlands,
however, who are able to purify their ſugars in this

manner, generally take this trouble. To a nation whose navy is weak, this method is extremely advantageous, as it enables it, in times of war, to convey into its own mother-country the most valuable cargoes with a less number of ships than if only raw sugars were sent.

One may judge from the species of sugars, but much better from that which has undergone the earthing, of what sort of salts it is composed. If the soil where the cane hath been planted be hard, stony, and sloping, the salts will be white, angular, and the grain very large. If the soil be marly, the colour will be the same; but the granulations, being cut on fewer sides, will reflect less light. If the soil be rich and spongy, the granulations will be nearly spherical, the colour will be dusky, the sugar will slip under the finger, without any unequal feel. This last kind of sugar is considered as the worst.

Whatever may be the reason, those places that have a northern aspect produce the best sugar; and marly grounds yield the greatest quantity. The preparations which the sugar that grows in these kinds of soil require, are less tedious and troublesome than those which the sugar requires that is produced in a rich land. But these observations admit of infinite variety, the investigation of which is properly the province of chemists, or speculative planters.

Beside sugar, the cane furnishes syrup, the value of which is only a twelfth of that of the price of sugars. The best syrup is that which runs from the first vessel into the second, when the raw sugar is made. It is composed of the grosser particles, which carry along with them the salts of sugar, whether it contain or separate them in its passage. The syrup of an inferior kind, which is more bitter, and less in quantity, is formed by the water which carries off the tartareous and earthy particles of the sugar when it is washed. By means of fire, some sugar is besides extracted from the first syrup, which, after this operation, is of less value than the second.

Both thefe kinds are carried into the north of Europe, where the people ufe them inftead of butter
and fugar. In North America they make the fame
ufe of them, where they are further employed to
give fermentation and an agreeable tafte to a liquor
called *Prufs*, which is only an infufion of the bark of
a tree.

This fyrup is ftill more ufeful, by the fecret that
hath been difcovered, of converting it by diftillation
into a fpirituous liquor, which the Englifh call *Rum*,
and the French *Taffia*. This procefs, which is very
fimple, is made by mixing a third part of fyrup with
two-thirds of water. When thefe two fubftances have
fufficiently fermented, which commonly happens at
the end of twelve or fifteen days, they are put into
a clean ftill, where the diftillation is made as ufual.
The liquor that is drawn off is equal to the quantity
of the fyrup employed.

Such is the method which, after many experiments
and variations, all the iflands have generally adopted
in the cultivation of fugar. It is undoubtedly a good
one ; but, perhaps, it hath not acquired that degree
of perfection of which it is capable. If, inftead of
planting canes in large fields, the ground were parcelled out into divifions of fixty feet, leaving between
two planted divifions a fpace of land uncultivated,
fuch a method would probably be attended with
great advantages. In the modern practice, none but
the canes which grow on the borders are good, and
attain to a proper degree of maturity. Thofe in the
middle of the field in part mifcarry, and ripen badly,
becaufe they are deprived of a current of air, which
only acts by its weight, and feldom gets to the foot
of thefe canes, that are always covered with the
leaves.

In this new fyftem of plantation, thofe portions of
land which had not been cultivated would be moft
favourable for reproduction ; when the crops of the
planted divifions had been made, which in their turn
would be left to recover. It is probable that by this

method as much fugar might be obtained as by the prefent practice; with this additional advantage, that it would require fewer flaves to cultivate it. One may judge what the cultivation of fugar would then produce, by what it now yields, notwithftanding its imperfections.

On a plantation fixed on a good ground, and fufficiently ftocked with Negroes, with cattle, and all other neceffaries, two men will cultivate a fquare of canes that is a hundred geometrical paces in every direction. This fquare muft yield, on an average, fixty quintals of raw fugar. The common price of a quintal in Europe will be twenty livres [16s. 8d.] after deducting all the expences. This makes an income of 600 livres [25l.] for the labour of each man. One hundred and fifty livres [6l. 5s.], to which the price of fyrup and rum muft be added, will defray the expences of cultivation; that is to fay, for the maintenance of flaves, for their lofs, for their diforders, for their clothes, for repairing their utenfils, and other accidents. The nett produce of an acre and a half of land will then be four hundred and fifty livres [18l. 15s.]. It would be difficult to find a culture productive of greater emoluments.

It may be objected, that this is ftating the produce below its real value, becaufe a fquare of canes doth not employ two men. But thofe who would urge fuch an objection ought to obferve, that the making of fugar requires other labours befide thofe of merely cultivating it, and confequently workmen employed elfewhere than in the fields. The eftimate and compenfation of thefe different kinds of fervice oblige us to deduct from the produce of a fquare of plantation the expence of maintaining two men.

It is chiefly from the produce of fugar that the iflands fupply their planters with all the articles of convenience and luxury. They draw from Europe flour, liquors, falt provifions, filks, linens, hardware, and every thing that is neceffary for apparel, food, furniture, ornament, convenience, and even luxury.

Their confumptions of every kind are prodigious, and muft neceffarily influence the manners of the inhabitants, the greateft part of whom are rich enough to fupport them.

Character of the Europeans fettled in the American iflands.
It fhould feem that the Europeans, who have been tranfplanted into the American iflands, muft no lefs have degenerated than the animals which they carried over thither. The climate acts on all living beings ; but men being lefs immediately fubject to the laws of nature, refift her influence the more, becaufe they are the only beings who act for themfelves. The firft colonifts who fettled in the Antilles corrected the activity of a new climate and a new foil, by the conveniences which it was in their power to derive from a commerce that was always open with their former country. They learnt to lodge and maintain themfelves in a manner the beft adapted to their change of fituation. They retained the cuftoms of their education, and every thing that could agree with the natural effects of the air they breathed. With thefe they carried into America the food and cuftoms of Europe, and familiarifed to each other beings and productions which Nature had feparated by an interval of the fame extent as a zone. But of all the primitive cuftoms, the moft falutary, perhaps, was that of mingling and dividing the two races by intermarriages.

All nations, even the leaft civilized, have profcribed an union of fexes between the children of the fame family ; whether it was that experience or prejudice dictated this law, or chance led them to it. Beings brought up together in infancy, accuftomed to fee one another continually, in this mutual familiarity rather contract that indifference which arifes from habit, than that lively and impetuous fenfation of fympathy which fuddenly affects two beings who never faw one another. If, in the favage life, hunger difunites families, love undoubtedly muft have reunited them. The hiftory, whether true or fabulous, of the rape of the Sabine women, fhows that marriage was the firſt alliance between nations. Thus the blood will have become gradually intermixed, either by the caſual meetings occaſioned by a wandering life, or by the conventions and agreements of ſettled communities. The natural advantage of croſſing the breed among men, as well as animals, in order to preſerve the ſpecies from degenerating, is the reſult of ſlow experience, and is poſterior to the acknowledged utility of uniting families, in order to cement the peace of ſociety. Tyrants ſoon diſcovered how far it was proper for them to ſeparate, or connect their ſubjects, in order to keep them in a ſtate of dependence. They formed men into ſeparate ranks, by availing themſelves of their prejudices ; becauſe this line of diviſion between them became a bond of ſubmiſſion to the ſovereign, who maintained his authority by their mutual hatred and oppoſition. They connected families to each other in every ſtation, becauſe this union totally extinguiſhed every ſpark of diſſenſion repugnant to the ſpirit of civil ſociety. Thus the intermixture of pedigrees and families by marriage, hath been rather the reſult of political inſtitutions, than formed upon the views of nature.

But whatever be the natural principle and moral tendency of this cuſtom, it was adopted by Europeans, who were deſirous of multiplying in the iſlands. The greateſt part of them either married in their own country before they removed into the New World, or with thoſe who landed there. The European married a Creole, or the Creole an European, whom chance or family connections brought into America. From this happy aſſociation hath been formed a peculiar character, which in the two worlds diſtinguiſhes the man born under the ſky of the New, from parents originally natives of both. The marks of this character will be pointed out with ſo much the more certainty, as they are taken from the writings of an accurate obſerver, from whom we have already drawn ſome particulars reſpecting natural hiſtory.

The Creoles are in general well made. There is scarce a single person among them afflicted with those deformities which are so common in other climates. They have all an extreme suppleness in their limbs; whether it is to be attributed to a particular organization adapted to hot countries, to the custom of their being reared without the confinement of swaddling clothes and stays, or to the exercises they are habituated to from their infancy. Their complexion, however, never has that air of vivacity and freshness, which contributes more to beauty than regular features do. As to their colour, when they are in health, it resembles that of persons just recovering from a fit of illness; but this livid complexion, more or less dark, is nearly that of our southern people.

Their intrepidity in war hath been signalized by a series of bold actions. There would be no better soldiers, if they were more capable of being disciplined.

History does not afford any of those instances of cowardice, treachery, and meanness among them, which fully the annals of all nations. It can hardly be alleged that a Creole ever did a mean action.

All strangers, without exception, find in the islands the most friendly and generous hospitality. This useful virtue is practised with a degree of ostentation, which shows, at least, the honour they attach to it. Their natural propensity to beneficence banishes avarice; and the Creoles are generous in their dealings.

They are strangers to dissimulation, craft, and suspicion. The pride they take in their frankness, the opinion they have of themselves, together with their extreme vivacity, exclude from their commercial transactions all that mystery and reserve which stifles natural goodness of disposition, extinguishes the social spirit, and diminishes our sensibility.

A warm imagination, incapable of any restraint, renders them independent and inconstant in their taste. It perpetually hurries them with fresh ardour into pleafures, to which they facrifice both their fortune B O O K and their whole exiftence. XI.

A remarkable degree of penetration, a quick facility in feizing all ideas, and expreffing themfelves
with vivacity ; the power of combining added to the
talent of obfervation ; a happy mixture of all the
qualities of the mind and of the heart, which render men capable of the greateft actions, will make
them attempt every thing when oppreffion compels
them to it.

The fharp and faline air of the Caribbee iflands
deprives the women of that lively colour which is
the beauty of their fex. But they have an agreeable
and fair complexion, which does not deprive the eyes
of all that vivacity and power that enables them to
convey into the foul fuch ftrong impreffions as are
irrefiftible. As they are extremely fober, they drink
nothing but chocolate, coffee, and fuch fpirituous liquors as reftore to the organs their tone and vigour,
enervated by the climate ; while the men are continually drinking in proportion to the heat that ex-
haufts them.

They are very prolific, and often mothers of ten or
twelve children. This fertility arifes from love, which
ftrongly attaches them to their hufbands ; but which
alfo throws them inftantly into the arms of another,
whenever death hath diffolved the union of a firft or
fecond marriage.

Jealous even to diftraction, they are feldom un-
faithful. That indolence which makes them neglect
the means of pleafing, the tafte which the men have
for Negro women, their particular manner of life,
whether private or public, which precludes the opportunities or temptations to gallantry ; thefe are the beft
fupports of the virtue of thefe females.

The folitary kind of manner in which they live in
their houfes, gives them an air of extreme timidity,
which embarraffes them in their intercourfe with the
world. They lofe, even in early life, the fpirit of
emulation and choice ; and this prevents them from

cultivating the agreeable talents of education. They
seem to have neither power nor taste for any thing
but dancing, which undoubtedly transports and animates them to higher pleasures. This instinct of pleasure attends them through their whole life ; whether
it be, that they still retain some share of their youthful sensibility, or are stimulated with the recollection
of it ; or from other reasons which are unknown to
us.

From such a constitution arises an extremely sensible and sympathising character, so that they cannot
even bear the sight of misery ; though they are, at
the same time, rigid and severe with respect to the
offices they require of those domestics that are attached to their service. More despotic and inexorable towards their slaves than the men themselves, they feel
no remorse in ordering chastisements, the severity of
which would be a punishment and a lesson to them,
if they were obliged to inflict them themselves, or
were witnesses to them.

This slavery of the Negroes is, perhaps, the cause
from whence the Creoles in part derive a certain
character, which makes them appear strange, fan-
tastic, and of an intercourse not much relished in Europe. From their earliest infancy they are accustom-
ed to see a number of tall and stout men about
them, whose business it is to conjecture and anticipate
their wishes. This first view must immediately inspire
them with the most extravagant opinion of themselves. Seldom meeting with any opposition to their
caprice, though ever so unreasonable, they assume a
spirit of presumption, tyranny, and disdain for a great
part of mankind. Nothing is more insolent than the
man who always lives with his inferiors ; but when
these happen to be slaves, habituated to wait upon
children, to dread even their cries, which must expose
them to punishment, what must masters become who
have never obeyed ; wicked men, who have never
been punished ; and madmen, who are used to put
their fellow-creatures in irons ?

So cruel an example of dependence gives the Ame- ricans that pride which muft neceffarily be detefted in Europe, where a greater equality prevailing among men, teaches them a greater fhare of mutual refpect. Educated without knowing either pain or labour, they are neither able to furmount difficulties or bear contradiction. Nature hath given them every ad- vantage, and fortune refufed them nothing. In this refpect, like moft kings, they are unhappy, becaufe they have never experienced adverfity. If the climate did not ftrongly excite them to love, they would be ig- norant of every real pleafure of the foul : and yet they feldom have the happinefs of forming an idea of thofe paffions, which, thwarted by obftacles and refufals, are nourifhed with tears and gratified with virtue. If they were not confined by the laws of Europe, which govern them by their wants, and reprefs or reftrain the extraordinary degree of independence they enjoy, they would fall into a foftnefs and effeminacy, which would in time render them the victims of their own tyranny, or would involve them in a ftate of anarchy, that would fubvert all the foundations of their com- munity.

But if they once ceafed to have Negroes for flaves, and kings who live at a diftance from them for ma- fters, they, perhaps, would become the moft afto- nifhing people that ever appeared on earth. The fpi- rit of liberty which they would imbibe from their earlieft infancy; the underftanding and abilities which they would inherit from Europe ; the activity, which the neceffity of repelling numerous enemies would infpire ; the large colonies they would have to form ; the rich commerce they would have to found on an immenfe cultivation ; the ranks and focieties they would have to create ; and the maxims, laws, and manners they would have to eftablifh on the princi- ples of reafon : all thefe fprings of action would, per- haps, make of an equivocal and mifcellaneous race of people, the moft flourifhing nation that philofophy

BOOK XI.
and humanity could wiſh for the happineſs of the world.

If ever any fortunate revolution ſhould take place in the world, it will begin in America. After having experienced ſuch devaſtation, this New World muſt flouriſh in its turn, and, perhaps, command the Old. It will become the aſylum of our people who have been oppreſſed by political eſtabliſhments or driven away by war. The ſavage inhabitants will be civilized, and oppreſſed ſtrangers will become free. But it is neceſſary that this change ſhould be preceded by conſpiracies, commotions, and calamities ; and that a hard and laborious education ſhould prediſpoſe their minds both to act and to ſuffer.

Young Creoles, come into Europe to excerciſe and practiſe what we teach you ; there to collect, in the valuable remains of our ancient manners, that vigour which we have loſt ; there to ſtudy our weakneſs, and draw from our follies themſelves thoſe leſſons of wiſdom which produce great events ; leave in America your Negroes, whoſe condition diſtreſſes us, and whoſe blood, perhaps, is mingled in all thoſe ferments which alter, corrupt, and deſtroy our population. Fly from an education of tyranny, effeminacy, and vice, which you contract from the habit of living with ſlaves, whoſe degraded ſtation inſpires you with none of thoſe elevated and virtuous ſentiments, which can only give riſe to a people that will become celebrated. America hath poured all the ſources of corruption on Europe. To complete its vengeance, it muſt draw from it all the inſtruments of its proſperity. As it hath been deſtroyed by our crimes, it muſt be renewed by our vices.

Nature ſeems to have deſtined the Americans to a greater ſhare of happineſs than the inhabitants of Europe. They have ſcarce any illneſs, except inflammations in the lungs, and pleuriſies, which are almoſt as common in the iſlands as in all other regions, where the tranſitions from heat to cold are frequent

and fudden. The gout, gravel, ftone, apoplexies, B O O K
and a multitude of other fcourges of the human race, ___XI.___
which are fo fatal in other countries, have never made
the leaft ravages there. If the air of the country can
be withftood, and the middle age be attained to, this
is fufficient to enfure a long and happy life. There
old age is not weak, languifhing, and befet with thofe
infirmities which affect it in our climate.

In the Caribbee iflands, however, new-born infants Difeafes to
are attacked with a difeafe which feems peculiar to Europeans
the torrid zone : it is called *tetanos*. If a child re- are fubject
ceive the impreffion of the air or wind, if the room iflands of
where it is juft born be expofed to fmoke, to too much America.
heat or cold, the diforder fhows itfelf immediately.
It firft feizes the jaw, which becomes rigid and fixed,
fo as not to be opened. This fpafm foon communicates itfelf to the other parts of the body ; and the
child dies for want of being able to take nourifhment.
If it efcape this danger, which threatens the nine firft
days of its exiftence, it has nothing to fear. The indulgences which are allowed to children before they
are weaned, which is at the end of the twelve months,
fuch as the ufe of coffee, chocolate, wine, but efpecially fugar and fweetmeats ; thefe indulgences that
are fo pernicious to our children, are offered to thofe
of America by nature, which accuftoms them in early
age to the productions of their climate.

The fair fex, naturally weak and delicate, has its
infirmities as well as its charms. In the iflands they
are fubject to a weaknefs, an almoft total decay of
their ftrength ; an unconquerable averfion for all kind
of wholefome food, and an irregular craving after
every thing that is prejudicial to their health. Salt
or fpiced food is what they only relifh and defire.
This difeafe is a true cachexy, which commonly degenerates into a dropfy. It is attributed to the diminution of the menfes in thofe women who come from
Europe, and to the weaknefs or total fuppreffion of
that periodical difcharge in Creoles. It might ftill
more properly be attributed to the exceffive heat, and

B O O K the immoderate dampnefs of the climate, which at
XI. length deftroys every fpring in the animal economy.
The men, more robuft, are liable to more violent
complaints. In this vicinity of the equator, they are
expofed to a hot and malignant fever, known under
different names, and indicated by hæmorrhages. The
blood, which is boiling under the fervent rays of the
fun, is difcharged from the nofe, eyes, and other parts
of the body. Nature, in temperate climates, does
not move with fuch rapidity, but that in the moft
acute diforders there is time to obferve and follow
the courfe fhe takes. In the iflands, her progrefs is
fo rapid, that if we delay to attack the diforder as
foon as it appears, its effects are certainly fatal. No
fooner is a perfon feized with ficknefs, but the phyfician, the lawyer, and the prieft, are all called to
his bed-fide.

The fymptoms of this terrible illnefs feem to indicate the neceffity of bleeding. This operation hath
therefore been repeated without meafure. Several
experiments have at length demonftrated that this expedient was fatal. Remedies are now preferred which
are capable of moderating this great rarefaction of
the blood, and which tend to the diffolution of it,
fuch as bathing, glyfters, oxycrate, and even blifters,
when the diforder is attended with delirium. We
have known a profeffional man of great underftanding, who thought that the immediate caufe of this
malady was the intenfe heat of the fun ; and who
affirmed, that thofe who did not expofe themfelves to
it, moft commonly efcaped this calamity.

Moft of thofe who furvive thefe attacks recover
very flowly and with difficulty. Several fall into an
habitual languor, occafioned by the debility of the
whole machine, which the noxious air of the country,
and the little nourifhment their food fupplies, are not
able to reftore. Hence obftructions, jaundice, and
fwellings of the fpleen are produced, which fometimes terminate in dropfies.

Almoft all the Europeans who go over to America

are expofed to this danger, and frequently the Cre- B O O K
oles themfelves, on their return from more temperate ___XI.___
climates. But it never attacks women whofe blood
has the natural evacuations, and Negroes, who, born
under a hotter climate, are inured by nature, and
prepared ·by free perfpiration, for all the ferments
that the fun can produce.

Thefe violent fevers are certainly owing to the
heat of the fun, the rays of which are lefs oblique,
and more conftant, than in our climates. This heat
muft undoubtedly thicken the blood, through the excefs of perfpiration, a want of elafticity in the folids,
and a dilatation of the veffels by the impulfe of the
fluids, whether in proportion to the rarefaction of the
air, or the lefs degree of compreffion which the furface of the bodies is expofed to in a rarefied atmofphere.

Far from having recourfe to thefe expedients, which
are known to be preventatives of the diforder, the inhabitants fall into fuch exceffes as are moft likely to
haften and increafe it. The ftrangers who arrive at
the Caribbee Iflands, are excited by the entertain-
ments they are invited to, the pleafures they partake of, and the kind reception they meet with ; every
thing induces them to an immoderate indulgence in
all the pleafures which cuftom renders lefs prejudicial
to thofe who are born under this climate. Feafting,
dancing, gaming, late hours, wine, cordials, and frequently the chagrin of difappointment in their chimerical expectations, confpire to add to the ferment
of an immoderate heat of the blood, which foon becomes inflamed.

With fuch indulgence, it is fcarce poffible to refift
the heats of this climate, when even the greateft precautions are not fufficient to fecure perfons from the
attack of thofe dangerous fevers ; when the moft fober
and moderate men, who are the moft averfe from
every kind of excefs, and the moft careful of all their
actions, are victims to the new air they breathe. In
the prefent ftate of the colonies, of ten men that go

B O O K into the iflands, four Englifh die, three French, three
XI.   Dutch, three Danes, and one Spaniard.

When it was obferved how many men were loft in
thefe regions, at the time they were firft occupied, it
was generally thought, that the ftates, who had the
ambition of fettling there would be depopulated in
the end.

Advantages   Experience hath altered the public opinion upon
of thofe na- this point. In proportion as thefe colonies have ex-
tions that
are in pof-   tended their plantations, they have had frefh means of
feffion of
the Ameri-   expence. Thefe have opened to their mother-coun-
can iflands. try new fources of confumption. The increafe in exportations could not take place without an increafe of
labour. Thefe labours have brought together a greater number of men, which will ever be the cafe when
the means of fubfiftence are multiplied. Even foreigners have reforted in great multitudes to thofe
kingdoms, which opened a vaft field to their ambition
and induftry.

Population hath not only increafed among the proprietors of the iflands, but the people have alfo become more happy. Our felicity in general is proportioned to our conveniences, and it muft increafe as we
can vary and extend them. The iflands have been
productive of this advantage to their poffeffors. They
have drawn from thefe fertile regions a number of
commodities, the confumption of which hath added
to their enjoyments. They have acquired fome, which,
when exchanged for others among their neighbours,
have made them partake of the luxuries of other climates. In this manner, the kingdoms which have
acquired the poffeffion of the iflands, by fortunate circumftances, or by well-combined projects, are become
the refidence of the arts, and of all the polite amufements which are a natural and neceffary confequence
of great plenty.

But this is not the only advantage : thefe colonies
have raifed the nations that founded them, to a fuperiority of influence in the political world, by the
following means: Gold and filver, which form the ge-

neral circulation of Europe, come from Mexico, Peru, B O O K and Brazil. They belong neither to the Spaniards XI. nor the Portuguese, but to people who give their merchandise in exchange for these metals. These people have commercial transactions with each other, that are ultimately settled at Lisbon and Cadiz, which may be looked upon as a common and universal repository. It is in these places that one must judge of the increase or decline of the trade of each nation. That nation, whose accounts of sale and purchase are kept in balance with the rest, receives the whole interest of its capital. That which hath purchased more than it hath sold, withdraws less than its interest; because it hath ceded a part of it, in order to satisfy the demands of the nation to which it was indebted : that which hath sold more to other nations than it hath purchased of them, does not only get what was owing from Spain and Portugal, but also the profit it hath derived from other nations with which it hath made exchanges. This last advantage is peculiar to the people who possess the islands. Their specie is annually increased by the sale of the valuable productions of these countries ; and the augmentation of their specie confirms their superiority, and renders them the arbiters of peace and war. But we shall explain, in the following Books, how far each nation hath increased its power by the possession of the islands.

BOOK XII.

Settlements of the Spaniards, the Dutch, and the Danes, in the American Islands.

I WAS going to say, that Spain had the glory of B O O K having discovered the great Archipelago of America, XII. and of having formed the first settlements there, Definition when I was checked by the consideration, that the of true glory. discovery of it could not possibly have been glorious

BOOK
XII.
to the Spaniards, unlefs it had been advantageous to the Antilles.

Glory is a fentiment which raifes us in our own eyes, and which increafes our confideration among enlightened men. The idea of it is infeparably connected with thofe of a great difficulty overcome, of great utility fubfequent to fuccefs, and of equal increafe of felicity for the univerfe or for one's country. Whatever mark of genius I may acknowledge in the invention of any deftructive weapon, I fhould excite a juft indignation, were I to fay, that fuch a man, or fuch a nation, had the glory of having invented it. Glory, at leaft according to the ideas I have formed of it, is not the reward of the greateft fuccefs in the fciences. If you invent a new calculation, compofe a fublime poem, or if you have excelled Cicero or Demofthenes in eloquence, Thucydides or Tacitus in hiftory, celebrity may be granted to you, but not glory. Neither is it any more to be obtained by the fuperiority of talents in the arts. Let us fuppofe, that from the block of marble you have cut out either the Gladiator, or the Apollo Belvidere ; that your pencil hath painted the transfiguration ; or that your fimple, expreffive, and melodious airs have equalled you with Pergolefi ; you will then enjoy a high reputation, but no glory. I will go further : If you fhould equal Vauban in the art of fortification, Turenne and Conde in that of commanding armies ; if you fhould gain battles, and conquer provinces, all thefe actions are undoubtedly great, and your name will be tranfmitted to the remoteft pofterity, but glory is referved for other qualities. We do not acquire glory by adding to that of our nation. A man may be the honour of his corps, without being the glory of his country. A private man may afpire to reputation, to fame, and to immortality ; but there are none but rare circumftances, and a fortunate hazard, that can conduct him to glory.

Glory belongs to God in heaven. Upon earth, it

is the lot of Virtue, and not of Genius ; of ufeful, B O O K great, beneficent, fplendid, and heroic virtue. It is XII. the lot of the monarch, who, throughout the courfe of a tumultuous reign, hath attended to the happinefs of his fubjects, and hath attended to it with fuccefs. It is the lot of a fubject, who fhall have facrificed his life for the prefervation of his fellow-citizens. It is the lot of a people, who fhall have chofen rather to die free, than to live enflaved. It is the lot, not of a Cæfar or of a Pompey, but of a Regulus or of a Cato. It is the lot of a Henry IV.

It is owing to the fpirit of humanity which philofophy hath infufed into the minds of all enlightened people, that conquerors, as well ancient as modern, are now put upon a level with the moft abhorred clafs of mankind. And I doubt not but that pofterity, which will judge with impartiality of the difcoveries we have made in the New World, will rank our navigators ftill below them. For, have they been guided by their regard for the human race, or by cupidity? And though an enterprife be in itfelf a good one, can it be laudable, if the motive of it be vicious?

The ifland which the Spaniards firft met with on Idea that their arrival in America, is called Trinidad. Colum- muft be bus landed on it in 1498, when he difcovered the the ifland Oroonoko ; but other objects interfering, both the of Trini- ifland, and the coafts of the neighbouring continent, dad. were at that time neglected.

It was not till 1535, that the court of Madrid took poffeffion of the ifland of Trinidad, which is fituated facing the mouth of the Oroonoko, as it were to moderate the rapidity of this river. It is faid to comprehend three hundred and eighteen fquare leagues. It hath never experienced any hurricane, and its climate is wholefome. The rains are very abundant there from the middle of May to the end of October : and the drynefs that prevails throughout the reft of the year is not attended with any inconvenience, becaufe the country, though deftitute of

navigable rivers, is very well watered. The earthquakes are more frequent than dangerous. In the
interior part of the ifland there are four groups of
mountains, which, togther with fome others formed
by nature upon the fhores of the ocean; occupy a
third part of the territory. The reft is in general
fufceptible of the richeft cultures.

The form of the ifland is fquare. To the North is
a coaft of twenty-two leagues in extent, too much
elevated, and too much divided, ever to be of any
ufe. The Eaftern coaft is only nineteen leagues in
extent, but in all parts as convenient as one could
wifh it to be. The Southern coaft hath five-and-
twenty leagues, is a little exalted, and adapted for
the fuccefsful cultivation of coffee and cacao. The
land on the Weftern fide is feparated from the reft of
the colony, to the South by the Soldier's Canal, and
to the North by the Dragon's Mouth, and forms, by
means of a recefs, a harbour of twenty leagues in
breadth and thirty in depth. It offers in all feafons
a fecure afylum to the navigators, who, during the
greateft part of the year, would find it difficult to
anchor any where elfe, except at the place called
the Galiote.

In this part are the Spanifh fettlements. They
confift only of the port of Spain, upon which there
are feventy-eight thatched huts ; and of Saint Jofeph,
fituated three leagues further up the country, where
eighty families, ftill more wretched than the former,
are computed.

The cacao was formerly cultivated near thefe two
villages. Its excellence made it be preferred even
to that of Caraccas. In order to fecure it the merchants ufed to pay for it before-hand. The trees
that produced it perifhed all in 1727, and have not
been replanted fince. The monks attributed this
difafter to the colonifts having refufed to pay the
tithes. Thofe who were not blinded by intereft or
fuperftition, afcribed it to the north winds, which
have too frequently occafioned the fame kind of ca-

lamity in other parts. Since this period, Trinidad hath not been much more frequented than Cubagua.

This little ifland, at the diftance of four leagues only from the continent, was difcovered, and ne- glected by Columbus, in 1498. The Spaniards, being afterwards informed that its fhores contained great treafures, repaired to it in multitudes in 1509, and and gave it the name of Pearl Ifland.

The pearl is a hard fhining body, more or lefs white, commonly of a round form, and which is found in fome fhells, but more frequently in that which is known by the name of mother-of-pearl. This rich production of nature is moftly attached to the infide of the fhell ; but it is moft perfect when found in the animal itfelf, which lives in the fhell.

The ancients were in an error with refpect to the ori- gin of the pearl, as well as with regard to many other phenomena, which we have obferved and underftood better, and which we have explained more fatisfac- torily. Let us not defpife them the more on this ac- count, neither let us be more vain. Their miftakes fometimes difplay a degree of fagacity, and have not been entirely ufelefs to us. They have been the firft fteps of fcience, which time, the efforts of human genius, and a number of fortunate and cafual cir- cumftances, were to improve. Attempts have been made to tear the veil that covers nature, before it was lifted up.

The Greeks and the Romans ufed to fay, that the fhell-fifh raifed itfelf every morning to the furface of the waters, and received the dew, which was chan- ged into pearl. This agreeable idea hath fhared the fate of numberlefs fables of the fame kind, when the fpirit of obfervation had made it known, that this fhell-fifh remained always at the bottom of the fea, or fixed to the rocks where it had been formed ; and when found philofophy had demonftrated, that it was impoffible it fhould be otherwife.

It hath fince been imagined, that pearls muft be the eggs, or the fperm of the fifh enclofed in the

BOOK shell.   But this idea hath likewife fallen into difcre-
XII. dit, when it hath been fully known, that the pearls
were found in all parts of the animal ; and when,
after the moft accurate inveftigations, anatomy hath
not been able to difcover the organs calculated for
generation in this fifh, which feems to add one to the
clafs of hermaphroditical animals.

At length, after a variety of fyftems lightly adopted, and fucceffively abandoned, it hath been imagined that pearls were produced from a difeafe in the
animal ; and that they were formed by a liquor ex-
travafated from fome veffels, and detained between
the membranes, or fpread along the interior furface
of the fhell.   This conjecture hath been ftill more
confirmed to accurate obfervers, in proportion as it
hath been afcertained that thefe treafures were not
to be found indifcriminately in all the fifh ; that thofe
which had them were not fo well tafted as the others ;
and that the coafts upon which this rich fifhery was
carried on were in general unwholefome.

Black pearls, fuch as are inclining to black, or fuch
as are of a lead colour, are univerfally defpifed.   In
Arabia, and in fome other parts of the Eaft, the yellow pearls are efteemed.   But the white ones are preferred in Europe, and throughout the greateft part of
the globe.   It is regretted only that they begin to
grow yellow after half a century.

Although pearls had been difcovered in the feas
of the Eaft Indies and in thofe of America, yet their
price was fufficiently kept up to induce people to
counterfeit them.   The imitation was at firft coarfe.
It was glafs covered with mercury.   Attempts have
been repeated, and in procefs of time, nature hath
been fo well copied, that it was eafy to be mifled.
The artificial pearls, which are made at prefent with
wax and ichthyocol, have much the advantage of the
others.   They are cheap ; and are made of every
fize and fhape, to fuit the women who ufe them for
ornament.

This difcovery was unknown when the Spaniards

fettled at Cubagua. They arrived there with fome B o o k
favages of the Lucaya Iflands, who had not been XII.
found proper for the labours of the mines, but who
had the faculty of remaining a long time under water
with great eafe. This talent procured to their oppreffors a great quantity of pearls. Thefe pearls were
not fpoiled, as thofe had been which had been hitherto collected by the Americans, who were only
acquainted with the mode of fire for opening the
fhell that contained them. They were preferved in
all their beauty, and found an advantageous mart.
But this fuccefs was momentary. The pearl bank
was foon exhaufted ; and the colony was transferred,
in 1524, to Margaretta, where the regretted riches
were found, and from whence they difappeared almoft as foon.

Yet this laft fettlement, which is fifteen leagues in Ideas re-
length and five in breadth, was not abandoned. It Margaret-
is almoft continually covered with thick fogs, although ta.
nature hath not beftowed upon it any current waters.
There is no village in it except Mon Padre, which is
defended by a fmall fort. Its foil would be fruitful
if it were cultivated.

It was almoft generally fuppofed, that the court of
Madrid, in preferving Margaretta and Trinidad, meant
rather to keep off rival nations from this continent,
than to derive any advantage from them. At prefent we are induced to think otherwife. Convinced
that the Archipelago of America was full of inhabitants loaded with debts, or who poffeffed but a fmall
quantity of indifferent land, the council of Charles III.
hath offered great conceffions, in thefe two iflands, to
thofe who fhould embrace their faith. The freedom
of commerce with all the Spanifh traders was enfured
to them. They were only obliged to deliver their
cacao to the Company of Caraccas, but at twenty-
feven fols [about 1s. 1½d.] per pound, and under the
condition that this Company fhould advance them
fome capital. Thefe overtures have only met with a
favourable reception at Granada, from whence fome

B O O K Frenchmen have made their efcape with a few flaves,
  XII.   either to fcreen themfelves from the purfuits of their
         creditors, or from averfion to the fway of the Englifh.
In every other part, they have had no effect, whether
from averfion for an oppreffive government, or whether it be that the expectations of all are at prefent
turned towards the North of the New World.

Trinidad and Margaretta are at prefent inhabited
only by a few Spaniards, who, with fome Indian women, have formed a race of men, who, uniting the
indolence of the favage to the vices of civilized nations, are fluggards, cheats, and zealots. They live
upon maize, upon what fifh they catch, and upon
bananas, which nature, out of indulgence as it were
to their flothfulnefs, produces there of a larger fize,
and better quality, than in any other part of the Archipelago. They have a breed of lean and taftelefs
cattle, with which they carry on a fraudulent traffic
to the French colonies, exchanging them for cam-
blets, black veils, linen, filk ftockings, white hats, and
hard-ware. The number of their veffels does not exceed thirty floops, without decks.

The tame animals of thefe two iflands have filled
the woods with a breed of horned cattle, which are
become wild. The inhabitants fhoot them, and cut
their flefh into flips of three inches in breadth and
one in thicknefs, which they dry, after having melt-
ed the fat out of them, fo that they will keep three
or four months. This provifion, which is called Taf-
fajo, is fold in the French fettlements for twenty
livres [16s. 8d.] a hundred weight.

All the money which the government fends to
thefe two iflands, falls into the hands of the com-
mandants, the officers civil and military, and the
monks. The remainder of the people, who do not
amount to more than fixteen hundred, live in a ftate
of the moft deplorable poverty. In time of war they
furnifh about two hundred men, who, for the fake
of plunder, offer themfelves, without diftinction, to
any of the colonies that happen to be fitting out

cruizers for fea. The inhabitants of Porto-Rico are B O O K
of a different turn. XII.

Although this ifland had been difcovered and vi- Conqueſt of
fited by Columbus in 1493, the Spaniards neglected Porto-Rico
it till 1509, when the thirſt of gold brought them niards.
thither from St. Domingo, under the command of
Ponce de Leon, to make a conqueſt, which afterwards coſt them dear.

It is generally known, that the ufe of poifoned
arms is of the higheſt antiquity. In moſt countries,
it preceded the invention of ſteel. When darts head-
ed with ſtones, bones of fiſh or other animals, proved
infufficient to repel the attacks of wild beaſts, men
had recourfe to poifonous juices, which, from being
originally defigned merely for the chafe, were afterwards employed in the wars of conquering or favage
people againſt their own fpecies. Ambition and revenge fet no limits to their outrages, till ages had
been fpent in drowning whole nations in rivers of
blood. When it was difcovered that this effufion of
blood produced no advantage, and that, in proportion
as the ſtream fwelled in its courfe, it depopulated
countries, and left nothing but deferts without animation and without culture; they then came to an
agreement to moderate, in fome degree, the thirſt of
fhedding it. They eftabliſhed what are called the
laws of war; that is to fay, injuſtice in injuſtice, or
the intereſt of kings in the maffacre of the people.
They do not now cut the throats of all their victims
at once; but referve fome few of the herd to propagate the breed. Thefe laws of war, or of nations,
required the abolition of certain abufes in the art of
killing. Where fire-arms are to be had, poifoned
weapons are forbidden; and, when cannon balls will
anfwer the end, chewed bullets are not allowed. O!
race, unworthy both of heaven or earth, deftructive,
tyrannical being, man, or devil rather, wilt thou never ceafe to torment this globe, where thou exiſteſt
but for a moment? Will thy wars never end but
with the annihilation of thy fpecies? Go then; if

thou wouldſt advance thy miſchief, go and provide thyſelf with the poiſons of the New World.

Of all the regions productive of venomous plants, none abounded ſo much in them as South America, which owed this malignant fertility to a ſoil in general rank, as if it were purging itſelf from the ſlime of a deluge.

The plants called Lianes, of which there were vaſt numbers in all damp and marſhy places, furniſhed the poiſon, which was in univerſal requeſt on the continent. The method of preparing it was by cutting them in pieces, then boiling them in water, till the liquor had acquired the conſiſtence of a ſyrup. After this, they dipped their arrows in it, which were immediately impregnated with the poiſonous quality. During ſeveral ages, the ſavages in general uſed theſe arms in their wars with each other. At length many of thoſe nations, from the deficiency of their numbers, found the neceſſity of renouncing ſo deſtructive a weapon, and reſerved it for beaſts, whether large or ſmall, which they could not overtake or overcome. Any animal, whoſe ſkin has been raiſed with one of theſe poiſoned arrows, dies a minute after, without any ſign of convulſion or pain. This is not occaſioned by the coagulation of the blood, which was a long time the general opinion ; recent experiments have proved, that this poiſon, mixed with blood newly drawn and warm, prevents it from coagulating, and even preſerves it ſome time from putrefaction. It is probable, that the effect of theſe juices is upon the nervous ſyſtem. Some travellers have imputed the origin of the venereal diſeaſe, among the inhabitants of the New World, to the habit of eating game killed with theſe poiſoned arms. At preſent it is univerſally known, that the fleſh of ſuch animals may be eaten for a continuance without any ill effect.

In the American iſlands, the natives draw their poiſon from trees, more than from the Lianes ; and of all the venomous ſorts of trees, the moſt deadly is the mancheneel.

This tree is rather lofty, and ufually grows by the BOOK water fide. It hath the figure and leaves of the pear- XII. tree. Its trunk, which is of a compact, heavy, veiny wood, fit for joiners work, is covered with a fmooth and tender bark. It bears two fpecies of flowers. Some are male, and difpofed in catkins at the extremity of the branches. They have in each calix but one thread furmounted with two antheræ. The female flowers are fingle. Their piftil becomes a ftraight flefhy fruit, of the form of a fig or a pear, and containing a very hard kernel, in which are five or fix feeds in fo many different cells. In all parts of the tree, and efpecially between the trunk and the bark, a milky juice is found, which is confidered as a very fubtile poifon, and which renders the cultivation of this tree, and even the coming near to it, very dangerous. One cannot fleep with impunity under the fhade of it, and the water which drops from its leaves after a fhower, raifes blifters upon the fkin, and excites a troublefome itching. The juice of the mancheneel is received into fhells, placed under various incifions that have been made in its trunk. As foon as this juice is grown a little thick, the points of the arrows are fteeped in it, which acquire from thence the property of conveying fudden death, be the wound ever fo flight. This poifon, as it appears from experience, preferves its venomous quality above a hundred years. Of all the fpots where this fatal tree is found, Porto-Rico is that in which it delights moft, and where it is found in the greateft abundance. Why were not the firft conquerors of America all fhipwrecked on this ifland? It is the misfortune of both worlds that they became acquainted with it fo late, and that they did not there meet with the death which their avarice merited.

The mancheneel feems to have been fatal only to the Americans. The inhabitants of the ifland where it grows, ufed it to repel the Caribs who made frequent defcents on their coafts. The fame arms they might have employed againft the Europeans; and,

B O O K
   XII.
as the Spaniards were ignorant at that time that falt, applied immediately, is an infallible cure, they would probably have fallen a facrifice to the firft effects of this poifon. But they did not meet with the leaft refiftance from the favage inhabitants of the ifland. Thefe had been informed of what had occurred in the conqueft of the neighbouring ifles; and they regarded thefe ftrangers as a fuperior order of beings, to whofe chains they voluntarily fubmitted themfelves. It was not long, however, before they wifhed to fhake off the intolerable yoke which had been impofed on them, and poftponed the enterprife only till they could be affured whether their tyrants were immortal. A Cacique, named Broyoan, was intrufted with this commiffion.

Chance favoured his defign, by bringing to him Salzedo, a young Spaniard, who was travelling. He received him with great refpect, and at his departure fent fome Indians to attend him on his way, and to ferve him in the quality of guides. When they came to the bank of a river, which they were to pafs, one of thefe favages took him on his fhoulder to carry him over. As foon as they had got into the midft of it, he threw him into the water, and, with the affiftance of his companions, kept him there till there was no appearance of life. They then dragged him to the bank, but, as they were ftill in doubt whether he was dead or living, they begged pardon a thoufand times for the accident that had happened. This farce lafted three days; till at length being convinced, by the ftench of the corpfe, that it was poffible for Spaniards to die, the Indians rofe on all fides upon their oppreffors, and maffacred a hundred of them.

Ponce de Leon immediately affembled all the Caftilians who had efcaped, and, without lofs of time, fell upon the favages, who were terrified with this fudden attack. In proportion as the number of their enemies increafed, their panic became more violent. They had even the folly to believe, that thefe Spaniards, which were juft arrived from St. Domingo, were

the fame that had been killed, and were come to life
again to fight them. Under this ridiculous perfuafion, dreading to continue a war with men who revive after their death, they fubmitted once more to
the yoke, and being condemned to the mines, in a
fhort time fell victims to the toils of flavery.

Porto-Rico hath thirty-fix leagues in length, eighteen in breadth, and one hundred in circumference.
We may venture to affirm, that it is one of the beft,
if not entirely the beft, of the iflands of the New
World, in proportion to its extent. The air is wholefome, and tolerably temperate, and it is watered by
the pure ftreams of a confiderable number of fmall
rivulets. Its mountains are covered with either ufeful or valuable trees, and its valleys have a degree of
fertility feldom to be met with elfewhere. All the
productions peculiar to America thrive upon this deep
foil. A fafe port, commodious harbours, and coafts
of eafy accefs, are added to thefe feveral advantages.

On this territory, deprived of its favage inhabitants
by ferocious deeds, the memory of which three centuries have not been able to obliterate, was fucceffively formed a population of forty-four thoufand eight
hundred and eighty-three men, either white or of a
mixed race. Moft of them were naked. Their habitations were nothing more than huts. Nature, with
little or no affiftance, fupplied them with fubfiftence.
The linens, and fome other things of little value,
which they clandeftinely obtained from the neighbouring or from foreign iflands, were paid for by the
colony with tobacco, cattle, and with the money
which was fent by government for the fupport of the
civil, religious, and military eftablifhment. They
received from the mother-country, annually, only
one fmall veffel, the cargo of which did not amount
to more than ten thoufand crowns [1250l.], and which
returned to Europe laden with hides.

Such was Porto-Rico, when, in 1765, the court of
Madrid carried their attention to St. John, an excel-

B O O K
   XII.
lent harbour, even for the royal navy, and which only
wants a little more extent. The town which commands it, was furrounded with fortifications. The
works were made particularly ftrong towards a narrow and marfhy neck of land, the only place by
which the town can be attacked on the land fide.
Two battalions, and one company of artillery, crof-
fed the fea for its defence.

At this period, a poffeffion which had annually
received from the treafury no more than 378,000
[15,750l.] coft them 2,634,433 livres [109,768l.
10d.], which fum was regularly brought from Mexico. This increafe of fpecie ftimulated the colonifts
to undertake fome labours. At the fame time, the
ifland, which till then had been under the yoke of
monopoly, was allowed to receive all Spanifh navigators. Thefe two circumftances united, imparted fome
degree of animation to a fettlement, the languifhing
ftate of which aftonifhed all nations. Its tithes, which
before 1765 did not yield more than 81,000 livres
[3375l.], have increafed to 230,418 livres [9680l.
15s.]

On the firft of January 1778, the population of
Porto-Rico amounted to fourfcore thoufand fix hundred and fixty inhabitants, of which number only
fix thoufand five hundred and thirty were flaves.
The inhabitants reckoned feventy-feven thoufand
three hundred and eighty-four head of horned cattle,
twenty-three thoufand one hundred and ninety-five
horfes, fifteen hundred and fifteen mules, and forty-
nine thoufand fifty-eight head of fmall cattle.

The plantations, the number of which were five
thoufand fix hundred and eighty-one, produced two
thoufand feven hundred and thirty-feven quintals of
fugar; eleven hundred and fourteen quintals of cotton; eleven thoufand one hundred and fixty-three
quintals of coffee; nineteen thoufand five hundred
and fifty-fix quintals of rice; fifteen thoufand two
hundred and fixteen quintals of maize; feven thou-

fand four hundred and fifty-eight quintals of tobac-co ; and nine thoufand eight hundred and fixty quintals of melaffes.

The cattle in the feveral pafture grounds, which were two hundred and thirty-four in number, produced annually eleven thoufand three hundred and fixty-four oxen ; four thoufand three hundred and thirty-four horfes ; nine hundred and fifty-two mules ; thirty-one thoufand two hundred and fifty-four head of fmall cattle.

All this is very trifling ; but great expectations are raifed from an arrangement which hath lately been made. No one citizen of Porto-Rico was in reality mafter of his poffeffions. The commanders who had fucceeded each other, had only granted the income of them. This inconceivable defect hath at length been remedied. The proprietors have been confirmed in their poffeffions, by a law of 14th of January 1778, upon condition of paying annually one real and a quarter, or fixteen fols fix deniers [8¼d.], for every portion of ground of twenty-five thoufand feven hundred and eight toifes, which they employed in cultures ; and three-quarters of a real, or ten fols one denier and a half [rather above 5d.], for that part of the foil that is referved for pafture ground. This eafy tribute is to ferve for the clothing of the militia, compofed of one thoufand nine hundred infantry, and two hundred and fifty cavalry. The remainder of the ifland is diftributed on the fame conditions to thofe who have little or no property. Thefe laft, who are diftinguifhed by the name of *Agregès*, are feven thoufand eight hundred and thirty-five in number.

This plan will not accomplifh the revolution which is expected by the council of Spain ; although, contrary to the precife determination of the laws, every colonift who choofes to eftablifh fugar plantations, is allowed to call in the affiftance of any foreigner who is able to teach him that kind of culture. Thefe colonifts ought to be authorized to fell openly to the

Means
which
would ren-
der Porto-
Rico flou-
rifhing.

BOOK French, the Dutch, the Englilh, and the Danes, the
XII. cattle which they have been hitherto obliged to difpofe of in a clandeftine manner only.

Man fuffers, only becaufe he knows not how to
put an end to his pain. If he fhould languifh in mifery, it is merely from being incapable of changing
his fituation. It would be a grofs error to imagine,
that in a ftate of nature we can fee man in perpetual agitation, inceffantly obferving and making all
kinds of experiments, as we fee him in a civilized
ftate. Experience hath proved, that it requires ages
for him to emerge from his natural torpid ftate; and
that when once his induftry is fubjeĉt to a certain invariable mode of proceeding, and from the fmall
number of his wants, reftrained within narrow and
circumfcribed limits, it will never be roufed of itfelf.
What method can then be contrived to fhorten the
duration of his indolence, of his ftupidity, and of
his mifery? For this purpofe, he muft be made acquainted with aĉtive beings, and muft be placed in
conftant intercourfe with laborious people. He will
foon open his eyes with aftonifhment; he will foon be
confcious that he likewife hath had hands given to
him, and will fcarce conceive how it could have been
poffible, that the idea of making ufe of them fhould
not have occurred to him fooner. The fight of the
enjoyments that are obtained by labour, will infpire
him with the defire of partaking of them, and he
will work. Invention is peculiar to genius, and imitation is peculiar to man. It is by imitation that all
fcarce things have become, and will hereafter become
common. This is the propenfity which the court of
Madrid ought to encourage, if not from motives of
humanity, at leaft from the profpeĉt of the political
advantages they might expeĉt to reap from it.

Matters perhaps might, and indeed ought to be
carried ftill further. Let Spain declare Porto-Rico a
neutral ifland, and let this neutrality be acknowledged by all the powers that have any poffeffions in
America. Let the lands, which are not yet cultivat-

ed, be granted to enterprifing men of all nations, who
fhall have a capital fufficient to eftablifh cultures.
Let perfons, lands, and productions, be exempted
from all taxes for the fpace of fifty years, or more.
Let the harbours be opened indifcriminately to all
traders, free from cuftoms, from reftraints, and from
formalities. Let no other troops be kept but thofe
neceffary for the police ; and let thefe be foreign
troops. Let a very plain code of laws be drawn up,
fuitable to a ftate of hufbandmen, or of merchants.
Let the citizens themfelves be the magiftrates, or the
magiftrates be chofen by them. Let property, that
firft and great bafis of all political focieties, be eftablifhed upon unmoveable foundations. Before half
a century fhall be elapfed, Porto-Rico will moft undoubtedly be one of the moft flourifhing colonies of
the New World. It may then again become, without inconvenience, a truly national poffeffion. Its
abundant productions, which will have coft neither
care, expence, anxiety, nor war to Spain, will increafe the mafs of national riches, and the public revenue.

But if even this plan of adminiftration were the in-
fpiration of wifdom itfelf ; if it were dictated by the
moft certain views of intereft ; if the fuccefs of it
could be geometrically proved, yet it would never be
carried into execution ; and for this reafon : It is becaufe it hath not been fuggefted by a native of Spain,
and that it fuppofes the concurrence of foreigners.
No country can do any thing of itfelf ; and yet, from
a deteftable, puerile, and ridiculous vanity, we wifh
to do every thing by ourfelves ; we are blind, and
yet we will not receive light from others. In mo-
narchical ftates, the way to exclude an able man from
an important fituation, is to anticipate, by popular
choice, the appointment of the court ; and this is a
mode which hatred and jealoufy feldom fail of employing. The fame method would fucceed as certainly between the refpective courts. In order to
prevent a minifter from purfuing any wife meafure,

BOOK
XII.

BOOK
XII.

nothing more is neceffary, than that another minifter fhould affume, by divulging it, the credit of having firft thought of it himfelf. Nothing is more fcarce, than to find among minifters of the fame court, one citizen, great, honeft, and good enough, to purfue a project begun by his predeceffor. Thus do abufes become perpetual in the nation. Thus is every thing begun, and nothing accomplifhed, from motives of a foolifh kind of pride, the influence of which extends itfelf over all the branches of adminiftration, which fufpends the progrefs of civilization, and would have fettled all nations in a ftate of barbarifm, had their chiefs been conftantly, and at all times, equally affected by it.

If, however, the meafures we have ventured to propofe to the court of Madrid fhould appear to them liable to inconveniences, which may have efcaped our notice, they might at leaft derive from themfelves part of thofe advantages which we fhould be happy to fee them obtain. The navigation to the Spanifh Indies is forbidden to the Bifcayans. As their ports are freed, both on the going out and coming in of the fhips, from the duties which are impofed upon all the other ports, the government have been apprehenfive that they might obtain too great a fuperiority over the fubjects of the monarchy, who do not enjoy the fame privileges. Let Porto-Rico be opened to thefe active men, where their competition cannot be prejudicial to rivals who have never attended to this trade, and the ifland will foon acquire fome degree of importance. The fame arrangement might be extended to St. Domingo.

What were the events that occafioned St. Domingo to degenerate from that ftate of fplendour to which that ifland had been raifed.

This ifland, famous for being the earlieft fettlement of the Spaniards in the New World, was at firft in high eftimation for the quantity of gold it fupplied. This wealth diminifhed with the inhabitants of the country, whom they obliged to dig it out of the bowels of the earth ; and the fource of it was entirely dried up, when the neighbouring iflands no longer fupplied the lofs of thofe wretched victims to the

avarice of the conqueror. A vehement defire of open- B O O K XII.
ing again this fource of wealth, infpired the thought
of getting flaves from Africa ; but, befides that thefe
were found unfit for the labours they were deftined
to, the multitude of mines, which then began to be
wrought on the continent, made thofe of St. Domingo no longer of any importance. An idea now
fuggefted itfelf, that their Negroes, which were healthy, ftrong, and patient, might be ufefully employed
in hufbandry ; and they adopted, through neceffity,
a wife refolution, which, had they known their own
intereft, they would have embraced by choice.

The produce of their induftry was at firft extremely
fmall, becaufe the labourers were few. Charles V.
who, like moft fovereigns, preferred his favourites
to his fubjects, had granted an exclufive right of the
flave trade to a Flemifh nobleman, who made over
his privilege to the Genoefe. Thofe avaricious republicans conducted this infamous commerce as all
monopolies are conducted ; they refolved to fell dear,
and they fold but little. When time and competition
had fixed the natural and neceffary price of flaves,
the number of them increafed. It may eafily be
imagined, that the Spaniards, who had been accuftomed to treat the Indians as beafts, though they
differed but little in complexion from themfelves, did
not entertain a higher opinion of thefe Negro Africans, who were fubftituted to them. Degraded ftill
further in their eyes by the price they had paid for
them, even religion could not reftrain them from aggravating the weight of their fervitude. It became
intolerable, and thefe wretched flaves made an effort
to recover the unalienable rights of mankind. Their
attempt proved unfuccefsful ; but they reaped this
benefit from their defpair, that they were afterwards
treated with lefs inhumanity.

This moderation (if tyranny, cramped by the apprehenfion of revolt, can deferve that name) was attended with good confequences. Cultivation was
purfued with fome degree of fuccefs. Soon after the

middle of the fixteenth century, the mother-country drew annually from this colony ten millions
weight of fugar, a large quantity of wood for dyeing,
tobacco, cocoa, caffia, ginger, cotton, and peltry in
abundance. One might imagine, that fuch favourable beginnings would give both the defire and
the means of extending this trade ; but a train of
events, each more fatal than the other, ruined thefe
fhips.

The firft misfortune arofe from the depopulation
of St. Domingo. The Spanifh conquefts on the continent fhould naturally have contributed to promote
the fuccefs of an ifland, which nature feemed to have
formed to be the centre of that vaft dominion arifing
round it, to be the ftaple of the different colonies :
but it happened quite otherwife. On a view of the
immenfe fortunes raifing in Mexico and other parts,
the richeft inhabitants of St. Domingo began to defpife their fettlements, and quitted the true fource of
riches, which is, in a manner, on the furface of the
earth, to go and ranfack the bowels of it for veins of
gold, which are foon exhaufted. The government
endeavoured in vain to put a ftop to this emigration ;
the laws were always either artfully eluded or openly
violated.

The weaknefs, which was a neceffary confequence
of fuch a conduct, leaving the coafts without defence,
encouraged the enemies of Spain to ravage them.
Even the capital of this ifland was taken and pillaged by that celebrated Englifh failor, Francis Drake.
The cruifers of lefs confequence contented themfeves
with intercepting veffels in their paffage through thofe
latitudes, the beft known at that time of any in the
New World. To complete thefe misfortunes, the
Caftilians themfelves commenced pirates. They attacked no fhips but thofe of their own nation, which
were more rich, worfe provided, and worfe defended,
than any others. The cuftom they had of fitting out
fhips clandeftinely, in order to procure flaves, prevented them from being known ; and the affiftance

they purchafed from the fhips of war, commiffioned
to protect the trade, infured to them impunity.

The foreign trade of the colony was its only refource in this diftrefs; and that was prohibited; but
as it was ftill carried on, notwithftanding the vigilance
of the governors, or perhaps by their connivance, the
policy of an exafperated and unenlightened court
exerted itfelf in demolifhing moft of the fea-ports,
and driving the miferable inhabitants into the inland
country. This act of violence threw them into a
ftate of dejection, which the incurfions and fettlement of the French on the ifland afterwards carried
to the utmoft pitch.

Spain, totally taken up with that vaft empire which
fhe had formed on the continent, ufed no pains to
diffipate this lethargy. She even refufed to liften to
the folicitations of her Flemifh fubjects, who earneft-
ly preffed that they might have permiffion to clear
thofe fertile lands. Rather than run the rifk of feeing them carry on a contraband trade on the coafts,
fhe chofe to bury in oblivion a fettlement which had
been of confequence, and was likely to become fo
again.

This colony, which had no longer any intercourfe
with the mother-country, but by a fingle fhip of no
great burden, received from thence every third year,
confifted in 1717 of eighteen thoufand four hundred
and ten inhabitants, including Spaniards, Meftees,
Negroes, or Mulattoes. The complexion and character of thefe people differed according to the different proportions of American, European, and African blood they had received from that natural and
tranfient union which reftores all races and conditions to the fame level; for love is not more a refpecter
of perfons than death. Thefe demi-favages, plunged in the extreme of floth, lived upon fruits and
roots, dwelt in cottages without furniture, and had
moft of them no clothes. The few among them, in
whom indolence had not totally fuppreffed the fenfe
of decency and tafte for the conveniences of life,

Prefent
ftate of
the Spanifh
portion of
St. Domin-
go.

B O O K purchafed clothes of their neighbours the French, in
XII.   return for their cattle, and the money fent to them
for the maintenance of two hundred foldiers, the
priefts, and the government. The company formed
at Barcelona in 1757, with exclufive privileges for
the re-eftablifhment of St. Domingo, hath had no
fuccefs. Since that ifland hath been opened, in 1766,
to all Spanifh navigators, it hath ftill remained in the
fame ftate. The quantity of fugar canes, of coffee
trees, and of tobacco, which may have been planted
there, is not fufficient for its own confumption, far
from being able to contribute to that of the mother-
country. The colony furnifhes annually to the national trade no more than five or fix thoufand hides,
and fome provifions, of fo little value, that they fcarce
deferve to be reckoned.

This deficiency of cultivation is univerfally felt in
the ifland. Sant Yago, La Vega, Seibo, and other
places in the inland parts, formerly fo renowned for
their riches, are no longer any thing more than ob-
fcure hamlets, where nothing revives the memory of
their ancient fplendour.

The coafts do not exhibit a more animated appearance. To the fouth of the colony is the narrow and
deep bay of Ocoa, which might be called a harbour.
It is in this place where the Spaniards have no fettlements, although they are near a falt-pit which is
fufficient for their neceffities, that the filver which is
fent from Mexico for the expences of government is
depofited, and from whence it is conveyed upon
horfes to St Domingo, which is at no more than fifteen leagues diftance.

This famous capital of the ifland received for a
long time its neceffaries directly from foreigners ; but
at that period the Lozama, with which its walls are
watered, was able to admit veffels of fix hundred
tons burden. Since the mouth of this river hath
been almoft choked by the fands, and by the ftones
it brings away from the mountains, the town is not
in a better condition than the harbour ; and magni-

ficent ruins are the only remains of it. The country **B O O K**
that furrounds it exhibits nothing but briars, and a **XII.**
fmall number of cattle.

The river Macouffis runs fourteen leagues above
that place, where the few American veffels that come
to trade in the ifland are ufed to land. They difembark their fmall cargoes by means of a few little
iflands, which afford a tolerable fhelter.

Further on, but ftill on the fame coaft, the Ruma-
na runs through the moft beautiful plains that can
poffibly be conceived. Neverthelefs, there is nothing
to be found upon this extenfive and fertile foil, except one hamlet, which would have a miferable appearance, even in thofe countries that are the moft
ill-treated by nature.

The North of the colony is no better than the
South. Porto de Plata, the beauty and excellence
of which it would be difficult to exaggerate, prefents
only a few huts, in its numerous creeks, and on its
rich territory.

The Ifabellica, which hath a beautiful river, immenfe plains, and forefts filled with precious woods,
doth not exhibit a more flourifhing appearance.

With as many, or even with more, means of profperity, Monte-Chrifto is nothing more than a ftaple,
where Englifh fmugglers come habitually to take in
the commodities of fome French plantations, fettled
in the neighbourhood. The hoftilities between the
courts of London and Verfailles render the fraudulent connections infinitely more confiderable ; and
this mart acquires at that time a great degree of
importance. But this incipient animation ceafes,
as foon as the miniftry of Madrid think it fuitable to
their interefts to take a part in the difputes between
the two rival nations.

The Spaniards have no fettlement in the weftern
part of the ifland, which is entirely occupied by the
French ; and it is only fince the laft war that they
have thought of fettling to the eaftward, which they
had long entirely neglected.

BOOK
XII.

The project of cultivation might be carried into execution in the plain of Vega-Real, which is situated in the inland part, and is fourscore leagues in length, by ten in its greatest breadth. It would be difficult to find, throughout the New World, a spot more level, more fruitful, or better watered. All the productions of America would succeed admirably there; but it would be impossible to remove them from thence without making roads; which is an undertaking that would alarm a people more enterprising than the Spaniards. These difficulties should naturally have led them to fix their attention on some exceeding good coasts, already a little inhabited, and where some subsistence would have been found. Probably it was apprehended that the new colonists would adopt the manners of the old, and therefore Samana was determined upon.

Samana is a peninsula, five leagues broad, and sixteen long; the soil of which, though rather uneven, is very fit for the richest productions of the New World. It hath, moreover, the advantage of affording to the ships that come from Europe, an easy landing and a safe anchorage.

These considerations induced the first adventurers from France, who ravaged St. Domingo, to settle at Samana; where they maintained their ground a long time, though surrounded by their enemies. At length it was found that they were too much exposed, and at too great a distance from the rest of the French settlements on the island, which were every day improving. In consequence of this they were recalled. The Spaniards rejoiced at their departure; but did not take possession of the spot they had quitted.

Within these few years, however, the court of Madrid have sent thither some people from the Canaries; the state have been at the expence of the voyage, of their establishment, and of their maintenance for several years. These measures, prudent as they were, have not been attended with success. The new inhabitants have for the most part fallen victims to the climate, to the clearing of the ground, undertaken without precautions, and, above all, to the difhonefty of the governors, who have appropriated to themfelves the funds they were intrufted with. The few that have furvived fo many evils, languifh under the expectation of approaching death. Let us fee whether the efforts made to render Cuba flourifhing, have been more fortunate.

The ifland of Cuba, which is feparated from St. Domingo by a narrow channel, is of itfelf equal in value to a kingdom : it is two hundred and thirty leagues in length, and in breadth from fourteen to twenty-four. None of its rivers are navigable : in three or four of them only, the boats can go up to the height of two, four, or fix leagues, during the greateft part of the year. To the north, the Havannah, Bahiabonda, Maiul, and Matanza, can receive men of war; but the fouthern harbours, as Cuba, Xaguas, Port au Prince, Bayamo, Bacacon, Nipe, Batabano, and Trinidad, admit only merchantmen.

Though Cuba was difcovered by Columbus in 1492, the Spaniards did not attempt to make themfelves mafters of it till 1511, when Diego de Velafquez came with four fhips, and landed on the eaftern point.

This diftrict was under the government of a Cacique named Hatuey. He was a native of St. Domingo, or Hifpaniola, and had retired hither to avoid the flavery to which his countrymen were condemned. Thofe who could efcape the tyranny of the Caftilians had followed him in his retreat, where he formed a little ftate, and ruled in peace. At a diftance he obferved the Spanifh fails, the approach of which he dreaded. On the firft news he received of their arrival he called together the braveft Indians, both of his fubjects and allies, to animate them to a defence of their liberty; affuring them, at the fame time, that all their efforts would be ineffectual, if they did not firft render the God of their enemies propitious to them : *Behold him there*, faid he, pointing to a veſſel filled with gold, *behold that mighty divinity, let us invoke his aid!*

This ſimple and credulous. people eaſily believed that gold, for the ſake of which ſo much blood was ſhed, was the God of the Spaniards. They danced and ſang before the rude and unfaſhioned ore, and re-ſigned themſelves wholly to its protection.

But Hatuey, more enlightened, and more ſuſpi-cious than the other Caciques, aſſembled them again. *We muſt not,* ſaid he to them, *expect any happineſs ſo long as the God of the Spaniards remains among us. He is no leſs our enemy than they. They ſeek for him in every place; and where they find him, there they eſtabliſh them-ſelves. Were he hidden in the cavities of the earth, they would diſcover him, Were we to ſwallow him, they would plunge their hands into our bowels, and drag him out. There is no place but the bottom of the ſea, that can elude their ſearch. When he is no longer among us, doubtleſs we ſhall be forgotten by them.* As ſoon as he had done ſpeaking, every man brought out his gold, and threw it into the ſea.

Notwithſtanding this, the Spaniards advanced. Their muſkets and cannons, thoſe tremendous deities, diſ-perſed with their thunder the ſavages who endeavour-ed to reſiſt: but, as Hatuey might reaſſemble them, he was purſued through the woods, taken, and con-demned to be burned. When he was faſtened to the ſtake, and waited only for the kindling of the fire, an inhuman prieſt advanced to propoſe the ceremony of baptiſm, and to ſpeak to him of paradiſe. *Are there,* ſaid the Cacique, *any Spaniards in that happy place?* *Yes,* replied the miſſionary; *but there are none but good ones. The beſt of them,* returned Hatuey, *are good for nothing. I will not go to a place where I ſhould be in danger of meeting one of them. Talk no more to me of your religion, but leave me to die.*

Thus was the Cacique burned, the God of the Chriſtians diſhonoured, and his croſs imbrued with human blood; but Velaſquez found no more enemies to oppoſe him. No reſiſtance was made, and yet the

nation did not long furvive the lofs of its liberty. In BOOK
thofe ferocious times, when to conquer was nothing XII.
but to deftroy, feveral inhabitants of Cuba were maffacred; a greater number of them ended their lives
in the gold mines, although they were not found
abundant enough to be worked for any length of
time. At laft the fmall-pox, that poifon which hath
been tranfmitted from the Old to the New World,
in exchange for a ftill more fatal poifon, completed
what had been fo much forwarded by the other calamities. The whole ifland was foon reduced to a
defert.

It was indebted for its revival to the pilot Alami- Import-
nos, who, in 1519, firft paffed the canal of Bahama, ance, go-
when he was carrying the firft intelligence of the population,
fuccefs of Cortez to the Emperor Charles V. It was culture,
foon underftood, that this would be the only conve- labours of
nient road for the fhips that fhould fail from Mexico Cuba.
to Europe, and the Havannah was built to receive
them. The utility of this celebrated port was afterwards extended to the veffels difpatched from Porto-
Bello and from Carthagena. They all put in there,
and waited reciprocally for each other, in order to
arrive together in the mother-country with a greater
degree of parade and of fecurity. The prodigious
expences which navigators, laden with the richeft
treafures of the world, incurred during their ftay,
occafioned an immenfe circulation of money in the
town, which was itfelf compelled to fend a part of
it into the countries, more or lefs diftant, from whence
it derived its fubfiftence. Cuba thus acquired fome
degree of animation, while the other iflands, under
the fame dominion, ftill continued in that ftate of
annihilation into which they had been plunged by
the conqueft. In order to accelerate the flow progrefs of this fettlement, a particular affociation was
formed in 1735. The funds of the new company
confifted of one million of piaftres, or of 5,400,000
livres [225,000l.]. They were divided into two thoufand fhares, one hundred of which belonged to the

crown. The privilege of this company was exclusive. They eſtabliſhed a factory at Cadix; but Cuba itſelf was the ſeat of the monopoly.

The directors, at a diſtance from the mother-country, attended only to the making of their own fortunes; they committed numberleſs malverſations; and the company, whoſe intereſts they managed, were ſo completely ruined in the ſpace of twenty years, that it was no longer poſſible for them to continue their tranſactions. The government then authoriſed a few merchants to carry on this trade, and in 1765, all the Spaniards were freely admitted into a poſſeſſion which ought never to have been ſhut againſt them.

A governor, who bears the title of Captain-general, preſides at preſent over the colony. He determines all matters relative to the civil and the military branches; but the finances are under the direction of an intendant. Magiſtrates, whoſe judgments may be ſet aſide by the audience of St. Domingo, diſtribute juſtice in the eighteen juriſdictions which divide the iſland.

The biſhop's ſee, and his chapter, are in the town of Cuba. Neither they, nor any other members of the clergy, receive the tithes; they belong, as in the reſt of the New World, to the crown; but in this, as well as in other places, without being a reſource for the treaſury. There are twenty-three convents of men, and three nunneries in the colony, the eſtates of which are valued, according to the moſt moderate calculation, at 14,589,590 livres [607,899l. 11s. 8d.] The funds which belong to the order of St. Jean de Dieu, and which are deſtined for public uſe, are not included in this calculation.

Children are either well or ill educated in moſt of theſe convents. There is, ever ſince 1728, an univerſity at the Havannah, which hath a revenue of 37,800 livres [1575l.], and leſs than two hundred ſcholars.

Nineteen hoſpitals are diſtributed over the iſland;

and there, as in all other parts, people are by no B O O K means unanimous with refpect to the utility of thefe XII. eftablifhments, or to the beft mode of regulating them. Alas! then, every thing that concerns government is ftill problematic, and the queftions which more particularly affect the happinefs of the human fpecies, are, perhaps, thofe which have been the leaft fatisfactorily folved.

The countries of the globe, which pretend to civilization, are full of indolent men, who choofe rather to fue for alms in the ftreets, than to employ their ftrength in the manufactures. Our intention is not certainly to harden the hearts of men, but we will pronounce, without hefitation, that thefe wretches are fo many robbers of the real poor; and that whoever grants them any affiftance becomes their accomplice. The knowledge of their hypocrify, of their vices, of their debaucheries, of their nocturnal faturnalia, leffens the commiferation that is due to real indigence. It is certainly a difagreeable tafk to deprive a citizen of his liberty, which is the only thing he poffeffes, and to add imprifonment to his mifery. And yet the man who prefers the abject ftate of a beggar, to an afylum where he might earn clothes and fubfiftence by his labour, is a vicious perfon who ought to be carried there by force. There are many countries where, from miftaken motives of compaffion, the profeffed beggars are fuffered to remain at liberty. The adminiftration of thofe countries difplays, in this inftance, more humanity than judgment.

But befide the ftate of beggary, which is brought on by a fpirit of idlenefs, there muft neceffarily be poor people without number in every place where there are multitudes of men, who have no protection againft mifery but in their labour. For all thefe unfortunate people, a day of ficknefs is a day of indigence. Every old man is poor. Every man who is difabled either by accident or by natural deformity, old or young, is a poor man. Every labourer, every fol-

B O O K dier, every failor, who hath either got no employment,
   XII.   or is unable to ferve, is a poor man. Poverty begets poverty; were it only from the impoffibility that indigent
perfons fhould give any kind of education, or furnifh
any employment to their children. A great conflagration, an inundation, a hail ftorm, a long and rigorous winter, an epidemical diforder, a famine, a
war, great and fudden reductions of rent, bankrupt-
cies, bad, and even fometimes good operations of finance, the invention of a new machine : every caufe,
in a word, which deprives the citizen of his ftate,
and which fufpends, or fuddenly diminifhes, the daily
labours, occafions an incredible number of people to
be reduced to poverty in an inftant.

And yet, who are thefe numerous unfortunate
people, who are reduced to inevitable poverty without any fault of their own, and perhaps from the injuftice of our conftitutional laws ? They are ufeful
men who have cultivated the lands, cut the ftones,
conftructed our edifices, nourifhed our children, worked in our mines and in our quarries, defended our
country, affifted the efforts of genius, and been fer-
viceable in all the branches of induftry.

In order to fuccour thefe interefting beings, hofpitals have been contrived. But do thefe eftablifhments anfwer the end of their inftitution ? Almoft
in all places they have a number of moral and natural effects, which render the utility of them doubtful
in their prefent ftate.

Particular and temporary fuccours, prudently difpenfed by government in a feafon of great popular
calamities, would perhaps be better than hofpitals
which are perpetually maintained. They would prevent beggary, while hofpitals encourage it. Thefe
afylums for misfortune, are almoft all in poffeffion of
landed property. This kind of property is liable to
too many embarraffments, and to difhonefty in the
management of it, and fubject to too many viciffi-
tudes in its produce. The directors of it are permanent. Hence their zeal is diminifhed, and the fpirit

of fraud and rapine, or at leaft that of indifference, B O O K
is fubftituted to it. Thefe facred depofits become at ___XII.___
laft the revenue of thofe who manage them. The
adminiftration of thefe eftablifhments is almoft always
a myftery to the government and to the public, while
nothing would be more honeft and more neceflary,
than that it fhould be expofed to public view: it is
alfo arbitrary, and it ought to be fubjected to the
moft careful and rigorous examination. The depredations that are committed in the palaces of kings,
are the fubject of much difcuffion. There at leaft
magnificence, abundance, and the etiquette which
compofes the falfe greatnefs of the throne, are in
fome fort an apology for this diffipation ; for where
there are kings, it is well known there muft likewife
be abufes. But hofpitals are liable to ftill greater
malverfations, and yet they are the houfes of the
poor! they are the fortunes of the poor! every thing
ought there to prefent the ftricteft ideas of economy
and order; every circumftance ought to render thefe
duties facred. You, who are the directors of thefe
afylums, if you be guilty of negligence, your hearts
muft be obdurate! But if you fhould allow yourfelves to commit extortions, by what name can you
be called? You are fit only to be trampled upon in
the duft, and to be drenched in blood.

The natural defects of our hofpitals are ftill more
deplorable than the moral vices of them. The air
is corrupted by a thoufand caufes, the detail of
which would be difgufting to all our fenfes. We
may form a judgment of this from one inconteftible
experiment. Three thoufand men, confined within
the limits of one acre, muft, by their perfpiration
alone, form an atmofphere of the height of fixty
inches, which becomes contagious if the air be not
perpetually renewed. All the people who are habitually employed in the fervice of the fick are pale,
and moftly attacked, even in a ftate of health, with
a peculiar kind of flow fever. How much greater
muft the fame caufe operate upon a fick perfon?

People are difcharged from the hofpital cured of one
difeafe, and carry away another along with them.
Patients are a long time recovering. How many fatal neglects, and unfortunate miftakes are committed? The frequency of them ftifles remorfe.

At the Hotel Dieu of Paris, and at Bicétre, the fifth
and the fixth part of the fick perifh ; at the hofpital
of Lyons, the eighth and the ninth part.

O thou! who, defcending from the firft throne of
Europe, haft vifited the principal countries of it with
the thirft of knowledge, and undoubtedly with the
defire of labouring for the good of thine own country ; tell us, how great was thy horror when thou
didft fee in one of our hofpitals, feven or eight fick
perfons heaped together in the fame bed, all maladies blended together, all the principles and degrees
of life and death confounded ; one wretch crying
out with acute pain, by' the fide of another who was
breathing his laft ; the dying man lain by the fide of
the dead one, and all of them reciprocally infecting
and curfing each other. Say, why didft thou not reprefent this picture to the imagination of thy young
and compaffionate fifter, our fovereign ? No doubt,
fhe would have been affected with it ; her compaffion
would have been communicated to her hufband, and
her tears would have interceded for thefe miferable
wretches. How noble a ufe would this have been
making of beauty!

The prefervation, therefore, of mankind, the watch-
ing over their days, and the removing from them the
horrors of mifery, is a fcience fo little underftood by
government, that even the eftablifhments they feem
to have made with a view of fulfilling thefe objects,
produce an oppofite effect. Aftonifhing perverfion
of mind! which ought not to be forgotten by any
one of our philofophers, who fhall write the immenfe
treatife on the barbarifm of civilized nations.

Some men, devoid of feeling, have afferted, that in
order to diminifh the number, already too great, of
idle, negligent, and vicious people, it was neceffary

that the poor and the fick fhould not be well treated B O O K
in the hofpitals. And indeed it cannot be denied, XII.
but that this barbarous expedient hath been purfued
to its utmoft extent ; neverthelefs, what are the effects produced by it ? Several men have been deftroyed, while no one hath been corrected.

Lazinefs and debauchery may poffibly be encouraged in hofpitals ; but if this defect be inherent in
thefe eftablifhments, it muft be borne with. If it can
be corrected, we muft endeavour to do it. Let hofpitals fubfift, but let us all exert ourfelves by diffuf-
ing general competency, in diminifhing the multitude of thofe unfortunate people who are compelled
to feek an afylum in them. Let them be employed
in charitable houfes, in fedentary labours ; let lazinefs
be punifhed there, but let induftry be rewarded.

With regard to the fick, let them be taken care of,
as men ought to be by men. Their country owes
them this relief from motives of juftice or of intereft.
If they be old, they have ferved mankind, they have
brought other citizens into the world ; if they be
young, they may ferve mankind again, they may be
the fource of a new generation. In a word, when
they are once admitted into thofe charitable afylums,
let hofpitality be exercifed in its full extent. Let
there be no more mean avarice, no murderous calculations. They ought to find there all the comforts
they would find in their own families, if their own
families were capable of receiving them.

This plan is not impracticable, it will not even be
expenfive, when better laws, when a more vigilant,
a more enlightened, and efpecially a more humane
adminiftration, fhall prefide over thefe eftablifhments.
The experiment hath been juft made with fuccefs, under our own immediate infpection, by the care of Ma-
dame Necker. While this lady's hufband is employing himfelf upon a larger fcale, in diminifhing the
number of unfortunate people, fhe enters into the
details which can alleviate the diftreffes of thofe who
are already unfortunate. She hath juft eftablifhed in

the fuburb of St. Germain, an hofpital, where fick
people, who have each a bed to themfelves, and are
attended in the fame manner as they would be at the
houfe of the moft affectionate mother, coft one third
lefs than in any of the hofpitals at Paris. Foreigners, who are become members of the nation, by the
moft meritorious of all naturalizations, by the good
you do to it ; Generous pair, I venture to name you,
although you are ftill alive, although you are furrounded with the influence of a high poft ; and I am
not apprehenfive of being accufed of adulation :—I
think I have given fufficient proofs, that I can neither fear nor flatter vice in power, and therefore I
have acquired the right of rendering public homage
to virtue.

Would to heaven, that the happy experiment we
have juft mentioned, might bring on a general reformation in all the hofpitals founded by the generofity
of our anceftors! Would to heaven, that fo fine an
eftablifhment might ferve as a model for thofe, which
a principle of foft compaffion, the defire of expiating
the poffeffion of wealth, or a benevolent fyftem of
philofophy, may one day excite fucceeding generations to found! This wifh of my heart extends to
the whole univerfe ; for my thoughts have no other
limits than thofe of the world, when they are employed about the happinefs of my fellow-creatures.
Citizens of the univerfe, unite yourfelves with me ;
it is your intereft that is in agitation.

What affurances have you, that none of your anceftors have died in an hofpital ? What affurances
have you that none of your defcendants will expire
in that retreat provided for mifery ? Might not an
unexpected misfortune oblige you to take refuge
there yourfelves ? Let your vows therefore be joined
to mine.

Let us now return to our fubject. According to
accounts taken in 1774, the ifland of Cuba reckons
one hundred and feventy-one thoufand fix hundred
and twenty-eight perfons, of whom twenty-eight

thoufand feven hundred and fixty-fix only are flaves.
The population muft even be rather more confiderable, becaufe the well-grounded apprehenfion of fome
new tax muft have prevented accuracy in the de-
clarations.

Few of the arts, except thofe of primary neceffity, are found in the ifland. Thefe are in the hands
of the Mulattoes, or free Negroes, and are in a very
imperfect ftate. Joiners work only hath been carried
on to a remarkable degree of perfection.

Other Mulattoes and blacks are employed in cultivating articles of fubfiftence. Thefe confift of fome
fruits of the New World, and fome vegetables of the
Old; of maize, and of manioc, the confumption of
which hath diminifhed in proportion as the freedom
of trade hath lowered the price of the flour brought
from Spain or Mexico, and fometimes alfo from North
America: they confift of tolerable good cacao, but in
fo fmall a quantity, that the inhabitants are obliged
to draw annually from Caraccas, or from Guayaquil,
more than two thoufand quintals of it: they confift alfo
of numerous herds of oxen, and efpecially of hogs, the
flefh of which hath been hitherto generally preferred, and will always be fo, unlefs the fheep, which
have lately been brought into the ifland, fhould make
them one day be neglected. All thefe animals wander about in the pafture grounds, each of which is
four, or at leaft two leagues in extent. Some mules
and horfes are likewife feen to graze there, which
ought to be ftill more multiplied, becaufe their prefent number doth not prevent the inhabitants from
purchafing a great quantity from the continent.

The articles deftined for exportation employ moft
of the flaves. From 1748 to 1753, the labour of thefe
unfortunate people did not produce annually to the
mother-country, more than eighteen thoufand feven
hundred and fifty quintals of tobacco, the value of
which in Europe was 1,293,570 livres [53,898l. 15s.];
one hundred and feventy-three thoufand eight hundred quintals of fugar, the value of which was 7,994,786

B O O K
XII.

livres [333,116l. 11s. 8d.] ; fifteen hundred and fix-
ty-nine hides, the value of which was 138,817 livres
[5784l. 10d.] ; and 1,064,505 livres [44,354l. 7s.
6d.] in gold and filver. Of this fum, amounting to
10,491,678 livres [437,153l. 5s.], the tobacco alone
was the property of government, all the reft belonged
to trade.

Since that period the labours have much increafed ;
they have not, however, been turned towards the
culture of indigo and of cotton, although thefe grow
naturally in the ifland.

The culture of coffee, which hath been lately undertaken, hath not made any confiderable progrefs,
nor will it increafe. Spain confumes but a fmall
quantity of that production, and the European marts
are and will be for a long time overftocked with it.
There is more to be expected from the wax.

When Florida was ceded, in 1763, by the court
of Madrid to that of London, the five or fix hundred
miferable people who lived in that ifland took refuge
at Cuba, and carried fome bees along with them.
Thefe ufeful infects flew to the forefts, fixed themfelves in the hollow of old trees, and multiplied with
a degree of celerity that feems incredible. The colony, which till then had bought a great deal of wax
for their religious folemnities, was foon able to collect a fufficient quantity for this pious ufe, and for
other confumptions. They had fome overplus in
1770 ; and feven years afterwards they exported feven thoufand one hundred and fifty quintals and a
half of it, for Europe and for America. This production muft neceffarily increafe, under a fky, and
on a foil, which are equally favourable to it ; in an
ifland where the hives yield four times in every year,
and where the fwarms fucceed each other without
interruption.

Tobacco is one of the moft important productions
of Cuba. Each crop furnifhes about fifty-five thoufand quintals. Part of this is confumed in the country, or fraudulently carried out of it. The govern-

ment purchafe annually, for their dominions in the
Old and in the New World, where they equally mo-
nopolize it, forty-fix thoufand feven hundred and fifty quintals, the price of which varies according to its
quality, but which coft, one with another, 48 livres
12 fols [2l. 6d.] the hundred weight. So that the
king pours annually into the ifland 2,272,050 livres
[94,668l. 15s.] for this production.

The progrefs made in the culture of tobacco hath
been lately ftopped at Cuba. This plant hath even
been rooted up in fome places where it did not thrive
fo well. The miniftry did not choofe that the crops
fhould exceed the demands of the monarchy. They
were certainly apprehenfive that foreigners, who might
have purchafed this production in the leaf, would introduce it clandeftinely in their provinces, after having manufactured it. It has been thought that the
induftry of the planters would be more ufefully employed in the culture of fugar.

This commodity was little known before the difcovery of the New World. It is gradually become
the object of an immenfe commerce. The Spaniards
were obliged to purchafe it of their neighbours, till
at length they thought of planting it at Cuba. The
mother-country receives annually from two hundred
to two hundred and fifty quintals of it, half of it white,
and half raw. It is not as much as its inhabitants
can confume ; but they will not be obliged to have
recourfe to foreign markets, when this cultivation
fhall be as firmly eftablifhed in the reft of the ifland,
as it already is in the territory of the Havannah.

Before 1765, Cuba did not receive annually more
than three or four large fhips from Cadiz ; and thofe
veffels, which, after having fold their cargoes upon
the coafts of the continent, came there in order to
take up a lading, which they had not been able to
find at Vera Cruz, at Honduras, and at Carthagena.
The ifland was at that time in want of the moft neceffary things, and the inhabitants were compelled
to purchafe them of their neighbours, with whom they

B O O K had formed fome fmuggling connections. Since the
XII.   reftraints have been diminifhed, the number of voyages hath multiplied the productions, which have alfo
reciprocally extended the navigation.

In 1774, one hundred and one veffels arrived from
Spain in the colony : thefe were laden with flour,
wines, brandies, and with every thing requifite for a
large fettlement ; and they carried away from thence
all the commodities which a better arrangement of
things had produced.

The fame year Cuba received, upon one hundred
and eighteen fmall veffels, from Louifiana, rice, and
the proper wood for their fugar chefts ; from Mexico,
flour, vegetables, Morocco leather, and copper ; from
the other parts of this large continent, oxen, mules,
and cacao; and from Porto Rico two thoufand flaves,
which had been diftributed among thefe fhips.

Thefe veffels of the Old and New World were not
allowed to choofe the ports where it would have been
moft convenient for them to put in. They were
obliged to land their cargoes at the Havannah, at
Port-au-Prince, at Cuba, and at Trinidad, the only
places where cuftoms were eftablifhed. None but
fifhing fmacks and coafting veffels are allowed to frequent all the harbours indifcriminately.

A man, who at this time does honour to Spain, and
who would do honour to any country whatever, Mr.
Campo Manes, fays, that the produce of the cuftoms,
which before 1765 had never exceeded 565,963
livres [23,581l. 15s. 10d.], amounts at prefent to
1,620,000 livres [67,500l.] ; and that the mother-
country draws from the colony, in metals, 8,100,000
livres [337,500l.], inftead of 1,620,000 livres [67,500l.]
which it formerly received. This is an argument in
favour of a free trade, of the force of which it were
to be wifhed that mankind could be made fenfible.

The taxes levied at Cuba, or thofe at leaft which
enter the coffers of the ftate, do not exceed 2,430,000
livres [101,250l.], and government circulates in the
ifland to the amount of 2,272,050 livres [94,668l,

15s.] for tobacco; 1,350,000 livres [56,250l.] for the B O O K maintenance of the fortifications, 2,160,000 livres XII. [90,000l.] for the ufual garrifons, and 3,780,000 livres [157,500l.] for the naval department.

Cedar woods, proper for fhip-building, were found all over the colony, though the idea had never occurred of making any ufe of them. At length docks were eftablifhed, in 1724, which have fent out, from that period to the prefent time, fifty-eight veffels, or frigates. This eftablifhment is kept up, notwithftanding the neceffity there is of importing the iron and the ropes ufed for thofe veffels, articles which the ifland doth not furnifh; and notwithftanding the cuftom which hath prevailed fince 1750, of bringing from the North of Europe the mafts, which were formerly obtained, though of inferior quality, from the Gulf of Mexico.

The fmall fleet deftined to clear the coafts of Spain of fmugglers or pirates, and which, in the intervals between the cruizing feafons ufed to remain at Vera Cruz, was fuppreffed in 1748. It was become ufelefs fince the government had refolved to maintain conftantly at Cuba fome maritime forces, more or lefs confiderable. In peace time thefe veffels carry to the iflands of Cumana, and to Louifiana, the funds that are deftined for the annual neceffities of thofe feveral fettlements; they prevent fmuggling as much as they can; and they caufe the name of their mafter to be refpected. In time of war they protect the traders and the territories of their country.

The Havannah, where thefe fhips are conftructed, hath juft been fupplied, by the care of the Marquis de la Torre, with fome conveniences and embellifhments which had been for a long time defired in vain. This active governor hath given the inhabitants a playhoufe, decorated with propriety, two delightful walks, convenient barracks, and five very well contrived bridges. Thefe ufeful or agreeable eftablifhments have coft the town no more than 482,066 livres [20,086l. 1s. 8d.],

Government have allotted, for the fortifications
with which the town hath been furrounded, from
1763 to 1777, 22,413,989 livres 18 fols 6 deniers
[933,916l. 4s. 11¼d.].   Thefe works have been conftructed by four thoufand one hundred and ninety-
eight blacks, by fifteen hundred malefactors fent from
Spain and Mexico, and by the freemen, who have
not difdained this kind of labour.

The harbour of the Havannah is one of the fafeft
in the univerfe ; the fleets of the whole world might
ride at anchor there together.   At the entrance of it
there are rocks, againft which the veffels that fhould
venture to deviate from the middle of the pafs would
infallibly be wrecked.   It is defended by the Moro
and the fort on the point.   The former of thefe fortreffes is raifed fo high above the level of the fea, that
even a firft rate man of war could not batter it.   The
other hath not the fame advantage ; but it can only
be attacked by a very narrow channel, where the
warmeft affailants could never withftand the numerous and formidable artillery of the Moro.

The Havannah, therefore, can only be attacked
on the land fide.   Fifteen or fixteen thoufand men,
which are the moft that could be employed in this
fervice, would not be fufficient to inveft the works,
which cover a vaft extent.   Their efforts muft be directed, either to the right or left of the port, againft
the town, or the Moro.   If the latter, they may eafily land within a league of the fort, and will come
within fight of it, without difficulty, by eafy roads,
through woods which will cover and fecure their
march.

The firft difficulty will be that of getting water,
which, in the neighbourhood of the camp the affailants muft choofe, is mortal.   To obtain fuch as is
drinkable, they muft go in boats to the diftance of
three leagues, and it will be neceffary to fend a confiderable force for this purpofe to the only river where
it is to be had, or to leave a detachment there in in-
trenchments ; which being at a diftance from the

camp, without communication or fupport, will be in perpetual danger of being cut off.

Previous to the attack of the Moro, the enemy muft make themfelves mafters of the Cavagna, which hath been lately built. It is a crown-work, com-pofed of a baftion, two curtains, and two demi-ba-ftions in front. Its right and left lie upon the bank of the harbour. It hath cafemates, refervoirs of wa-ter, and powder magazines that are bomb-proof, a good covered-way, and a wide ditch cut in the rock. The way which leads to it is compofed of ftones and pebbles, without any mixture of earth. The Cavag-na is placed on an eminence which commands the Moro, but is itfelf expofed to attacks from a hill which is of an equal height, and not more than three hundred paces diftant from it. As it would have been eafy for an enemy to open their trenches under the cover of this hill, the Spaniards have levelled it, and the Cavagna can now extend its view and its batteries to a great diftance. If the garrifon fhould find them-felves fo preffed, as not to be able to maintain this poft, they would blow up the works, which are all undermined, and retreat into the Moro, the commu-nication with which cannot poffibly be cut off.

The famous fortrefs of the Moro had towards the fea, on which fide it is impregnable, two baftions; and on the land fide two others, with a wide and deep ditch cut out of the rock, Since it was taken, it hath been entirely rebuilt, and its parapets made higher and thicker. A good covered-way hath been added, and every thing that was wanting to fecure the gar-rifon and the ftores. It is not eafier to open trenches before this place than the Cavagna. Both of them are built with a foft ftone, which will be lefs dange-rous to the defenders than the common fort of free-ftone.

Independent of thefe advantages, the two fortref-fes have in their favour a climate extremely hazar-dous to befiegers, and an eafy communication with the town for receiving all forts of provifions, without

BOOK a poſſibility of being intercepted. Thus circumſtan-
XII. ced, theſe two places may be conſidered as impregnable, at leaſt as very difficult to be taken, provided
they be properly ſtocked with proviſions, and defended with courage and ability. The preſervation of
them is of ſo much greater importance, as their loſs
would neceſſarily occaſion the ſurrender of the harbour and town, which are both of them commanded,
and may be battered, from theſe eminences.

After having explained the difficulties of taking
the Havannah by attacking the Moro, we muſt next
ſpeak of thoſe which muſt be encountered on the ſide
of the town.

It is ſituated near the bottom of the harbour. It
was defended, as well towards the harbour as towards
the country, by a dry wall, which was good for nothing, and twenty-one baſtions, which were not much
better. It had a dry ditch, and of little depth. Before this ditch was a kind of covered-way, almoſt in
ruins. The place, in this ſtate, could not have reſiſted a ſudden attempt, which, had it been made in
the night, and ſupported by ſeveral attacks, true or
falſe, would certainly have carried it. Wide and
deep ditches have been made, and an exceeding
good covered-way added.

Theſe defences are ſupported by the fort at the
point ; which is a ſquare, built of ſtone, and, though
ſmall, is provided with caſemates. It hath been rebuilt, having been very much damaged during the
ſiege. There is a good dry ditch round it, digged
out of the rock. Independent of its principal deſti-
nation, which is to co-operate with the Moro in defending the port, and for which it is perfectly well
calculated, it hath ſeveral batteries which open upon
the country, and flank ſome parts of the town wall.

Its fire croſſes that of a fort of four baſtions, which
hath a ditch, covered-way, powder magazine, caſemates, and reſervoirs of water. This new fortification,
which is erected at three quarters of a mile from the
place on an eminence called Aroſteguy, will require

a fiege in form, if the town is to be attacked on that
fide, particularly as it is fo conftructed as to have a
view of the fea, to command a confiderable track on
the land fide, and to difturb an enemy exceedingly
in getting water, which they muft fetch from its
neighbourhood.

In fkirting the city onward, we come to the fort
of Atarès, which has been conftructed fince the fiege.
It is of ftone, hath four baftions, a covered-way, a half-
moon before the gate, a wide ditch, a good rampart,
refervoirs, cafemates, and a powder magazine. It is bare-
ly three quarters of a league diftant from the town,
and is fituated on the other fide of a river and an impracticable morafs, which cover it in that direction.
The rifing ground upon which it is built, is entirely
occupied by it, and has been infulated by the digging of a broad ditch, into which the fea hath a paffage from the bottom of the harbour. Befides its
commanding the communication between the town
and the interior part of the ifland, it defends the cir-
cuit of the place by croffing its fires with thofe of
Arofteguy. The Spaniards have conftructed a large
redoubt in the interval of thefe two forts, which is
an additional protection to the town. The Atarès
alfo croffes its fire with that of the Moro, which is
very high, and fituated at the extreme point of the
fort.

If it were allowable to form an opinion upon a fubject, which we do not profeffionally underftand, we
might venture to affert, that thofe who would undertake the fiege of the Havannah, fhould begin by the
Cavagna and the Moro ; becaufe thefe forts once
taken, the town muft of courfe furrender, or be deftroyed by the artillery of the Moro. On the contrary, if they fhould determine for the town fide, the
befiegers woule fcarcely find themfelves in a better
condition, even after they had taken it. Indeed,
they would have it in their power to deftroy the dock-
yards, and the fhips that might happen to be in the
harbour ; but this would produce no permanent ad-

vantage. In order to eſtabliſh themſelves, they muſt ſtill be obliged to take the Cavagna and the Moro, which in all probability they would find impoſſible; after the loſs they muſt have ſuſtained in the attack of the town and its fortreſſes.

But whatever plan may be purſued in the ſiege of this place, the aſſailants' will not only have to combat the numerous garriſon encloſed within its works ; there will be a corps likewiſe of twelve thouſand four hundred and ſeventy-two militia, who have been ac-cuſtomed to manœuvre in a ſurpriſing manner, who would take the field, and continually interrupt their operations. Theſe troops, armed, clothed, and ac-coutred at the expence of the government, and paid in time of war upon the footing of regulars, are train-ed and commanded by non-commiſſioned officers ſent from Europe, and; choſen from the moſt diſtinguiſhed regiments. The forming of this militia hath coſt an immenſe ſum. The court of Spain is in expectation of future events, to form a judgment of the utility of theſe expences. But whatever may be the mili-tary ſpirit of theſe troops, we may pronounce before-hand, that this eſtabliſhment, in a political view, is inexcuſable ; and for the following reaſons :

The project of making ſoldiers of all the coloniſts of Cuba, a moſt unjuſt and deſtructive project to all colonies, has been purſued with uncommon ardour. The violence they have been forced to uſe with the inhabitants, to make them ſubmit to exerciſes which they were averſe from, has produced no other effects than that of increaſing their natural love of repoſe. They deteſt thoſe mechanical and forced movements, which, not contributing in any reſpect to their hap-pineſs, appear doubly inſupportable ; not to mention their ſeeming frightful or ridiculous to a people, who probably think they have no intereſt in defending a government by which they are oppreſſed. The rage of keeping up an army ; that madneſs, which, under pretence of preventing wars, encourages them; which by introducing deſpotiſm into governments, paves the

way for rebellion among the people ; which continually dragging the inhabitant from his dwelling, and
the hufbandman from his field, extinguifhes in them
the love of their country, by driving them from their
home; which fubverts nations, and carries them over
land and fea : that mercenary profeffion of war, fo
different from the truly military fpirit, fooner or later
will be the ruin of Europe ; but much fooner of the
colonies, and perhaps, firft of all, of thofe which belong to Spain.

The moft extenfive and moft fertile part of the Hath Spain
American Archipelago is poffeffed by the Spaniards. taken pro-
These flands, in the hands of an induftrious nation, fures to
would have proved a fource of unbounded wealth. ifland ufe-
In their prefent ftate, they are vaft forefts, exhibiting ful, and
only a frightful folitude. Far from contributing to ftill purfue
the ftrength and riches of the kingdom they belong them?
to, they ferve only to weaken and to exhauft it by
the expences required to maintain them. If Spain
had attended properly to the political improvements
of other nations, fhe would have difcovered, that
feveral of them owed their influence folely to the advantages they have drawn from iflands, in every refpect inferior to thofe which have hitherto only ferved the ignominious purpofe of fwelling the lift of the
numberlefs and ufelefs poffeffions of the Spanifh
crown. She would have learned, that there is no
other rational foundation of colonies, efpecially of
thofe which have no mines, but agriculture.

It is not doing juftice to the Spaniards to fuppofe
that they are naturally incapable of labour. If we
give the leaft attention to the exceffive fatigues which
thofe of them who are concerned in contraband trade
fubmit to with the utmoft patience, we fhall find that
their toils are infinitely more grievous than any that
attend the management of a plantation. If they neglect to enrich themfelves by agriculture, it is the
fault of their government. Alas! might the difin-
terefted hiftorian, who neither feeks nor defires any
thing but the general good of mankind, be permit-

BOOK ted to furnish them with those sentiments and ex-
XII. pressions, which the habit of sloth, the rigour of government, and prejudices of every kind, seem to have
precluded them from the use of, thus would he in
their name address the court of Madrid, and the
whole Spanish nation :

" Reflect on the sacrifices we require from you,
" and see, if you will not reap a centuple advantage
" by the valuable commodities we shall supply to
" your now expiring commerce. Your navy, increas-
" ed by our labours, will form the only bulwark that
" can preserve to you those possessions, which are now
" ready to escape from your hands. As we become
" more rich, our consumption will be greater ; and
" then the country which you inhabit, and which
" droops with you, though Nature herself invites it
" to fertility ; those plains, which present to your
" eyes only a desert space, and are a disgrace to
" your laws and to your manners, will be converted
" into fields of plenty. Your native land will flou-
" rish by industry and agriculture, which have now
" forsaken you. The springs of life and activity,
" which ye will have conveyed to us through the
" channel of the sea, will flow back, and encompass
" your dwellings with rivers of plenty. But if ye prove
" insensible to our complaints and misfortunes ; if ye
" do not govern us for our sakes ; if we be only the
" victims of our loyalty ; recal to your minds that
" ever celebrated era, in which a nation of unfor-
" tunate and discontented subjects shook off the yoke
" of your dominion ; and by their labours, their suc-
" cess, and their opulence, justified the revolt in the
" eyes of the whole world. They have been free for
" near two centuries ; and shall we still have to la-
" ment that we are governed by you ? when Holland
" broke in pieces the rod of iron, which crushed
" her ; when she rose from the depth of the waters
" to rule over the sea ; heaven, without doubt, rais-
" ed her up as a monument of freedom, to point out
" to the nations of the world the path of happiness,

" and to intimidate faithlefs kings who would exclude
" them from it."

It might be fufpected that the court of Madrid
have difcovered that it would be poffible to pafs this
cenfure upon them. In 1735, their miniftry fuggefted a company for Cuba. Twenty years after they
conceived the idea of a new monopoly for St. Domingo and for Porto-Rico. The fociety which was
to clear thefe deferts, was eftablifhed at Barcelona,
with a capital of 1,785,000 livres [74,375l.] divided
into fhares, of the value of a hundred piftols each [83l.
15s.]. This company never paid any intereft to its
members ; they made no dividend ; they obtained
the important permiffion of fitting out feveral veffels
for the Honduras. Notwithftanding this, on the 30th
of April 1771, their debts, including their capital,
amounted to 3,121,692 livres [130,070l. 10s.], and
they had no more than 3,775,540 livres [157,314l.
3s. 4d.]. So that in the courfe of fifteen years, with
an exclufive privilege, and with very fignal favour,
they had gained no more than 653,848 livres
[27,243l. 13s. 4d.]. Their affairs have fince been in
great diforder, and at prefent they have no degree of
activity. They are endeavouring to liquidate their
debts, but they cannot difpofe of their fhares even
at fifty per cent. lofs.

The miniftry had not waited for this reverfe of fortune, to judge that they had miftaken the means
they had adopted to render thefe iflands flourifhing.
From 1765, the adminiftrators of that large empire
were obliged to acknowledge that their poffeffions
had not acquired the fmalleft degree of improvement
under the yoke of monopoly. They underftood that
they would never improve under fuch fatal reftraints.
This conviction determined them to have recourfe to
the only principle of profperity, a free trade : but
they had not the courage or the wifdom to remove
the obftacles which muft neceffarily have impeded
the happy effects of it.

In the year 1778, thefe prohibitions, reftraints, and

impofitions, which checked their labours, were partly abolifhed; but there ftill remain too many of thofe
oppreffive fcourges, to give reafon to expect much
exertion.   Were they even totally removed, this
would ftill be only a preliminary ftep.

All the cultures of the New World require fome
advances; but confiderable capitals are wanted to
make that of fugar fuccefsful.   Excepting at Cuba,
there are not perhaps in the other iflands five or fix
inhabitants wealthy enough to cultivate this production.   If the Spanifh miniftry do not beftow liberally
their treafures upon thefe iflanders, they will not
awake from that long and profound lethargy in which
they are plunged.   This generofity would be very
practicable in an empire where the public revenue
amounts to 140,400,000 livres [5,850,000l.], where
the expences do not exceed 129,600,000 livres
[5,400,000l.], and where there remains a balance of
10,800,000 livres [450,000l.], which may be laid out
in improvements.   It is true, that without receiving
fuch powerful affiftance from their refpective governments, other nations have founded flourifhing colonies; but befides that they had not been debafed
during the courfe of three centuries, by pride, languor, and poverty, they were alfo in more favourable and different circumftances.

Happy is the man, who is borne after the extinction of this long feries of errors which have infected
his nation!   Happy is the nation, that fhould rife up
in the centre of the moft enlightened nations, if it
were prudent enough to profit by the faults which
they had committed, and to avail itfelf of the knowledge they had acquired.   Such a nation would only
have to caft her eyes about her, in order to difcern
the fcattered materials that would conftitute her
happinefs, and to attend to the collecting of them.
One of the principal advantages which fhe would
owe, either to the novelty of her origin, or to the
tardinefs of her labours, or to the long duration of
her infant ftate, would be, that fhe would be fpared

the trouble of conquering thofe rooted prejudices, B O O K
which were the refult of the inexperience of the firft   XII.
legiflators, which had been confecrated by time, and
which had been maintained againft reafon and facts;
either from pufillanimity, which is apprehenfive of
any innovation; or from pride, which dreads the being obliged to retract; or from a weak veneration for
every thing of ancient date.

Let the court of Madrid haften to lay open its treafures, and the iflands fubject to its empire will foon
be covered with productions. Their fubjects, placed
upon an extenfive and virgin foil, will not only be
difpenfed from buying at a high price what ferves
for their confumption; but, in a little time, they will
fupplant in all the markets their mafters in this career. The moft active, the moft induftrious, and the
moft enlightened nations, will have laboured for ages
in improving their cultures, their mode of managing
them and their manufactures, for the advantage merely of a rival, more favoured by nature than themfelves. But it can fcarce be expected, that they will
fubmit patiently to fuch a misfortune.

Since the origin of focieties, a fatal jealoufy prevails Would the
among them, which muft, it fhould feem, be per- that have
petual, unlefs by fome inconceivable revolution they colonies in
fhould be feparated from each other by immenfe de- fuffer the
fert intervals. Hitherto they have fhowed themfelves Spanifh
in the fame light as a citizen in our towns, who become
fhould be convinced, that the more his fellow-citizens flourifhing?
were indigent and weak, the more he would become
rich and powerful, and the more he fhould be able to
check their undertakings, to thwart their induftry, to
limit their cultures, and to confine them to what is
abfolutely neceffary for their fubfiftence.

But it will be urged, that a citizen enjoys his wealth
under the protection of the laws. The profperity of
his neighbour may increafe without inconvenience to
his own, but this is not the cafe with nations—and
wherefore is it not?—It is becaufe there doth not
exift any tribunal before which they can be fummon-

BOOK XII.

ed.—But what need have they of such a tribunal?—Because they are unjust and pusillanimous.—And what advantage do they derive from their injustice and pusillanimity?—Perpetual wars, and misery which is incessantly renewed.—And can it be supposed, that experience will not correct them?—We are perfectly convinced of it,—and for what reason?—Because one madman is sufficient to disconcert the wisdom of all other powers, and there will always be more than one at a time upon the several thrones of the universe.

Nevertheless, we hear on every side the nations, and especially those that are commercial, crying out for peace, while they still continue to conduct themselves towards one another, in a manner that excludes them from ever obtaining that blessing. They will all aspire to happiness, and each of them would enjoy it alone. They will all equally hold tyranny in detestation, and they will all exercise it upon their neighbours. They will all consider the idea of universal monarchy as extravagant, and yet they will most of them act as if they had either attained it, or were threatened with it.

Could I expect any good to result from my discourse, I would address myself to the most turbulent and the most ambitious among the nations, in the following terms :

" Let us suppose, that you have at length acquired
" a sufficient degree of authority among the nations,
" to reduce them to that state of degradation and
" poverty that is suitable to you, what can you ex-
" pect from this despotism? For how long a time,
" and at what price, will you maintain it ; and what
" advantages will accrue to you from it ?—Do you
" expect that security, with which one is always suf-
" ficiently rich, and without which one is never suf-
" ficiently so?—And can you really think yourself
" not sufficiently secure? You know, as well as I do,
" that the times of invasion are past, and it is thus
" you disguise an inordinate ambition, under the mask
" of a ridiculous phantom. You prefer the vain splen-

" dour of this ambition to the enjoyment of real hap-
" pinefs, which you lofe in order to deprive others of
" it. What right have you to prefcribe limits to their
" happinefs, you who pretend to extend yours be-
" yond all bounds ? You are an unjuft people, while
" you attribute to yourfelves the exclufive right of
" profperity. You are a people erroneous in your
" calculations, when you hope to enrich yourfelves
" by reducing others to˙poverty. You are ftill a
" blind people, if you do not conceive that the power
" of a nation which raifes itfelf upon the ruins of all
" thofe that furround it, is a Coloffus of clay, which
" aftonifhes for a moment, but which crumbles into
" duft."

I fhould afterwards fay to the Spanifh miniftry :
" All the ftates of Europe are interefted in the pro-
" fperity of your continent in the New World, be-
" caufe the more thefe vaft ftates fhall be flourifhing,
" the more will their merchandife and their manu-
" factures find advantageous marts ; but this is not
" the cafe with the iflands. The powers that have
" appropriated to themfelves the fertility of fome of
" them, are fufficient to provide for their prefent
" wants, and a new competitor would ftrongly excite
" their jealoufy. They would attack this competitor
" either together or feparately, would not lay afide
" their arms without having obliged him to give up
" the clearing of the lands, perhaps, even not with-
" out having made him experience ftill greater evils.
" It is yours to judge, whether thefe views be falfe,
" or whether your ftrength and your courage will
" allow you to bid defiance to fuch a combination."
The Dutch colonies will never have any thing of this
kind to fear.

Before the difcovery of the weftern coaft of Africa, Political
of the paffage to India by the Cape of Good Hope, fteps taken
and particularly before that of America, the Euro- public of the
pean nations fcarcely knew or vifited each other, ex- vinces at its
cept in making barbarous incurfions, the aim of which firft rife.
was plunder, and the confequence deftruction. Ex-

BOOK cepting a fmall number of tyrants, who, by oppref-
XII. fing the weak, found means to fupport a luxury dearly purchafed, all the inhabitants of the different ftates
were obliged to content themfelves with the meagre
fubfiftence furnifhed them by lands ill cultivated, and
a trade which extended only to the frontiers of each
province. Thofe great events towards the end of the
fifteenth century, which form one of the moft brilliant epochas of the hiftory of the world, did not
produce fo fudden a change of manners as might naturally be fuppofed. Some of the Hanfe towns and
fome Italian republics, it is true, ventured as far as
Cadiz and Lifbon, which were become great marts,
to purchafe the rare and valuable productions of the
Eaft and Weft Indies; but the confumption was very
fmall, through the inability of the feveral nations to
pay for them. Moft of them were languifhing in a
ftate of abfolute lethargy; they were totally ignorant
of the advantages and refources of the countries that
belonged to them.

To roufe them from this ftate of infenfibility, there
was wanting a people, who, fpringing from nothing,
fhould infpire every mind with activity and intelligence, and diffufe plenty through every market; that
fhould offer the produce of all countries at a lower
price, and exchange the fuperfluities of every nation
for thofe commodities which they want; that fhould
give a quick circulation to produce merchandife and
money; and, by facilitating and increafing confumption, fhould encourage population, agriculture, and
every branch of induftry. For all thefe advantages,
Europe is indebted to the Dutch. The blind multitude may be excufed in confining themfelves to the
enjoyment of their profperity, without knowing the
fources of it; but it is incumbent on the philofopher
and the politician to tranfmit to pofterity the fame of
the benefactors of mankind; and to trace out, if it
be poffible, the progrefs of their beneficence.

When the generous inhabitants of the United Provinces freed themfelves from the dominion of the fea

and of tyranny, they perceived that they could not fix the foundation of their liberty on a foil which did not afford even the neceffaries of life. They were convinced, that commerce, which to moft nations is no more than an acceffion, a means only of increafing the quantity and value of the produce of their refpective countries, was to them the fole bafis of their exiftence. Without territory and without productions, they determined to give a value to thofe of other nations, fatisfied that their own would be the refult of the general profperity. The event juftified their policy.

Their firft ftep eftablifhed, among the nations of Europe, an exchange of the commodities of the north with thofe of the fouth. In a fhort time the fea was covered with the fhips of Holland. In her ports were collected all the commercial effects of different countries, and from thence they were difperfed to their refpective deftinations. Here the value of every thing was regulated, and with a moderation which precluded all competition. The ambition of giving greater ftability and extent to her enterprifes, excited in the republic a fpirit of conqueft. Her empire extended itfelf over a part of the Indian continent, and over all the iflands of confequence in the fea that encompaffes it. By her fortreffes, or her fleets, fhe kept in fubjection the coafts of Africa, towards which her ambition, ever directed to ufeful objects, had turned its attentive and prudent views. Her laws were acknowledged only in thofe countries of America where cultivation had fowed the feeds of real wealth. The immenfe chain of her connections embraced the univerfe, of which, by toil and induftry, fhe became the foul. In a word, fhe had attained the univerfal monarchy of commerce.

Such was the ftate of the United Provinces in 1661, when the Portuguefe, recovering themfelves from that languor and inaction which the tyranny of Spain had thrown them into, found means to repoffefs themfelves of that part of Brafil which the Dutch had taken from

BOOK
XII.

them. From this firft ftroke, that republic would have
loft all footing in the New World, had it not been for
a few fmall iflands, particularly that of Curaffou, which
they had taken in 1634 from the Caftilians, who had
been in poffeffion of it ever fince 1527.

Defcription
oftheDutch
ifland of
Curaffou.

This rock, which is not above three leagues off the
coaft of Venezuela, is about ten leagues long and five
broad. It has an excellent harbour, but the entrance
is difficult. The bafon is extremely large, and convenient in every refpect; and it is defended by a fort
fkilfully conftructed, and always kept in good repair.

The French, in 1673, having previoufly bribed the
commandant, landed there to the number of five or
fix hundred men: but the treafon having been difcovered, and the traitor punifhed, they were received
by his fucceffor in a very different manner from what
they expected, and reimbarked with the difgrace of
having expofed only their own weaknefs, and the ini-
quity of their meafures.

Lewis the XIVth, whofe pride was hurt by this
imprudent check, fent out d'Eftrees five years after
with eighteen fhips of war, and twelve buccaneering
veffels, to wipe off the ftain, which in his eyes tar-
nifhed the glory of a reign filled with wonders. The
admiral was not far from the place of his deftination,
when by his rafhnefs and obftinacy he ran his fhips
aground on Davis's Ifland; and, after collecting the
fhattered remains of his fleet, returned in very bad
condition to Breft, without having attempted any
thing.

From this period neither Curaffou, nor the little
iflands Aruba and Bonaire, which are dependent on
it, have met with any difturbance. No nation has
thought of feizing upon a barren fpot, where they
could find only a few cattle, fome manioc, fome vegetables proper to feed flaves, and not one article
for commerce. St. Euftatia is of ftill lefs confequence.

This ifland, which is only five leagues in length and one in breadth, is formed by two mountains, with a narrow vale between them. The eaftern mountain bears evident traces of an ancient volcano, and is hollowed almoft to the level of the fea. The borders of this gulf, which hath the figure of an inverted cone, are compofed of rocks calcined by the fire they muft have experienced. However plentiful the rains may be, there is never any collection of water in this crater. It is carried off undoubtedly through the channels of the volcano that ftill remain open, and may one day, perhaps, contribute to the rekindling of it, if its focus be not extinguifhed or at too great a diftance.

Some Frenchmen, who had been driven from St. Chriftopher's, took refuge, in 1629, in this almoft uninhabitable place, and abandoned it fome time after; perhaps becaufe there was no frefh water, but what they got from rain collected in cifterns. The exact time of their quitting it is not known; but it is certain, that in 1639 the Dutch were in poffeffion of it. They were afterwards driven out by the Englifh, and thefe by Lewis the XIVth, who caufed his right of conqueft to be recognized in the negotiation of Breda, and would not liften to the reprefentations of the republic, with which he was then in alliance, and which preffed ftrongly for the reftitution of this ifland, as having been in poffeffion of it before the war. When the figning of the peace had put an end to thefe reprefentations, the French monarch, whofe pride more readily fubmitted to the dictates of generofity than of juftice, thought it not confiftent with his dignity to take advantage of the misfortunes of his friends. He of his own accord reftored to the Dutch their ifland, although he knew that it was a natural fortrefs, which might be of fervice in defending that part of St. Chriftopher's which belonged to him.

Thefe republicans, before their difafter, cultivated only tobacco upon this territory. Since their re-eftablifhment, they have planted in the places that were

BOOK
XII.
susceptible of this kind of culture, a few sugar-canes,
from which they have only received annually eight
or nine hundred thousand weight of raw sugar.

Description
of the
Dutch
island of
Saba.
Soon after this, the colony sent some of its inhabitants to a neighbouring island, known by the name
of Saba. This is a steep rock, on the summit of
which is a little ground, very proper for gardening.
Frequent rains which do not lie any time on the soil,
give growth to plants of an exquisite flavour, and
cabbages of an extraordinary size. Fifty European
families, with about one hundred and fifty slaves,
here raise cotton, spin it, make stockings of it, and
sell them to other colonies for as much as ten crowns
[1l. 5s.] a pair. Throughout America there is no
blood so pure as that of Saba; the women there preserve a freshness of complexion, which is not to be
found in any other of the Caribbee islands. Happy
colony! elevated on the top of a rock, between the
sky and sea, it enjoys the benefit of both elements
without dreading their storms; it breathes a pure air,
lives upon vegetables, cultivates a simple commodity,
from which it derives ease, without the temptation of
riches; is employed in labours less troublesome than
useful, and possesses in peace all the blessings of moderation, health, beauty, and liberty. This is the
temple of peace from whence the philosopher may
contemplate at leisure the errors and passions of men,
who come, like the waves of the sea, to strike and
dash themselves on the rich coasts of America, the
spoils and possession of which they are perpetually
contending for, and wresting from each other; hence
may he view at a distance the nations of Europe
bearing thunder in the midst of the ocean, and burning with the flames of ambition and avarice under
the heats of the tropics; devouring gold without ever
being satisfied; wading through seas of blood to
amass those metals, those pearls, those diamonds,
which are used to adorn the oppressors of mankind;
loading innumerable ships with those precious casks,
which furnish luxury with purple, and from which

flow pleafures, effeminacy, cruelty, and debauchery. The tranquil inhabitant of Saba views this mafs of follies, and fpins his cotton in peace.

Under the fame climate lies the ifland of St. Martin, which hath feventeen or eighteen leagues in circumference, but lefs territory than might be expected from fuch dimenfions, becaufe its bays are deep and numerous. The ocean hath formed, by pufhing the fands from one cape to another, feveral lakes, more or lefs extenfive, and moft of them abounding in fifh. The inland part of the country is filled with high mountains, which extend almoft every where as far as the fea. They were covered with valuable trees, before they were ftripped of that ornament, to make room for cultures, which they were found to be better adapted to than the plains and the valleys. The foil is generally light, ftony, too much expofed to frequent droughts, and not very fertile; but the fky is pure, and the climate remarkably healthy. The navigation is fafe and eafy in thefe latitudes; and the multiplicity and excellence of the anchoring places that are found there, occafions the want of harbours to be lefs fenfibly felt.

The Dutch and French landed, in 1638, in this defert ifland, the firft to the fouth, and the latter towards the north. They lived there in peace, but feparate from each other, when the Spaniards, who were at open war with both nations, attacked them, beat them, made them prifoners, and took poffeffion of the place themfelves : but the conquerors foon grew weary of an eftablifhment, the prefervation of which was very expenfive, and from which they did not derive the leaft advantage. They therefore quitted it in 1648, after having deftroyed every thing they could not carry with them.

Thefe devaftations did not hinder the former poffeffors from fending fome vagabonds to the ifland, as foon as they knew that it was evacuated. Thefe colonifts fwore a mutual faith to each other ; and their defcendants have been faithful to this engagement

BOOK XII.

Defcription of the ifland of St. Martin, part of which belongs to the Dutch, and part to the French.

notwithſtanding the animoſities that have ſo often
diſunited the two mother-countries. But the diviſion
of the territory, originally too unequal, hath been
more equitably adjuſted. Of ten thouſand one hundred and eighty ſquares of ground, comprehending
each two thouſand five hundred ſquare toiſes, which
the iſland contains, the French poſſeſs no more than
five thouſand nine hundred and four ; and the Dutch
have ſucceeded in appropriating to themſelves four
thouſand one hundred and ſeventy-ſix.

The culture of tobacco was the firſt which the
ſubjects of the court of Verſailles undertook at St.
Martin. They abandoned it for indigo, which was
ſucceeded by cotton, to which ſugar hath been added, ſince foreigners have been permitted, from the
year 1769, to ſettle in this iſland. It reckons at preſent nineteen plantations, which yield annually one
million weight of raw ſugar, of a beautiful white colour, but of little conſiſtence ; and a ſtill greater number of dwellings, which produce two hundred thouſand weight of cotton. Theſe labours are managed
by fourſcore families, thirty-two of which are French,
and the reſt Engliſh, and which form together a population of three hundred and fifty-one white perſons, of every age and ſex. They have but twelve
thouſand ſlaves. This is too little for the extent of
the cultures : but the coloniſts of the Dutch part,
who were proprietors of the beſt lands in the French
part, have adopted the cuſtom of ſending their Negroes to the north, when the labours on the ſouth are
at an end. Before 1763, there had not been any regular ſyſtem of authority in this feeble and miſerable
ſettlement. At this period a governor was given to
it, who hath not yet attracted any trade from any
other country. The French always go in queſt of
what they want to their neighbour, and always deliver to him their productions.

The Dutch colony is inhabited by ſix hundred
and thirty-nine white men, and three thouſand five
hundred and eighteen blacks, employed in the culti-

vation of thirty-two fugar plantations, which com-
monly produce fixteen hundred thoufand weight of fugar ; and in the growth of one hundred and thirty thoufand cotton trees. This revenue, which is too infufficient, is increafed by the produce of a falt marfh, in the feafons which are not exceffively rainy. At the morning dawn, fome foldiers embark upon flat-bottomed boats ; they collect, during the courfe of the day, the falt which floats upon the furface of the water ; and at night they return to fhore, in order to begin again the next day this operation, which can only be continued during the months of June, July, and Auguft. The neighbouring iflands purchafe a fmall quantity of this production, the total value of which may amount to one hundred thoufand crowns [12,500l.] : but it is principally fent to the provinces of North America, who carry off likewife the rum and the fugar of the colony, while the cotton is delivered to the traders of Great Britain. Nothing, or fcarce any thing, is left for the active merchants of the republic, and for the following reafons :

The fettlement of St. Martin, although it belong to the Dutch, is not inhabited by Dutchmen. There are fcarce five or fix families of that nation to be found there, and thofe are even almoft afhamed of their origin. All the reft is Englifh, the people, the language, and the manners. Prejudice hath been carried fo far, as to induce the women often to go and lay in at Anguilla, a Britifh ifland, which is only two leagues diftant, in order that their children may not be deprived of an origin, which is confidered in the country as the only one that is illuftrious.

The domain of the United Provinces, in the great Advantages which the Archipelago of America, doth not offer any thing trade of either curious or interefting, at the firft afpect. Pof- Holland acfeffions, which fcarce furnifh a cargo for fix or feven quires from her iflands. fmall veffels, do not appear worthy of any attention. Accordingly, they would be buried in total oblivion, if fome of thefe iflands, which are nothing as places

BOOK for cultivation, were not very considerable as com-
XII. mercial islands. We mean those of St. Eustatia and
of Curassou.

The desire of forming contraband connections with
the Spanish provinces of the New World, decided
the conquest of Curassou. A great number of Dutch
vessels soon arrived there. They were strong, well
armed, and their crews consisted of choice men,
whose bravery was supported by powerful motives of
interest. Each of them had a share, more or less
considerable, in the cargo, which he was determined
to defend with his life against the attacks of the
Guarda Costas.

The Spaniards did not always wait for the smug-
glers. They often resorted of themselves to a staple,
which was constantly well supplied, in order to barter
their gold, their silver, their bark, their cacao, their
tobacco, their hides, and their cattle, for Negroes,
linens, silks, Indian stuffs, spices, quicksilver, and iron
or steel manufactures. This was a reciprocal connection of wants and of assistance, of labours and of
expeditions, between two nations, greedy of riches,
and rivals of each other.

The settlement of the company of Caraccas, and
the substitution of the register ships to the galleons,
hath much diminished this communication : but the
connections which have been formed with the south
part of the French colony of St. Domingo, have made
up in some measure for this deficiency. Every thing
is revived, when the two crowns are plunged into the
horrors of war, either by their own ambition, or by
the ambition of their rivals. Even in time of peace,
the republic receives annually from Curassou, twelve
vessels laden with sugar, coffee, cotton, indigo, tobacco, and hides, which have been cultivated in a
foreign soil.

Every commodity, without exception, that is landed at Curassou, pays one per cent. port-duty. Dutch
goods are never taxed higher ; but those that are
shipped from other European ports pay nine per cent.

more. Foreign coffee is fubject to the fame tax, in order to promote the fale of that of Surinam. Every other production of America is fubject only to a payment of three per cent. but with an exprefs ftipulation, that they are to be conveyed directly to fome port of the republic.

St. Euftatia was formerly fubject to the fame impofitions as Curaffou; and yet it carried on moft of the trade of Guadaloupe and of Martinico, during the time that thefe French fettlements remained under the odious yoke of monopoly. This bufinefs diminifhed in proportion as the proprietors of thofe iflands adopted found principles of commerce, and extended their navigation. The free port of St. Thomas was even carrying off from the Dutch the fmall fhare of trade they had ftill retained, when in 1756 it was refolved to abolifh moft of the eftablifhed taxes. Since this neceffary alteration, St. Euftatia, during the divifions between the minifters of London and Verfailles, is become the ftaple of almoft all the merchandife of the French colonies in the Leeward Iflands, and the general magazine of fupply for them. But this great operation was not conducted fingly by the Dutch; both Englifh and French united in the harbour of this ifland, to form, under fhelter of its neutrality, commercial engagements. A Dutch paffport, which coft lefs than 300 livres [12l. 10s.], concealed thefe connections, and was granted, without inquiring of what nation the perfon was who applied for it. This great liberty gave rife to numberlefs tranfactions and to fingular combinations. Thus it is that commerce found the art of pacifying or eluding the vigilance of difcord.

The end of hoftilities doth not render St. Euftatia of lefs importance. It ftill fends annually to the United Provinces, twenty-five or thirty veffels, laden with the productions of the Spanifh and Danifh, and efpecially of the French iflands, which it pays for with the merchandife of the two hemifpheres, or with bills of exchange upon Europe.

All thefe tranfactions have brought together, at St. Euftatia, fix thoufand white people, of various nations, five hundred Negroes or Mulattoes, and eight thoufand flaves. A governor, affifted by a council, without which nothing material can be decided, directs, under the authority of the Weft India Company, this fingular fettlement, as well as thofe of Saba and St. Martin. He refides near a very dangerous anchorage, which, however, is the only one of the ifland where the veffels can land and take in their cargoes. This bad harbour is protected by a fmall fort, and by a garrifon of fifty men. If it were defended with vigour and fkill, the moft daring enemy would, in all probability, fail in attempting a defcent, which, if even effected, the befieger would ftill find an almoft infurmountable difficulty to conquer, in afcending from the lower town, where the magazines are kept, to the upper town, where all the inhabitants are affembled in the night-time.

The Dutch, however, equally ingenious in finding out the means of turning to their own advantage both the profperity and the misfortunes of others, are not entirely confined, in the New World, to the fluctuating profits of a precarious trade. The republic poffeffes and cultivates, on the continent, a large territory in the country known by the name of Guyana.

Philofophical confiderations on Guyana.
This is a vaft country, wafhed on the Eaft by the fea, on the South by the Amazon, on the North by the Oroonoko, and on the Weft by Rio-Negro, which joins thefe two rivers, that are the largeft in South America.

This fingular ifland prefents three remarkable circumftances. The feveral fpecies of earth are not here difpofed, as they are elfewhere, in layers, but cafually mixed, and without any order. In the correfpondent hills, the falient angles of the one are not anfwerable to the re-entering angles of the others. The fubftances, which have been generally taken for flints, are nothing more than pieces of lava, that are beginning to be decompounded.

It follows from thefe obfervations, that fome revolutions have happened in this part of the globe, and that they have been the work of fubterraneous fires, at prefent extinguifhed ; that the conflagration has been general, becaufe maffes are every where feen, filled with the fcoriæ of iron ; and that calcareous ftones, which probably have been all calcined, are not to be found in any part ; that the explofion muft have been very confiderable, and muft have levied a great quantity of earth, becaufe volcanoes are only to be found upon the higheft mountains, and that the only one on which the crater hath been perceived in thefe regions, is raifed little more than a hundred feet above the level of the fea.

At the period of thefe great accidents of nature, every thing muft have been fubverted. The fields muft have remained uncovered, alternately expofed to the action of torrents of rain, or to the effects of exceffive heat. In this ftate of revolution, many centuries muft have elapfed before the foil can have again become fit to nourifh the plants, and after them the trees. We might however be liable to miftake, if we were to compute this change at an exceffive diftance. The fmall quantity of vegetating earth found in Guyana, although fome be continually formed there by the decompofition of the trees, would furnifh an unanfwerable argument againft the idea of a very remote antiquity.

In the inland parts of the country, the foil is therefore, and will continue for a long time, ungrateful. The upper lands, that is to fay, thofe which are not under water, or marfhy, are for the moft part nothing more than a confufed mixture of clay and chalk, where nothing can grow but manioc, yams, potatoes, and fome other plants, which do not turn round on the ftem ; and even thefe are too frequently rooted in the feafon of heavy rains, becaufe the water cannot be drained off. Even in thofe lands, which are

B O O K   neceffarily looked upon as good, the coffee, the cacao,
XII.   the cotton plants, and all the ufeful trees, laft but
for a very fhort time, and not fufficiently to reward
the labours of the cultivator. Such is, without exception, the interior part of Guyana.

Its fhores prefent another fpectacle. The numerous rivers, which from this vaft fpace precipitate
themfelves in the ocean, depofit inceffantly upon their
borders, and upon the whole coaft, a prodigious quantity of feeds, which germinate in the flime, and produce, in lefs than ten years, lofty trees, known by
the name of mangroves. Thefe large vegetables,
attached to their bafis by deep roots, occupy all the
fpace where the tide is perceptible. They form vaft
forefts, covered with four or five feet of water during
flood, and at the time of ebb, with an equal depth
of a foft and inacceffible mud.

This fpectacle, which is perhaps not to be equalled
in the univerfe, varies every year upon the coaft. In
the places where fands are brought and accumulated
by the currents, the mangrove perifhes with great
rapidity, and the forefts are carried away by the
waves, and difappear. Thefe revolutions are lefs frequent on the borders of the rivers, where the fands,
brought from the mountains during the ftorms, are
conveyed to a diftance by the rapidity of the waters.

The revolutions are the fame upon the coaft of four
hundred leagues, which extends from the Amazon to
the Oronooko. There is every where found, upon
the fhore, a line of mangroves, alternately deftroyed
and renewed by the flime and by the fand. Behind
this row, at the diftance of four or five hundred feet,
are found favannahs, deluged by the rain waters, which
have no drain ; and thefe favannahs are always extended laterally towards the fhore, to a depth more or lefs
confiderable, according to the diftance or nearnefs
of the mountains.

Thefe immenfe moraffes have never been paffed by
any thing but reptiles fince the creation. The genius
of man, prevailing over an ungrateful and rebellious

foil, hath altered their primitive deftination. It is in
the midft of thefe ftagnating, infectious, and muddy
waters, that the fpirit of liberty hath formed three
ufeful fettlements, the moft confiderable of which is
Surinam.

Six years afterwards, there appeared in this forfaken fpot fome of thofe Frenchmen, whom a reft-
lefs difpofition then hurried into all climates, and
whom their volatile turn prevented from fettling in
moft of them. They maffacred the natives of the
country, began to conftruct a fort, and difappeared.

Settlement
formed by
the Dutch
in Guyana,
upon the
river Suri-
nam. Re-
markable
events

Their retreat brought back, in 1650, the nation
that had firft turned their attention to that fo long
neglected part of the New Hemifphere. The colony
had formed forty or fifty fugar plantations, when it
was attacked and taken by the Dutch, who were fecured in their conqueft by the treaty of Breda.

Zealand pretended to have the exclufive right over
this ufeful acquifition, becaufe it had been gained by
their troops and their fhips. The other provinces,
who had fhared the expences of the expedition, infifted that it fhould belong in common to them all.
This difcuffion had for a long time inflamed the
minds of the people, when it was refolved in 1682,
that Surinam fhould be given up to the Weft India
Company, but upon condition that they fhould pay
572,000 livres [23,833l. 6s. 8d.] to the Zealanders;
that the trade of the Company fhould be limited to
the fale of flaves; and that the country fhould be
open to all the fubjects and to all the traders of the
republic.

Although the imagination of this great Company
was filled with remembrance of their former profperity, they foon comprehended, that the expences
required to eftablifh cultures throughout an immenfe
region were above their exhaufted ftrength. The
year following they ceded one third of their right
to the city of Amfterdam, and one-third to a rich
citizen, whofe name was Van Aarfen, at a price proportioned to what they themfelves paid for it. This

B O O K extraordinary arrangement lafted till 1772, at which
XII. period the defcendants of Van Aarfen fold their property for 1,540,000 livres [64,166l. 13s. 4d.] to the
two other members of the affociation.

The Company found Surinam plunged into thofe
diforders which are the neceffary confequence of a
long ftate of anarchy. Their reprefentative wanted
to eftablifh fome kind of police, fome kind of juftice.
He was accufed of tyranny to the States General,
and maffacred in 1688 by the troops.

The colony was attacked the year following by the
French, under the command of Ducaffe. The fkill
of this chief, and the efforts of the brave adventurers
who attended him, were not powerful enough againft
a fettlement, where the civil and military troubles
had caufed a fermentation in the minds of men, who
had juft been reconciled by a profpect of imminent
danger. Caffard, a native of St. Malo, was more
fortunate in 1712. He laid Surinam under contributions, and carried off to the amount of 1,370,160
livres [57,290l.], in fugar, or in bills of exchange.
This difafter, fo much more unexpected as it happened at a time when the arms of the republic were triumphant every where elfe, diftreffed the planters,
who were obliged to give a tenth of their capitals.

The fociety were accufed of having neglected the
fortifications, and of having employed, to defend
them, only a few troops, and thofe ill-difciplined.
Thefe complaints were foon extended to more ferious
objects. The reafons, or the pretences for difcontent,
were multiplied daily. The States General, wearied
with all thefe contefts, charged the Stadtholder to
put an end to them in whatever manner he might
think the moft proper. This firft magiftrate had not
yet fucceeded in conciliating the minds of the people, when it became neceffary to attend to the fafety of the colony.

Scarce had the Englifh fettled on the banks of the
Surinam, before feveral of their flaves took refuge
in the inland countries. The defertion was ftill more

considerable under the Dutch dominion, becaufe they required more conftant labours, becaufe the quantity of fubfiftence was diminifhed, and more fevere punifhments were inflicted. Thefe fugitives, in procefs of time, became numerous enough to form a colony. They ufed to quit their place of refuge in a body, in order to fupply themfelves with provifions, arms, and inftruments of agriculture ; and they brought back with them the Negroes who chofe to go with them. Some attempts were made to put a ftop to thefe excurfions; but they were fruitlefs, and could not be otherwife. Soldiers grown effeminate, officers without merit and without a fenfe of honour, had an infurmountable averfion for a war, where deep moraffes and thick forefts were to be paffed, in order to get within reach of a bold and implacable enemy.

The danger became at laft fo urgent, that the republic thought proper to fend, in 1749, in 1772, and in 1774, fome of their beft battalions to the affiftance of the colony. All that thefe brave men, arrived from Europe, have been able to accomplifh, after various and bloody engagements, has been to procure fome kind of tranquillity to the planters, who were before every day in danger of being either ruined or murdered. It hath been neceffary fucceffively to acknowledge the independence of feveral numerous hordes, but which have no communication with each other, and are feparated by confiderable diftances. Annual prefents are fent them, and it hath been ftipulated that they fhould enjoy all the advantages of a free trade. Thefe new nations have on their part agreed only to affift their ally, if it be neceffary ; and to return them every flave who fhall take refuge upon their territory. To give a fanction to thefe feveral treaties, the plenipotentiaries of the contracting parties have caufed an incifion to be made in their arms. The blood was received in vafes filled with water and earth. This difgufting mixture hath been drunk on both fides, in token of fidelity. If they

B O O K had refufed to fubmit to this extreme humiliating ftep,
XII. thefe oppreffive mafters would never have obtained a
peace from their former flaves.

Caufes of   After fo many fatal events, the colony is ftill be-
the profpe- come more flourifhing than could have been expect-
rity of the
colony of ed. The caufes of this furprifing profperity cannot
Surinam. but be curious and interefting.

The firft Europeans who fettled in thofe barbarous
regions, eftablifhed their cultures at firft upon heights,
which were commonly barren. It was foon fufpected
that their faline particles had been detached by the
torrents ; and that it was from thefe fucceffive layers
of an excellent flime, that the lower grounds had
been formed. Some fortunate experiments confirmed this judicious conjecture ; and it was determined
to take advantage of fo great a difcovery. This was
not an eafy undertaking, but the defire of fuccefs furmounted all obftacles.

Thefe vaft plains are overflowed by the rivers with
which they are watered, but not during the whole
year. Even in the feafon of the overflowings, the
waters are diffufed a little before and a little after the
times of high water. During the ebb, the rivers retire gradually, and at low water are fometimes feveral feet below the foil, which they covered fix hours
before.

The drying up of thefe grounds muft be begun
when the rains are not abundant, and when the rivers are low. This feafon begins in Auguft, and ends
in the month of December. During this period, the
fpace which is to be fecured from inundations is furrounded with a dyke, fufficient to refift the waters.
It is feldom neceffary to raife it above three feet high,
becaufe it is not ufual to choofe a territory that is
more than two feet under water, to fettle a plantation
upon.

At one of the corners of the dyke, which is made
of the earth of the ditch digged for that purpofe, is
an hydraulic machine, entirely open on one fide, cut
on the other in the fhape of a beak, and furnifhed

with a flood-gate, which is opened by the impulse of the waters from below upwards, and which shuts again by its own weight. When the agitation of the sea swells the waves, the rivers press upon this flood-gate, and close it so effectually, that the waters on the outside cannot get into it. When, on the contrary, the rivers are low, the internal and rain waters, if there be any, raise the gate up, and the waters run off very easily.

In the inner part of the dyke, at different distances from each other, a few slight trenches are made. They all terminate in a ditch, which surrounds the plantation. This precaution contributes to raise the soil, and to carry off any superfluous moisture that might remain.

The labours of one year are sufficient to surround the territory which is intended to be enclosed. It is ploughed the second year, and might be cultivated at the beginning of the third, if it were not absolutely necessary to leave it for a sufficient length of time exposed to the influence of the fresh water, in order to counteract the action of the marine salts. This circumstance necessarily retards the crops more than could be wished ; but the abundance of them compensates for the delay.

The coffee-tree, which is generally planted in other colonies upon the sloping grounds, leaves sooner or later a void, which cannot be filled up, either by another coffee-tree, or by any other plant, because the storms have successively deprived this soil of every thing that rendered it fertile. This is not the case at Surinam. This valuable tree doth not, indeed, preserve its vigour more than about twenty years ; but the young plants, put between the old ones, and intended to succeed them, prevent the planter from being sensible of this premature decay. This is the reason that the crops are never interrupted. They are even more plentiful than in the other settlements.

The disposition of the sugar plantations, in those singular marshes, have this peculiarity attending them,

that the territory is interfected by feveral fmall canals, deftined for the conveyance of the fugar-canes.
They all terminate in the great canal, which receives the waters when they rife, by one of its outlets ; and by the other works a mill, when they defcend. The firft production in thefe plantations is
very indifferent ; but it acquires, in procefs of time,
the proper degree of perfection. This may be waited
for with lefs impatience in a region where the canes,
at their fifth or fixth crop, yield as much fugar as is
obtained elfewhere from the new-planted canes. One
of the principles of this fertility muft be, the facility
with which the planters can furround their habitations with water during the dry feafon. The habitual
moifture which this method keeps up in the grounds,
appears preferable to the watering of them, which is
practifed in other parts at a confiderable expence, and
which cannot even be always done every where.

Since the Dutch have fucceeded in fubduing the
ocean in the New World as well as in the Old, their
cultures have profpered. They have carried them on
twenty leagues beyond the fea, and given to their plantations an agreeable afpect and convenience, which
are not to be perceived in the moft flourifhing poffeffions of the Englifh or French. Spacious and well-
contrived buildings, terraces perfectly ftraight, kit-
chen-gardens exquifitely neat, delightful orchards,
and walks planted with fymmetry, ftrike the eye on
all fides. So many wonders, accomplifhed in lefs than
a century, in floughs that were originally difgufting
and unwholefome, cannot be viewed without emotion. But the fevere eye of reafon puts a reftraint on
the tranfports excited by this enchanting fcene. The
capitals employed in thefe fuperfluities would be more
wifely laid out in the multiplication of vendible productions.

One of the means by which labour, and that kind
of luxury that hath been introduced, have been chiefly encouraged, has been the extreme facility which
the colonifts have found in getting a capital. They

have obtained all the money they could make ufe of, at the rate of five or fix per cent. but with the exprefs condition, that their plantations fhould remain mortgaged to their creditor ; and that till the fum was entirely paid off, they fhould be obliged to give up to him all their productions at the current price in the colony.

With the affiftance of thefe loans, four hundred and thirty plantations have been formed on the banks of the Surinam, of the Commenwine, of the rivers of Cottica and of Perica. In 1775, they yielded twenty-four millions one hundred and twenty thoufand weight of rough fugar, which was fold in Holland for 8,333,400 livres [347,225l.] ; fifteen millions three hundred and eighty-feven pounds weight of coffee, which were fold for 8,580,934 livres [357,538l. 18s. 4d.] ; nine hundred and feventy thoufand pounds weight of cotton, which were fold for 2,372,255 livres [98,843l. 19s. 2d.] ; feven hundred and ninety thoufand eight hundred and fifty-four pounds weight of cacao, which were fold for 616,370 livres [25,682l. 1s. 8d.] ; one hundred and fifty-two thoufand eight hundred and forty-four pounds weight of wood for dyeing, which were fold for 14,788 livres [616l. 13s. 4d.]. The fum total of thefe productions amounted to 19,917,747 livres [822,905l. 19s. 2d.], and was brought into the harbours of the republic upon feventy veffels. The number of thefe veffels would have increafed, if the five hundred and fixty thoufand gallons of molaffes, and the hundred and fixty-fix gallons of rum, fent to North America, had been conveyed to Europe ; and they will ftill increafe, if the tobacco which hath juft begun to be planted, fhould thrive as well as is expected.

The united labours of thefe fettlements, employed in 1775 fixty thoufand flaves of every age and fex. They belonged to two thoufand eight hundred and twenty-four mafters, exclufive of the women and children. The white people were of feveral countries and of different religions.

BOOK
XII.

Such is the influence of the fpirit of trade, that it forces all national and religious prejudices to fubmit to that general intereft, which fhould be the bond of union among mankind. What are thofe idle nominal diftinctions of Jews or Chriftians, French or Dutch? Miferable inhabitants of a fpot, which ye cultivate with fo much toil and forrow, are ye not all brethren? Why then do ye drive each other from a world, where ye live but for an inftant? And what a life too is. it, that ye have the folly and cruelty to difpute with each other the enjoyment of? Is it not fufficient, that the elements, the heavens, and even the earth, combat againft you, but ye muft add to thofe fcourges, with which nature hath furrounded you, the abufe of that little ftrength fhe has left you to refift them?

Paramabiro, the principal place of the colony of Surinam, is a fmall town pleafantly fituated. The houfes are pretty and convenient; though they are only built of wood upon a foundation of European bricks. Its port, which is five leagues diftant from the fea, has every requifite that can be defired. It is the rendezvous of all the fhips difpatched from the mother-country to receive the produce of this colony. The Company to which this large fettlement belongs, is obliged to defray the public expences. The fovereign hath enabled them to fulfil this obligation, by permitting them to levy fome taxes, which cannot be increafed without the confent of the ftate and of the inhabitants. A poll-tax of one hundred fols [4s. 2d.] upon every free adult or flave, and of fixty fols [2s. 6d.] for every child, was formerly the higheft of thefe contributions. In 1776, it hath been changed for another lefs degrading, of fix per cent. upon the productions of the country, upon the profits of trade, and upon the wages of the feveral occupations. Neverthelefs, the payment of two and a half per cent. for the commodities which were exported from the colony, and of one and a half per cent. for thofe which were imported, hath not been difcontinued. Thefe taxes united, are fcarce fufficient for the great object for which they are defigned, and there is feldom any thing remaining for the benefit of the Company.

Befide the taxes levied for the Company, there is one which is rather confiderable, upon the productions of the colony, which the citizens have agreed to eftablifh themfelves for their refpective wants, and efpecially for the pay of three hundred free Negroes, who are employed in protecting the cultures from the incurfions of the fugitive Negroes.

Notwithstanding all thefe impofts, and notwithftanding the obligation of paying the intereft of 77,000,000 livres [3,208,333l. 6s. 8d.], the colony was in a flourifhing ftate, while its productions had a certain and advantageous mart. But fince coffee hath loft in trade one half of its former price, every thing is fallen into extreme confufion ; the debtor is become infolvent, hath been driven from his plantation. Even the moft mercilefs creditor hath not been able to recover his capital, and they have both been ruined. Men have become ftill more exafperated againft each other, their minds have been depreffed, and it is difficult to forefee at what period concord and induftry will revive. Let us examine what hath been the fate of Berbice, during this fatal crifis.

This fettlement, bounded on the eaft by the river Corentin, and on the weft by the territory of Demerary, extends no more than ten leagues along the coaft. In the inland part of the country it might reach as far as that part of the Cordeleras, known by the name of the Blue Mountains. The great river from which it hath derived its name, being choked up at its mouth by a bank of mud and fand, hath at firft no more than fourteen or fifteen feet in depth ; but it foon acquires forty, and its navigation is eafy as far as thirty-fix leagues from the fea, which is the utmoft extent of the moft diftant plantations.

The foundations of this colony were laid in 1626. As it was formed in a diftrict included in the grant given to the Weft India Company, that body, which was at that time powerful and ftrongly protected, re-

BOOK
XII.
served to themselves some privileges, and more especially the exclusive sale of slaves. The culture of sugar and arnotto, which were the only articles attended to, had not made any considerable progress, when, in 1689, some French adventurers ravaged the country, and did not leave it till they had extorted the promise of 44,000 livres [1833l. 6s. 8d.], which were never paid. Some Frenchmen invaded the colonies again in 1712. In order to escape pillage, and to get rid of these foreigners, the inhabitants engaged to give them 660,000 livres [27,500l.]. The Negroes, the sugar, and the provisions which were delivered amounted to 28,654 livres 4 sols [1193l. 18s. 6d.], the remainder was to be paid in Europe by the proprietors of the habitations, who all belonged to the province of Zealand. Whether from inability, or through design, they refused to ratify an engagement entered into without their consent. Three rich individuals of Amsterdam fulfilled the obligation, and became sole proprietors of Berbice.

They conducted themselves with prudence and moderation. They restored the ancient plantations, they introduced a better method among those who cultivated them ; they added the culture of cacao to to those which were already known : but their capital was not sufficient to raise the colony to that degree of prosperity of which it appeared to be susceptible; 7,040,000 livres [293,333l. 6s. 8d.] were thought necessary for this great object, and sixteen shares, each of 4400 livres [183l. 6s. 8d.], were created. They were not able to dispose of more than nine hundred and forty-one, upon which even the purchasers did not furnish more than 42 per cent. Thus the new capital was reduced to 1,573,352 livres [65,556l. 6s. 3d.], out of which 1,320 000 livres [55,000l.] belonged to the former Company for the cession of all their property ; so that the remainder of the money amounted to no more than 273,352 livres [11,389l. 13s. 4d.].

This was a very small sum to answer the intended purpose. The proprietors were themselves so well

convinced of it, that in 1730 they required that every B O O K
fubject of the ftate fhould be allowed to trade to Ber- XII.
bice and to fettle there, upon condition of paying in
America fix livres [5s.] poll-tax for every white man,
and for every Negro they fhould place upon their habitation 55 livres [2l. 5s. 10d.] per plantation, towards the ecclefiaftical contribution; two and a half
per cent. for all the merchandife which fhould enter
the colony, or for the provifions which fhould be carried out of it; and in Europe 3 livres [2s. 6d.] per
ton, for every thing they fhould receive from the
ports of the republic, and 3 livres [2s. 6d.] per ton for
every article they fhould fend there. With thefe af-
fiftances, the Company engaged to defray all the expences that fhould be wanted for government, for defence, for the police, and for the legiflation of that
fettlement. The States General approved of this plan,
and gave it the fanction of their laws, by a decree of
the 6th December 1732.

A tolerable degree of activity was the fortunate
refult of thefe new arrangements. Every thing was
in a profperous ftate, when, in 1756, the white people, and they alone, were attacked with an epidemical diforder which lafted feven years, and deftroyed
the greateft number of them. The ftate of weaknefs
to which Berbice was reduced by this calamity, encouraged the flaves to rebel in 1763. Upon the firft
intimation of this infurrection, twenty foldiers, and a
few colonifts who had efcaped the contagion, took
refuge upon four veffels that were in the river, and
foon after fecured themfelves in a redoubt built near
the ocean. They were at length enabled, by the
affiftance fent from all quarters to them, to return to
their plantations, and even to fubdue the Negroes;
but their authority was eftablifhed only upon ruins
and upon dead bodies.

The Company being ruined, as well as the inhabitants, were obliged to call upon the holders of
fhares for a contribution of eight per cent. which
made up the fum of 330,000 livres [13,750l.], and to

B O O K
XII.

borrow 1,100,000 livres [45,833l. 6s. 8d.] of the province of Holland, at the intereſt of two and a half
per cent. Theſe ſums not being yet ſufficient to fulfil their obligations, they obtained of the republic in
1774, that the taxes levied till this period ſhould for
the future be doubled. The new taxes threw the
planters, already too much diſcouraged by the total
loſs of their cacao trees, and by the enormous reduction of the price of their coffee, into deſpair. Accordingly this ſettlement, upon which ſo great hopes
had been founded, is continually decreaſing.

There are but one hundred and four plantations
in the colony, moſt of which are inconſiderable, ſcattered at great diſtances upon the banks of the river
Berbice, or upon that of Canje, which empties itſelf
in the firſt, at three leagues diſtance from the ſea.
Their population conſiſts of ſeven thouſand ſlaves of
every age and ſex, and of two hundred and fifty
white men, excluſive of the ſoldiers, who ought to
amount to the ſame number. The coffee, the ſugar,
and cotton they produce annually, is conveyed to the
mother-country upon four or five ſhips, and is not
ſold for more than one million, or twelve hundred
thouſand livres [from 41,666l. 13s. 4d. to 50,000l.].
From this ſum an intereſt of ſix per cent. ought to be
deducted, which the coloniſts have engaged to pay
for about 1,760,000 livres [73,333l. 6s. 8d.], which
they have borrowed ; but this is an obligation which
it is not in their power to fulfil. The lenders are
obliged to be ſatisfied with four, three, or two per
cent. Several of them even do not receive any
thing.

Although, according to the calculations delivered
in 1772 to the States General, the annual expences
of ſovereignty do not exceed in Europe and in America 190,564 livres [7940l. 3s. 4d.] ; the Company
are neverthelefs in a deſperate ſituation. From 1720
to 1763, the united dividends have not amounted to
more than 61 per cent. which makes, one year with
another, no more than $1\frac{18}{43}$. After this period there

hath been no more dividend. Accordingly, the
shares, which have cost 2200 livres [9l. 13s. 4d.],
are no longer marketable, they would not sell for
110 livres [4l. 11s. 8d.]. A very different idea must
be formed of the colony of Essequibo.

This river, twelve leagues distant from that of Berbice, first attracted the attention of the Dutch, who,
as well as the other Europeans, infested Guyana with
their plunders towards the end of the sixteenth century, in hopes of finding gold there. It is unknown
at what precise period they settled at Essequibo ; but
it is certain that they were driven from it by the Spaniards in 1595.

It is evident that these republicans returned to
their post, since they were again expelled from it in
1666 by the English, and even they could not maintain themselves there for one whole year. This settlement, which had always been inconsiderable, was
reduced to nothing when the Dutch retook possession
of it. In 1740 its productions did not form more
than the cargo of one single vessel.

Two or three years after, some of the colonists
of Essequibo turned their attention towards the
neighbouring river of Demerary. Its borders were
found very fertile, and this discovery was attended
with fortunate circumstances.

For some time past the clearing of the lands had
been suspended at Surinam, by the bloody and ruinous war which the colonists sustained against the Negroes assembled in the woods. Berbice was likewise
disturbed by the revolt of its slaves. The West India
Company seized this favourable opportunity of invit-
ing enterprising men of all nations, to share in the
grant that had been made to them. Those who arrived there with a small share of property, received
gratuitously a certain extent of territory, with some
other encouragements. They were even assured,
that after their first labours, they should obtain a loan
of the value of three fifths of the settlements they
should have formed upon moderate terms. This ar-

Antiquity
of the colo-
ny of Esse-
quibo.
Cause of its
prosperity,
after hav-
ing remain-
ed for a long
time in a
languid
state.

B O O K rangement became a fruitful fource of induftry, of
XII.   activity, and of economy. In 1769, there were already eftablifhed upon the banks of the Demerary,
one hundred and thirty habitations, in which fugar,
coffee, and cotton, were cultivated with fuccefs. The
number of plantations hath much increafed fince
that period, and it will ftill increafe a great deal
more.

Confufion   Such is the ftate of the three colonies which the
that pre-
vails in the Dutch have fucceffively formed in Guyana. It is
Dutch co- deplorable, and will remain fo for a long while, per-
lonies.   haps for ever, unlefs government in their wifdom, in
their generofity, and in their courage, can fuggeft
fome expedient to relieve the planters from the oppreffive burden of the debts which they have contracted.

In modern times, the governments themfelves have
fet the example of loans. The facility of obtaining
them at an intereft more or lefs burdenfome, hath
engaged or fupported almoft all of them, in wars, in-
compatible with their natural refources. This folly
hath infected the cities, the provinces, and the feveral affociations of men. The large trading companies
have alfo greatly extended this cuftom ; and it hath
afterwards become familiar to bold men, urged by
their difpofition to extraordinary enterprifes.

The Dutch, who, in proportion to their territory
and to their population, had accumulated a greater
quantity of metals than any other people, and who
did not find a ufe for them in their own tranfactions,
extenfive even as they were, have endeavoured to
place them to advantage in the public funds of all
nations, and even in the fpeculative undertakings of
individuals. Their money hath ferved particularly
to cultivate fome foreign colonies in America, and
principally their own. But the precaution they had
taken of having the plantations of their debtors mortgaged to them, hath not produced the effect which
they expected from it. They have never been reimburfed their capital, and have even never received

the intereſt of their money, ſince the proviſions of thoſe ſettlements have been reduced in their price. The contracts made with the planters, who are reduced to a ſtate of indigence, have fallen fifty, ſixty, eighty per cent. below their original value.

This is a matter totally ruinous. It would be in vain to examine, whether it muſt be attributed to the avidity of the merchants ſettled at Amſterdam, or to the inactivity and idle expences of the coloniſts removed beyond the ſeas. Theſe diſcuſſions would not diminiſh the evil. We will leave ſuch idle queſtions to be diſcuſſed by idle men, let them write and diſpute ; if no good ſhould reſult from this, there is not much harm in it. But it is exertion, and not diſcourſe, that is required in a conflagration. While time would be loſt in examining what hath been the cauſe of the fire, what ravages it hath made, and what its progreſs hath been, the building would be reduced to aſhes. A matter of a very urgent nature ſhould engage the attention of the States General. Let them relieve that vaſt extent of country ſubject to Holland, from the river Poumaron to that of Marony, from the anxiety it labours under, and from the miſery with which it is oppreſſed, and let them afterwards remove the other obſtacles which ſo obſtinately impede its advancement.

That difficulty which ariſes from the climate, appears the moſt unſurmountable. In this region, the year is divided between continual rains and exceſſive heats. Diſguſting reptiles are inceſſantly attacking the crops purchaſed by the moſt aſſiduous labours. The coloniſts run the riſk of periſhing, either by dropſies, or by fevers of all kinds. Authority is unavailing againſt theſe ſcourges of nature. The only remedy, if there can be one, muſt be the work of time, of population, and of the clearing of the lands.

What the laws can, and what they ought to do, would be to unite to the body of the republic, poſſeſſions which are in a manner caſually abandoned to private aſſociations, who do not attend ſufficiently

BOOK
XII.
or in a proper manner, to the feveral parts of adminiftration in the countries fubject to their monopoly.
States have been all convinced, fooner or later, of
the inconvenience of leaving the provinces they have
invaded in the other hemifphere to chartered companies, whofe interefts feldom coincided with thofe of
the public. They have at length underftood, that
the diftance did not alter the nature of the exprefs
or tacit covenant made between adminiftration and
the fubjects; and that when the fubjects have faid,
we will obey, we will ferve, we will contribute to the
formation and to the maintenance of the public
ftrength, and that the miniftry have anfwered, we
will protect you within by our police and by our
laws, and without by negotiations and by arms, thefe
conditions ought equally to be fulfilled on both fides,
from one bank of a river to the oppofite fide, from
one fhore of the fea to that which is oppofed to it:
they have underftood, that the ftipulated protection
being withdrawn, the obedience and the promifed
fuccours were of courfe fufpended; that if the affift-
ances fhould be required, when the protection had
ceafed, adminiftration would degenerate into a tyrannical fyftem of plunder; and that the people were
releafed from the oath of fidelity towards them; that
they were entitled to free themfelves from a bad mafter, and at liberty to choofe another; that they returned to a ftate of abfolute freedom, and recovered
the prerogative of inftituting any form of government
that might be thought moft fuitable to them. From
thefe circumftances, ftates have concluded, that their
fubjects of the New World had as much right as thofe
of the Old, to depend upon government only; and
that their colonies would be in a more flourifhing
condition under the immediate protection of the ftate,
than under that of any intervening power. The fuccefs hath generally demonftrated the folidity of thefe
views. None but the United Provinces have adhered
to the original plan. This infatuation cannot laft;
whenever it fhall be diffipated, the revolution will be

effected without commotion, becaufe none of the af- fociations which muft be abolifhed have any intereft in oppofing it : it will even be accomplifhed without embarraffment, becaufe none of thofe affociations have one fingle veffel, or carry on the leaft trade. The Dutch poffeffions in Guyana will then form one en- tire ftate, capable of making fome refiftance.

In the prefent ftate of things, Berbice and Effe- quibo are fcarce able to repulfe an enterprifing pirate, and would be obliged to capitulate at the appearance of the fmalleft fquadron. The eaftern part, which by its wealth is expofed to greater danger, is better de- fended. The entrance of the Surinam river is not very practicable, on account of its fand-banks. Ships, however, that do not draw more than twenty feet water, can come in at flood. At two leagues from its outlet, the Commenwine joins the Surinam. This point of union the Dutch have principally fortified. They have erected a battery on the Surinam, another on the right bank of the Commenwine, and on the left bank a citadel called Amfterdam. Thefe works form a triangle ; and their fires, which crofs each other, are contrived to have the double effect of pre- venting fhips from proceeding further up one river, and from entering into the other. The fortrefs is fi- tuated in the middle of a fmall morafs, and is inac- ceffible, except by a narrow caufeway entirely com- manded by the artillery. It requires no more than eight or nine hundred men to garrifon it completely. It is flanked with four baftions, and furrounded with a mud rampart, a wide ditch full of water, and a good covered-way : for the reft, it is unprovided with powder magazines, hath no vaults, nor any kind of cafement. Three leagues higher up on the Surinam, is a mafked battery, intended to cover the harbour and town of Paramabiro. It is called Fort Zealand. A battery of the fame kind, which they call Somme- fwelt fort, covers the Commenwine at nearly the fame diftance. The forces of the colony confift of its mi-

B O O K litia, and twelve hundred regulars, and of two com-
XII. panies of artillery.

If this fettlement were united to the two others,
and if all thefe divided territories were joined, they
would mutually affift each other. The republic itfelf,
accuftomed to caft a watchful eye upon a domain become more particularly its own property, would protect it with all its power. The fea and land forces
would be employed to fhelter it from the dangers
with which it might be threatened on the fide of Europe, and to relieve it from the ftate of anxiety with
which it is continually agitated even on the continent.·

The Dutch exercifed againft the Negroes in Guyana, cruelties unknown in the iflands. The facility
of defertion in an immenfe territory, hath probably
occafioned this excefs of barbarity. A flave is put
to death by his mafter upon the flighteft fufpicions,
in prefence of all the other flaves, but with the precaution of keeping the white men out of fight, becaufe they alone might give their teftimony in a court
of juftice againft this ufurpation of public authority.

Thefe cruelties have fucceffively driven to the forefts a confiderable multitude of thefe deplorable victims of an infamous avarice. A fharp and bloody
war hath been carried on againft them without a poffibility of deftroying them. Their independence hath
at length been neceffarily acknowledged, and fince
thefe remarkable treaties they have formed feveral
hamlets, where they cultivate in peace, upon the
back fettlements of the colony, the provifions they
are abfolutely in want of for their fubfiftence.

Other Negroes have forfaken their manufactures.
Thefe fugitives fall unexpectedly, fometimes upon one
fide of the colony, fometimes upon another, in order
to carry off fupplies for their own fubfiftence, and to
lay wafte the wealth of their former tyrants. It is
in vain that the troops are kept continually upon the
watch, to check or to furprife fo dangerous an enemy.

By means of private information, they contrive to efcape every fnare, and direct their incurfions towards thofe parts which happen to be left defencelefs.

Methinks I fee thofe people who were flaves in Egypt, and who, taking refuge in the deferts of Arabia, wandered for the fpace of forty years, attempted to make incurfions upon all the neighbouring people, haraffed them, penetrated alternately among fome of them, and by flight and frequent inroads paved the way for the invafion of Paleftine. If nature fhould chance to add a great foul, and a powerful underftanding, to the outward form of a Negro ; if fome European fhould afpire to the glory of being the avenger of nations that have been oppreffed during two centuries ; if even a miffionary fhould know how to avail himfelf properly of the continual and progreffive afcendant of opinion over the variable and tranfient empire of ftrength,—but alas ! muft the cruelty of our European policy infpire fanguinary ideas, and fuggeft plans of deftruction to an equitable and humane man, whofe thoughts are engaged in fecuring the peace and happinefs of all mankind ?

The republic will prevent the fubverfion of their fettlements, by laying a falutary reftraint on the caprices and extravagances of their fubjects. They will alfo take effectual meafures to bring into their own ports the fruits of their labours, which hitherto have been too often thrown into another channel.

The principal proprietors of Dutch Guyana refide in Europe. There are fcarcely to be found in the colony any inhabitants, but the factors of thefe wealthy men, and fuch proprietors, whofe fortunes are too moderate to admit of their intrufting the care of their plantations to other hands. The confumption of fuch inhabitants muft be extremely confined. Accordingly, the veffels which are fent from the mothercountry to bring home their produce, carry out nothing but abfolute neceffaries ; very feldom any articles of luxury, and but few of them. Even this

BOOK
XII.
scanty supply the Dutch traders are forced to share with the English of North America.

Those foreigners were at first admitted only because the colony was under a necessity of purchasing horses of them. The difficulty of breeding, and perhaps other causes, have established this permission. The bringing of horses is so indispensable a passport for the men, that a ship which does not carry a number proportionate to its size is not admitted into their harbours. But if the horses happen to die in their passage, it is sufficient that their heads are produced, to entitle the owners to expose to sale all kinds of provisions. There is a law forbidding payments to be made otherwise than by barter of molasses and rum; but this law is little attended to. The English, newly arrived, who have usurped the right of importing thither whatever they choose, take care to export the most valuable commodities of the colony, and even exact payments in money or bills of exchange on Europe. Such is the law of force, which republics apply, not only to other nations, but to each other. The English treat the Dutch nearly in the same manner as the Athenians did the people of Melos. *It has ever been the case*, said they to the inhabitants of that island, *that the weakest should submit to the strongest: this law is not of our making; it is as old as the world, and will subsist as long as the world endures.* This argument, which is so well calculated to suit the purposes of injustice, brought Athens in its turn under the dominion of Sparta, and at length destroyed it by the hands of the Romans.

The losses incurred by the Dutch, must render the republic very careful of their American possessions. The United Provinces have not given to their American settlements that attention they deserved, although they have met with strokes so severe, and so closely following upon each other, as ought to have opened their eyes. If they had not been blinded by the rapidity of their success, they would have discovered the beginning of their ruin in the loss of Brazil. Deprived of that vast acquisition, which in their

hands might have become the firſt colony of the uni- B O O K
verſe, and might have compenſated the weakneſs or XII.
inſufficiency of their territory in Europe, they ſaw
themſelves reduced to the condition they were in before they had made this conqueſt, of being factors
for other nations; and thus was created, in their
maſs of real wealth, a void which hath never ſince
been filled up.

The conſequences of the act of navigation, paſſed
in England, were not leſs fatal to the Dutch. From
this time that iſland, ceaſing to be a tributary to the
trade of the republic, became her rival, and in a
ſhort time acquired a deciſive ſuperiority over her in
Africa, Aſia, and America.

Had other nations adopted the policy of Britain,
Holland muſt have ſunk under the ſtroke. Happily
for her, their kings knew not, or cared not for the
proſperity of their people. Every government, however, in proportion as it has become more enlightened, has aſſumed to itſelf its own branches of commerce. Every ſtep that has been taken for this purpoſe, hath been an additional check upon the Dutch;
and we may preſume, from the preſent ſtate of things,
that ſooner or later every people will eſtabliſh a navigation for themſelves, ſuited to the nature of their
country and to the extent of their abilities. To this
period the courſe of events in all nations ſeems to
tend; and whenever it ſhall arrive, the Dutch, who
are indebted for their ſucceſs, as much to the indolence and ignorance of their neighbours, as to their
own economy and experience, will find themſelves
reduced to their original ſtate of poverty.

It is not certainly in the power of human prudence
to prevent this revolution; but there was no neceſſity to anticipate it, as the republic has done, by
chooſing to interfere as a principal in the troubles
which ſo frequently have agitated Europe. The intereſted policy of our times would have afforded a
ſufficient excuſe for the wars ſhe hath commenced or
ſuſtained for the ſake of her trade. But upon what

B O O K principle can fhe juftify thofe in which her exorbitant
  XII.   ambition, or ill-founded apprehenfions, have engaged
her ? She has been obliged to fupport herfelf by immenfe loans ; if we fum up together all the debts feparately contracted by the generalities, the provinces,
and the towns, which are all equally public debts,
we fhall find they amount to two thoufand millions of
livres [83,333,333l. 6s. 8d.]; the intereft of which,
though reduced to two and a half per cent. hath
amazingly increafed the load of taxes.

Others will perhaps examine, whether thefe taxes
have been laid on with judgment, and collected with
due economy. It is fufficient here to remark, that
they have had the effect of increafing fo confiderably
the price of neceffaries, and confequently that of labour, that the induftrious part of the nation have fuffered feverely from them. The manufactures of wool,
filk, gold, filver, and a variety of others, have funk,
after having ftruggled for a long time under the growing weight of taxes and fcarcity. When the fpring
equinox brings on at the fame time high tides and
the melting of the fnow, a country is laid under water by the overflowing of the rivers. No fooner does
the increafe of taxes raife the price of provifions, than
the workman, who pays more for his daily confumption, without receiving any addition to his wages,
forfakes the manufacture and workfhop. Holland
hath not preferved any of its internal refources of
trade, but fuch as were not expofed to any foreign
competition.

The hufbandry of the republic, if we may be allowed to call it by that name, that is to fay, the her-
ring fifhery, hath fcarce fuffered lefs. This fifhery,
which for a long time was intituled the gold mine of
the ftate, on account of the number of perfons who
derived their fubfiftence, and even grew rich from it,
is not only reduced to one-half, but the profits of it,
as well as thofe of the whale fifhery, are dwindled by
degrees to nothing. Nor is it by advances of fpecie,
that thofe who fupport thefe two fifheries embark in

the undertaking. The partnerships consist of merchants, who furnish the bottoms, the rigging, the utensils, and the stores. Their profit consists almost entirely in the vent of these several merchandises : they are paid for them out of the produce of the fishery, which seldom yields more than is sufficient to defray its expences. The impossibility there is in Holland of employing their numerous capitals to better advantage, has been the only cause of preserving the remains of this ancient source of the public prosperity.

The excessive taxes, which have ruined the manufactures of the republic, and reduced the profits of their fisheries so low, have greatly confined their navigation. The Dutch have the materials for building at the first hand. They seldom cross the sea without a cargo. They live with the strictest sobriety. The lightness of their ships in working is a great saving in the numbers of their crews ; and these crews are easily formed, and always kept in the greatest perfection, and at a small expence, from the multitude of sailors swarming in a country which consists of nothing else but sea and shore. Notwithstanding all these advantages, which are further increased by the low rate of money, they have been forced to share the freight-trade of Europe with Sweden, Denmark, and especially the Hamburghers, with whom the neneffary requisites for navigation are not encumbered with the same impositions.

With the freights have diminished the commissions which used to be sent to the United Provinces. When Holland was become a great staple, merchandise was sent thither from all parts, as to the market where the sale of it was most ready, sure, and advantageous. Foreign merchants were the more ready oftentimes to send them thither, as they obtained, at an easy rate, credit to the amount of two-thirds, or even three-fourths, of the value of their goods. This management ensured to the Dutch the double advantage of employing their capitals without risk, and obtaining a commission besides. The profits of com-

B O O K   merce were at that time fo confiderable, that they
   XII.   could eafily bear thefe charges ; they are now fo
greatly leffened, fince experience has multiplied the
number of adventurers, that the feller is obliged to
convey his commodity himfelf to the confumer, without the intervention of any agent.   But if upon certain occafions an agent muft be employed, they will
prefer, *cæteris paribus*, thofe ports where commodities
pay no duty of import or export.

The republic hath likewife loft the trade of in-
furance, which fhe had in a manner monopolized
formerly.   It was in her ports that all the nations of
Europe ufed to enfure their freights, to the great profit
of the enfurers, who, by dividing and multiplying their
rifks, feldom failed of enriching themfelves.   In proportion as the fpirit of inquiry introduced itfelf into
all our ideas, whether of philofophy or economy, the
utility of thefe fpeculations became univerfally known.
The practice became familiar and general ; and what
other nations have gained by it, was of courfe loft to
Holland.

From thefe obfervations it is evident, that all the
branches of commerce the republic was in poffeffion
of, have been very greatly diminifhed.   Perhaps the
greater part of them would have been annihilated, if
the quantity of her fpecie, and her extraordinary
economy, had not enabled her to be fatisfied with a
profit of three per cent. which we look upon to be
the value of the product upon all her trade.   This
great deficiency has been made up to them by veft-
ing their money in the Englifh, French, Auftrian,
Saxon, Danifh, and even Ruffian funds, the amount
of which, upon the whole, is about fixteen hundred
millions of livres [66,666,666l. 13s. 4d.].

Formerly the ftate made this branch of commerce
unlawful, which is now become the moft confiderable
of any.   Had this law been obferved, the fums they
have lent to foreigners would have lain unemployed
at home ; their capitals for the ufe of trade being already fo large, that the leaft addition to them, fo far

from giving an advantage, would become detrimen- B O O K
tal, by making the amount too great for ufe. The XII.
fuperfluity of money would immediately have brought
the United Provinces to that period, in which excefs
of wealth begets poverty. Millions of opulent perfons, in the midft of their treafures, would not have
had a fufficiency to fupport themfelves.

The contrary practice hath been the principal refource of the republic. The money fhe has lent to
neighbouring nations, has procured her an annual
balance in her favour, by the revenue accruing from
it. The credit is always the fame, and produces always the fame intereft.

We fhall not prefume to determine how long the
Dutch will continue to enjoy fo comfortable a fituation. Experience authorifes us only to declare, that
all governments which have, unfortunately for the
people, adopted the deteftable fyftem of borrowing,
will fooner or later be forced to give it up; and the
abufe they have made of it will moft probably oblige
them to defraud their creditors. Whenever the republic fhall be reduced to this ftate, her great refource
will be in agriculture.

This, though it be capable of improvement in the
county of Breda, Bois-le-Duc, Zutphen, and Guel-
ders, can never become very confiderable. The territory belonging to the United Provinces is fo fmall,
that it will almoft juftify the opinion of a Sultan, who
feeing with what obftinacy the Dutch and Spaniards
difputed with each other the poffeffion of it, declared,
if it belonged to him, he would order his pioneers to
throw it into the fea. The foil is good for nothing
but fifh, which, before the Dutch, were the only inhabitants of it. It has been faid with as much truth
as energy, that the four elements were but in embryo
there.

The exiftence of the republic in Europe is precarious, from their pofition in the middle of a capricious
and boifterous element which furrounds them, which
perpetually threatens them, and againft which they

B O O K are obliged to maintain means of defence as expen-
XII. five as a numerous army; from formidable neighbours, fome on the feas, and others on the continent;
from the barrennefs of the foil, which produces nothing of what is abfolutely required for daily fubfiftence. Without any wealth of their own, their
magazines, which are at prefent filled with foreign
merchandife, may be to-morrow either empty or overftocked, whenever the nations fhall either choofe to
ceafe the furnifhing of them with any, or fhall no
longer require any from them. Expofed to every
kind of want, their inhabitants will be forced to
leave their country, or to die with hunger upon their
treafures, if they cannot be relieved, or if fuccours
be refufed to them. If it fhould happen that the
nations fhould become enlightened with refpect to
their interefts, and fhould refolve to carry their productions themfelves to the different regions of the
earth, and to bring back upon their own fhips thofe
which they fhall receive from thence in exchange,
what will become of thefe ufelefs carriers? Deprived
of original materials, the poffeffors of which are at
liberty to prohibit the exportation of, or to fix them
at an exorbitant price, what will become of their
manufactures? Whether the deftiny of any power
fhould depend upon the wifdom or upon the folly of
others, that power is almoft equally an object of compaffion. Without the difcovery of the New World,
Holland would be nothing, England would be inconfiderable, Spain and Portugal would be powerful,
and France would be what fhe is, and what fhe will
ever remain, under whatever mafter, and under whatever form of government fhe may be placed. A long
feries of calamities may plunge her into misfortunes,
but thofe misfortunes will be only temporary, fince
nature is perpetually employed in repairing her difafters. And this is the enormous difference there
is between the condition of an indigent people and
that of a people rich in their territory. The latter
can exift without all other nations, while thefe can

scarce exist without them. Their population must be
incessantly increasing, if a bad administration do not
retard the progress of it. Several successive years of
general dearth will only bring on a transient inconvenience, if the wisdom of the sovereign should provide against it. They scarce stand in need of any
allies. If the combined policy of all the powers
should concur in refusing to purchase their commodities, they would still experience nothing more than
the inconvenience of superfluity, and the diminution
of their luxury ; an effect which would turn to the
advantage of their strength, which is enervated,
and of their manners, which are corrupted. True
riches they are in possession of, and have no need to go
in search of them at a distance : so that the superabun-
dance or scarcity of the metal which represents their
felicity, can be of no avail either for or against it.

Deprived of these advantages in Europe, the republic must seek them in America. Her colonies,
though very inferior to the settlements formed there
by most of the other nations, would furnish productions, the whole profits and property of which will
centre in her. By her territorial acquisitions she will
be enabled in every market to rival those nations,
whose commodities she formerly served only to convey. Holland, raised to the dignity of a state, will
cease to be a warehouse. She will find in another
hemisphere that consistence which Europe hath denied her. It remains to see, if Denmark can have
the same wants and the same resources.

Denmark and Norway, which are at present united Revolu-
under the same government, formed, in the eighth tions which have chan-
century, two different states. While the former sig- ged the
nalized itself by the conquest of England, and other state of Denmark.
bold enterprises, the latter peopled the Orcades, Fero,
and Iceland. Urged by that restless spirit, which had
always actuated their ancestors the Scandinavians,
this active nation, so early as the ninth century, formed an establishment in Greenland, which country,

BOOK
XII.

there is good reason to suppose, is attached to the American continent. It is even thought, notwithstanding the darkness which prevails over all the historical records of the north, that there are sufficient traces to induce a belief, that their navigators in the eleventh century were hardy enough to penetrate as far as the coasts of Labrador and Newfoundland, and that they left some small colonies on them. Hence it is probable, that the Norwegians have a right to dispute with Columbus the glory of having discovered the New World ; at least, if those may be said to have made the discovery, who were there without knowing it.

The wars which Norway had to sustain, till the time it became united to Denmark ; the difficulties which the government opposed to its navigation ; the state of oblivion and inaction into which this enterprising nation fell ; not only lost it its colonies in Greenland, but also whatever settlements or connections it might have had on the coasts of America.

It was not till more than a century after the Genoese navigator had begun the conquest of that part of the world under the Spanish banner, that the Danes and Norwegians, who were then become one nation, cast their eyes upon that hemisphere, which was nearer to them than to any of those nations who had already possessed themselves of different parts of it. They chose, however, to make their way into it by the shortest course, and therefore, in 1619, they sent captain Monk to find out a passage by the northwest into the Pacific Ocean. His expedition was attended with as little success as those of many other navigators, both before and after him.

It may be presumed, that a disappointment in their first attempt would not entirely have disgusted the Danes ; and that they would have continued their American expeditions till they had succeeded in forming some settlements, that might have rewarded them for their trouble. If they lost sight of those

diftant regions, it was becaufe they were forced to it
by an unfortunately obftinate war, which humbled
and tormented them, and lafted till the year 1660.

The government feized the firft moment of tranquillity to examine the condition of the ftate. Like
all other Gothic governments, it was divided between
an elective chief, the nobility or fenate and the com-
mons. The king enjoyed no other pre-eminence
than that of prefiding in the fenate, and commanding the army. In the intervals between the Diets
the government was in the hands of the fenate: but
all great affairs were referred to the Diets themfelves,
which were compofed of the clergy, nobility, and
commonalty.

Though this conftitution be formed upon the model of liberty, no country was lefs free than that of
Denmark. The clergy had forfeited their influence
from the time of the Reformation. The citizens had
not yet acquired wealth fufficient to make them confiderable. Thefe two orders were overwhelmed by
that of the nobility, which was ftill influenced by the
fpirit of the original feudal fyftem, that reduces every
thing to force. The critical fituation of the affairs
of Denmark did not infpire this body of men with
that juftice or moderation, which the circumftances
of the time required. They refufed to contribute
their proportion to the public expences; and by this
refufal exafperated the members of the Diet. But,
inftead of exterminating this proud race, which was
defirous of enjoying the advantages of fociety, without partaking the burden of it, they refolved to fubmit to unlimited fervitude, and voluntarily put on
chains themfelves, which the nobles would never have
ventured to impofe upon them by force, or with which
they would perhaps have in vain attempted to load
them.

At this ftrange and humiliating fpectacle, is there
any one who will not afk, what is man? What is that
original and deep fenfe of dignity which he is fuppofed to poffefs? Is he born for independence or for fla-

BOOK
XII.

very? What is that fenfelefs herd of men which we call a nation? And when, on reviewing the globe, the fame phenomenon, and the fame meannefs, are difplayed in a greater or lefs degree from one pole to the other, is it poffible that pity fhould not be extinguifhed, and that in the contempt which fucceeds to it we fhould not be tempted to exclaim : Bafe and ftupid people, fince the continuity of oppreffion doth not reftore to you any energy ; fince you confine yourfelves to unavailing groans, when you might make your oppreffors tremble ; fince there are millions of you, and that yet you fuffer yourfelves to be led at pleafure by a few infants, armed with defpicable weapons, continue ftill to obey. Go on without troubling us with your complaints ; and learn at leaft how to be unhappy, if you know not how to be free.

The Danes had no fooner fubmitted to one fingle chief, than they fell into a kind of lethargic ftate. To thofe great convulfions, which are occafioned by the clafhing of important rights, fucceeded the delufive tranquillity of fervitude. A nation, which had filled the fcene for feveral ages, appeared no more on the theatre of the world. In 1671, it juft recovered fo far from the trance, into which the acceffion of defpotifm had thrown it, as to look abroad, and take poffeffion of a little American ifland, known by the name of St. Thomas.

The Danes form fettlements in the iflands of St. Thomas, St. John, and Santa Cruz.

This ifland, the fartheft of the Caribbees towards the weft, was totally uninhabited, when the Danes undertook to form a fettlement upon it. They were at firft oppofed by the Englifh, under pretence that fome emigrants of that nation had formerly begun to clear it. The Britifh miniftry ftopped the progrefs of this interference ; and the colony were left to form plantations of fugar, fuch as a fandy foil, of no greater extent than five leagues in length, and two and a half in breadth, would admit of. Thefe improvements, which were at that time very rare in the American Archipelago, were brought on by particular caufes.

The Elector of Brandenburg had formed, in 1681,

a company for the weftern part of Africa. The ob- ject of this affociation was to purchafe flaves ; but they were to be fold again ; and that could be done in no other place than in the New World. It was propofed to the court of Verfailles to receive them in their poffeffions, or to cede Santa-Cruz. Thefe two propofals being equally rejected, Frederic William turned his views towards St. Thomas. Denmark confented in 1685, that the fubjects of this enter- prifing prince fhould eftablifh a factory in the ifland, and that they fhould carry on a free trade there, upon condition of paying the taxes eftablifhed, and of agreeing to give an annual ftipend.

They were then in hopes of furnifhing the Spanifh colonies, which were diffatisfied with England and Holland, with the Negroes which thofe provinces were continually in want of. The treaty not hav- ing taken place, and the vexations being inceffantly multiplied, even at St. Thomas's, the tranfactions of the inhabitants of Brandenburg were always more or lefs unfortunate. Their contract, however, which had been only made at firft for thirty years, was re- newed. Some few of them ftill belonged to it, even in 1731 ; but without any fhares or any charter.

Neverthelefs, it was neither to the productions, nor to the undertakings of the inhabitants of Branden- burg, that the ifland of St. Thomas was indebted for its importance.

The fea has hollowed out from its coaft an excel- lent harbour, in which fifty fhips may ride with fe- curity. This advantage attracted both the Englifh and French Buccaneers, who were defirous of ex- empting their booty from the duties they were fub- ject to pay in the fettlements belonging to their own nations. Whenever they had taken their prizes in the lower latitudes, from which they could not make the Windward Iflands, they put into that of St. Tho- mas to difpofe of them. It was alfo the afylum of all merchant-fhips which frequented it as a neutral port in time of war. It was the mart, where the neigh-

bouring colonies bartered their refpective commmo-
dities which they could not do elfewhere with fo much
eafe and fafety.   It was the port from which were
continually difpatched veffels richly laden to carry on
a clandeftine trade with the Spanifh coafts ; in return
for which, they brought back confiderable quantities
of metal and merchandife of great value.   In a word,
St. Thomas was a market of very great confequence.

Denmark, however, reaped no advantage from this
rapid circulation.   The perfons who enriched themfelves were foreigners, who carried their wealth to
other fituations.   The mother-country had no other
communication with its colony than by a fingle fhip,
fent out annually to Africa to purchafe flaves, which
being fold in America, the fhip returned home laden
with the productions of that country.   In 1719 their
traffic increafed by the clearing of the ifland of St.
John, which is adjacent to St. Thomas, but not half
fo large.   Thefe flender beginnings would have required the addition of Crab Ifland, or Bourriquen,
where it had been attempted to form a fettlement
two years before.

This ifland, which is from eight to ten leagues in
circumference, has a confiderable number of hills ;
but they are neither barren, fteep, nor very high.
The foil of the plains and valleys, which run between
them, feems to be very fruitful ; and is watered by
a number of fprings, the water of which is faid to
be excellent.   Nature, at the fame time that fhe has
denied it a harbour, has made it amends by a multitude of the fineft bays that can be conceived.   At
every ftep fome remains of plantations, rows of o-
range and lemon trees, are ftill found ; which make
it evident, that the Spaniards of Porto-Rico, who are
not further diftant than five or fix leagues, had formerly fettled there.

The Englifh, obferving that fo promifing an ifland
was without inhabitants, began to raife fome plantations there towards the end of the laft century ; but
they had not time to reap the fruit of their labour.

They were furprifed by the Spaniards, who murdered all the men, and caried off the women and children to Porto-Rico. This accident did not deter the
Danes from making fome attempts to fettle there in
1717. But the fubjects of Great Britain, reclaiming
their ancient rights, fent thither fome adventurers,
who were at firft plundered, and foon after driven off,
by the Spaniards. The jealoufy of thefe American
tyrants extends even to the prohibiting of fifhing-
boats to approach any fhore where they have a right
of poffeffion, though they do not exercife it. Too
idle to profecute cultivation, too fufpicious to admit
induftrious neighbours, they condemn the Crab Ifland
to eternal folitude ; they will neither inhabit it themfelves, nor fuffer any other nation to inhabit it.
Such an exertion of exclufive fovereignty has obliged
Denmark to give up this ifland for that of Santa
Cruz.

Santa Cruz had a better title to become an object
of national ambition. It is eighteen leagues in length,
and from three to four in breadth. In 1643 it was
inhabited by Dutch and Englifh. Their rivalfhip in
trade foon made them enemies to each other. In
1646, after an obftinate and bloody engagement, the
Dutch were beat, and obliged to quit a fpot from
which they had formed great expectations. The conquerors were employed in fecuring the confequences
of their victory, when, in 1650, they were attacked
and driven out in their turn by twelve hundred Spaniards, who arrived there in five fhips. The triumph
of thefe lafted but a few months. The remains of
that numerous body, which were left for the defence
of the ifland, furrendered without refiftance to a hundred and fixty French, who had embarked in 1651,
,from St. Chriftopher's, to make themfelves mafters of
the ifland.

Thefe new inhabitants loft no time in making themfelves acquainted with a country fo much difputed.
On a foil, in other refpects excellent, they found only one river of a moderate fize, which, gliding gently

B O O K almoſt on a level with the ſea through a flat country,
  XᴵI   furniſhed only a brackiſh water. Two or three ſprings,
which they found in the innermoſt parts of the iſland,
made but feeble amends for this defect. The wells
were for the moſt part dry. The conſtruction of reſervoirs required time. Nor was the climate more in-
viting to the new inhabitants. The iſland being flat,
and covered with old trees, ſcarce afforded an opportunity for the winds to carry off the poiſonous vapours,
with which its moraſſes clogged the atmoſphere.
There was but one remedy for this inconvenience;
which was to burn the woods. The French ſet fire
to them without delay; and, getting on board their
ſhips, became ſpectators from the ſea, for ſeveral
months, of the conflagration they had raiſed in the
iſland. As ſoon as the flames were extinguiſhed, they
went on ſhore again.

They found the ſoil fertile beyond belief. Tobacco, cotton, arnotto, indigo, and ſugar, flouriſhed
equally in it. So rapid was the progreſs of this colony, that, in eleven years from its commencement,
there were upon it eight hundred and twenty-two
white perſons, with a proportionable number of ſlaves.
It was rapidly advancing to proſperity, when ſuch
obſtacles were thrown in the way of its activity as
made it decline again. This decay was as ſudden as
its riſe. In 1696 there were no more than one hundred and forty-ſeven men, with their wives and children, and ſix hundred and twenty-three blacks remaining; and theſe were tranſported from hence to
St. Domingo.

Some obſcure individuals, ſome writers unacquaint-
ed with the views of government, with their ſecret
negotiations, with the character of their miniſters,
with the intereſts of the protectors and the protected,
who flatter themſelves that they can diſcern the reaſon of events, amongſt a multitude of important or
frivolous cauſes, which may have equally occaſioned
them; who do not conceive, that among all theſe
cauſes, the moſt natural may poſſibly be the fartheſt

from the truth ; who after having read the news, or B O O K
journal of the day, with profound attention, decide XII.
as peremptorily as if they had been placed all their
life-time at the helm of the ftate, and had affifted at
the council of kings ; who are never more deceived
than in thofe circumftances, in which they difplay
fome fhare of penetration ; writers as abfurd in the
praife as in the blame which they beftow upon nations, in the favourable or unfavourable opinion they
form of minifterial operations : thefe idle dreamers,
in a word, who think they are perfons of importance,
becaufe their attention is always engaged on matters
of confequence, being convinced that courts are always governed in their decifions by the moft compre-
henfive views of profound policy, have fuppofed, that
the court of Verfailles had neglected Santa Cruz,
merely becaufe they wifhed to abandon the fmall
iflands, in order to unite all their ftrength, induftry,
and population, in the large ones ; but this is a miftaken notion : this determination, on the contrary, arofe
from the farmers of the revenue, who fóund, that the
contraband trade of Santa Cruz with St. Thomas was
detrimental to their interefts. The fpirit of finance
hath in all times been injurious to commerce ; it hath
deftroyed the fource from whence it fprang. Santa
Cruz continued without inhabitants, and without cultivation, till 1733, when it was fold by France to
Denmark for 738,000 livres [30,750l.]. Soon after
the Danes built there the fortrefs of Chriftianftadt.

Then it was, that this northern power feemed likely to take deep root in America. Unfortunately, fhe
laid her plantations under the yoke of exclufive privileges. Induftrious people of all fects, particularly
Moravians, ftrove in vain to overcome this great difficulty. Many attempts were made to reconcile the
interefts of the colonifts and their oppreffors, but without fuccefs. The two parties kept up a continual
ftruggle of animofity, not of induftry. At length
the government, with a moderation not to be expected from its conftitution, purchafed, in 1754, the pri-

vileges and effects of the Company. The price was fixed at 9,900,000 livres [412,500l.], part of which was paid in ready money, and the remainder in bills upon the treasury, bearing interest. From this time the navigation to the islands was opened to all the subjects of the Danish dominions.

Unfortunate state of the Danish islands. Measures proper to be adopted by government to relieve them. On the first January 1773, there was reckoned in St. John sixty-nine plantations, twenty-seven of which were devoted to the culture of sugar, and forty-two to other productions of less importance. There were exactly the same number at St. Thomas, and they had the same destination, but were much more considerable. Of three hundred and forty-five plantations, which were seen at Santa Cruz, one hundred and fifty were covered with sugar-canes. In the two former islands, the plantations acquire what degree of extent it is in the power of the planter to give them, but in the last, every habitation is limited to three thousand Danish feet in length, and two thousand in breadth.

St. John is inhabited by one hundred and ten white men, and by two thousand three hundred and twenty-four slaves: St. Thomas, by three hundred and thirty-six white men, and by four thousand two hundred and ninety-six slaves: Santa Cruz, by two thousand one hundred and thirty-six white men, and by twenty-two thousand two hundred and forty-four slaves. There are no freed men at St. John's, and only fifty-two at St. Thomas, and one hundred and fifty-five at Santa Cruz ; and yet the formalities required for granting liberty, are nothing more than a simple enrolment in a court of justice. If so great a facility hath not multiplied these acts of benevolence, it is because they have been forbidden to those who had contracted debts. It hath been apprehended, that the debtors might be tempted to be generous at the expence of their creditors.

This law appears to me a very prudent one ; with some mitigation it might be of service, even in our countries. I should very much approve, that all citizens invefted with honourable functions, either at court, in the army, in the church, or in the magiftracy, fhould be fufpended whenever they fhould be legally fued by a creditor, and that they fhould be unremittingly deprived of their rank whenever they fhould be declared infolvent by the tribunals. It appears to me that money would then be lent with more confidence, and borrowed with greater circumfpection. Another advantage which would accrue from fuch a regulation, would be, that the fubaltern orders of men, who imitate the cuftoms and the prejudices of the higher clafs of citizens, would foon be apprehenfive of incurring the fame difgrace ; and that fidelity in engagements would become one of the characteriftics of the national manners.

The annual productions of the Danifh iflands are reduced to a fmall quantity of coffee, to a great deal of cotton, to feventeen or eighteen millions weight of raw fugar, and to a proportionate quantity of rum. Part of thefe commodities are delivered to the Englifh, who are proprietors of the beft plantations, and in poffeffion of the flave trade. We have before us at prefent, very authentic accounts, which prove that from 1756 to 1773, that nation hath fold in the Danifh fettlements of the New World, to the amount of 2,307,686 livres 11 fols [96,153l. 12s. 1¼d.], and carried off to the value of 3,197,047 livres 5 fols 6 deniers [133,210l. 6s. 0¾d.]. North America receives likewife fome of thefe productions in exchange for its cattle, for its wood, and for its flour. The remainder is conveyed to the mother-country upon forty fhips of one hundred, and from that to four hundred tons burden. The greateft part is confumed in Denmark, and there is fcarcely fold in Germany, or in the Baltic, for more than the value of one million of livres [41,666l. 13s. 4d.].

The lands fufceptible of cultivation in the Danifh iflands are not all tilled, and thofe which are, might be improved. According to the opinion of the beft-informed men, the produce of thefe poffeffions might

BOOK XII. easily be increased by one third, or perhaps by one half.

One great obstacle to this increase of riches, is the extremely narrow circumstances of the colonists. They owe 4,500,000 livres [187,500l.] to government, 1,200,000 livres [50,000l.] to the trade of the mother-country, and 26,630,170 livres [1,109,590l. 8s. 4d.] to the Dutch, who, from the immensity of their capitals, and the impossibility of employing them all themselves, necessarily become the creditors of all nations.

The avidity of the treasury puts fresh restraints upon industry. The provisions and merchandise which are not peculiar to the country, or which have not been brought upon Danish vessels, are obliged to pay four per cent. upon their departure from Europe. The national and foreign commodities equally pay six per cent. on their arrival in the islands; 18 livres [15s.] are required for every fresh Negro brought in, and a poll-tax of 4 livres 10 sols [3s. 9d.]. Some heavy duties are laid upon stampt paper; an impost of 9 livres [7s. 6d.] for each thousand foot square of ground, and the tenth of the price of every habitation that is sold. The productions are all subjected to five per cent. duty on their leaving the colonies, and to three per cent. on their arrival in any of the ports of the mother-country, exclusive of the duties which are paid for rum when consumed in retail. These tributes collectively bring in to the crown an income of eight or nine hundred thousand livres, [from 33,333l. 6s. 8d. to 37,500l.]

It is time that the court of Copenhagen should give up these numerous and oppressive taxes. Well-grounded motives of interest ought certainly to suggest the same kind of conduct to all the powers that have possessions in the New World. But Denmark is more particularly compelled to this act of generosity. The planters are loaded with such enormous debts, that they will never be able to repay the capitals, and cannot even make good the arrears, unless

the treafury fhould entirely drop every kind of claim B O O K
upon them.

But can fuch a prudent meafure be expected, either in Denmark or elfewhere, as long as the public
expences fhall exceed the public revenues ; as long as
the fatal events, which, in the prefent order, or rather
diforder, of things, are perpetually renewed, fhall
compel adminiftration to double or to treble the burden of their unfortunate, and already overloaded fubjects; as long as the councils of the fovereigns fhall
act without any certain views, and without any fettled plan ; as long as minifters fhall conduct themfelves, as if the empire, or their functions, were to
end the next day ; as long as the national treafures
fhall be exhaufted by unparalleled depredations, and
that its indigence fhall only be removed by extravagant fpeculations, the ruinous confequences of which
will not be perceived, or will be neglected, for the
trifling advantages of the moment? and to make ufe
of an energetic, but true metaphor, one that is terri-
fying, but fymbolical of what is practifed in all countries ; as long as the folly, the avarice, the diffipation,
the degradation, or the tyranny of the rulers, fhall
have rendered the treafury fo much exhaufted or rapacious, as to induce them to *burn the harveft, in order the more fpeedily to collect the price of the afhes!*

If the treafury were by chance to become wifer
and more generous in Denmark than they have been,
or than they are in any other part of the globe, the
iflands of St. Thomas, of St. John, and of Santa
Cruz, might poffibly profper, and their productions
might, in fome meafure, compenfate for the trifling
value of thofe of the mother-country.

The provinces which at prefent conftitute the do- Rapid
mains of this ftate in Europe, were formerly inde- fketch of
the Danifh
pendent of each other. Revolutions, moft of them power.
of a fingular nature, have united them into one kingdom. In the centre of this heterogeneous compofi-
tion are fome iflands, the principal of which is called
Zealand. It has an excellent port, though in the

eleventh century it was but a little fifhing town ; it
became a place of importance in the thirteenth ; in
the fifteenth, the capital of the kingdom ; and, fince
the fire in 1728, which confumed fixteen hundred
and fifty houfes, it is a handfome city. To the fouth
of thefe iflands is that long and narrow peninfula,
which the ancients called the Cimbrian Cherfonefus.
Jutland, Slefwick, and Holftein, the moft important
and extenfive parts of this peninfula, have been fucceffively added to the Danifh dominions. They have
been more or lefs flourifhing, in proportion as they
have felt the effects of the reftleffnefs of the ocean,
which fometimes retires from their coafts and fometimes overwhelms them. In thefe countries, one may
fee a perpetual ftruggle between the inhabitants and
the fea, an inceffant conteft, the fuccefs of which
hath always been equivocal. The inhabitants of fuch
a country will be free from the moment they feel
that they are not fo. Mariners, iflanders, and moun-
taineers, will not long remain under the yoke of defpotifm.

Nor is Norway, which conftitutes part of the Danifh dominions, more adapted to fervitude. It is covered with ftones or rocks, and interfected by chains
of high and barren mountains. Lapland contains
only a few wild people, either fettled upon the fea-
coafts, for the fake of fifhing, or wandering through
frightful deferts, and fubfifting by the chafe, by their
furs, and their rein-deer. Iceland is a miferable
country, which has been many times overturned by
volcanos and earthquakes, and conceals within its
bowels a quantity of combuftible matter, which in an
inftant may reduce it to a heap of ruins. With refpect to Greenland, which the common people look
upon as an ifland, and which geographers confider as
united towards the weft to the American continent ;
it is a vaft and barren country, condemned by nature
to be eternally covered with fnow. If ever thefe
countries fhould become populous, they would be independent of each other, and of the king of Den-

mark, who thinks at prefent that he rules over their
wild inhabitants, becaufe he calls himfelf their king,
while they know nothing of the matter.

The climate of the Danifh iflands in Europe is not
fo fevere as might be conjectured from the latitude
they lie in. If the navigation of the gulfs which
furround them be fometimes interrupted, it is not fo
much by ice formed there, as by what is driven thither by the winds, and by degrees collects into a
mafs. All the provinces which make part of the
German continent, except Jutland, partake of the
German temperature. The cold is very moderate
even on the coafts of Norway. It rains there often
during the winter, and the port of Berghen is fcarcely once clofed by ice, while thofe of Amfterdam, Lu-
bec, and Hamburgh, are fhut up ten times in the
courfe of the year. It is true, that this advantage is
dearly purchafed by thick and perpetual fogs, which
make Denmark a difagreeable and melancholy refidence, and its inhabitants gloomy and low-fpirited.

The population of this empire is not proportioned
to its extent. In the earlier ages it was ruined by
continual emigrations. The piratical enterprifes which
fucceeded to thefe, kept up this ftate of poverty, and
anarchy prevented the government from remedying
evils of fuch magnitude and importance. The double
tyranny of the prince over one order of his fubjects,
who fancy themfelves to be free, under the title of
nobles, and of the nobility over a people entirely deprived of liberty, extinguifhes even the hopes of an
increafe of population. The bills of mortality of all
the ftates of Denmark, excepting Iceland, taken together, make the deaths in 1771 amount only to
55,125; fo that, upon the calculation of thirty-two
living to one dead perfon, the whole number of inhabitants does not amount to more than 1,764,000.

Independent of many other caufes, the weight of
impofts is a great obftacle to their profperity. There
are fixed taxes payable on land, arbitrary ones collected by way of capitation, and daily ones levied on

BOOK consumption. This oppreffion is the more unjuft, as
XII. the crown poffeffes a very confiderable domain, and
hath likewife a certain refource in the ftraits of the
Sound. Six thoufand nine hundred and thirty fhips,
which, if we may judge from the accounts of the year
1768, annually pafs into or out of the Baltic, pay at
the entrance of that fea about one per cent. upon all
the commodities they are laden with. This fpecies
of tribute, which, though difficult to collect, brings
in to the ftate two millions five hundred thoufand
livres [104,166l. 13s. 4d.], is received in the bay of
Elfinoor, under the guns of the caftle of Chronen-
burg. It is aftonifhing that the fituation of this bay,
and that of Copenhagen, fhould not have fuggefted
the idea of forming a ftaple here, where all the commercial nations of the north and fouth might meet,
and exchange the produce of their climates and their
induftry.

With the funds arifing from tributes, domains, cuftoms, and foreign fubfidies, this ftate maintains an
army of twenty-five thoufand men, which is compofed of foreigners, and is reckoned the very worft body
of troops in Europe. On the other hand, its fleet is
in the higheft reputation. It confifts of twenty-feven
fhips of the line, and of one-and-thirty fhips of war,
but of inferior rates. Twenty-four thoufand regiftered
feamen, moft of whom are continually employed, form
a certain refource for their navy. To their military
expences, the government have of late years added
others, for the encouragement of manufactures and
arts. If we add to thefe, four millions of livres
[166,666l. 13s. 4d.] for the neceffary expences and
amufements of the court, and about the fame fum
for the intereft of the national debt, amounting to
feventy millions [2,916,666l. 13s. 4d.]; we fhall account for the diftribution of twenty-three millions of
livres [958,333l. 6s. 8d.], which form the revenue of
the crown.

It was with a view of fecuring thefe feveral
branches, that the government, in 1736, prohibited

the ufe of jewels, and gold and filver ftuffs, we may venture to fay, there were plainer and eafier means to be ufed for that purpofe. They fhould have abolifhed that multitude of difficulties, which clog the commercial intercourfe of the citizens, and hinder a free communication between the different parts of the kingdom. The trade of Iceland, of Greenland, of the States of Barbary, and the whale-fifhery, fhould have been laid open to all the traders of the nation. The trade of the iflands of Fero, abfurdly given up to the fovereign, fhould have been reftored to the people. All the members of the ftate fhould have been freed from the obligation that was impofed upon them in 1726, of providing themfelves with wine, falt, brandy, and tobacco, from Copenhagen itfelf.

In the prefent ftate of affairs, their exportations are but fmall. In the provinces on the German continent, they confift of five or fix thoufand beeves, three or four thoufand horfes fit for cavalry, and fome rye, which is fold to the Swedes and Dutch. For fome years paft, Denmark hath confumed all the wheat which Fionia and Aland ufed to export to other nations. Thofe two iflands, as well as Zealand, have now no other traffic but in thofe magnificent harneffes which are purchafed at fo dear a rate by all who love fine horfes. The trade of Norway confifts of herrings, timber, mafts, tar, and iron. Lapland and Greenland produce furs. From Iceland is procured cod, whale blubber, the oil of feals, and manatees, fulphur, and that luxurious down fo celebrated under the name of eider-down.

We fhall clofe here the details into which the commerce of Denmark hath neceffarily led us; and which are fufficient to convince that power, that nothing contributes fo much to her intereft as having the fole poffeffion and traffic of all the productions of her American iflands. Let us warn her, that the more limited her poffeffions are in the New World, the more attentive ought fhe to be, not to fuffer any

B O O K of the advantages fhe may derive from them to efcape
XII.   her: let us warn her, as well as all the governments
of the earth, that the difeafes of empires are not
among the number of thofe which are cured of themfelves; that they grow more inveterate with age, and
that it is feldom their cure is facilitated by fortunate
circumftances; that it is almoft always dangerous to
put off, to a diftant period, either the accomplifhing
of any good purpofe we may have in view, or the
removal of any evil we may expect to remedy at the
time; that for one inftance of fuccefs obtained by
temporifing, hiftory affords a thoufand, where the favourable opportunity hath been miffed for having
been too long waited for; that the ftruggles of a fovereign are always thofe of a fingle man againft all,
unlefs there be feveral fovereigns, who have one common intereft between them; that alliances are nothing more than preparations for treachery; that the
power of a feeble nation grows only by imperceptible
degrees, and by efforts which are always thwarted by
the jealoufy of other nations, unlefs it fhould emerge
at once from its ftate of mediocrity by the daring
exertions of fome impatient and formidable genius;
that a man of fuch genius may be waited for a long
time, and that even he rifks every thing, fince his attempts may terminate equally in the aggrandizement
of the ftate or in its total ruin. Let us warn Denmark in particular, that while fhe is expecting the
appearance of this man of genius, the fafeft thing for
her is to be fenfible of her pofition, and the wifeft,
is to be convinced, that if powers of the firft clafs
feldom commit faults without impunity, the leaft negligence on the part of fubaltern fovereignties, which
have not any fpeedy or great refource in the poffeffion of immenfe and opulent territories, cannot but
be attended with fatal confequences. Let us not
conceal from her, that all petty ftates are deftined to
aggrandize themfelves or to difappear, and that the
bird which dwells in a barren climate, and lives
amidft arid rocks, ought to act as a bird of prey.

BOOK XIII.

Settlement of the French in the American Iſlands.

HISTORY entertains us with nothing but the accounts of conquerors, who have employed themſelves
at the expence of the lives and the happineſs of their
ſubjects in extending their dominions; but it doth
not ſet before our eyes the example of one ſovereign
who hath thought of reſtraining the limits of them.
Would not this meaſure, however, have been as prudent as the other has been fatal, and may we not
judge of the extent of empires in the ſame manner
as we do of the increaſe of population? A vaſt empire, and an immenſe population, may be two great
evils. Let there be few men, but let them be happy; let the empire be ſmall, but well governed. The
fate of ſmall ſtates is to be extended, and of large
ones to be diſmembered.

The increaſe of power, which moſt of the governments of Europe have flattered themſelves with, from
their poſſeſſions in the New World, hath for too long
a time engaged my attention, not to have induced
me frequently to conſider within myſelf, or to inquire of men more enlightened, what idea it was
proper to entertain of ſettlements formed at ſo much
expence, and with ſo much labour, in another hemi-
ſphere.

Doth our real happineſs require the enjoyment of
the things which we go in ſearch of at ſuch a diſtance? Is it our fate for ever to perſevere in ſuch
factitious inclinations? Is man born eternally to
wander between the ſky and the waters? Is he a
bird of paſſage, or doth he reſemble other animals,
whoſe moſt diſtant excurſions are exceedingly limited? Can the articles of commerce we derive from
thence be an adequate compenſation for the loſs of
the citizens who leave their country, to periſh, either
by the diſorders with which they are attacked dur-

BOOK
XIII.
ing their voyage, or by the climate at their arrival? At fuch confiderable diftance, what influence can the laws of the mother-country have upon the fubjects? and how will their obedience to thofe laws be enforced? Will not the abfence of the witneffes and judges of our actions neceffarily induce corruption in our manners, and occafion in time the fubverfion of the moft wife inftitutions, when virtue and juftice, which are the bafis on which they are founded, fhall no longer fubfift? By what firm tie fhall we fecure a poffeffion, from which we are feparated by an immenfe interval? Hath the individual, who paffes his whole life in voyages, any idea of the fpirit of patriotifm? and among all the countries he is obliged to traverfe, is there any one which he ftill confiders as his own? Can colonies intereft themfelves to a certain degree in the misfortunes or profperity of the mother-country? and can the mother-country be very fincerely rejoiced or afflicted at the fate of the colonies? Do not the people feel a ftrong propenfity, either of governing themfelves, or of giving themfelves up to the firft power which hath ftrength enough to get poffeffion of them? Are not the directors, fent over to govern them, confidered as tyrants, who would be deftroyed, were it not for the refpect borne to the perfon whom they reprefent? Is not this extenfion of empire contrary to nature? and muft not every thing that is contrary to nature have an end?

Would the man be confidered as bereft of underftanding, who fhould fay to the nations: Your authority muft either ceafe on the other continent, or you muft make it the centre of your empire? This is the alternative you have to choofe: you muft either remain in this part of the world, and increafe the profperity of the land on which you are placed, and upon which you dwell; or if the other hemifphere fhould offer you more power, ftrength, fecurity, or happinefs, you muft go and fettle upon it. Convey to it your authority, and your arms, your manners and your laws will profper there. Do ye think that your commands will be obeyed upon a fpot where you do not refide, when the abfence even of the mafter is always attended with fome difagreeable circumftance in the narrow limits of his own family? The fway of a monarch can only be eftablifhed in the kingdom where he dwells; and it is ftill no eafy matter to reign there with propriety. Wherefore, O fovereign! haft thou affembled numerous armies in the centre of thy kingdom? Wherefore are thy palaces furrounded with guards? It is becaufe the perpetual threats of thy neighbours, the fubmiffion of thy people, and the fecurity of thy facred perfon, require thefe precautions. Who will be refponfible for the fidelity of your diftant fubjects? Your fceptre cannot reach to thoufands of leagues, and your fhips can but imperfectly fupply this authority. This is the decree pronounced by fate upon your colonies: You muft either renounce them, or they will renounce you. Confider, that your power ceafes of itfelf, beyond the natural limits of your own dominions.

These ideas, which begin to arife in the minds of men, would have excited them to revolt at the commencement of the feventeenth century. Every thing was then in commotion in moft of the countries of Europe. The thoughts of all men were generally turned towards the concerns of the New World, and the French appeared as impatient as other nations to take a fhare in them.

Ever fince the fatal cataftrophe of the affaffination of the beft of their kings, that nation had been in perpetual confufion, from the caprices of an intriguing queen, the oppreffions of a rapacious foreigner, and the fchemes of a weak-minded favourite. A defpotic minifter began to enflave her; when fome of her failors, excited as much by a defire of independence, as by the allurement of riches, failed towards the Caribbee Iflands, in hopes of making themfelves

First expeditions of the French to the American iflands.

B O O K masters of the Spanish vessels that frequented those
XIII. seas. Their courage had been successful on many
occasions ; but they were at last obliged, in order to
refit, to seek for an asylum, which they found at St.
Christopher's in 1625. This island appeared to them
a proper place for securing the success of their expeditions, and they were therefore desirous of procuring
a settlement upon it. Desnambuc, their chief, not
only obtained leave to form an establishment there,
but likewise to extend it as far as he was either desirous or was able to do, in the great Archipelago of
America. Government required, for this permission
merely, without giving any assistance to the project,
or encouraging it with any protection, the tenth
part of the produce of every colony that might be
founded.

The French   A company was formed in 1626, in order to reap
islands are   the benefit of this concession. Such was the custom
oppressed
under ex-   of those times, when trade and navigation were yet
clusive pri- in too weak a state to be intrusted to private hands.
vileges.
This company obtained the greatest privileges. The
government gave them, for twenty years, the property of all the islands they should cultivate, and
empowered them to exact a hundred weight of tobacco, or fifty pounds of cotton, of every inhabitant
from sixteen to sixty years of age. They were likewise to enjoy an exclusive right of buying and selling.
A capital of forty-five thousand livres [1875l.] only,
and which was never increased to three times that
sum, procured them all these advantages.

It seemed impossible to rise to any degree of prosperity with such inadequate means. Considerable
numbers, however, of bold and enterprising men
came from St. Christopher's, who hoisted the French
flag in the neighbouring islands. Had the company,
which excited this spirit of invasion by a few privileges, acted upon a consistent and rational plan, the
state must soon have reaped some benefit from this
restless disposition. But, unfortunately, an inordi-

sate thirst of gain rendered them unjust and cruel; a consequence that ever has, and ever will attena a spirit of monopoly.

The Dutch, apprised of this tyranny, came and offered provisions and merchandise on far more moderate terms, and made proposals which were readily accepted. This laid the foundation of a connection between those republicans and the colonists, that could never afterwards be broken; and formed a competition, not only fatal to the company in the New World, where it prevented the sale of their cargoes, but even pursued them in all the markets of Europe, where the contraband traders undersold all the produce of the French islands. Discouraged by these deserved disappointments, the company sunk into a total state of inactivity, which deprived them of most of their emoluments, without lessening any of their expences. In their despair, they gave up, in 1631, their charter to a new company, who in their turn ceded it also to another, in 1642. In vain did the ministry sacrifice to the last company the duties they had reserved to themselves; this indulgence could not change the pernicious system which had been hitherto the perpetual cause of all the calamities. A new revolution therefore soon became necessary. The exhausted company, to prevent their total ruin, and that they might not sink under the weight of their engagements, put their possessions up to auction : they were mostly bought up by their respective governors.

In 1649, Boisseret purchased, for seventy-three thousand livres [3041l. 13s. 4d.], Guadalupe, Marigalante, the island called *The Saints*, and all the effects belonging to the company on these several islands : he afterwards parted with half in favour of Houel, his brother-in-law. In 1650, Duparquet paid but sixty thousand livres [2500l.] for Martinico, St. Lucia, Granada, and the Granadines. Seven years after, he sold Granada and the Granadines to Count Cerillac, for one third more than he had given for

B O O K his whole purchafe. In 1651, Malta purchafed St.
XIII. Chriftopher's, St. Martin, St. Bartholomew, Santa
Cruz, and Tortuga, for forty thoufand crowns [5000l.],
which were paid by the commandant De Poincy, who
governed thofe iflands. The knights of Malta were
to hold them in fief of the crown, and were not allowed to intruft any but a Frenchman with the adminiftration of them.

The new poffeffors enjoyed an unlimited authority,
and difpofed of the lands. All places, both civil and
military, were in their gift. They had the right of
pardoning thofe whom their deputies condemned to
death ; in a word, they were fo many petty fovereigns.
It was natural to expect, as their domains were under
their own infpection, that agriculture would make a
rapid progrefs. This conjecture was in fome meafure
realized, notwithftanding the contefts, which were
neceffarily fharp and frequent under fuch mafters.
However, this fecond ftate of the French colonies did
not prove more beneficial to the nation than the firft.
The Dutch continued to furnifh them with provifions,
and to carry away the produce, which they fold indifcriminately to all nations, even to that which ought
to have reaped the fole advantage of it, becaufe it
was her own property.

The mother-country fuffered confiderably from this
evil, and Colbert miftook the means of redrefs. That
great man, who had for fome time prefided over the
finances and trade of the kingdom, had begun upon
a wrong plan. The habit of living with the farmers
of the revenue under the adminiftration of Mazarin,
had accuftomed him to confider money, which is but
an inftrument of circulation, as the fource of every
thing. He imagined that manufactures were the
readieft way to draw it from abroad ; and that in the
workfhops were to be found the beft refources of the
ftate, and in the tradefmen the moft ufeful fubjects
of the monarchy. To increafe the number of thefe
men, he thought it proper to keep the neceffaries of
life at a low price, and to difcourage the exportation

of corn. The production of materials was the leaft object of his care, and he bent his whole attention to the manufacturing of them. This preference of induftry to agriculture became the reigning tafte, and unfortunately this deftructive fyftem ftill prevails.

Had Colbert entertained juft notions of the improvement of lands, of the encouragement it requires, and of the liberty the hufbandman muft enjoy, he would have purfued, in 1664, a very different plan from that which he adopted. It is well known that he redeemed Guadalupe, and its dependent iflands, for one hundred and twenty-five thoufand livres [5208l. 6s. 8d.] ; Martinico for forty thoufand crowns [5000l.] ; Granada for a hundred thoufand livres [4166l. 13s. 4d.] ; and all the poffeffions of Malta for five hundred thoufand livres [20,833l. 6s. 8d.]. So far his conduct deferved commendation : it was fit that he fhould reftore fo many branches of fovereignty to the body of the ftate. But he ought never to have fubmitted poffeffions of fuch importance to the oppreffions of an exclufive company ; a meafure forbidden as much by paft experience, as by reafon. It is probable, that the miniftry expected that a company, which was to be incorporated into thofe of Africa, Cayenne, and North America, and interefted in the trade that was beginning to be carried on upon the coafts of St. Domingo, would obtain a ftrong and permanent power, as well from the great connections it would have an opportunity of forming, as from the facility with which it might repair, in one part, the misfortunes it had fuftained in another. They thought to fecure the future fplendour of the company, by lending them the tenth part of the amount of their capital, free from intereft for four years, by permitting the exportation of all provifions duty-free into their fettlements, and by prohibiting, as much as they could, the competition of the Dutch.

Notwithftanding all thefe favours, the company was never in any flourifhing ftate. The errors they fell into feemed to increafe, in proportion to the num-

ber of conceffions that had been injudicioufly granted to them. The knavery of their agents, the dejection of the colonifts, the devaftations of war, with
other caufes, concurred to throw their affairs into the
utmoft confufion. Their ruin was advancing, and
appeared inevitable in 1674, when the ftate judged it
proper to pay off their debts, which amounted to
three millions five hundred and twenty-three thoufand livres [146,791l. 13s. 4d.], and to reimburfe
them their capital of one million two hundred eighty-
feven thoufand one hundred and eighty-five livres
[53,632l. 14s. 2d.]. Thefe generous terms reftored
to the body of the ftate thofe valuable poffeffions
which had been hitherto, as it were, alienated from
it. The colonies became entirely French, and all the
citizens, without diftinction, were at liberty to go
and fettle there, or to open a communication with
them.

The French
iflands re-
cover their
liberty.
Obftacles
which pre-
vent their
fuccefs.
It would be difficult to exprefs the tranfports of
joy which this event excited in the iflands. They
were now freed from the chains under which they
had fo long been oppreffed, and nothing feemed capable of abating for the future, the active fpirit of
labour and induftry. Every individual gave a full
fcope to his ambition, and thought himfelf at the
eve of making an immenfe fortune. If they were
deceived in thefe expectations, this cannot be attributed either to their prefumption or their indolence.
Their hopes were very natural, and their whole conduct was fuch as juftified and confirmed them. Unfortunately, the prejudices of the mother-country
threw infurmountable difficulties in their way.

Firft, it was required, even in the iflands, that
every free man, and every flave of either fex, fhould
pay an annual poll-tax of a hundred weight of raw
fugar. It was in vain urged, that the condition impofed upon the colonies, to trade only with the mother-country, was of itfelf a fufficient hardfhip, and
a reafon why they fhould be exempted from all other
taxes. Thefe reprefentations were not attended to,

as they ought to have been. Whether from necef- B O O K
fity, or from ignorance on the part of government, ___XIII.___
thofe cultivators who ought to have been affifted with
loans without intereft, or with gratuities, faw part of
their harveft collected by greedy farmers of the revenue ; which, had it been returned into their own
fertile fields, would gradually have increafed their
produce.

While the iflands were thus deprived of part of
their produce, the fpirit of monopoly was taking effectual meafures in France to reduce the price of
what was left them. The privilege of buying it up,
was limited to a few fea-ports. This was a manifeft
infringement of the effential rights vefted in the other
harbours of the kingdom ; but to the colonies it proved a very unfortunate reftriction, becaufe it leffened
the number of buyers and fellers on the coafts.

To this difadvantage another foon fucceeded. The
miniftry had endeavoured to exclude all foreign veffels from thofe diftant poffeffions, and had fucceeded,
becaufe they were in earneft. Thefe navigators obtained, from motives of intereft, the privilege that
was denied them by the laws. They purchafed of
the French merchants paffes to go to the colonies,
where they took in their ladings, and carried them
directly to their own country. This difhonefty might
have been punifhed and fuppreffed by a variety of
methods ; but the moft deftructive one was adopted.
All fhips were required to give in their return, not
only at home but likewife at the ports from whence
they had failed. This reftraint neceffarily occafioned
a confiderable expence to no purpofe, and could not
fail of enhancing the price of American commodities.

Their increafe was alfo checked by the duties with
which they were overladen ; tobacco was fubjected
to a duty of twenty fols [10d.] per pound. The ufe
of indigo was at firft prohibited in the dyes of the
kingdom, under a pretence that it fpoiled them, and
that it would be prejudicial to one of the cultures of

B O O K the mother-country. But when the moſt obſtinate
XIII. perſons had been convinced by repeated experiments,
that indigo, when mixed with paſtel, or even when
uſed alone, rendered the colours more beautiful and more laſting, government confined itſelf to
the loading of it with taxes. They were ſo heavy
as to render the exportation of it impoſſible. It was
not till 1693, that the tax was taken off the indigo
which was intended for foreigners.

The cacao was taken out of the hands of monopoly, only to be ſubjected, in 1693, to a duty of 15
ſols [7½d.] per pound, although it was ſold for no
more than 5 ſols [2½d.] in the colonies. Its intro-
duction in the kingdom was at firſt allowed only by
Rouen and Marſeilles, and by this latter port alone,
ſince the pretended liberty granted to it.

Cotton, which had at firſt eſcaped the rigours of the
treaſury, was taxed 3 livres [2s. 6d.] per hundred
weight in 1664. It was to no purpoſe that half of
this impoſt was taken off in 1691. This modifica-
tion could not renew the plants that had been extir-
pated.

The conſumption of ginger, which hath ſome of
the qualities of pepper, and which might eaſily be
uſed as a ſuccedaneum, ought to have been encouraged. A ſtop was put to it by a duty of 6 livres [5s.]
per quintal. It was afterwards reduced to 15 ſols
[7½d.]; but at that period, the loweſt claſs of citizens had contracted a diſlike for that ſpice, which it
was impoſſible to conquer.

The American caſſia was purchaſed in France for
one quarter of the price that was paid for that of the
Levant. If a proper analyſis had been made of it, it
would have diſpelled the prejudices which were the
cauſe of this enormous difference in the price. But
government never thought of any expedient which
might tend to increaſe the riches of their poſſeſſions.

Sugar was the richeſt production of the iſlands till
1669 : the direct exportation of it into all the ports
of Europe had been allowed, as well as that of all the

provisions of the colonies. At this period it was ordered, that it should be only deposited in the harbours of the kingdom. This arrangement necessarily
enhanced its price, and foreigners, who could purchase it at a cheaper rate in other parts, contracted
the habit of going there in search of it. The resolu-
tion, however, that was taken of liberating the sugar from the duty of 3 per cent. which it had paid
on its arrival, was the means of preserving some purchasers. A fresh mistake completed the ruin of this
branch of trade.

The refiners, in 1682, petitioned that the exportation of raw sugar might be prohibited ; in which they
seemed to be influenced merely by public good.
They alleged that it was repugnant to all sound principles, that the original produce should be sent away
to support foreign manufactures, and that the state
should voluntarily deprive itself of the profits of so
valuable a labour. This plausible reasoning made too
great an impression on Colbert ; and the consequence
of it was, that the refining of sugar was kept up at
the same exorbitant price, and the art itself never received any improvement. This was not approved
by the people who consumed this article ; the French
sugar-trade sank, and that of the rival nations was
visibly increased.

Some of the colonists, observing that the system was
not dropped, notwithstanding this fatal experiment,
solicited leave to fine their own sugars. They were
supplied with so many conveniences to go through
this process at a trifling expence, that they flattered
themselves they might soon recover that preference
they had lost in the foreign markets. This change
was more than probable, had not every hundred weight
of refined sugar they sent home been clogged with a
duty of eight livres [6s. 8d.] on entering the kingdom.
All that could be done, notwithstanding this heavy
imposition, was to support the competition of the
French refiners residing in the kingdom. The produce of the sugar-houses in France, and of those in

B o o k the colonies, were entirely confumed within the em-
XIII. pire ; and thus an important branch of trade was given up, rather than it fhould be acknowledged, that
a miftake had been committed in prohibiting the exportation of raw fugars.

From this period the colonies, which fupplied twenty-feven millions weight of fugar, could not difpofe
of the whole of it in the mother-country, which confumed but twenty millions. As the confumption of
it decreafed, no more was cultivated than was abfolutely neceffary. This medium could only be fettled
in procefs of time ; and before this was effected, the
commodity fell to an exceeding low price. This decreafe in the value, which was alfo owing to the negligent manner of making it, was fo great, that raw
fugar, which fold for fourteen or fifteen livres [from
11s. 8d. to 12s. 6d.] per hundred in 1682, fetched
no more than five or fix [from 4s. 2d. to 5s.] in 1713.

The low price of the ftaple commodity would have
made it impoffible for the colonifts to increafe the
number of their flaves, even if the government, by
its conduct, had not contributed to this misfortune.
The Negro trade was always in the hands of exclufive companies, who imported but few, in order to
be certain of felling them at a better price. We have
good authority to affert, that in 1698 there were not
twenty thoufand Negroes in thofe numerous fettlements ; and it may fafely be affirmed, that moft of
thefe had been brought in by contraband traders.
Fifty-four fhips of a moderate fize were fufficient to
bring over the whole produce of thefe colonies.

The French iflands could not but fink under fo
many difficulties. If the inhabitants did not forfake
them, and carry the fruit of their induftry to other
places, their perfeverance muft be attributed to refources that did not depend upon adminiftration.
When fome production was oppreffed, the planter
turned his attention fuddenly to another, which had
not yet attracted the notice of the treafury, or which
they were apprehenfive of crufhing in its infancy

The coasts were never sufficiently guarded to prevent B O O K
all the connections formed with foreign navigators. XIII.
The plunders of the freebooters were sometimes converted into advances for culture. At length the propensity which was daily increasing in the Old World
for the productions of the New, greatly encouraged
the multiplication of them. These means, however,
would never have been sufficient to raise the French
colonies from their state of languor. A great revolution was necessary, and it was brought about in
1716.

At this period, a plain and simple regulation was Measures
substituted in lieu of a multitude of equivocal orders, adopted by
which rapacious officers of the revenue had, from Verfailles,
time to time, extorted from the wants and weakness to render
of government. The merchandise destined for the nies useful.
colonies was exempted from all taxes. The duties
upon American commodities designed for home consumption were greatly lowered. The goods brought
over for exportation were to be entered and cleared
out freely, upon paying three per cent. The duties
laid upon foreign sugars were to be levied every where
alike, without any regard to particular immunities,
except in cases of re-exportation in the ports of Bay-
onne and Marseilles.

In granting so many favours to her remote possessions, the mother-country was not unmindful of her
own interests. All merchandise prohibited at home,
was also forbidden in the colonies. To secure the
preference to its own manufactures, it was enacted,
that even such commodities as were not prohibited
should pay duty on their entry into France, although
they were destined for the colonies. Salt beef alone,
which the mother-country could not furnish in competition, was exempted from this duty.

This regulation would have been as beneficial a
one as the times would admit of, if the edict had allowed that the trade from America, which till then
had been confined to a few sea-ports, should be general; and if it had released ships from the necessity

BOOK of returning to the place from whence they came.
XIII. These restraints limited the number of seamen, raised
the expences of navigation, and prevented the exportation of the productions of the country. The
persons who were then at the head of affairs ought to
have been sensible of these inconveniences, and no
doubt intended one day to restore to trade that freedom and spirit which alone can make it flourish.
They were probably forced to sacrifice their own
views to the clamours of men in power, who openly
disapproved of whatever opposed their own interest.

Notwithstanding this weakness, the colonists, who
had reluctantly given up the hopes of an excellent
soil, bestowed their utmost industry upon it, as soon
as they were allowed that liberty. Their success
astonished all nations. If government, on the arrival
of the French in the New World, had only foreseen
what they learned from experience a century later,
the state might soon have enjoyed, from the advantages of cultivation, that wealth which would have
added more to its prosperity than conquests ; it would
not then have been as much ruined by its victories
as by its defeats. Those prudent ministers, who repaired the losses of war by a happy revolution in
trade, would not have had the mortification to see
that Santa Cruz was evacuated in 1696, and St. Christopher's given up at the peace of Utrecht. Their
concern would have been greatly heightened, could
they have foreseen that in 1763 the French would be
reduced to deliver up the Granades to the English.
Strange infatuation of the ambition of nations, or rather of kings ! After sacrificing thousands of lives
to acquire and to preserve a remote possession, a greater number must still be lavished to lose it. Yet France
has some important colonies left : let us begin with
Guiana, which lies to windward of all the rest.

Notions   The people who roved about this vast tract before
concerning the arrival of the Europeans, were divided into se-
Guiana.
Motives   veral nations, none of which were very numerous.
which in-   Their manners were the same as those of the savages
duced the

of the fouthern continent. The Caribs only, who from their numbers and courage were more turbulent than the reft, diftinguifhed themfelves by a remarkable cuftom in the choice of their chiefs. To be qualified to govern fuch a people, it was neceffary a man fhould have more ftrength, more intrepidity, and more knowledge, than the reft of his brethren; and that he fhould give evident and public proofs of thefe fuperior qualifications.

The man, who afpired to the honour of commanding his brethren, was previoufly to be well acquainted with all the places fit for hunting and fifhing, and with all the fprings and roads. He was obliged to endure long and fevere fafts; and was afterwards expofed to carry burdens of an enormous weight. He ufed to pafs feveral nights as a centinel, at the entrance of the carbet or principal hut. He was buried up to the waift in an ant's neft, where he remained for a confiderable time expofed to fharp and bloody ftings. If in all thefe fituations he fhowed a ftrength and fortitude fit to fupport the dangers and hardfhips incident to the lives of favages; if he was one who could endure every thing, and fear nothing; he was declared fit to be their chief. He withdrew, however, as if confcious of what his intended dignity required, and concealed himfelf under thick bufhes. The people went out to feek him in a retreat, which made him more deferving of the poft he feemed to decline. Each of the affiftants trod upon his head, to fhow him, that, being raifed from the duft by his equals, it was in their power to fink him into it again, if ever he fhould be forgetful of the duties of his ftation. Such was the ceremony of his coronation. Here we behold favages who had jufter notions of fovereignty, and were better acquainted with their privileges, than moft civilized nations are. After this political leffon, all the bows and arrows were thrown at his feet; and the nation was obedient to his laws, or rather to his example.

Such were the inhabitants of Guiana, when the

Spaniard Alphonſo de Ojeda firſt landed there in 1499, with Americus Veſpucius and John de la Coſa. He went over a part of it ; but this experiment afforded him only a ſuperficial knowledge of ſo vaſt a country. Many others were undertaken at a greater expence, but they proved ſtill more unſucceſsful. They were, however, ſtill continued, from a motive which ever did and ever will deceive mankind.

A report had prevailed, though its origin could not be diſcovered, that in the interior parts of Guiana there was a country known by the name of *El Dorado*, which contained immenſe riches in gold and precious ſtones ; more mines and treaſures than ever Cortez and Pizarro had found. This fable not only inflamed the ardent imagination of the Spaniards, but fired every nation in Europe.

Sir Walter Raleigh in particular, one of the moſt extraordinary men that ever appeared in a country abounding in ſingular characters, was ſeized with this enthuſiaſm. He was paſſionately fond of every thing that was magnificent ; he enjoyed a reputation ſuperior to that of the greateſt men ; he had more knowledge than thoſe whoſe immediate purſuit was learning ; he poſſeſſed a freedom of thinking uncommon in thoſe days ; and had a kind of romantic turn in his ſentiments and behaviour. This determined him, in 1595, to undertake a voyage to Guiana ; but he returned without diſcovering any thing relative to the object of his voyage. On his return, however, he publiſhed an account, full of the moſt brilliant impoſtures that ever amuſed the credulity of mankind.

So ſplendid a teſtimony, determined ſome Frenchmen, in 1604, to ſail towards thoſe countries under the direction of La Ravardiere. Other adventurers of their nation ſoon followed their example. They all ſubmitted to incredible fatigues. At length ſome of them, rather diſcouraged by the infinite labours they underwent, than undeceived in their expectations, ſettled on the iſland of Cayenne.

Some merchants of Rouen, thinking that this rising settlement might prove advantageous, united their stock in 1643. They intrusted their affairs in the hands of a man of a ferocious disposition, named Poncet de Britigny, who, having declared war both against the colonists and the savages, was soon massacred.

BOOK XIII.

The French settle in Guiana, and languish there during a century.

This catastrophe having checked the ardour of the associates, a new company was established in 1651, which seemed to promise to be much more considerable than the former. They set out with so large a capital as to enable them to collect, in Paris itself, seven or eight hundred colonists. These embarked on the Seine, in order to sail down to Havre de Grace. Unfortunately, the virtuous Abbé de Marivault, who was the principal promoter of this undertaking, and was to have had the management of it as director-general, was drowned as he was stepping into his boat. Roiville, a gentleman of Normandy, who was going over to Cayenne as general, was assassinated in the passage. Twelve of the principal adventurers, who were the perpetrators of this act, and had undertaken to put the colony into a flourishing condition, behaved there in as atrocious a manner as might be expected from so horrid a beginning. They hanged one of their own number ; two died ; three were banished to a desert island ; the rest abandoned themselves to every kind of excess. The commandant of the citadel deserted to the Dutch, with part of his garrison. The remainder, that had escaped hunger, poverty, and the fury of the savages, which had been roused by numberless provocations, thought themselves happy in being able to get over to the Leeward Islands in a boat and two canoes. They abandoned the fort, ammunition, arms, and merchandise, with five or six hundred dead bodies of their wretched companions, fifteen months after they had landed on the island.

A new company was formed in 1663, under the direction of La Barre, master of requests. Their capi-

B O O K tal was no more than two hundred thoufand livres
  XIII. [8333l. 6s. 8d.]. The affiftance they obtained from
the miniftry, enabled them to expel the Dutch, who,
under the conduct of Spranger, had taken poffeffion
of the lands granted to them, after they had been
evacuated by the firft poffeffors. A year after, this
inconfiderable body made a part of the great company, to which were united all thofe that the nation
had formed for Africa and the New World. In 1667,
Cayenne was infulted, pillaged, and abandoned by
the Englifh ; the colonifts, who had fled from it, took
poffeffion of it again ; and it was again taken from
them in 1672 by the fubjects of the United Provinces, who could not keep it longer than to the year
1676. At this period they were driven out by the
Marfhal D'Etrees ; but the colony hath not been attacked fince.

This fettlement, fo often overturned, had but juft
begun to be re-eftablifhed, and to enjoy fome tranquillity, when great hopes were entertained of its
fuccefs. Some pirates, laden with fpoils they had
gathered in the South Seas, came and fixed there ;
and, what was of greater confequence, refolved to
employ their treafures in the cultivation of the lands.
It was probable that their plan would be profecuted
with vigour, becaufe their means were great ; when
Ducaffe propofed to them in 1688, the plundering of
Surinam. This excited their natural turn for plunder ; the new colonifts became pirates again, and almoft all the inhabitants followed their example.

The expedition proved unfortunate. Some of the
befiegers fell in the attack ; the reft were taken prifoners, and fent to the Caribbee Iflands, where they
fettled. The colony has never recovered this lofs.
Far from extending into Guiana, it has never been in
a profperous ftate at Cayenne.

This ifland, which is only parted from the continent by one river, which is divided into two branches,
may be about fourteen or fifteen leagues in circumference. By a particular formation, very rarely to be

met with in iflands, the land is high near the water- B O O K
fide, and low in the middle. Hence it is interfected XIII.
with fo many moraffes, that all communication is almoft impracticable. The only town in the colony is
built in a plain of two miles in extent, where navigable canals might have been made with eafe, though
care hath not even been taken to drain the waters
from it. This village confifts of a number of barracks,
heaped upon one another without order or convenience, where fevers are rather frequent in fummer,
notwithftanding the boafted falubrity of the fpot. It
is defended by a covered way, a large ditch, a mud
rampart, and five baftions. In the middle of the
town is rather a confiderable eminence, of which a
redoubt has been made, that is called the fort, where
forty men might be able to capitulate after the place
had been taken. The entrance into the harbour hath
not much more than thirteen feet water. The fhips
might touch the ground at fourteen feet, but fortunately the mud is foft, and the keel may be driven
into it without danger.

The firft productions of Cayenne were, the arnotto,
cotton, and fugar. It was the firft of all the French
colonies that cultivated coffee ; which was brought
thither, as it hath always been, and perhaps is ftill
believed, in 1721 by fome deferters, who purchafed
their pardon by conveying it from Surinam, where
they had taken refuge. An accurate hiftorian hath
lately affirmed, probably from authentic information,
that this plant was a prefent of M. de la Motte
Aigron, who, in 1722, had the dexterity to bring
away from this Dutch fettlement fome frefh coffee
berries, notwithftanding the ftrict prohibition there is
againft exporting any of them in the pods. Ten or
twelve years after, cocoa was planted.

In 1752, 260.541 pounds weight of arnotto, 80,363
pounds of fugar, 17,919 pounds of cotton, 26,881
pounds of coffee, 91,016 pounds of cocoa, and 618
trees for timber, were exported from the colony. All
thefe articles were the refult of the labour of ninety

B O O K   French families, a hundred and twenty-five Indians,
XIII.   and fifteen hundred blacks ; which made up the
whole of the colony.

The court   Such, and weaker still, was the state of Cayenne,
of Ver-   when, in 1763, the court of Versailles endeavoured
failles in-
tend to ren-   to render it extremely flourishing, by a system which
der Guiana   occasioned a general astonishment. The French had
flourishing.
Inquiry   then just emerged from the horrors of an unsuccessful
whether
this plan   war. The situation of affairs had determined the mi-
was a judi-   nistry to purchase peace with the cession of several
cious one,
and whe-   important colonies. It appeared equally necessary to
ther it was   make the nation forget her distresses, and the errors
prudently
executed.   that had been the cause of them. The prospect of
better fortune might amuse the people, and silence
their clamours ; while their attention was removed
from possessions the nation had lost, and turned towards Guiana, which, it was pretended, would compensate all their misfortunes.

This was not the opinion of the citizens who appeared to be the best informed of the situation of
things. A settlement formed a century and a half
before, at a period when the minds of men were im-
petuously urged to great undertakings ; a settlement,
the labours of which had not been ruined by civil
discords, nor by foreign wars ; a settlement, which
had been ruled by prudent directors, with attention
and disinterestedness ; a settlement, which had always experienced the favours of government and the
assistance of trade ; a settlement, where there was a
constant and certain mart for the productions ; yet,
with all these advantages, this settlement was of no
consequence. No plantation had ever been seen to
flourish ; no fortune had ever been raised in it. Misery and obscurity had obstinately attended at those
periods, when the other French possessions in America astonished the Old and the New World by their
splendour and by their riches. Its fate, far from
being amended by time and by the advancement of
knowledge, was become daily more unfortunate.
How therefore could it possibly fulfil the important

deftiny that was prepared for it? Thefe confiderations BOOK
did not reftrain the miniftry. Let us hear what hath XIII.
been faid in juftification of their views.

America, when it was firft invaded by Europe,
exhibited to it two regions entirely different from
each other, the torrid zone, and the temperate zone
of the North. The firft prefented to the thirft of
gold, innumerable objects of gratification; various
allurements to cupidity, to idlenefs, repofe; to voluptuoufnefs its incitement; to luxury its refources.
That nation which firft took poffeffion of it, muft
have dazzled by its fplendour, and feduced men by
the image of its happinefs. An opulence as ftriking
as it was rapid, could not fail of giving it in the Old
World an influence fo much the more extenfive, as
the nature of true riches was unknown there, and as
its rivals found themfelves fuddenly plunged into a
ftate of relative indigence, as infupportable as that
which is real. Its new domain was the country calculated for defpotifm. The heat prevailing there exhaufted the ftrength of the body; and indolence,
the neceffary confequence of a fertility which fupplies all wants without labour, deprived the foul of
all its energy. This country fubmitted to its deftiny.
The people who inhabited it were flaves who waited
for a mafter; he came, and ordered them to obey,
and his commands were refpected. The fpirit of abfolute monarchy was a production of the foil, which
he found already formed there; but he alfo found
an impending enemy which nothing can refift, and
which, in its turn, muft neceffarily fubdue him; this
was the climate. In the firft intoxication of conqueft,
the ufurper formed the moft extenfive projects, and
conceived hopes apparently the beft founded. He
confidered the fign of wealth as the plaftic and preferving principle of political ftrength; and how is it
poffible that he fhould not have been deceived in this
particular? If we have got rid of this prejudice, it is
perhaps to the difafters of that power that we owe
this great leffon. They imagined, that with gold

BOOK they could keep the nations in their pay, as they
XIII. kept the Negroes in their chains; and never confidered that this gold, which procured them jealous
allies, would turn them into fo many powerful adver-
faries; who, uniting their arms with the riches they
received, would make ufe of this double power to effect their ruin.

The temperate zone of North America could only
attract free and laborious people. It furnifhes no productions but what are common and neceffary; and
which, for that very reafon, are a conftant fource of
wealth and ftrength. It favours population, by fupplying materials for that quiet and peaceful fpecies
of hufbandry which fixes and multiplies families; and,
as it does not excite inordinate defires, is a fecurity
againft invafion. It reaches through an immenfe continent, and prefents a large extent of country, on
every fide, open to navigation. Its coafts are wafhed
by a fea which is generally navigable, and abounds
with harbours. The colonifts are not at fo great a
diftance from the mother-country; they live in a
climate more analogous to their own; and in a fituation that is fit for hunting, fifhing, hufbandry, and
for all the manly exercifes and labours which improve
the ftrength of the body, and are prefervatives againft
the vices that taint the mind. Thus, in America,
as in Europe, the North will have the fuperiority
over the South. The one will be covered with inhabitants and plantations; while the other will lavifh
its voluptuous liquors and its golden mines. The one
will be able to civilize the favage nations by its intercourfe with a free people; the other will only produce a monftrous mixture of a race of flaves with a
nation of tyrants, which can never acquire any degree of ftrength.

It was of great importance to the fouthern colonies
to have their refources for population and ftrength in
the North, where they might exchange the commodities of luxury for thofe of neceffity, and keep open
a communication that might afford them fuccours if

they were attacked; a retreat in cafe they were de- feated, and a fupply of land-forces to balance the weaknefs of their naval refources.

Before the laft war, the French fouthern colonies enjoyed this advantage. Canada, by its fituation, the warlike genius of its inhabitants, their alliances with the Indian nations in friendfhip with the French, and fond of the franknefs and freedom of their manners, might balance, or at leaft give umbrage to New England. The lofs of that great continent determined the French miniftry to feek for fupport from one another. Guiana was thought a very proper fituation for this purpofe, if a free and national population could be eftablifhed there, which might be able to refift foreign attacks, and, in courfe of time, to furnifh a fpeedy affiftance to the other colonies, when circumftances might require it.

Such was evidently the fyftem of the minifter. It never occured to him, that a part of the world, thus inhabited, could never enrich the mother-country by the produce of fuch commodities as are peculiar to the fouthern colonies. He was too intelligent not to know, that there is no fuch thing as felling, without complying with the general run of the market; and that this cannot be done but by producing falcable commodities at the fame rate as other nations can afford them; and that labours, executed by free men, muft of neceffity bear a much higher price than thofe that are exacted from flaves.

The meafures were directed by an active minifter. As a wife politician, who does not facrifice fafety to wealth, he only propofed to raife a bulwark to protect the French poffeffions. As a philofopher, who feels for his fellow-creatures, who knows and refpects the rights of humanity, he wifhed to people thefe fertile but defert regions with free men. But genius, efpecially when too impatient of fuccefs, cannot forefee every circumftance. The miftake proceeded from fuppofing, that Europeans would be able to undergo the fatigues of preparing lands for cultivation under the torrid zone ; and that men, who quitted their own country only in hopes of living with greater fatisfaction in another, would accommodate themfelves to the precarious fubfiftence of a favage life, in a worfe climate than that which they had left.

This bad fyftem, which the government was drawn into by a fet of enterprifing men, who were either mifled by their prefumption, or who facrificed the public good to their own private views, was as extravagantly executed as it had been inconfiderately adopted. Every thing was blended together, without any principle of legiflation, and without confidering in what manner Nature had adapted the feveral lands to the men who were to inhabit them. The inhabitants were divided into two claffes, the proprietors and the mercenaries. It was not confidered that this divifion, at prefent eftablifhed in Europe, and in moft civilized nations, was the confequence of wars, of revolutions, and of the numberlefs chances which time produces ; that it was the effect of the progrefs of civilization, not the bafis and foundation of fociety, which in its origin requires that all its members fhould have fome property. Colonies, which are new populations and new focieties, ought to adhere to this fundamental rule. It was broken through at the very firft eftablifhment of the colony, by allotting lands in Guiana to thofe only who were able to advance a certain fund for the cultivation of them. Others, whofe defires were tempted with uncertain hopes, were excluded from this divifion of lands. This was an error equally contrary to found policy and humanity. Had a portion of land been given to every new inhabitant that was fent over to this barren and defert country, each perfon would have cultivated his own fpot, in proportion to his ftrength or abilities ; one, by the means his money would have afforded him ; another, by his own labour. It was neceffary that thofe, who were poffeffed of a capital, fhould neither be difcouraged, because they were men of great importance to a rising colony; nor that they should have an exclusive preference given them, left it should prevent them from having affistants who might be willing to be dependent on them. It was alfo indifpenfably neceffary, that every member of the new colony should be offered fome property, with which he might employ his labour, his induftry, his money, in a word, his greater or lefs powers to his advantage. It ought to have been forefeen, that Europeans, in whatever fituation they were, would not quit their own country, but with the hopes of improving their fortune; and that deceiving their hopes and confidence in this refpect, would be an effectual way to ruin the colony intended to be eftablifhed.

Men, who are tranfplanted into uncultivated regions, are furrounded with wants of every kind; the beft-directed, and moft continued labours, cannot prevent thofe, who go into thofe deferts to clear the lands, from being deprived of every refource, till the period, more or lefs diftant, of the harveft arrives. Accordingly, the court of Verfailles, by whom fo ftriking a truth could not be unnoticed, engaged to fupport, indifcriminately, all the Germans, and all the French, who were intended to eftablifh the population of Guiana. But this, though an act of juftice, was not an act of prudence. It ought to have been forefeen, that the provifions would be ill-chofen by the agents of government. It ought to have been forefeen, that if they had even been chofen with zeal, prudence and difintereftednefs, moft of them muft unavoidably have been fpoiled, either in the paffage or on their arrival. It ought to have been forefeen, that falt meats, either well or ill preferved, would never be a proper food for unfortunate refugees, who had forfaken a wholefome and temperate climate, to live among the burning fands of the torrid zone, and to breathe the damp and rainy air of the tropics.

A judicious plan of policy ought to have attended

BOOK to the multiplication of cattle, before it had thought
XIII of fettling men there. This precaution would not
only have enfured a wholefome fubfiftence to the firft
colonifts, it would likewife have fupplied them with
convenient inftruments for the undertakings which
are required in the formation of a new colony. With
this affiftance, they would have thought nothing of
labours, which the miniftry would have undertaken
to pay liberally, and would have prepared habitations
and provifions for thofe who were to come after them.
By purfuing fuch meafures, which could not require
any depth of thought, the fettlement which it was
intended to form, would have acquired, in a fhort
time, the confiftence of which it was fufceptible.

Thefe very plain and natural reflections were never
fuggefted. Twelve thoufand men, after a tedious
voyage, were landed upon dreary and inhofpitable
fhores. It is well known, that, almoft throughout
the torrid zone, the year is divided into two feafons,
the dry and the rainy. In Guiana, fuch heavy rains
fall from the beginning of November to the end of
May, that the lands are either overflowed, or at leaft
unfit for tillage. Had the new colonifts arrived there
in the beginning of the dry feafon, and been placed
on the lands deftined for them, they would have had
time to put their habitations in order, to cut down
or burn the woods, and to plough and fow their fields.

For want of thefe precautions, they knew not where
to beftow fuch multitudes of people as were conftantly pouring in juft at the rainy feafon. The ifland of
Cayenne might have been a proper place for the reception and refrefhm nt of the new-comers, till they
could have been difpofed of; there they might have
found lodging and affiftance. But the falfe opinion
which prevailed, that the new colony muft not be intermixed with the old, deprived them of this refource.
In confequence of this prejudice, twelve thoufand
unfortunate men were landed on the iflands *Du Salut*,
or on the banks of the Kourou, and were placed under tents, or under miferable fheds. In this fituation,

totally inactive, weary of exiftence, and in want of all neceffaries, expofed to contagious diftempers, which are always occafioned by tainted provifions, and to all the irregularities which idlenefs neceffarily produces among men of the loweft clafs, removed far from their native country, and placed under a foreign fky; they ended their wretched life in all the horrors of defpair. Their fate will ever call aloud for vengeance on thofe who either invented or promoted fo deftructive a fcheme, to which fo many victims were facrificed; as if the devaftations of war, which they were intended to repair, had not fwept away a fufficient number in the courfe of eight years.

That nothing might be wanting to complete this difafter, and that 25,000,000 of livres [1,041,666l. 13s. 4d.], employed in the fuccefs of this abfurd fyftem, might be entirely loft, the man who was commiffioned to put an end to thefe various calamities, thought proper to bring back into Europe two thoufand men, whofe robuft conftitution had refifted the inclemency of the climate, and had enabled them to fupport greater miferies than are to be defcribed.

The ftate hath fortunately had fufficient ftrength to bear thefe heavy loffes. But how dreadful is it for our country, for the fubjects, for every man who is interefted in the lives of his fellow-citizens, to fee them thus lavifhed upon ruinous enterprifes, by an abfurd jealoufy of authority, which enjoins the moft rigorous fecrecy upon all public tranfactions! Is it not then the intereft of the whole nation, that her rulers fhould be well informed? And how can they be fo, but from collecting general information? Why fhould projects, of which the people are to be both the object and the inftrument, be concealed from them? Can the will be commanded without the judgment, or can we infpire courage without confidence? The only true information is to be obtained from public writings, where truth appears undifguifed, and falfehood fears to be detected. Secret memoirs, private fchemes, are commonly the work of

BOOK
XIII.

artful and interefted men, who infinuate themfelves into the cabinets of perfons in adminiftration, by dark, oblique, and indirect ways. When a prince or a miniſter has acted according to the opinion of the public, or of enlightened men, if he be unfortunate, he cannot on any account be blamed. But, when enterprifes are undertaken without the advice, or againſt the fenfe of the people ; when events are brought on unknown to thofe whofe lives and fortunes are expofed by them ; what can this be but a fecret league, a combination of a few individuals againſt fociety in general? Can it be poffible, that authority fhould think itfelf degraded by an intercourfe with the citizens ? Or will men in power for ever treat the reft of mankind with fo great a degree of contempt, as not even to defire that the injuries they have done them fhould be forgiven ?

What has been the confequence of that cataftrophe, in which fo many fubjects, fo many foreigners, have been facrificed to the illufions of the French miniftry with refpect to Guiana ? This unhappy climate has been inveighed againſt with all the rancour with which refentment and misfortune can aggravate its real evils. Fortunately, the obfervations of a few enlightened men enable us to clear up this confufion.

Idea that muft. be formed of the coafts and of the foil of Guiana.

This vaſt country, which was decorated with the magnificent title of Equinoctial France, is not the fole property of the court of Verfailles, as they formerly pretended. The Dutch, by fettling to the North, and the Portuguefe to the South, have confined the French between the rivers of Marony and Vincent Pinçon, or Oyapock, which interval ſtill forms a fpace of more than a hundred leagues.

The feas which water this long extent of coaſt, are fafe, open, and free from any obftacle which might impede navigation. There are only the iflands *Du Salut*, at three leagues diſtance from the continent, to be feen in them. As they are divided only by a channel of fourfcore toifes, they might be eafily united, and after their junction they would form a fufficient fhelter for the largeft fhips. Nature hath dif- pofed things in fuch a manner, that the poft might be rendered impregnable at a trifling expence, with the materials which are to be found upon the fpot. From this harbour, which abounds in turtles part of the year, and which is fituated to windward of the Archipelago of America, a 1quadron might, in time of war, fail in the fpace of feven or eight days to the affiftance of the national poffeffions, or to attack thofe belonging to the enemies of France.

There is no danger to be feared in thefe latitudes. The winds are generally favourable for approaching the coafts, as much or as little as one may choofe. If the contrary fhould happen, which is extremely uncommon ; or if there fhould be a calm, the fhips have the refource of anchoring every where upon an excellent bottom.

Thefe advantages are unfortunately accompanied with a few inconveniencies. The navigators are ob-ftructed, on their coming in, by rapid currents. If, in order to avoid them, they fhould go too near the land, they would find almoft every where a deficiency of water. There is not any to be found, even at the mouth of the rivers, which can receive none but very fmall fhips. The river Aprouague is the only one which is twelve feet deep. In this river the veffels may be run aground upon a foft bottom, and may undergo all the neceffary repairs, without creating any anxiety. It is neceffary, however, to make great difpatch, becaufe the beft conftructed and beft fitted out veffels, are deftroyed in a fmall fpace of time, by the worms, by the muddy waters, by the rains, and by the heats.

In this region, though near the equator, the climate is very fupportable. This temperature may be attributed, perhaps, to the length of the nights, and to the abundance of fogs and dews. Guiana never experiences thofe fuffocating heats which are fo common in many other countries of America.

Unfortunately, this colony is deftroyed by deluges

of water, during the firſt ſix months of the year, and
ſometimes longer. Theſe ſuperabundant rains level
the elevated ſituations, drown the plains, deſtroy the
plants, and frequently ſuſpend the moſt urgent labours. Vegetation is at that time ſo powerful, that
it is impoſſible to reſtrain it within proper limits,
whatever numbers of people may be emplcved for
that purpoſe. To this calamity ſucceeds anuther,
and that is a long drought, which opens and parches
up the ground.

Various have, for a long time, been the opinions
concerning the ſoil of Guiana. It is known at preſent, that it is moſtly a ſtony turf, covered over with
ſand, and with the remains of ſome vegetables. Theſe
grounds are worked with facility, but their produce
is very trifling, and even does not laſt longer than
five or ſix years. The planter is then obliged to till
new grounds, which undergo the ſame fate as the
former. Thoſe tillages even, which are executed
in ſome parts of a deeper ſoil, which is to be found
at intervals, do not laſt long, becauſe the repeated
rains, which fall in torrents in thoſe regions, ſoon
waſh away the juice that might render them fruitful.

It was upon theſe meagre plains that the firſt French,
who were driven to Guiana by a fatal deſtiny, formed a ſettlement. The generations which ſucceeded
them ſearched for more fertile territories in all parts,
but could not find any. In vain did the treaſury
make ſeveral great ſacrifices to improve this colony.
Theſe expences were unavailing, becauſe they could
not alter the nature of things. The example of the
Dutch, who, after having languiſhed in the neighbourhood upon the high grounds, had at laſt ſucceeded upon plantations formed in moraſſes, which were
drained off with immenſe labour, did not make any
impreſſion. At length M. Mallouet, being intruſted
with the adminiſtration of this unfortunate ſettlement,
hath himſelf carried into execution what he had ſeen
practiſed at Surinam ; and the place which he had
reſcued from the ocean was immediately covered with

provifions. This circumftance hath infpired the co- B o o K lonifts with a fpirit of emulation, of which they were ̲ ̲XIII.̲ ̲ not thought to be fufceptible, and they wait only for the favourable affiftance of government, to enrich the mother-country with their productions.

The plantations will be hereafter eftablifhed upon thofe territories that are formed by levelling of the mountains, and by the fea. It will be neceffary to dry up the moraffes, to dig canals, and to conftruct dykes. But why fhould the French be apprehenfive of undertaking what they have executed with fo much fuccefs upon their own frontiers? Why fhould the court of Verfailles refufe to encourage, by loans and by gratifications, labours of tillage that are really ufeful? It is in the clearing of the lands that confifts the true conqueft over chaos, for the advantage of all mankind; and not in the obtaining of provinces, which are depopulated and laid wafte, in order that we may acquire them; which lavifh the blood of two nations, without enriching either; and which muft be maintained at a great expence, and covered for ages with troops, before we can flatter ourfelves with the peaceable poffeffion of them.

Every thing invites the French miniftry to purfue the plan which we have ventured to propofe. The fubterraneous fires, which are fo common in the reft of America, are at prefent extinguifhed in Guiana. There are never any earthquakes, neither do hurricanes exercife their ravages upon thofe coafts. The accefs to this country is attended with fo many difficulties, that we may foretel it will not be conquered. The French iflands, on the contrary, which have already been once taken, attract the attention, and incite the cupidity of a nation, highly diffatiffied with having reftored them. This circumftance makes us prefume, that they will always be difpofed to repair, by force of arms, the defects of their negotiations. The well-grounded confidence they repofe in their navy, may perhaps foon precipitate them into a new war, in order that they may regain what

they have reſtored, and extend their uſurpations ſtill
further. Should fortune again favour their enter-
priſes ; ſhould a people, encouraged by victories, of
which the citizens alone reap the advantages, be for
ever triumphant over a nation which fights for their
kings only ; Guiana would at leaſt prove a great reſource, where all the productions which are become
neceſſary by habit, might be cultivated ; for which an
enormous tribute muſt be paid to foreigners, if the
colonies of the nation were unable to furniſh them.

The drying up of the coaſts of Guiana would require long and difficult labours. Where can a ſufficient number of men be found for the accompliſh-
ment of this undertaking?

What men
could be
employed
for the cul-
tures of
which Gui-
ana is ſuſ-
ceptible.

It was thought in 1763, that the Europeans would
be fit for this purpoſe. Twelve thouſand of them
were the victims of this opinion. About ſixty German, or Acadian families, alone eſcaped the cata-
ſtrophe. They ſettled upon the Sinamary, the banks
of which are never overflowed by the ſea, and where
there are ſome natural meadows, and a great quantity of turtles. This ſmall colony increaſes, and lives
happily along the ſide of that river. Their reſources
conſiſt of fiſhing, hunting, breeding of cattle, and
the culture of a ſmall quantity of rice and of maize.
Some ſpeculative perſons have concluded from this
inſtance, that white people might be able to cultivate Guiana ; but they have not conſidered, that colonies have been founded only for the purpoſe of obtaining vendible commodities ; and that theſe commodities require labours, more conſtant and more fatiguing
than thoſe which are cultivated on the borders of the
Sinamary.

The natives of the country might, it is ſaid, execute without inconvenience thoſe labours which are
fatal to us. Theſe ſavages were ſufficiently numerous upon the coaſt when it was diſcovered ; but their
number hath been ſo much diminiſhed by European
cruelties, that there are at preſent no more than
four or five hundred of them capable of bearing arms.

But some adventurers, who have lately penetrated B O O K
into the inland countries, have difcovered feveral XIII.
fmall nations, each more barbarous than the other.
They have every where perceived the oppreffion of
the women, fuperftitions which prevent the increafe of
population, animofities which can only be exftinguifh-
ed by the entire deftruction of families and of colo-
nics; the fhocking neglect of old and of fick people ; the habitual ufe of the moft various and the
moft fubtile poifons, and a multitude of other evils,
the hideous fpectacle of which is too generally difplayed in a ftate of nature. Travellers, however,
are received with refpect, and affifted with the moft
unbounded generofity and the moft affecting fimplicity. They enter into the hut of the favage, fit
down by the fide of his naked wife and daughters,
partake of their repaft, and repofe upon the fame
bed. The next day they are laden with provifions,
and accompanied to fome diftance on their journey
by the favages, from whom they part with demonftrations of friendfhip. But this hofpitable fcene may become bloody in an inftant. The favage is jealous to
excefs, and on the leaft fign of familiarity which
would alarm him, he would put his gueft to death.

The firft ftep to be taken would be, to collect thefe
perpetually wandering people. This meafure might
be facilitated, by diftributing in a proper manner a few
prefents, fuited to their tafte. The moft fcrupulous attention fhould be exerted, to avoid bringing together
in the fame place fuch of thefe nations as have an
infurmountable averfion to each other.

Thefe colonies fhould not be cafually formed. It
would be proper to diftribute them in fuch a manner
as to be able to penetrate, with eafe, into the inland
parts. In proportion as thefe fettlements fhall acquire ftrength, they will facilitate the eftablifhment
of new habitations.

No confideration hath yet been powerful enough
to fix thefe Indians. The beft way to fucceed, would
be to diftribute cows among them, which they would

not be able to feed, without cutting down woods, in order to form pasture grounds. The vegetables and the fruit trees with which their habitation would be enriched, might prove a further inducement to them to give up their wandering life. It is probable that these resources, the advantage of which they have never known, might disgust them, in time, of hunting and fishing, which are at present the only support of their miserable and precarious existence.

There would still remain a much more fatal prejudice to subdue. It is an idea generally adopted among nations, that sedentary occupations are suitable to women only. This senseless pride degrades all kinds of labours in the eyes of the men. An intelligent missionary might employ his time to advantage, in combating this infatuation. He would ennoble the labours of agriculture, by exercising them himself with his children; and by this great and fortunate stratagem, he would succeed in diffusing a new system of morality among the young men. It might, perhaps, be also possible to overcome the indolence even of the parents, if it could be contrived to excite their desires. It is not improbable but that they would cultivate provisions, in order to barter them against some other mercantile articles, which might have become necessary to them from habit.

This salutary end would be far from being answered, if the savages, when collected together, were subjected to a poll-tax, and to the labours of vassalage, as they have been by the Portuguese and the Spaniards, upon the borders of the Amazon, of the Rio-Negro, and of the Oroonoko. These people must have been suffered to enjoy, for ages, the benefits of cultivation, before they should be obliged to bear the burdens of it.

But even after this happy revolution, Guiana would still but very imperfectly fulfil the extensive views which the court of Versailles may have. The feeble hands of the Indians will only bring forth commodities of moderate value. In order to obtain rich productions, it will be neceffary to have recourfe to the B O O K ftrong arms of the Negroes.

XIII.

The facility which thefe flaves will have of deferting their manufactures, excites apprehenfions. They will take refuge, they will gather together, they will intrench themfelves, it is faid, in vaft forefts, where the plenty of game and of fifh will fupply them with an eafy fubfiftence ; where the heat of the climate will allow them to go without clothes ; and where they will never want for wood fit to make bows and arrows. One hundred of them had taken this refolution about thirty years ago. .The troops fent to reduce them again to fubjection were repulfed. This check excited the apprehenfions of a general defertion, and confternation prevailed throughout the colony. They were uncertain what meafures to purfue ; when a miffionary fet out, attended by a fingle Negro, arrived at the fpot where the engagement had taken place, raifed up an altar, affembled all the deferters by ringing a bell, faid mafs to them, harangued them, and brought them all back, without exception, to their former mafters. But the Jefuits, who had merited and obtained the confidence of thefe unfortunate people, are no longer in the colony ; and their fucceffors have not fhown either the fame activity, or an equal knowledge of the human heart. Neverthelefs, it would not, perhaps, be impoffible to prevent the evafion of thefe unhappy victims of our cupidity, by rendering their condition fupportable. The law of neceffity, which commands even tyrants, will eftablifh in this region a fpirit of moderation, which humanity alone ought to excite every where.

This new arrangement of things would engage the Before any government in confiderable expences. Before they beftowed enter upon them, they will examine whether the co- upon Guilony hath hitherto obtained from nature that kind of would be conftitution which was neceffary to make it profper, proper to and whether Cayenne be the moft fuitable place to whether become the capital of a large eftablifhment. This the colony

funds are
ana, it
confider,

B O O K indeed is our opinion : but some able men think
XIII. otherwise, and their arguments must be discussed.

be well   These views may be excellent : and yet it is not a
constituted, matter of surprise that the advantages of them should
and its li-
mits must not have been sooner perceived. The discernment
be regulat- of some things is attended with so much difficulty,
ed. that it can only be surmounted by experience, or by
genius. But the progress of experience is slow, and
requires time ; and genius, which, like the coursers
of the gods, clears an immense interval at one leap,
may be expected for ages. When it appears, it is
either rejected or persecuted ; and when it speaks, it
is not heard. If it should by chance be attended to,
the spirit of jealousy inveighs against its projects, and
traducing them as sublime reveries, makes them abortive. The general interest of the multitude might,
perhaps, supply the penetration of genius, if it were
suffered freely to exert its influence : but it is incessantly thwarted by authority ; the depositaries of
which, while they understand nothing, pretend to
regulate every thing. Who is the man whom they
will honour with their confidence, and with their in-
timacy ? It is the impudent flatterer, who, without
believing it, will be continually repeating to them,
that they are a set of wonderful beings. The mischief is first done by their folly, and is perpetuated
by a spirit of false shame, which prevents them from
acknowledging their errors. False combinations are
exhausted, before they have discovered the true ones,
or before they can resolve to approve, after having
rejected them. Thus it is that the evil prevails, by
the childishness of the sovereigns, by the incapacity
and pride of the ministers, and by the impatience of
the victims. One might be comforted with respect
to past and present misfortunes, if the future were to
produce an alteration in this destiny : but this is a
hope with which it is impossible to flatter ourselves.
And if the philosopher were asked, of what use are
the counsels which he persists in giving to nations,
and to those who govern them, and that he were to

anfwer with fincerity, he would fay, that he is only
fatisfying an invincible propenfity to declare the
truth, at the rifk of exciting general indignation, and
even of being obliged to drink the cup of Socrates.

It would be proper to fix the yet unfettled boundaries of Guiana, before any final refolution be taken
refpecting this colony. The Dutch are very defirous
of extending the frontiers of Surinam to the North,
as far as the banks of the Sinamary ; but the military
poft which the court of Verfailles have caufed to be
eftablifhed upon the right bank of the river Maroni,
feems entirely to have fet afide this ancient pretenfion. Towards the South, the difficulties are ftill
greater. The Amazon was formerly, without difpute, the boundary of the French poffeffions ; fince
by a treaty of the 4th March 1700, the Portuguefe
engaged to demolifh the forts which they had erected upon the left bank of that river. At the peace
of Utrecht, France, which was under fubjection, was
compelled to cede the navigation of that river, together with the lands which extend as far as the
river Vincent Pinçon, or the Oyapock. When the
time fixed for the execution of the treaty arrived, it
was found, that thefe two words, which were employed as fynonymous, were defcribed in the country, as
well as in ancient maps, as two rivers thirty leagues
diftant from each other. Both courts were equally
defirous of turning this error to their own advantage.
The court of Lifbon wifhed to extend its boundaries
as far as the Oyapock, and that of Verfailles as far
as Vincent Pinçon. Nothing could be determined
upon, and the contefted lands have remained defert
ever fince that rather remote period.

We will not prefume to decide this important que-
ftion. The only obfervation we fhall allow ourfelves
to make, will be, that the motive of the ceffion required by Portugal, was to fecure to it the exclufive
trade upon the Amazon. The fubjects of this crown
will therefore poffibly enjoy this advantage ; by reftraining the limits of the French poffeffions only

twenty leagues, and as far as to the river of Vincent Pinçon; without its being neceffary to pufh them back to the diftance of fifty leagues, as far as the Oyapock.

Every thing ftill remains to be done at Guiana; there are no more than thirty plantations at Cayenne itfelf, and almoft all of them are in a miferable condition. The continent is in a ftill worfe ftate than the ifland. The habitations are often moved. They are feparated by immenfe deferts. Placed at a great diftance from the general mart, they have no facility for bartering their commodities. They enjoy none of the conveniences which men, when collected together, mutually procure to one another. The laws, the police, decency, emulation, the influence of the miniftry; none of thefe advantages are known there. In 1775 there were no more than thirteen hundred free men, and eight thoufand flaves, for the clearing of an extent of one hundred leagues of coaft. The productions of the colony were even inadequate to thefe trifling means, becaufe in the manufactures there were none but white men without underftanding, and Negroes who were under no kind of fubordination. The commodities which were taken away, by the veffels that came from North America, from Guadaloupe and from Martinico, did not amount to 100,000 livres [4166l. 13s. 4d.], and France received upon fix veffels only forty quintals of fugar, which were fold in Europe for 2156 livres [89l. 16s. 8d.]; fix hundred and fifty-eight quintals, fourfcore and eight pounds of coffee, which were fold for 31,296 livres 16 fols [1304l. 8d.]; three quintals thirty-four pounds of indigo, which were fold for 2839 livres [118l. 5s. 10d.]; one hundred and fifty-two quintals forty-one pounds of cacao, which were fold for 10,668 livres 16 fols [444l. 10s. 8d.]; three thoufand and three quintals fifty-five pounds of arnotto, which were fold for 187,706 livres 7 fols 6 deniers [7821l. 11s. 11¼d.]; nine hundred and feventy-two quintals fixty pounds of cotton, which were fold for 243,150 livres

[10,131l. 5s.]; three hundred and fifty-three hides, which were fold for 3177 livres [132l. 7s. 6d.]; fourteen hundred and twenty-two quintals eight pounds of wood, which were fold for 7604 livres three fols nine deniers [316l. 16s. 10d.]; which made, upon the whole, 488,598 livres 3 fols 3 deniers [about 20,388l. 5s. 2d.]. The 600,000 livres [25000l.] which were fpent by the court, in this as well in other years, for this ancient eftablifhment, ferved to pay for what had been received beyond thefe exportations. At this period Cayenne was indebted 2,000,000 livres [83,333l. 6s. 8d.] to the government, or to the merchants, of the mother-country.

Something may be expected from the knowledge which M. de Mallouet hath diffufed through the colony, and from the encouragements which this able adminiftrator hath granted in 1777 to thofe coloniits who fhould devote their labours to the felling of wood for fhip-building, to the culture of articles of fubfift-ence, to the falting of fifh, and to fome other productions of little value, for which he hath enfured them a market. Greater expectations are ftill raifed from the fpice trees. The clove tree hath already yielded cloves, which are very little inferior to thofe that come from the Moluccas; and every thing feems to promife that the nutmeg tree will thrive as well. But nothing great can be undertaken without a capital; and, indeed, without a confiderable one.

This capital is in the hands of a rich company, which hath been formed, but without any exclufive privilege for this part of the world. This affociation, the original funds of which confift of 2,400,000 livres [100,000l.], hath obtained from government the vaft fpace which extends from the river Aprouage to the Oyapock; and every encouragement which could reafonably be granted them, to fertilize this foil, which is confidered as the beft of Guiana. Till their fuc-cefs fhall enable them to employ themfelves in draining the moraffes, and in cultures of importance, this powerful affociation have turned their views towards

BOOK
XIII.
the felling of wood, the multiplication of cattle, and the cultivation of cotton, and of cacao, but principally of tobacco.

Some flaves have for a long time cultivated, for their own ufe, round their huts, this laft mentioned plant. It hath the fame properties as the tobacco of the Brazils, which fells to advantage in all the European markets, and which is abfolutely requifite for the purchafe of Negroes, upon a great part of the coafts of Africa. If this undertaking fhould fucceed, the wants of France will be diminifhed, and its navigators will not be obliged to go to Lifbon for that part of their cargo. The expectations arifing from St. Lucia are founded upon a different bafis.

The poffef-
fion of St.
Lucia, for
a long time
difputed, is
at laft ceded
to the
French.
The Englifh took poffeffion of this ifland, without oppofition, in the beginning of the year 1639. They lived there peaceably for a year and a half, when a fhip of their own nation, which had been overtaken by a calm off Dominica, carried off fome Caribs, who were come in their canoes to bring them fruit. This violence occafioned the favages of St. Vincent and Martinico to join the offended favages; and in Auguft 1640, they all attacked the new colony. In their fury, they maffacred every one that oppofed them. The few who efcaped their vengeance, quitted, for ever, a fettlement that was only in its infant ftate.

In the firft ages of the world, before civil focieties were formed and polifhed, all men in general had a common right to every thing upon earth. Every one was free to take what he chofe for his own ufe, and even to confume it, if it were of a perifhable nature. The ufe that was thus made of a common right, fupplied the place of property. As foon as any one had in this manner taken poffeffion of any thing, it could not be taken from him by another without injuftice. It was in this point of view, which can only be applied to the primitive ftate of nature, that the European nations confidered America when it was firft difcovered. They paid no regard to the natives, and imagined they were fufficiently authorifed to feize

upon any country, if no other nation of our hemisphere were in poffeffion of it. Such was conftantly
and uniformly the only public right obferved in the
New World, and which men have not fcrupled to
avow, and attempt to juftify, in this century during
the late hoftilities.

Is not then the nature of property the fame every
where ; is it not every where founded upon poffeffion
acquired by labour, and upon a long and peaceable
enjoyment ? Europeans, can you then informs us, at
what diftance from your refidence the facred title
becomes abolifhed ? Is it at the diftance of a few
fteps, of one league, or of ten leagues ? You will anfwer in the negative ; in which cafe it cannot poffibly
be even at the diftance of ten thoufand leagues. Do
you not perceive, that while you arrogate to yourfelves
this imaginary right over a diftant people, you confer
it at the fame time to thofe diftant people over yourfelves ? Neverthelefs, what would you fay, if it were
poffible that the favages fhould enter upon your country, and reafoning in the fame manner as you do,
fhould fay, this land is not inhabited by our own
people, and therefore it belongs to us. You hold the
fyftem of Hobbes in abhorrence among your neighbouring country ; and yet this fatal fyftem, which
makes of ftrength the fupreme law, you practife it at
a diftance. After having been thieves and affaffins,
nothing remained to complete your character, but
that you fhould become, as you really are, a fet of
execrable fophifts.

According to thefe principles, which muft always
be reprobated by juft and upright men, St. Lucia was
to belong to any power that could or would people
it. The French attempted it firft. They fent over
forty inhabitants in 1650, under the conduct of
Rouffeban, a brave, active, prudent man, and fingularly beloved by the natives, on account of his having
married one of their women. His death, which happened four years after, put a ftop to the general
good he had begun to effect. Three of his fucceffors

B O O K were murdered by the Caribs, who were diffatisfied
XIII. with their behaviour to them ; and the colony was
declining when it was taken in 1664 by the Englifh,
who evacuated it in 1666.

They had fcarce left it, when the French appeared
again on the ifland. Whatever was the caufe, they
had not greatly increafed their number, when the
enemy, that had before driven them out, again forced
them to quit their habitations twenty years after.
Some, inftead of evacuating the ifland, took refuge in
the woods. As foon as the conquerors, who had made
only a temporary invafion, were gone, they refumed
their labours only for a fhort time. The war, which
foon after raged in Europe, made them apprehenfive
that they might fall a prey to the firft privateer that
fhould be defirous of plundering them ; with a view,
therefore, of obtaining greater tranquillity, they removed to other French fettlements, which were
either ftronger, or might expect to be better defended. There was then no regular culture or colony in
St. Lucia. It was only frequented by the inhabitants of Martinico, who came hither to cut wood and
to build canoes, and who had confiderable docks on
the ifland.

Some foldiers and failors having deferted thither
after the peace of Utrecht, Marfhal d'Eftrees petitioned for a grant of the ifland. No fooner was it obtained in 1718, then he fent over a commandant,
troops, cannon, and inhabitants. This gave umbrage
to the court of London, which had a kind of claim to
this ifland from prior fettlement, as that of Verfailles
had from almoft uninterrupted poffeffion. Their complaints determined the French miniftry to order that
things fhould be put into the fame condition they
were in before the grant. Whether this compliance
did not appear fufficient to the Englifh, or whether it
gave them room to think they might attempt any
thing, they themfelves gave St. Lucia, in 1722, to
the duke of Montague, who was fent to take poffeffion of it. This clafhing of interefts occafioned fome

disturbance between the two courts ; which was set B o o k
tled, however, by an agreement made in 1731, that, XIII.
till the respective claims should be finally adjusted,
the island should be evacuated by both nations ; but
that both should have the liberty to wood and water
there.

This agreement did not prevent the French from
fixing there again a commandant, a garrison, and batteries. The court of London were either not informed of this breach of faith, or they overlooked it, because this channel was useful to their navigators, to
affist them in carrying on with richer colonies a
smuggling trade, which the subjects of both governments thought equally advantageous to them. This
trade has been more or less considerable till the treaty
of 1763, which secured to France the long and obstinately contested property of St. Lucia.

The first use which the court of Versailles propos- First tranf-
ed to make of their acquisition, was to establish a ma- actions of
gazine there. Since their windward islands had cut at St. Lu-
down their forests, extended their cultures, and lost cia.
the resources they used to derive from Canada and
from Louisiana, it had been impossible for them to do
without the woods and cattle of North America. It was
thought great inconveniences would attend the direct
admission of these foreign assistances ; and St. Lucia was
fixed upon as a very proper place for the exchange
of these commodities against the molasses of Martinico and Guadaloupe. Experience soon showed that
this scheme was impracticable.

In order that this arrangement might be carried
into execution, it would be necessary that the Americans should either deposit their cargoes in store-
houses, keep them on board, or sell them to traders
settled on the island ; three things equally impossible.

These sailors will never consent to land their cattle, as the expences they would incur for having
them taken care of, for their food, or to secure them
from accidents, would infallibly ruin them. Neither

will they pay for warehoufes for their wood, which is too cheap and too bulky a commodity to be worth the charge of ftore-room. They will never wait on board their fhips for diftant purchafers who might not arrive, nor will they ever meet with intermediate purchafers, whofe profits would neceffarily abforb fo much, that it would be impoffible to employ them.

The proprietors of molaffes have the fame reafons to diflike this mart. The carriage, the leakage, and commiffion, would reduce their commodities to nothing. If the Englifh fhould determine to pay a higher price for the molaffes, they muft confequently raife that of their own merchandife ; and after this advance, the confumer would not purchafe them.

The French miniftry, undeceived as to their firft notion, without entirely giving it up, attended, fince 1763, to the formation of cultures in St. Lucia. This plan was a prudent one, but it was not executed in a proper manner. Had the governor and the intendant of Martinico, from which this ifland is no more than feven leagues diftant, been intrufted with this bufinefs, the colonifts, who would have been fent there, would have obtained the fuccours which can be furnifhed with eafe, by a fettlement that hath exifted more than a century. Precipitation, a paffion for novelty, the defire of providing for friends or favourites, and other motives perhaps ftill more blameable, made the government prefer the fending of an independent adminiftration, who were to have no connections but with the mother-country. This erroneous fyftem coft the treafury 7,000,000 of livres [291,666l. 13s. 4d.], and to the ftate feven or eight hundred men, whofe unhappy fate is more a matter of pity than furprife. Under the tropics, the beft eftablifhed colonies always deftroy one third of the foldiers that are fent thither, though they are healthy ftout men, and find good accommodations. It is not furprifing then, that a fet of miferable wretches, the refufe of Europe, and expofed to all the hardfhips of

indigence and all the horrors of defpair, fhould moft
of them perifh in an uncultivated and uninhabited ifland.

The advantage of peopling this colony was referved to the neighbouring fettlements. Some Frenchmen, who had fold, upon very profitable terms, their plantations at the Granades to the Englifh, brought part of their capital to St. Lucia. Several planters from St. Vincent's, incenfed at being obliged to buy lands which they themfelves had been at incredible pains to clear and fertilize, took the fame ftep. Martinico alfo furnifhed fome inhabitants, whofe poffeffions were either not fufficiently fertile, or too much confined, and merchants who have withdrawn part of their ftock from trade in order to devote it to hufbandry. Lands have been gratuitoufly diftributed to all of them.

This would have been but a fatal prefent, if the prejudice which prevailed againft St. Lucia had had any foundation. It was faid, that nature had refufed it every advantage neceffary to form a colony of any importance. In the opinion of the public, its dry, uneven, and ftony foil, could never pay the expences of manuring. The inclemency of the climate would infallibly deftroy every man, who, from a ftrong defire of enriching himfelf, or who driven by defpair, fhould be bold enough to go there. Thefe notions were generally received.

The fact is, that the foil of St. Lucia is not bad on the borders of the fea, and that it becomes better the further one advances in the country. The whole of the ifland may be cultivated, except fome high and craggy mountains, which bear evident marks of ancient volcanoes. In one deep valley there are ftill eight or ten hollow places of fome feet in diameter, where the water boils up in a moft dreadful manner. There are not indeed many extenfive plains in the ifland, but feveral fmall ones, where fugar may be cultivated with fuccefs. The fhape of the ifland, which is long and narrow, will make the carriage easy wherever the canes are planted.

The air in the inland parts of St. Lucia, is the same as it was in all the other islands before they were inhabited ; foul and unwholesome at first, but less noxious, as the woods are cleared, and the ground laid open. The air, on some part of the sea-coast, is more unhealthy. On the leeward side the lands receive some small rivers, which springing from the foot of the mountains, have not a slope sufficient to wash down the sands with which the influx of the ocean chokes up their mouths. Stopped by this insurmountable barrier, they spread themselves into unwholesome morasses upon the neighbouring grounds. So obvious a reason had been sufficient to drive away the few Caribs who were upon the island when it was first discovered. The French, driven into the New World by a more powerful motive than even self-preservation, have been less careful than the savages. It is upon this very spot that they chiefly fixed their plantations. Several of them have been punished for their rapaciousness. Others will be so hereafter, unless they construct dykes and dig channels to drain off the waters. Government hath already set the example of this in the principal part of the island ; some citizens have followed it, and it is to be imagined, that so useful a practice will in time become general.

Present
state of the
colony of
St. Lucia. There are already eleven parishes in the colony, almost all of them to leeward. This preference given to one part of the island, is not for the sake of a better soil, but for the conveniency of the shipping. In time that part that was neglected at first, will likewise be inhabited, as bays are continually discovered, in which canoes may put in and receive all kinds of commodities on board.

A road which goes all round the island, and two others that cross it from east to west, are very convenient for carrying the produce of the plantations to the landing-places. In process of time, and with

fome expence, thefe roads will be brought to a much B O O K
greater degree of perfection than it was poffible they XIII.
fhould be at firft, without running into expences too
burdenfome for a fettlement in an infant ftate. The
labours of vaffalage required for making the roads,
have unavoidably retarded the culture of the lands,
and excited great complaints ; but the colonifts now
begin to blefs the wife and fteady hand that has ordered and conducted this work for their benefit.
Their burden hath been in fome degree alleviated in
latter times, by the attention which the directors
have had to apply to thefe labours the taxes required
to procure an exemption from them.

On the firft of January 1777, the number of white
people at St. Lucia amounted to two thoufand three
hundred fouls, men, women, and children.

There were fifty thoufand blacks, or free mulattoes. The cattle confifted of eleven hundred and
thirty mules, or horfes ; two thoufand and fifty-three
head of horned cattle, and three thoufand feven hundred and nineteen fheep, or goats.

There were fifty-three fugar plantations, which
occupied fifteen hundred and forty-one pieces of
land ; five millions forty thoufand nine hundred and
fixty-two coffee-trees ; one million nine hundred and
forty-five thoufand feven hundred and twelve cacao
plants ; and five hundred and ninety-feven plots of
cotton.

Thefe united productions were fold in the ifland
for little lefs than 3,000,000 of livres [125,000l.].
Two thirds of them were delivered to the Americans,
to the Englifh, and to the Dutch, who were allowed a free trade with the colony. The remainder was
carried to Martinico, upon which this ifland was dependent, and from whence it received fome merchandife
and fome liquors, brought from the mother-country.

The character and abilities of the Earl of Ennery,
the founder of this colony, authorifed us to affirm,
that when St. Lucia, which is about forty leagues
in circumference, hath attained the degree of culti-

vation it is capable of, it may employ fifty or fixty thoufand flaves, and yield to the value of nine or ten millions [from 375,000l. to 416,666l. 13s. 4d.] in commodities. This great teftimony hath been confirmed fince by other directors. By what fatality is it, that this fettlement hath acquired fo fmall a degree of improvement, notwithftanding all the encouragements, which it hath received?

The reafon of this is, that from the beginning properties were precipitately given to vagabonds, who had neither the habit of labour nor the means for cultivation: It is becaufe an immenfe territory was granted to greedy fpeculators, who were only able to cultivate a few acres: it is becaufe the inland parts were diftributed before the borders had been cleared: it is becaufe the ants, which fo cruelly infefted Martinico, have conveyed the fame ravages in the rifing fugar plantations of St. Lucia: it is becaufe coffee hath experienced there the fame diminution in value as every where elfe: in a word, it is becaufe the adminiftration hath been neither fufficiently regular, nor fufficiently continued, nor fufficiently enlightened. What remedy can be employed againft fo many errors, againft fo many calamities?

It will be neceffary to eftablifh a more firm fyftem of government, a more ftrict police. It will be neceffary to deprive of their territory thofe who have not at leaft partly fulfilled the engagement they had contracted, of rendering it ufeful. It will be neceffary, by modes of union prudently contrived, to bring together, as much as poffible, fome of the plantations that are feparated by diftances, which deprive their owners of the will, of the inclination, and of the facility of affifting each other. It will be neceffary legally to compel all debtors to pay proper attention to their creditors, with whom it had been cuftomary to fport. It will be neceffary, by a long feries of years, and by authentic acts, to fecure to the traders of all nations a free intercourfe with this ifland. Matters ought indeed to be carried ftill further.

The French of the mother-country cannot, and those of the iflands will not, cultivate St. Lucia. Many foreigners, on the contrary, have offered to convey their induftry and their capitals there, if the barbarous right of efcheat were fupprefled ; a right which impedes reciprocal commerce of nations ; which repels the living man, and fpoils the dead one ; which difinherits the child of the foreigner ; which obliges him to leave his wealth in his own country ; and which prohibits him from obtaining elfewhere any acquifition of perfonal or real eftate : a right which a people who have the leaft idea of good policy will abolifh among themfelves, and the extinction of which they will carefully abftain from foliciting in other countries. It is to be hoped that the court of Verfailles will no longer perfift in rejecting the only method of raifing an interefting colony from that languid ftate into which it hath been plunged by calamities which it was impoffible to avert, and by the vices of a bad adminiftration.

BOOK XIII.

When the proper fteps have been taken to render St. Lucia flourifhing, the French miniftry may purfue the fyftem which they feem to have adopted, of defending their colonies by fortreffes. To keep poffefion of this ifland, it will be fufficient to defend the Carenage harbour.

Meafures which the court of Verfailles propofes to adopt, in order to fecure St. Lucia from an invafion.

This harbour, which is the beft in the Antilles, unites many advantages. It hath a great deal of water every where, with an excellent bottom. Nature hath provided it with three complete careening places, one for the largeft fhips, and the two others for frigates. Thirty fhips of the line might ride fafely there, and be fheltered from the moft terrible hurricanes. They have never yet been injured by the worms. The winds are always favourable for failing out, and the largeft fquadron would be cleared out in lefs than an hour.

So favourable a fituation is capable of defending not only all the national poffeffions, but alfo of threatening thofe of the enemy throughout America. The naval forces of England cannot cover all parts. The smalleft fquadron fent out from St. Lucia would in a few days invade thofe colonies which, being leaft expofed, would think themfelves quite fecure. The only way to prevent this danger, would be to block up the Carenage ; and even then, the purport of fo expenfive and tirefome a cruize might be defeated by a man who fhould be bold enough to undertake any enterprife that can be effected at fea.

This harbour, which is fubject to the inconvenience of expofing every fhip that comes within view to be taken, has never appeared worthy the attention of the Britifh nation, though too powerful and too enlightened not to confider, that fhips are to protect the roads, and not the roads the fhips. With regard to France, this harbour affords the greateft maritime defence, that is to fay, a pofition that will not allow a fhip under fail to enter. She muft be warped for a confiderable fpace before fhe can get into it. There is no plying to windward between the two points. The foundings increafing fuddenly near the land from twenty-five to a hundred fathom, will not permit the affailants to come to an anchor. Only one fhip can come in at a time, and fhe would be expofed to the fire of three mafked batteries in front and on both fides.

A fhip that would attack the harbour would be under the neceffity of landing at Shoque Bay, a fhore a leage long, which is only parted from the Carenage by the point called Vigie, which forms this bay. If the enemy were once mafters of the Vigie, they would fink every fhip in the harbour, or at leaft compel them to bring to, and that without any lofs on their fide ; becaufe this peninfula, though commanded by a citadel built on the other fide of the harbour, would cover the affailants by its own back. It would only have occafion for mortars, and neither fire a fingle gun, nor endanger the life of one man.

If the fhutting up of the entrance of the harbour againft the enemy were fufficient, it would be needlefs to fortify the Vigie. The enemy might be kept out without this precaution ; but the fhips of the French muft be protected. It is neceffary that a fmall fquadron fhould be able to fet the Englifh forces at defiance ; compel them to block up the place ; take advantage of their abfence, or of fome error they might fall into ; all which cannot be effect-ed without fortifying the top of the peninfula. It muft be confidered, that by thus multiplying the points of defence, a greater number of men will be wanted ; but if there be any fhips in the harbour, their failors and gunners may be employed in defend-ing the Vigie, which they would do with the greater alacrity, as on this would depend the fafety of the fquadron. If there be no veffels in the harbour, the Vigie will be abandoned, or ill defended, and that for the following reafon :

On the other fide of the harbour there is an emi-nence, called *Morne Fortuné*. The flat on the top offers one of thofe favourable fituations, that are fel-dom to be met with for erecting a citadel, which would require almoft as great a force to attack it as the beft fortified place in Europe. This fortification, the plan of which is already laid, and will certainly one day be carried into execution, will have the advantage of defending the Carenage bay on all fides, of com-manding all the eminences that furround it, and of making it impoffible for the enemy to enter ; of fe-curing the town which is to be built on the back of the mountain ; in fhort, of hindering the affailants from penetrating into the ifland, even if they had actually landed at Shoque Bay, and made themfelves mafters of the Vigie. Further difcuffions on the means of preferving St. Lucia muft be left to the profeffors of the military art.

It is not, in truth, a motive of vanity that hath engaged us in the difcuffion of this matter, which is fo contrary to our profeffion, and which implies fo many ftudies to which we are ftrangers, and fo long an experience in thofe who follow it. But zeal, the

B O O K desire of doing good, and the spirit of patriotism, di-
XIII. rect the thoughts of the man and of the citizen upon
every object. His heart grows warm ; he reflects ;
and if he thinks he has not discovered what is right
to be done, he must speak, because his silence would
be reproachful to himself. " If my ideas be just,"
saith he to himself, " perhaps government may avail
" themselves of them ; if they be erroneous, the worst
" that can happen will be, that I shall excite a smile,
" and that I shall be called the good man, a name
" which the venerable Abbé of St. Pierre took so
" much pride in. I would rather run the risk of be-
" ing ridiculous, than lose the opportunity of being
" useful." Whether this duty be well fulfilled or
not, let us fix the attention of the reader on Martinico.

The French   This island hath sixteen leagues in length, and for-
settle at   ty-five in circumference, exclusive of the capes, which
Martinico,
upon the   sometimes extend two or three leagues into the sea.
ruins of the It is very uneven, and intersected in all parts by a
Caribs.   number of hillocks, which are mostly of a conical
form. Three mountains rise above these smaller eminences. The highest bears the indelible marks of an
ancient volcano. The woods with which it is covered, continually attract the clouds, which occasions
noxious damps, and contributes to make it horrid and
inaccessible, while the two others are in most parts
cultivated. From these mountains, but chiefly from
the first, issue the many springs that water the island.
These waters, which flow in gentle streams, are
changed into torrents on the slightest storm. Their
quality partakes of the nature of the soil they pass
through ; in some places they are excellent, in others
so bad, that the inhabitants are obliged to drink the
water they have collected in the rainy season.

Denambuc, who had sent to reconnoitre Martinico,
sailed from St. Christopher's in 1635, to settle his nation there ; for he would not have it peopled from
Europe. He foresaw that men, tired with the fatigue
of a long voyage, would mostly perish soon after their

arrival, either from the effects of a new climate, or BOOK from the hardships incident to most emigrations. The XIII. sole founders of this new colony were a hundred men, who had long lived in this government of St. Chriftopher's. They were brave, active, inured to labour and fatigues; skilful in tilling the ground and erecting habitations; abundantly provided with potato plants, and all necessary seeds.

They completed their first settlement without any difficulty. The natives, intimidated by the fire-arms, or seduced by the promises that were made them, gave up to the French the western and southern parts of the island, and retired to the other. This tranquillity was of short duration. The Caribs, when they saw these enterprising strangers daily increasing, were convinced that their ruin was inevitable, unless they could extirpate them; and they therefore called in the savages of the neighbouring islands to their affiftance. They fell jointly upon a little fort that had been accidentally erected; but they met with such a warm reception, that they thought proper to retreat, leaving seven or eight hundred of their best warriors dead upon the spot. After this check they difappeared for a long while; and when they returned, they brought with them presents, and expressed their concern for what had happened. They were received in a friendly manner; and the reconciliation was fealed with some bottles of brandy that were given them to drink.

The labours had been carried on with difficulty till this period. The fear of a surprise obliged the colonists of three different habitations to meet every night in that which was in the centre, and which was always kept in a state of defence. There they slept fecure, guarded by their dogs and a centinel. In the day-time no one ventured out without his gun, and a brace of pistols at his girdle. These precautions were needless when the two nations came to be on friendly terms; but the one, whose friendship and favour had been courted, took such undue advantages

B O O K of her fuperiority, to extend her ufurpations, that fhe
  XIII. foon rekindled in the others a hatred that had never
entirely fubfided. The favages, whofe manner of life
requires a vaft extent of land, finding themfelves
daily more ftraitened, had recourfe to ftratagem, to
weaken an enemy whom they dared not attack by
force. They feparated into fmall bands, way-laid
the French, who frequented the woods, waited till
the fportfman had fired his piece, and, before he had
time to load it again, rufhed upon him and deftroyed
him. Twenty men had been thus deftroyed before
any one was able to account for their difappearance.
As foon as this particular was difcovered, the agref-
fors were purfued and beaten, their carbets burnt,
their wives and children maffacred, and thofe few
that efcaped the carnage, fled from Martinico, and
never appeared there again.

First la-   The French, by this retreat now become fole ma-
bours of the fters of the ifland, lived quietly upon thofe fpots
French in
Martinico. which beft fuited their plantations. They were then
divided into two claffes. The firft confifted of fuch
as had paid their paffage to America ; and thefe were
called inhabitants. The government diftributed lands
to them, which became their abfolute property upon
paying a yearly tribute. They were obliged to keep
watch by turns, and to contribute, in proportion to
their abilities, towards the neceffary expences for the
public welfare and fafety. Thefe had under their
command a multitude of miferable people brought
over from Europe at their expence, whom they called *engagés*, or bondfmen. This engagement was a
kind of flavery for the term of three years. When
that time was expired, the bondfmen, by recovering
their liberty, became the equals of thofe whom they
had ferved.

They all confined themfelves at firft to the cultivation of tobacco and cotton ; to which was foon added that of the arnotto and indigo. That of fugar
was not begun till about the year 1650. Benjamin
Dacofta, one of thofe Jews who are beholden for their

induſtry to that very oppreſſion which their nation is B O O K
now fallen under, after having exerciſed it upon $\underbrace{\text{XIII.}}$
others, planted ſome cocoa trees ten years after. His
example was not followed till 1684, when the chocolate grew more common in France. Cocoa then became the principal dependence of the coloniſts, who
had not a ſufficient fund to undertake ſugar plantations. One of thoſe calamities which ariſe from the
ſeaſons, and which ſometimes affect men, and ſometimes vegetables, deſtroyed all the cocoa trees in
1727. This ſpread a general conſternation among
the inhabitants of Martinico. The coffee tree was
then propoſed to them, as a plank is held out to mariners after a ſhipwreck.

The French miniſtry had received, as a preſent
from the Dutch, two of theſe trees, which were carefully preſerved in the king's botanical garden. Two
ſhoots were taken from theſe. Mr. Deſclieux, who
was intruſted to carry them over to Martinico, in
1726, happened to be on board a ſhip which wanted
water. He ſhared with his young trees the portion
that was allotted him for his own drinking ; and by
this generous ſacrifice ſaved half of the valuable truſt
that had been put into his hands. His magnanimity
was rewarded. The culture of coffee was attended
with the greateſt and moſt rapid ſucceſs ; and this
virtuous patriot enjoyed, till the end of 1774, the
pleaſing ſatisfaction, the uncommon felicity, of having as it were ſaved an important colony, and enriched it with a freſh branch of induſtry.

Independent of this reſource, Martinico was poſſeſſed of thoſe natural advantages which ſeemed to
promiſe a ſpeedy and great proſperity. Of all the
French ſettlements, it is the moſt happily ſituated
with regard to the winds that prevail in thoſe ſeas.
Its harbours poſſeſs the ineſtimable advantage of affording a certain ſhelter from the hurricanes which
annoy theſe latitudes. Its ſituation having made it
the ſeat of government, it has obtained the greateſt
marks of favour, and enjoyed the ableſt and moſt up-

BOOK right adminiftration of them all. The enemy has
XIII. conftantly refpected the valour of its inhabitants, and
has feldom attacked it, without having caufe to re-
pent. Its domeftic peace has never been difturbed,
not even in 1717, when, urged by a general difcontent, the inhabitants ventured, boldly indeed, but
prudently, to fend back to France a governor and
an intendant, who oppreffed the people under their
defpotifm and rapacioufnefs. The order, tranquillity, and harmony, which they found means to preferve in thofe times of anarchy, were a proof that
they were influenced rather by their averfion from
tyranny, than by their impatience of authority;
and ferved in fome meafure to juftify to the mother-
country, a ftep, which in itfelf might be confidered
as irregular, and contrary to the eftablifhed principles.

Notwithftanding all thefe advantages, Martinico,
though in greater forwardnefs than the other French
colonies, had made but little progrefs at the end of
the laft century. In 1700, it contained but 6597
white men in all. The favages, Mulattoes, and free
Negroes, men, women, and children, amounted to
no more than 507. The number of flaves was but
14,566. All thefe together made a population of
21,640 perfons. The whole of the cattle was 3668
horfes or mules, and 9217 head of horned cattle.
They grew a great quantity of cocoa, tobacco, and
cotton, and had nine indigo houfes, and one hundred
and eighty-three fmall fugar plantations.

Profperity On the ceffation of the long and obftinate wars,
of Marti- which had ravaged all the continents, and been car-
nico.
Caufe of it. ried on upon all the feas of the world, and when
France had relinquifhed her projects of conquefts and
thofe principles of adminiftration by which fhe had
been fo long mifled; Martinico emerged from that
feeble ftate in which all thefe calamities had kept
her, and foon rofe to a great degree of profperity.
She became the general mart for all the windward
national fettlements. It was in her ports that the

neighbouring iflands fold their produce, and bought **B O O K** the commodities of the mother-country. The French navigators loaded and unloaded their fhips no where elfe. Martinico was famous all over Europe. She was the objeét of fpeculation, confidered under the different views of a planter, an agent to the other colonies, and a trader with Spanifh and North America.

As a planter, it employed, in 1736, feventy-two thoufand flaves, upon a foil, great part of which was newly cleared, and which conftantly yielded very abundant crops.

The conneétions of Martinico with the other iflands entitled her to the profits of commiffion, and the charges of tranfport, as fhe alone was in poffeffion of carriages. This profit might be rated at the tenth of the produce, which was increafing daily. This ftanding debt, feldom called in, was left them for the improvement of their plantations. It was increafed by advances in money, flaves, and other neceffary articles. Martinico, thus becoming more and more a creditor to the other iflands, kept them in conftant dependence, but without injuring them. They all enriched themfelves by her affiftance, and their profit was beneficial to her.

Her conneétions with Cape Breton, with Canada, and with Louifiana, procured her a market for her ordinary fugars, her inferior coffee, her molaffes and rum, which would not fell in France. They gave her, in exchange, falt fifh, dried vegetables, deals, and fome flour.

In her clandeftine trade on the coafts of Spanifh America, confifting wholly of goods manufaétured by the nation, fhe was well paid for the rifks which the French merchants did not choofe to run. This traffic, lefs important than the former as to its objeét, was much more lucrative in its effeéts. It commonly brought in a profit of fourfcore or ninety per cent. upon the value of three or four millions of livres [from 125,000l. to 166,666l. 13s. 4d.], yearly fent to the Caraccas, or the neigbouring colonies.

BOOK
XIII.

So many profperous tranfactions had brought immenfe fums into Martinico. Twelve millions of livres
[500,000l.] were conftantly circulated there with
amazing rapidity. This is, perhaps, the only country in the world where the fpecie has been fo confiderable, as to make it a matter of indifference to
them whether they dealt in gold or filver, or in commodities.

Her extenfive trade annually brought into her ports
two hundred fhips from France, fourteen or fifteen
fitted out by the mother-country for the `coaft of
Guinea, thirty from Canada, ten or twelve from the
iflands of Margaretta and Trinidad; befide the Englifh and Dutch fhips that come to carry on a fmuggling trade. The private navigation from the ifland
to the northern colonies, to the Spanifh continent,
and to the Windward Iflands, employed a hundred
and thirty veffels, from twenty to feventy tons burden, manned with fix hundred European failors of
all nations, and fifteen hundred flaves long inured to
the fea fervice.

Manner in
which the
trade is car-
ried on in
Martinico.

At firft, the fhips that frequented Martinico ufed
to land in thofe parts where the plantations lay.
This practice, feemingly the moft natural, was liable
to great inconveniences. The north and north-eaft-
erly winds which blow upon part of the coafts, keep
the fea in a conftant and violent agitation. Though
there are many good roads, they are either at a confiderable diftance from each other, or from moft of
the habitations. The floops, deftined to coaft along
this interval, were frequently forced by the weather
to anchor, or to take in but half their lading. Thefe
difficulties retarded the loading and unloading of the
fhip; and the confequence of thefe delays was, a
great lofs of men, and an increafe of expence to the
buyer and feller.

Commerce, which muft always reckon among its
greateft advantages that of procuring a quick return,
could not but be impeded by another inconvenience,
which was the neceffity the trader lay under, even

in the beſt latitudes, of diſpoſing of his cargo in ſmall parcels. If ſome induſtrious man undertook to ſave him that trouble, this enhanced the price of the goods to the coloniſts. The merchant's profit is to be rated in proportion to the quantity he ſells. The more he ſells, the more is he able to abate of the profit which another muſt make who ſells leſs.

A greater inconvenience than either of theſe was, that ſome places was overſtocked with ſome ſorts of European goods, while others were in want of them. The owners of the ſhips were equally at a loſs to take in a proper lading. Moſt places did not afford all ſorts of commodities, nor every ſpecies of the ſame commodity. This deficiency obliged them to touch at ſeveral places, or to carry away too great or too ſmall a quantity of what was fit for the port where they were to unload.

The ſhips themſelves were expoſed to ſeveral difficulties. Many of them wanted careening, and moſt required at leaſt ſome repair. The proper aſſiſtance on theſe occaſions was not to be found in the roads that were but little frequented, where workmen did not chooſe to ſettle, for fear of not getting ſufficient employment. They were therefore obliged to go and refit in ſome particular harbours, and then return to take in their lading at the place where they had made their ſale. Theſe different expeditions took up at leaſt three or four months.

Theſe and many more inconveniences made it very deſirable to ſome of the inhabitants, and to all the navigators, to eſtabliſh a magazine, where the colonies and the mother-country might ſend their reſpective articles of exchange. Nature ſeemed to point out Fort Royal as a fit place for this purpoſe. Its harbour was one of the beſt in all the Windward Iſlands, and ſo celebrated for its ſafety, that, when it was open to the Dutch veſſels, they had orders from the republic to ſhelter there in June, July, and Auguſt, from the hurricanes which are ſo frequent and ſo violent in thoſe latitudes. The lands of the

B O O K   Lamentin are diſtant but a league, and are the moſt
   XIII.   fertile and richeſt of all the colony. The numerous
rivers which water this fruitful country, convey loaded canoes to a certain diſtance from the place where
they empty into the ſea. The protection of the fortifications ſecured the peaceable enjoyment of ſo
many advantages; which, however, were balanced
by a ſwampy and unwholeſome ſoil. This capital of
Martinico was alſo the aſylum of the men of war;
which branch of the navy at that time deſpiſed, and
even oppreſſed, the merchantmen. On this account,
Fort Royal was an improper place to become the
centre of trade, which was therefore turned to St.
Peter's.

   This little town, which, notwithſtanding the fires
that have reduced it four times to aſhes, ſtill contains
eighteen hundred houſes, is ſituated on the weſtern
coaſt of the iſland, in a bay or inlet which is almoſt circular. One part of it is built on the ſtrand
along the ſea-ſide; which is called the Anchorage;
and is the place deſtined for the ſhips and warehouſes.
The other part of the town ſtands upon a low hill:
it is called the Fort, from a ſmall fortification that
was built there in 1665, to check the ſeditions of the
inhabitants againſt the tyranny of monopoly; but it
now ſerves to protect the road from foreign enemies.
Theſe two parts of the town are ſeparated by a rivu-
let, or fordable river.

   The anchorage is at the back of a pretty high and
perpendicular hill. Shut up, as it were, by this hill,
which intercepts the eaſterly winds, the moſt conſtant
and moſt ſalubrious in theſe parts; expoſed, without
any refreſhing breezes, to the ſcorching beams of
the ſun, reflected from the hill, from the ſea, and
the black ſand on the beach; this place is extremely
hot, and always unwholeſome. Beſides, there is no
harbour; and the ſhips, which cannot winter ſafely
upon this coaſt, are obliged to take ſhelter at Fort
Royal. But theſe diſadvantages are compenſated by
the conveniency of the road of St. Peter's, for load-

ing and unloading of goods; and by its fituation, B O O K
which is fuch, that fhips can freely go in and out at XIII.
all times, and with all winds.

This village was the firft that was built, and the
firft that was cultivated on the ifland. It hath not
been, however, fo much on account of its antiquity
as of its convenience, that it enjoys the advantage of
having become the centre of communication between
the colony and the mother-country. At firft, St.
Peter's was the ftorehoufe for the commodities of fome
diftricts, which lay along fuch dreary and tempeftu-
ous coafts, that no fhip could ever get at them; fo
that the inhabitants could carry on no trade without
removing elfewhere. The agents for thefe colonifts
in thofe early times, were only the mafters of fmall
veffels, who having made themfelves known, by continually failing about the ifland, were enticed, by
the profpect of gain, to fix upon a fettled place for
their refidence. Honefty was the only fupport of
this intercourfe : moft of thefe agents could not read.
None of them kept any books or journals. They
had a trunk, in which they kept a feparate bag for
each perfon, whofe bufinefs they tranfacted. Into
this bag they put the produce of the fales, and took
out what money they wanted for the purchafes.
When the bag was empty, the commiffion was at an
end. This confidence, which muft appear fabulous
in our days of degeneracy and difhonefty, was yet
common at the beginning of this century. There
are fome perfons ftill living, who have carried on this
trade, where the employer had no other fecurity for
the fidelity of his agent, but the benefit refulting
from it.

Thefe plain men were fucceffively replaced by
more enlightened perfons from Europe. Some had
gone over to the colony, when it was taken out of
the hands of the exclufive companies. Their number increafed as the commodities multiplied ; and
they themfelves contributed greatly to the extending
of the plantations by the loans they advanced to the

planters; whofe labours had, till then, gone on but flowly for want of fuch help. This conduct made them the neceffary agents for their debtors in the colony, as they were already for their employers at home. Even the colonift, who owed them nothing, was in fome meafure dependent on them, as he might poffibly hereafter ftand in need of their affiftance. If his crop fhould fail, or be retarded, a plantation of fugar-canes be fet on fire, or a mill blown down ; if his buildings fhould fall, mortality carry off his cattle or his flaves ; or if every thing fhould be deftroyed by drought or heavy rains ; where could he find the means of fupporting himfelf during thefe calamities, or of repairing the lofs occafioned by them ? Thefe means are in twenty different hands. If only one refufes his affiftance, the diftrefs muft neceffarily increafe. Thefe confiderations induced fuch as had not yet borrowed money, to truft the agents of St. Peter's with their concerns, in order to fecure a refource in times of diftrefs.

The few rich inhabitants, whofe fortunes feemed to place them above thefe wants, were in fome degree compelled to apply to this factory. The trading captains, finding a port where they might with advantage complete their bufinefs, without ftirring out of their warehoufes, or even of their fhips, forfook Fort Royal, Trinity Fort, and all the other places where an arbitrary price was put upon the commodities, and where the payments were flow and uncertain. By this revolution, the colonifts, being confined to their works, which require a conftant and daily attendance, could no longer go out to difpofe of their produce. They were therefore obliged to intruft it to able men, who, being fettled at the only frequented fea-port, were ready to feize the moft favourable opportunities for buying and felling ; an ineftimable advantage this, in a country where trade is continually fluctuating. Guadalupe and Granada followed this example, induced by the fame motives.

The war of 1744 put a ftop to this profperity ; not

that the fault was in Martinico itſelf. Its navy, conſtantly exerciſed, and accuſtomed to frequent engagements, which the carrying on of a contraband trade
required, was prepared for action. In leſs than ſix
months, forty privateers, fitted out at St. Peter's,
ſpread themſelves about the latitudes of the Caribbee
Iſlands. They ſignalized themſelves in a manner
worthy of the ancient freebooters. They were conſtantly returning in triumph, and laden with an immenſe booty. Yet, in the midſt of theſe ſucceſſes,
an entire ſtop was put to the navigation of the colony,
both to the Spaniſh coaſt and to Canada, and they
were conſtantly diſturbed even on their own coaſts.
The few ſhips that came from France, in order to
compenſate the hazards they were expoſed to by the
loſe of their commodities, ſold them at a very advanced price, and bought them at a very low one.
By this means the produce decreaſed in value, the
lands were but ill cultivated, the works neglected,
and the ſlaves periſhing for want. Every thing was
in a declining ſtate, and tending to decay. The
peace at laſt reſtored the freedom of trade, and with
it the hopes of recovering the ancient proſperity of
the iſland. The event did not anſwer the pains that
were taken to attain it.

Two years had not yet elapſed ſince the ceſſation
of hoſtilities, when the colony loſt the contraband
trade ſhe carried on with the American Spaniards.
This revolution was not owing to the vigilance of the
guarda-coſtas. As it is more the intereſt of the traders to ſet them at defiance, than theirs to defend
themſelves ; the former are apt to deſpiſe men who
are ill paid to protect ſuch rights, or enforce ſuch
prohibitions, as are often times unjuſt. The ſubſti-
tution of regiſter ſhips to the ſleets was the cauſe that
confined the attempts of the ſmugglers within very
narrow limits. In the new ſyſtem, the number of
ſhips was undetermined, and the time of their arrival uncertain, which occaſioned a variation in the
price of commodities unknown before. From that

Book XIII.

Decline of Martinico, and the cauſe of it.

BOOK XIII. time the fmuggler, who only engaged in this trade from the certainty of a fixed and conftant profit, would no longer purfue it, when it did not fecure him an equivalent to the rifks he ran.

But this lofs was not fo fenfibly felt by the colony, as the hardfhips brought upon them by the mother-country. An unfkilful adminiftration clogged the reciprocal and neceffary connection between the iflands and North America with fo many formalities, that in 1755 Martinico fent but four veffels to Canada. The direction of the colony, now committed to the care of avaricious and ignorant clerks, foon loft its importance, funk into contempt, and was proftituted to venality.

In the meanwhile the trade of France was not yet affected by the decay of Martinico. The French found traders in the road of St. Peter's, who purchafed their cargoes at a good price, and fent their fhips home with expedition, and richly laden; and they never inquired from what particular colony the confumption and produce arofe. Even the Negroes who were carried there were fold at a high price; but few remained. The greateft part were fent to the Granades, to Guadalupe, and even to the Neutral Iflands, which, notwithftanding the unlimited freedom they enjoyed, preferred the flaves brought by the French to thofe the Englifh offered, though apparently on better terms. They were convinced, from long experience, that the chofen Negroes, who coft the moft, enriched their lands, while the plantations did not flourifh in the hands of the Negroes bought at a lower price. But thefe profits of the mother-country were foreign and rather hurtful to Martinico.

She had not yet repaired her loffes during the peace, nor paid off the debts which a feries of calamities had obliged her to contract; when war, the greateft of all evils, broke out afrefh. A feries of misfortunes for France, after repeated defeats and loffes, made Martinico fall into the hands of the Englifh. It was

reſtored in July 1763, ſixteen months after it had been
conquered; but deprived of all the neceſſary means
of proſperity, that had made it of ſo much importance.
For ſome years paſt, the contraband trade carried on
to the Spaniſh coaſts was almoſt entirely loſt. The
ceſſion of Canada and of Louiſiana had precluded all
hopes of opening again a communication, which had
only been interrupted by temporary miſtakes. The
productions of the Granades, St. Vincent, and Dominica, which were now become Britiſh dominions,
could no longer be brought into their harbours; and
a new regulation of the mother-country, which for-
bade her having any intercourſe with Gaudalupe, left
her no hopes from that quarter.

The colony, thus deſtitute, could depend upon
nothing but its cultures; unfortunately, at the period
when its inhabitants began to attend to them with
advantage, there appeared in the iſland a ſpecies of
ant unknown in America, before it had exerciſed ſuch
ravages in Barbadoes, that it was deliberated, whether
it would not be proper to abandon a colony formerly
ſo flouriſhing. It is not known whether this inſect
was transferred to Martinico from the continent, or
from this iſland. It is however certain, that it occaſioned inexpreſſible ravages in all the ſugar plantations in the iſland where it appeared. This calamity,
which had been too ineffectually reſiſted, had laſted
for eleven years, when the coloniſts aſſembled on the
9th of March 1775, announced a reward of 666,000
livres [27,750l.], for the perſon who ſhould find a
remedy againſt theſe deſtructive ſcourges. This important ſecret hath been already diſcovered and practiſed by an officer named Deſvouſe, upon one of the
plantations the moſt infeſted with ants. This excellent cultivator had obtained plentiful crops by multiplying the labours, the manure, and the weedings,
by burning the ſtraw in which this inſect concealed
itſelf, by replanting the ſugar-canes after every crop,
and by diſpoſing them in ſuch a manner as to facilitate the circulation of the air. This example hath

BOOK at length been followed by the rich colonists; others
XIII. will imitate it in proportion to their means; and it is
to be hoped that in procefs of time, the recollection
only will remain of this great difafter.

This calamity was raging in its greateft force, when
the hurricane of 1766, the moft furious of thofe which
had ravaged Martinico, deftroyed the provifions and
the harvefts, rooted up the trees, and even overthrew
the buildings. The deftruction was fo general, that
fcarce a few inhabitants remained able to adminifter
comfort to fo many unfortunate people, and to relieve
fo many miferies.

The high price to which for fome time coffee had
rifen, affifted them in fupporting thefe misfortunes.
This production, which had been too much cultivated, fell into difgrace, and the planters preferved only the regret of having devoted their lands to a commodity, the value of which was no more fufficient for
their fubfiftence.

To complete thefe misfortunes, the mother-country fuffered the colony to be in want of the perfons
neceffary for the labours of it; for from the year
1764 to 1774 the trade of France did not introduce
into Martinico more than three hundred and forty-
five flaves, one year with another. The inhabitants
were reduced to the neceffity of renewing their men
from the refufe of the Englifh cargoes clandeftinely
introduced.

An enlightened minifter, whofe watchful care
would have extended itfelf to all parts of the empire,
would have alleviated the fate of a great fettlement
fo cruelly afflicted, but this was not the cafe. New
offices eftablifhed on the colony were fubftituted to
thofe fuccours it had a right to expect.

In the French fettlements in the New World, and
undoubtedly in thofe of other nations likewife, the
Africans grew extremely depraved; and this was,
becaufe they were certain of impunity. Their mafters, feduced by a blind motive of intereft, never
brought the criminals to juftice. In order to put a

ftop to this great mifchief, the black code regulated
that the price of every flave who fhould be condemned to death, after information lodged againft him
with the magiftrate by the proprietor, fhould be paid
for by the colony.

Collections were immediately made for this ufeful
purpofe ; but part of them was foon employed in expences foreign to their inftitution. That of Martinico was ftill more oppreffed than the others with thefe
acts of injuftice ; when in 1771 it was burdened with
the expences incurred by the chamber of agriculture
belonging to the colony, and with the falary of a de-
puty, which its council keeps to no purpofe in the
mother-country.

Oppreffion was carried ftill further. The duties
which the government collected at Martinico, were
originally very trifling, and were paid in provifions,
which were changed into metals, when thefe univerfal agents of commerce were multiplied in the ifland.
Neverthelefs, the impoft was moderate till 1763,
when it was raifed to eight hundred thoufand livres
[833,333l. 6s. 8d.]. Three years after, it became
neceffary to lower it, but this diminution, extorted
by the calamities of the times, was put a ftop to in
1762. The tribute was lowered again in 1778, to
the fum of 666,000 livres [27,750l.], which is equal
to a million [41,666l. 13s. 4d.] in the iflands. It is
paid by a poll-tax upon the white people and upon
the Negroes, by a tax of five per cent. on the rent
of houfes, by a duty of one per cent. on all heavy
merchandife which enters the colony, and an equal
duty upon all provifions that are exported from it,
except coffee, which pays three per cent.

On the firft of January 1778, the population of
Martinico confifted of twelve thoufand white people
of all ages and of both fexes ; three thoufand free
Negroes or Mulattoes, and upwards of fourfcore thoufand flaves, though its calculations did not amount
to more than feventy-two thoufand.

Prefent
ftate of
Martinico.

BOOK
XIII.
Its cattle confifted of eight thoufand two hundred mules or horfes ; nine thoufand feven hundred head of horned cattle, and thirteen thoufand one hundred hogs, fheep, or goats.

Its fugar plantations amounted to two hundred and fifty-feven, which occupied ten thoufand three hundred and ninety-feven fquares of land. It cultivated fixteen millions fix hundred two thoufand eight hundred and feventy coffee plants ; one million four hundred thirty thoufand and twenty cacao plants ; and one million fix hundred forty-eight thoufand five hundred and fifty cotton plants.

In 1775, the French navigators loaded at Martinico one hundred and twenty-two veffels, with two hundred and forty-four thoufand four hundred and thirty-eight quintals fifty-eight pounds of clayed or raw fugar, which were fold in the mother-country for 9,971,155 livres 3 fols 7 deniers [about 415,465l. 16s.] ; with ninety-fix thoufand eight hundred and eighty-nine quintals fixty-eight pounds of coffee, which were fold for 4,577,259 livres 16 fols [190,719l. 3s. 2d.] ; eleven hundred and forty-feven quintals eight pounds of indigo, which were fold for 975,018 livres [40,625l. 15s.] ; eight thoufand fix hundred and fifty-fix quintals fixty-three pounds of cacao, which were fold for 605,964 livres 12 fols [25,248l. 10s. 6d.] ; eleven thoufand and twelve quintals of cotton, which were fold for 2,753,100 livres [114,712l. 10s.] ; nine hundred and nineteen hides, which were fold for 8271 livres [344l. 12s. 6d.] ; twenty-nine quintals ten pounds of rope-yarn, which were fold for 29,100 livres [1212l. 10s.] ; nineteen hundred fixty-fix quintals thirty-five pounds of black caffia, which were fold for 52,980 livres 10 fols [2207l. 10s.] ; one hundred and twenty-five quintals of wood, which were fold for 3125 livres [130l. 4s. 2d.]. The total amount of thefe articles was 18,975,974 livres 1 fol 7 deniers [about 790,665l. 11s. 9d.] ; but this fum did not entirely belong to the colony ; a little more

than a quarter of it belonged to St. Lucia and Gua- B O O K
dalupe, which had fent part of their productions to   XIII.
Martinico.

All thofe who from inftinct or duty are concerned Hath Mar-
tinico any
for the intereft of their country, would wifh to fee profpect of
the productions multiplied at Martinico. It is well improving?
known, indeed, that the centre of the ifland, full of
horrid rocks, is unfit for the culture of fugar, coffee,
or cotton ; that too much moifture would be hurtful
to thefe productions ; and that, fhould they fucceed,
the charges of carriage acrofs mountains and preci-
pices would abforb the profits of the crops. But in
this large fpace meadows would turn to very good account. The foil is excellent for pafture, and only
wants the attention of government to furnifh the inhabitants with the neceffary increafe of cattle both
for labour and food. There are other fpots on the
ifland where the foil is ungrateful : craggy territories,
which have been levelled by the torrents and the
rains ; fwampy grounds, which it would be difficult,
and perhaps impoffible, to dry up ; and ftony lands,
which cannot be fertilized by any kind of labour.
The obfervers, however, who are the moft acquainted with the colony, unanimoufly agree, that thefe
cultures are capable of being increafed nearly by one-
third, and that even this improvement might be
brought about by a better and more fteady method
of cultivation, without any further clearing of lands.
But in order to attain to this improvement, a greater
number of flaves would be required. It is a confiderable thing that the inhabitants have been able to
preferve, till our time, their works in the fame ftate
as they had received them from their anceftors. We
do not think that it will be in their power to increafe
them.

The proprietors of the lands at Martinico may be
divided into four claffes. The firft are poffeffed of a
hundred large fugar plantations, in which twelve
thoufand Negroes are employed. The fecond have
one hundred and fifty, worked by nine thoufand

blacks. The third clafs poffefs thirty-fix, with two thoufand blacks. The fourth, devoted to the culture of coffee, cotton, cocoa, and caffava, may employ twelve thoufand Negroes. The remaining flaves of both fexes are engaged in domeftic fervices, in fifhing, or in navigation ; they are children or infirm perfons

The firft clafs confifts entirely of rich people. Their culture is carried to the higheft degree of perfection, and they are able to preferve it in the flourifhing ftate to which they have brought it. Even the expences they muft be at for replacing deficiencies, are not fo great as thofe of the lefs wealthy planter, as the flaves born upon thefe plantations fupply the place of thofe deftroyed by time and labour.

The fecond clafs, which is that of planters in eafy circumftances, have but half the hands that would be neceffary to acquire a fortune equal to that of the opulent proprietors. If they were even able to buy the number of flaves they want, they would be deterred from it by fatal experience. Nothing can be more imprudent than the cuftom of putting a great number of frefh Negroes upon a plantation. The ficknefs thofe miferable wretches are liable to, from a change of climate and diet ; the trouble of inuring them to a kind of labour to which they are not accuftomed, and which they diflike, cannot but difguft a planter, from the conftant and laborious attention he muft pay to this training up of men for the cultivation of land. The moft active proprietor is he, who is able to increafe his works by one-fixth of the number of flaves every year. Thus the fecond clafs might acquire fifteen hundred blacks yearly, if the nett produce of their lands would admit of it. But they muft not expect to meet with credit. The merchants in France do not feem difpofed to truft them ; and thofe who circulated their ftock in the colony, no fooner found that they could not make ufe of it without running confiderable rifks, than they removed it to Europe, or to St. Domingo.

The third clafs, which are but little removed from indigence, cannot change their fituation by any means which the natural courfe of trade can fupply. It is a matter of difficulty for them to be able to fubfift. The indulgence of government can alone put then into fuch a flourifhing condition as to render them ufeful to the ftate, by lending them, without intereft, the fums they may want, to raife their plantations. This clafs might employ a greater number of frefh Negroes than we have allotted to the fecond, without the fame inconveniencies; becaufe each planter, having fewer flaves to look after, will be able to pay a greater attention to thofe he may purchafe.

The fourth clafs, who are employed in cultures of lefs importance than that of fugar, do not ftand in need of fuch powerful helps, to recover that eafe and plenty from which they are fallen, by war, hurricanes, and other misfortunes. Could thefe two laft claffes but make an acquifition of fifteen hundred flaves every year, it would be fufficient to raife them to that degree of profperity to which their induftry naturally entitles them.

Thus Martinico might hope to revive her declining plantations, and to recover the firft fplendour to which her diligence had raifed her, if fhe could get a yearly acceffion of three thoufand Negroes. But it is well known that fhe is not in a condition to pay for thefe recruits. She owes the mother-country, for balance of trade, about a million [41,666l. 13s. 4d.]. A feries of misfortunes has obliged her to borrow four millions [166,666l. 13s. 4d.] of the merchants fettled in the town of St. Peter. The engagements fhe has entered into on account of divided inheritances, and thofe fhe has contracted for the purchafe of a number of plantations, have made her infolvent. This defperate ftate will neither allow her the means of foon recovering her former fituation, nor the ambition of purfuing that road to fortune which once lay open to her.

Add to this, that fhe ftands expofed to invafion. Whether

But though there are a number of places where the enemy may land, yet they will never make the attempt. It would indeed be fruitlefs, becaufe of the impoffibility of bringing up the artillery and amunition, acrofs fuch a rugged country, to Fort Royal, which defends the whole colony. It is in this latitude only that the enemy would fail, in order to make fuch an attempt.

In the front of this ftrong and principal place of defence is a famous harbour, fituated on the fide of a broad bay, that cannot be entered without many tackings, which muft decide the fate of any fhip that is forced to avoid an engagement. If fhe happens to be unrigged, or is a bad failer, or meets with fome accident from the variations of the fqualls of wind, the currents, or whirlpools, fhe will fall into the hands of an affailant that is a better failer. The garrifon of the fortrefs itfelf may become a ufelefs and inglorious fpectator of the defeat of a whole fquadron, as it has been often of the taking of merchant-fhips.

The infide of the harbour is much injured, on account of the hulks of feveral fhips that have been funk there, to keep out the Englifh in the laft war. Thefe veffels have been taken up again; but it will ftill require a confiderable expence to remove the heaps of fand which had gathered about them, and to put the harbour in the fame ftate it was before. This work will not admit of any delay ; for the port, though not very fpacious, is the only one where fhips of all rates can winter; the only one where they can be fupplied with mafts, fails, cables, and excellent water, which is brought there from the diftance of a league by a very well contrived canal, and which may be eafily procured.

An enemy will always land near to this harbour, and there is no poffibility of preventing them, whatever precaution be taken. The war could only be carried on againft them in the field ; it could not be continued for any time, and the people would foon

be reduced to fhut themfelves up in their fortifications.

They formerly had no other fortification than Fort
Royal, where immenfe fums had been buried through
want of fkill under a ridge of mountains. All the
knowledge of the ableft engineers has never been
fufficient to give any degree of ftrength or folidity to
works occafionally erected by the moft unfkilful
hands, and without any fort of plan. They have
been obliged to content themfelves with adding a
covered-way, a rampart, and flanks, to fuch parts of
the place as would admit of them. But the work of
the moft confequence has been to cut into the rock,
which eafily gives way; and to dig fubterraneous
rooms, which are airy, wholefome, and fit to fecure
warlike ftores and provifions; as alfo to fhelter the
fick, and to defend the foldiers, and fuch of the inhabitants whofe attachment to their country would
infpire them with courage to defend the colony. It
has been thought, that men who were fure of finding a fafe retreat in thefe caverns, after having expofed their lives on the ramparts, would foon forget
their fatigues, and face the enemy with frefh vigour.
This idea was fortunate and fenfible, and muft have
been fuggefted, if not by a patriotic government, at
leaft by fome fenfible and humane minifter.

But the bravery this muft infpire could not be fufficient to preferve a place, which is commanded on
all fides. It was therefore thought advifable to fix
upon fome more advantageous fituation; and the
point called *Morne Garnier* was chofen for this purpofe, which is higher by thirty-five or forty feet than
the higheft tops of Patate, Tortenfon, and Cartouch,
all which overlook Fort Royal.

Upon this eminence a citadel has been raifed, confifting of four baftions. The baftions in front, the
covered-way, the refervoirs for water, the powder
magazines; all thefe means of defence are ready.
The cazernes, and other neceffary buildings, will

foon complete the work. If even the redoubts and
the batteries, intended to force the enemy to make
their defcent at a greater diftance than Cafco bay,
where they landed at the laft invafion, fhould not
be attended with the effect that is expected from
them ; yet ftill the colony would be able to refift
about three months. Fifteen hundred men will defend the *Morne Garnier* for thirty or fix-and-thirty
days againft an army of fifteen thoufand ; and twelve
hundred men will fuftain themfelves for twenty or
five-and-twenty days in Fort Royal, which cannot
be attacked till *Garnier* has been taken. This is all
that can be expected from an expence of ten millions of livres [416,666l. 13s. 4d.].

Thofe who are of opinion that the navy alone
ought to protect the colonies, think that fo confiderable an expence hath been mifapplied. As it was
not poffible, in their opinion, to erect fortifications
and to build fhips at the fame time, the preference
ought to have been given to the latter, as being indifpenfably neceffary ; efpecially if the impetuofity
in the character of the French difpofes them to attack rather than to defend, they ought fooner to deftroy than erect fortreffes ; or none but fhips fhould
be built, thofe moveable ramparts which carry war
with them, inftead of waiting for it. Any power that
aims at trade, and the eftablifhment of colonies, muft
have fhips, which bring in men and wealth, and increafe population and circulation ; whereas baftions
and foldiers are only fit to confume men and provifions. All that the court of Verfailles can expect
from the expence they have incurred at Martinico,
is, that if the ifland fhould be attacked by the only
enemy it has to fear, there will be time enough to
relieve it. The Englifh proceed flowly in a fiege ;
they always go on by rule, and nothing diverts them
from completing any works that concern the fafety
of the affailants ; for they efteem the life of a foldier
of more confequence than the lofs of time. This
maxim, fo fenfible in itfelf, is, perhaps, mifapplied in

the deftructive climate of America ; but it is the B O O K
maxim of a people, whofe foldiers are engaged in the XIII.
fervice of the ftate, not mercenaries paid by the
prince. But whatever be the future fate of Martinico,
it is now time to inquire into the prefent ftate of Guadalupe.

This ifland, which is of an irregular form, may be The French
about eighty leagues in circumference. It is divided invade
Guadalupe.
into two parts by a fmall arm of the fea, which is not Calamities
above two leagues long, and from fifteen to forty they experience
toifes broad. This canal, known by the name of the there.
Salt River, is navigable, but will only carry Indian
boats.

That part of the ifland which gives its name to the
whole colony, is, towards the centre, full of craggy rocks, and fo cold, that nothing will grow there
but fern, and fome ufelefs fhrubs covered with mofs.
On the top of thefe rocks, a mountain called *La
Souphriere*, or the Brimftone mountain, rifes to an immenfe height into the middle region of the air. It
exhales, through various openings, a thick black
fmoke, intermixed with fparks that are vifible by
night. From all thefe hills flow numberlefs fprings,
which fertilize the plains below, and moderate the
burning heat of the climate by a refrefhing ftream,
fo celebrated, that the galleons, which formerly ufed
to touch at the Windward Iflands, had orders to renew their provifion with this pure and falubrious water. Such is that part of the ifland properly called
Guadalupe. That which is commonly called Grande
Terre, has not been fo much favoured by nature.
The foil is not fo fertile, or the climate fo wholefome
or fo pleafant. It is, indeed, lefs rugged ; but it
wants fprings and rivers. There are even no fprings
to be found there. Aqueducts, which would not be
very expenfive, would undoubtedly, in procefs of
time, enable it to enjoy this advantage in common
with the other part of the colony.

No European nation had yet taken poffeffion of
this ifland, when five hundred and fifty Frenchmen,

B O O K led on by two gentlemen named Loline and Dupleffis,
  XIII. arrived there from Dieppe on the 28th of June 1635.
They had been very imprudent in their preparations.
Their provifions were fo ill chofen, that they were
fpoiled in the paffage ; and they had fhipped fo few,
that they were exhaufted in two months. They were
fupplied with none from the mother-country. St.
Chriftopher's, whether from fcarcity or defign, refufed
to fpare them any ; and the firft attempts in hufbandry they made in the country, could not yet afford
any thing. No refource was left for the colony but
from the favages ; but the fuperfluities of a people
who cultivate but little, and therefore had never laid
up any ftores, could not be very confiderable. The
new-comers, not content with what the favages might
freely and voluntarily bring, came to a refolution to
plunder them ; and hoftilities commenced on the 16th
of January 1636.

The Caribs, not thinking themfelves in a condition
openly to refift an enemy who had fo much the advantage from the fuperiority of their arms, deftroyed
their own provifions and plantations, and retired to
Grande Terre, or to the neighbouring iflands. From
thence the moft defperate came over to the ifland
from which they had been driven, and concealed
themfelves in the thickeft parts of the forefts. In
the day-time they fhot with their poifoned arrows, or
knocked down with their clubs, all the French who
were fcattered about for hunting or fifhing. In the
night, they burned the dwellings, and deftroyed the
plantations, of their unjuft fpoilers.

A dreadful famine was the confequence of this
kind of war. The colonifts were reduced to graze in
the fields, to eat their own excrements, and to dig up
dead bodies for their fubfiftence. Many who had
been flaves at Algiers, held in abhorrence the hands
that had broken their fetters ; and all of them curfed
their exiftence. It was in this manner that they
atoned for the crime of their invafion, till the government of Aubert brought about a peace with the

favages at the end of the year 1640. When we confider the injuftice of the hoftilities which the Europeans have committed all over America, we are almoft tempted to rejoice at their misfortunes, and at
all the judgments that purfue thofe inhuman oppreffors. We are ready, from motives of humanity, to
renounce the ties that bind us to the inhabitants of
our own hemifphere, to change our conne&ions, and
to contra& beyond the feas, with the favage Indians,
an alliance which unites all mankind, that of misfortune and compaffion.

The remembrance, however, of hardfhips endured
in an invaded ifland, proved a powerful incitement
to the cultivation of all articles of immediate neceffity ; which afterwards induced an attention to thofe
of luxury confumed in the mother-country. The
few inhabitants who had efcaped the calamities they
had drawn upon themfelves, were foon joined by fome
difcontented colonifts from St. Chriftopher's, by Europeans fond of novelty, by failors tired of navigation,
and by fome fea-captains, who prudently chofe to
commit to the care of a grateful foil the treafures
they had faved from the dangers of the fea. But
ftill the profperity of Guadulupe was ftopped, or impeded, by obftacles arifing from its fituation.

The facility with which the pirates from the neighbouring iflands could carry off their cattle, their flaves,
their very crops, frequently brought them into a very
defperate fituation. Inteftine broils, arifing from jea-
loufies of authority, often difturbed the quiet of the
planters. The adventurers who went over to the
Windward Iflands, difdaining a land that was fitter
for agriculture than for naval expeditions, were eafily attra&ed to Martinico, by the convenient roads it
abounds with. The prote&ion of thofe intrepid pirates, brought to that ifland all the traders who flattered themfelves that they might buy up the fpoils
of the enemy at a low price, and all the planters who
thought they might fafely give themfelves up to
peaceful labours. This quick population could not

B O O K fail of introducing the civil and military government
XIII. of the Caribbee Iflands into Martinico. From that
time, the French miniftry attended more ferioufly to
this than to the other colonies, which were not fo immediately under their direction; and, hearing chiefly
of this ifland, they turned all their encouragements
into that channel.

It was in confequence of this preference, that in 1700
the number of inhabitants in Guadalupe amounted
only to 3825 white people ; 325 favages, free Negroes,
or Mulattoes ; and 6725 flaves, many of whom were
Caribs. Her cultures were reduced to 60 fmall plantations of fugar, 66 of indigo, a little cocoa, and a
confiderable quantity of cotton. The cattle amount-
to 1620 horfes and mules, and 3699 head of horned
cattle. This was the fruit of fixty years labour.

The colony did not make any rapid progrefs till
after the peace of Utrecht. Its population confifted
of 9643 white men ; 41,140 flaves ; and its cattle
and provifions were proportioned to it, when, in the
month of April 1759, it was conquered by the arms
of Great Britain.

France lamented this lofs ; but the colony had reafon to comfort themfelves for this difgrace. During
a fiege of three months they had feen their plantations deftroyed, the buildings that ferved to carry on
their works burnt down, and fome of their flaves carried off. Had the enemy been forced to retreat after
all thefe devaftations, the ifland was ruined. Deprived of all affiftance from the mother-country, which
was not able to fend her any fuccours, and expecting
nothing from the Dutch, who on account of their
neutrality came into her roads, becaufe fhe had nothing to offer them in exchange, fhe could never
have fubfifted till the enfuing harveft.

The conquerors delivered the colonifts from thefe
apprehenfions. The Englifh, indeed, are no merchants in their colonies. The proprietors of lands,
who moftly refide in Europe, fend their reprefenta-
tives whatever they want, and draw the whole pro-

duce of the eftate by the return of their fhip. An
agent fettled in fome fea-port of Great Britain, is intrufted with the furnifhing of the plantation, and
with receiving the produce. This was impracticable
at Guadalupe ; and the conquerors in this refpect
were obliged to adopt the cuftom of the conquered.
The Englifh, informed of the advantage the French
made of their trade with the colonies, haftened, in
imitation of them, to fend their fhips to the conquered ifland ; and fo multiplied their expeditions, that
they overftocked the market, and fank the price of
all European commodities. The colonift bought them
at a very low price, and, in confequence of this plenty, obtained long delays for the payment.

To this credit, which was neceffary, was foon added another arifing from fpeculation, which enabled
the colony to fulfil its engagements.

The victorious nation fent there eighteen thoufand
feven hundred and twenty-one flaves, in the expectation of reaping in time great advantages from their
labour. But their ambition was fruftrated, and the
colony was reftored to its former poffeffors in July
1763.

The flourifhing ftate to which Guadalupe had been Various
raifed by the Englifh, was remarked by all the world, fyftems a-
when they reftored it. It acquired that degree of the mini-
confideration, which opulence always infpires at pre- ftry of
fent. The mother-country beheld it with a kind of the govern-
refpect. Till that time it had been fubordinate to ment of
Martinico, as were all the French Windward Iflands. Guadalupe.
The ifland was releafed from thefe fhackles, which it
confidered as a difgrace, by giving it an independent
adminiftration. · This arrangement lafted till 1768, at
which period it was again fubjected to the former
yoke, from which it was releafed in 1772, and placed
under it again fix months after. In 1775, a governor of its own was again granted to it ; and it is to
be hoped, that after fo many variations, the court of
Verfailles will no more depart from this arrangement,
the only one which is comfortable to the principles

B O O K of an enlightened policy. Should adminiftration ever
XIII. fwerve from this fortunate plan, the governors and
the intendants would again beftow their care, their
credit, and their regard, upon the metropolitan ifland
immediately under their infpection, while the dependent ifland would be abandoned to fubalterns, without influence or without confideration, and confequently without the power or the will of doing any
thing ufeful.

The military men, who have been of opinion that
the two colonies fhould be united under one governor, have been led into it from confidering the advantages that would arife from collecting the forces
of both iflands, for their mutual defence. But they
have not reflected, that at an equal diftance between
Martinico and Guadalupe, there is Dominica, an Englifh fettlement, which cannot be avoided, and whi c
overlooks equally the double canal that divides it
from the French poffeffions. Should the French naval forces be inferior to the Englifh, the communication would be impracticable, becaufe the refpective
fuccours would infallibly be intercepted ; if, on the
contrary, they fhould be fuperior, the communication
would become ufelefs, becaufe no invafion could be
apprehended. In either of thefe cafes, the fyftem
propofed is chimerical.

It would be very different, if it were neceffary to
carry on offenfive meafures. The union of the powers
belonging to each of thefe iflands might become ufeful, and even neceffary, under fuch circumftances. In
that cafe, the command of the whole would be intrufted to one of the governors, and this command
would ceafe at the conclufion of the projected enterprife.

But is it proper to leave a free trade between the
territorial productions of one colony and thofe of the
other ? Till the conqueft of Guadalupe by the Englifh, the immediate connections of that ifland with
the ports of France had been limited to fix or feven
veffels annually. Its provifions, from motives more

or lefs maturely confidered, were moftly fent to Mar- B O O K
tinico. When, at the period of the reftitution, the XIII.
adminiftration of the two colonies was feparated, their
trade became likewife diftinct. The communications
have fince been opened again, and are ftill permitted
at this prefent time.

This arrangement is cenfured by fome people in
France. It is neceffary, fay they with acrimony, that
the colonies fhould fulfil their deftination, which is,
to confume a great quantity of merchandife from the
mother-country, and to fend back a great abundance
of productions. And yet, notwithftanding her abilities to fulfil this double obligation, Guadalupe will
neither do the one nor the other, as long as fhe fhall
be allowed to carry her commodities to Martinico.
This intercourfe will always be the caufe or the occafion of an immenfe trade in foreign markets, and
at Dominica in particular. This fraudulent trade can
only be ftopped, and the habit of fmuggling eradicat-
ed, by prohibiting this communication.

Thefe arguments, which are founded upon motives
of private intereft, ought not to prevent the con-
firmation of the connections which Guadalupe and
Martinico have formed with each other. Liberty is
the wifh of all mankind ; and every proprietor hath
a natural right to fell the productions of his foil to
whom he choofes, and to as much advantage as he
can. This fundamental principle of all well-regulated focieties hath been fet afide in favour of the mother-country ; and it was perhaps neceffary in the
prefent ftate of affairs. But to be defirous of extending farther the prohibitions to which the colonifts are fubjected ; to wifh to deprive them of the
conveniences and advantages which they may derive
from a lafting or a temporary communication with
their own fellow-citizens, is an act of tyranny which
the merchants of France will one day be afhamed of
having folicited, and which will never be granted but
by an ignorant, corrupt, or weak minifter. If, as it
is pretended, the intercourfe permitted at prefent be-

B O O K tween the two iflands, fhould give part of their com-
XIII. modities to artful and rapacious rivals, government
may find fome fair means of introducing into the
kingdom the territorital riches of Guadalupe, and of
the fmall iflands which are under its dependence.

Iflands de-   Defeada, at the diftance of four or five leagues
pendent   from Guadalupe, is one of thefe iflands.   Its territory
upon Gua-
dalupe.   is exceedingly barren, and is ten leagues in circumference.   It reckons but few inhabitants, who are all
employed in the culture of a few coffee and cotton
trees.   It is not known at what precife time this fettlement was begun, but it is a modern one.

The Saints, three leagues diftant from Guadalupe,
are two very fmall iflands, which, with another yet
fmaller, form a triangle, and have a tolerable harbour.   Thirty Frenchmen were fent thither in 1648,
but were foon driven away by an exceffive drought,
which dried up their only fpring, before they had
time to make any refervoirs.   A fecond attempt was
made in 1652, and lafting plantations were eftablifhed, which now yield fifty thoufand weight of coffee,
and one hundred thoufand of cotton.

At the diftance of fix leagues from Guadaloupe is
Marigalante, which hath fifteen leagues in circumference.   The numerous favages by whom it was inhabited, were driven from it in 1645, by the French,
who were obliged to fuftain and repel feveral warm
attacks, in order to maintain themfelves in their ufurpation.   It hath an excellent foil, upon which a population hath fucceffively been formed, of feven or
eight hundred white people, and of fix or feven
thoufand Negroes, moft of whom are employed in
the culture of fugar.

St. Martin and St. Bartholomew are likewife dependent upon Guadalupe, though at the diftance of
forty-five or fifty leagues from it.   The former of
thefe iflands hath been fpoken of in the hiftory of the
Dutch fettlements.   It remains to fay fomething of
the latter.

It is faid to be eleven leagues in circumference.

Its mountains are nothing but rocks, and its valleys nothing but fands, which are never watered by fprings or by rivers, and much too feldom by the waters of the fky. It is even deprived of a good harbour, although all geographers have beftowed this advantage upon it. In 1646, fifty Frenchmen were fent there from St. Chriftopher's; they were maffacred by the Caribs in 1656, and were replaced only three years after. The barrennefs of the foil obliged them to have recourfe to the Guyacum wood, which covered their new country, and of which they made fome fmall works, that were in great requeft. This refource was foon exhaufted, and it was fucceeded by the care of a few cattle, which fupplied the neighbouring iflands. Soon after this, the culture of cotton was introduced; and the crop of this amounts to fifty or fixty thoufand weight, when not checked by obftinate droughts, which are very frequent. Till thefe prefent times, the labours have all been carried on by white people; and it is ftill the only one of the European colonies eftablifhed in the New World, where free men do not difdain to partake of the labours of agriculture with their flaves. The numbers of the latter do not exceed four hundred and twenty-feven, nor thofe of the former three hundred and forty-five. The ifland could not, without difficulty, maintain a greater number, even in the moft profperous times.

The wretchednefs of the inhabitants is fo well known, that the enemy's privateers, which frequently put in there, have always paid punctually for what few refrefhments they could fpare them, though the miferable inhabitants were too weak to compel them. There is then fome humanity left even in the breaft of enemies and pirates; man is not naturally cruel; and only becomes fo from fear or intereft. The armed pirate, who plunders a veffel richly laden, is not deftitute of equity, nor even of compaffion for a fet of poor defencelefs iflanders.

On the firft of January 1777, the population of Guadalupe, and of the iflands more or lefs fertile,

B O O K
XIII.

and of the
finall
iflands un-
der its de-
pendence. under its dependence, amounted to twelve thoufand
feven hundred white perfons of all ages and of both
fexes, thirteen hundred and fifty free Negroes, or
Mulattoes, and a hundred thoufand flaves; although,
in the account of the colony, there were only fourfcore and four thoufand one hundred mentioned.

Their cattle confifted of nine thoufand two hundred and twenty horfes or mules, fifteen thoufand
feven hundred and forty head of horned cattle, and
twenty-five thoufand four hundred fheep, hogs, or
goats.

Their cultures confifted only of four hundred and
forty-nine-thoufand fix hundred and twenty-two cacao trees; eleven million nine hundred feventy-four
thoufand and forty-fix cotton plants; eighteen million feven hundred and ninety-nine thoufand fix hundred and fourfcore coffee trees; and three hundred
and eighty-eight fugar plantations; which occupied
twenty-fix thoufand and eighty-eight fquares of land.

Their government, taxes, and impofts, were the
fame as at Martinico.

If thefe frequent calculations be difgufting to the
idle reader, it is hoped that they will not be fo difagreeable to political calculators; who, difcovering, in the
population and in the productions of the lands, the
exact proportion of the ftrength of the ftate, will be
the better enabled to compare the natural refources
of all nations.

It is only by a well-regulated regifter of fuch a
nature, that we can judge, with fome degree of pre-
cifion, of the prefent ftate of the maritime and commercial powers that have fettlements in the New
World. The merit of the work, in this point, confifts in its accuracy; and fome allowances ought,
perhaps, to be made to the author, for the want of
embellifhments, in favour of the ufeful information
which is fubftituted to them. There are eloquent
defcriptions, and ingenious reprefentations enough of
diftant countries, which ferve to amufe and to deceive
the multitude. It is time to appreciate the truth,

which refults from the hiftory of them, and to be in-B o o K
formed, not fo much of what they have been, as of XIII.
what they are at prefent: for the hiftory of what is
paffed, efpecially from the manner in which it is
written, is almoft as much applicable to future ages,
as to the prefent. Let me be allowed, therefore,
once again to declare, that no man fhould be furprifed at the numerous repetitions of the quantity of
Negroes, of animals, of lands, and of productions ;
and at details, in a word, which, however dry and
unentertaining they may be to the mind, are neverthelefs the natural foundations of fociety.

Guadalupe muft obtain from its cultures, a very
confiderable mafs of productions, and more confiderable even than Martinico. It hath a greater number
of flaves ; it employs lefs of them in its navigation
and in its commerce ; it hath placed a number of
them upon a foil which is inferior to that of its rival,
but great part of which being newly manured, yields
more abundant crops than the grounds which are
fatigued by a long continuance of tillage. Accordingly, it is evident, that fuch of its plantations as are
not devoured by ants, yield an income much fuperi-
or to that which is obtained at Martinico. Neverthelefs, eighty-one veffels of the mother-country did
not carry away, in 1775, from this ifland, more than
one hundred and eighty-eight thoufand three hundred and eighty-fix quintals fix pounds of raw or
clayed fugar, which were fold in Europe for
7,137,930 livres 16 fols [297,413l. 15s. 8d.] ; fixty-
three thoufand twenty-nine quintals and two pounds
of coffee, which were fold for 2,993,860 livres 19 fols
[124,744l. 4s. 1¼d.] ; fourteen hundred thirty-eight
quintals and twenty-feven pounds of indigo, which
were fold for 1,222,529 livres 10 fols [50,938l. 14s.
7d.] ; one thoufand twenty-three quintals fifty-nine
pounds of cacao, which were fold for 71,651 livres 6
fols [2985l. 9s. 5d.] ; five thoufand one hundred
and ninety-three quintals feventy-three pounds of
cotton, which were fold for 1,298,437 livres 10 fols

BOOK [54,101l. 11s. 3d.] ; feven hundred and twenty-feven
XIII. hides, which were fold for 6973 livres [290l. 10s.
10d.] ; fixteen quintals and fifty-fix pounds of rope-
yarn, which were fold for 16,560 livres [690l.] ;
twelve quintals and fixty-two pounds of black caffia,
which were fold for 336 livres 15 fols 10 deniers
[about 14l. 8d.] ; one hundred and twenty-five quintals of wood, which were fold for 3125 livres [130l.
4s. 2d.]. Thefe fums, collectively, amounted to no
more than 12,751,404 livres 16 fols 10 deniers [about
531,291l. 14s. ¼d.

Some of the productions of the colony were fent
to Martinico. Its molaffes, and fome other commodities, were bartered with the Americans, for wood,
cattle, flour, and falt fifh : its cottons were fent to
Dominico, from whence it received flaves ; and its
fugars to St. Euftatius, which paid for them in fpecie, or with bills of exchange, and with merchandife
from the Eaft Indies.

The vigilance of its laft directors hath put fome
ftop to thefe fmuggling connections, and the French
veffels intended for the exportation of thefe commodities, have immediately been multiplied. Many of
them have been induced by habit to go to Guadalupe, properly fo called, and to St. Charles of the
Baffe Terre, where all the cargoes were formerly
taken in, although it be but a foreign harbour, the
accefs of which is difficult, and in which it is dangerous to remain : but the greateft number of them go
to Pitre Point.

This is a deep and tolerably fafe harbour, fituated
at one of the extremities of Grande Terre : it was
difcovered by the Englifh at the time when they were
in poffeffion of the colony ; and they were employed
in rendering it healthy, when they were deprived of
this acquifition by the peace. The court of Verfailles
purfued this idea of an enlightened conqueror, and,
without delay, had the plan of a town traced, which
hath rapidly increafed. Nature, the winds, the bearing of the coafts, all feem to concur in concentrating

in this staple almost the whole trade of so beautiful a possession. St. Charles can preserve no more trade than it can be supplied with from the fine sugars of the Three Rivers collected, and from the coffees which are gathered in the districts of the Bailiff, of Deshays, of Buillante, and of Pointe Noire. This town will, however, continue to be the seat of government, since the forces of the colony, and the fortifications, are there.

If some observers are to be believed, the colony must expect to decline. That part of it which is called Guadalupe, and hath been cultivated for a long time, is not susceptible, say they, of much improvement. On the other hand, they affirm, that Grande Terre will not support itself in the flourishing state to which a fortunate hazard hath brought it. That vast space, which was almost entirely covered with briars seventeen or eighteen years ago, and which furnishes at present three fifths of the territorial riches, hath not a good soil. Its sugars are of a very inferior quality; it is destitute of forests, of dews, and of rivers, and is exposed to frequent droughts, which destroy its cattle and its productions: calamities which cannot but be increased by time.

We are very far from adopting these anxieties; and our readers may judge of the reasons we have for our security. The calamities of an unfortunate war had almost annihilated Guadalupe. But scarce had it submitted to a foreign yoke, in 1759, than its planters hastened to restore the ruins of their manufactures, in order to profit by the high price which the conquerors put upon their productions. The three years subsequent to its restitution were employed in the restoration of the buildings, that had been constructed with precipitation. In the years 1767 and 1768, the roads of the colony were all mended, and an easy communication was opened between Guadalupe and Grande Terre, by means of two causeways of three thousand toises each, which it was necessary to raise

BOOK
XIII.
in the moraffes. Before and after this period, confiderable fortifications, and more than one hundred
batteries, were erected upon the coafts. Thefe labours have deprived the lands, for a long while, of
part of the hands deftined to fertilize them. At prefent, that the flaves are all reftored to their manufactures, is it not fortunately a neceffary confequence,
that the commodities fhould increafe?

The colony hath ftill other reafons to expect a rapid advancement. It hath fome territories which
have not yet been manured; and thofe which are already cultivated are capable of improvement. Its
debts are not confiderable. With fewer wants than
the fettlements have, where opulence hath for a long
time multiplied propenfities and defires, it can beftow more upon the improvement of its cultures. The
Englifh iflands will continue to furnifh it with flaves,
if the French navigators ftill limit themfelves to convey to it annually no more than five or fix hundred,
as they have hitherto done. All thefe circumftances
united, fuggeft the idea that Guadalupe will foon rife
of itfelf to the height of its profperity, without the
affiftance, and notwithftanding the fhackles, of government.

Meafures
taken by
France to
preferve
Guadalupe
from inva-
fion.
But can France be affured of enjoying a long and
quiet poffeffion of this ifland? If the enemy that might
attack the colony, chofe only to plunder the Grande
Terre, and to carry off the flaves and cattle from
thence, it would be impoffible to prevent this, or
even to retaliate, unlefs an army were oppofed to
them. Fort Lewis, which defends this part of the
fettlement, is but a wretched ftar-fort, incapable of
much refiftance. All that could poffibly be expected, would be to prevent the devaftation from extending any further. The nature of the country prefents
feveral fituations, fome more favourable than others,
by which the progrefs of an affailant may be fecure-
ly ftopped, whatever his courage or his forces may
be. He would, therefore, be forced to reimbark and

proceed to the attack of what is properly called Guadalupe.

The landing of the enemy could be effected nowhere but at the bay of the Three Rivers, and at
that of the Bailiff; or rather these two places would
be moft favourable to the fuccefs of his enterprife ;
becaufe they would bring him nearer than any other
to Fort St. Charles of the Baffe Terre, where he
would have lefs difficulties to encounter.

Let the enemy choofe whichever of thefe landings
they prefer, they will find nothing more than a fpot
covered with trees, interfected with rivers, hollow
ways, narrow paffes, and fteep afcents, which they
muft march over expofed to the French fire. When,
by the fuperiority of their forces, they have furmounted thefe difficulties, they will be ftopped by
the eminence of the great camp. This is a platform
furrounded by nature with the river Galleon, and
with dreadful ravines, to which art hath added parapets, barbettes, flanks, and embrafures, to direct the
artillery in the moft advantageous manner. This intrenchment, though formidable, muft be forced. It
is not to be imagined that an intelligent general
would ever leave fuch a poft as this behind him : his
convoys would be too much expofed, and he would
not get up what would be neceffary for carrying on
the fiege of Fort St. Charles without much difficulty.

If thofe who were firft employed in fortifying Guadalupe, had underftood the art of war, or even been
only engineers, they would not have failed choofing
the pofition between the river of the great Bay and
that of Galleon, for erecting their fortifications. The
place then would have had towards the fea-fide a
front, that would have enclofed a harbour capable of
containing forty fail of fhips, which would have annoyed the enemy's fleet, without being themfelves
in the leaft expofed. The fronts towards the river
Galleon and that of the Great Bay would have been in-

acceffible, being placed upon the fummit of two very fteep afcents. The fourth front would have been the only place open to an attack ; and it would have been an eafy matter to ftrengthen that as much as might have been thought proper.

By choofing the prefent pofition of Fort St. Charles, the works, which were conftructed there, ought at leaft to have flanked each other from the fea, and from the heights. But the principles of fortification were fo much neglected, that the fire was pointed entirely in a wrong direction, that the internal works were in all parts open to the view, and that the re-vetments might be battered from the bottom.

Such was the condition of Fort St. Charles, when, in 1764, it was thought proper to put it in a ftate of defence. Perhaps, it might have been beft to deftroy it totally, and to place the new fortifications on the pofition juft pointed out. It was however thought neceffary to cover the bad fort, conftructed by un-fkilful perfons, with out-works ; adding two baftions towards the fea-fide ; a good covered-way, which goes all round, together with a glacis, partly cut and partly in a gentle flope; two large places of arms with re-entering angles, having each a good redoubt, and behind thefe, good tenailles, with caponieres and po-fterns of communication with the body of the place ; two redoubts, one on the prolongation of the capital of one of the two places of arms, and the other at the extremity of an excellent intrenchment made along the river Galleon, the platform of which is de-fended by the cannon from another intrenchment made on the top of the bank of the other fide of the fame river ; large and deep ditches, a refervoir for wa-ter, and a powder magazine, bomb proof ; in a word, a fufficient quantity of works under ground to lodge a third part of the garrifon. All thefe out-works, well contrived, being added to the fort, will enable an active and experienced commander to hold out a fiege of two monhs, and perhaps more. But what-

ever may be the refiftance that Guadalupe can oppofe to the attacks of the enemy, it is time to pafs
on to St. Domingo.

B O O K
XIII.

This ifland is one hundred and fixty leagues in
length; its main breadth is about thirty; and its circumference three hundred and fifty, or fix hundred
in coafting round the feveral bays. It is parted length-
ways, from eaft to weft, by a ridge of mountains,
from which gold was extracted, before the continent
of America had difclofed mines infinitely richer.

Short de-
fcription of
the ifland of
St. Domin-
go.

The navigator who draws near to, or who ap-
proaches the Spanifh part of the ifland, perceives nothing but an irregular mafs of lands, heaped one upon another, covered with trees, and divided towards
the fea-fide by bays or promontories: but he is in-
demnified for this profpect, which is none of the moft
agreeable, by the perfume of the flowers of acacia,
and of the orange and lemon trees, which are conveyed to him every morning and evening, from the
midft of the woods, by the land breezes.

The French part of the coaft, although cultivated,
doth not exhibit a much more fmiling afpect. There
is a famenefs in all the horizon; the fame accidents
of nature, the fame cultures, the fame colours, and
the fame edifices, prefent themfelves on all fides.
The eye, fatigued, cannot fix itfelf on any fpot, without meeting with the fame object, and without feeing
what it had feen before. There is only the northern
part, which, being full of rich plantations, from the
fea-fide to the tops of the hills, exhibits a profpect
worthy of fome attention. This is the only landfcape
in the ifland; but it cannot be compared to thofe in
Europe, where nature and art abound much more in
interefting beauties.

The heats are always confiderable in the plains.
Although the temperature of the valleys depend partly upon their opening to the eaft or to the weft, it
may be faid in general that the air, which is damp
and frefh before and and after fun-fet, is very hot in
the courfe of the day. The difference of climate is

indeed only to be felt upon the mountains ; where the thermometer is at feventeen degrees in the fhade, when, with the fame expofure, it rifes to twenty-five in the plain.

Some French adventurers take refuge at St. Domingo. Spain was the fole and ufelefs proprietor of this large poffeffion, when fome Englifh and French, who had been driven out of St. Chriftopher's, took refuge there in 1630. Though the northern coaft, where they firft lettled, was in a manner forfaken, they confidered, that being liable to be attacked by a common enemy, it was but prudent to fecure a retreat. For this purpofe they pitched upon Tortuga, a fmall ifland within two leagues of the great one ; and twenty-five Spaniards, who were left to guard it, retired on the firft fummons.

The adventurers of both nations, now abfolute mafters of an ifland eight leagues long and two broad, found a pure air, but no river, and few fprings. The mountains were covered with valuable woods, and the fertile plains only wanted the hand of the cultivator. The northern coaft appeared to be inacceffible ; but the fouthern had an excellent harbour commanded by a rock, which required only a battery of cannon to defend the entrance of the ifland.

This happy fituation foon brought to Tortuga a multitude of thofe people who are in fearch either of fortune or liberty. The moft moderate applied themfelves to the culture of tobacco, which grew into repute, while the more active went to hunt the buffaloes at St. Domingo, and fold their hides to the Dutch. The moft intrepid went out to cruife, and performed fuch bold exploits as will be long remembered.

This fettlement alarmed the court of Madrid. Judging, by the loffes they had already fuftained, of the misfortunes they had ftill to expect, they gave orders for the deftruction of the new colony. The general of the galleons chofe, for executing his commiffion, the time when the brave inhabitants of Tortuga were out at fea or a-hunting, and with that barbarity which was then fo familiar to his nation, hanged or put to the fword all thofe who were left at home. He then withdrew, without leaving any garrifon, fully perfuaded that fuch a precaution was needlefs, after the vengeance he had taken. But he foon found that cruelty is not the method to fecure dominion.

The adventurers, informed of what had paffed at Tortuga, and hearing at the fane time that a body of five hundred men, deftined to harafs them, was getting ready at St. Domingo, judged that the only way to efcape the impending ruin, was to put an end to that anarchy in which they lived. They therefore gave up perfonal independence to focial fafety, and made choice of one Willis to be at their head ; an Englifhman, who had diftinguifhed himfelf on many occafions by his prudence and valour. Under the guidance of this chief, at the latter end of 1638, they re-took an ifland which they had poffeffed for eight years, and fortified it, that they might not lofe it again.

The French foon felt the effects of national partiality. Willis having fent for as many of his countrymen as would enable him to give the law, treated the reft as fubjects. Such is the natural progrefs of dominion ; in this manner moft monarchies have been formed. Companions in exile, war, or piracy, have chofen a leader, who foon ufurps the authority of a mafter. At firft he fhares the power or the fpoils with the ftrongeft ; till the multitude, crufhed by the few, embolden the chief to affume the whole power to himfelf ; and then monarchy degenerates into defpotifm. But fuch a feries of revolutions can only take place in many years in great ftates. An ifland of fixteen leagues fquare is not calculated to be peopled only with flaves. The commander De Poincy, governor-general of the Windward Iflands, being informed of the tyranny of Willis, immediately fent forty Frenchmen from St. Chriftopher's, who collected fifty more on the coaft of St. Domingo. They landed at Tortuga ; and having joined their countrymen on the ifland, they all together fummoned the Englifh to withdraw. The Englifh, difconcerted at fuch an unexpected and vigorous action, and not doubting but that fo much haughtinefs was fupported by a much greater force than it really was, evacuated the ifland and never returned.

The Spaniards were not fo tractable. They fuffered fo much from the depredations of the pirates who were daily fent out from Tortuga, that they thought their peace, their honour, and their intereft, were equally concerned in getting that ifland once more in their own power. Three times they recovered it, and were three times driven out again. At laft it remained in the hands of the French, in 1659, who evacuated it when they were firmly eftablifhed at St. Domingo, but without giving up the property of it. The government have always drawn from thence the woods neceffary for fhip-building, for the ufe of the artillery, and for the troops, till a rapacious minifter took the ifland out of the hands of the treafury, in order to increafe his family inheritance with it.

Their progrefs, however, was but flow; and they firft attracted the attention of the mother-country in 1665. Huntfmen, indeed, and pirates were continually feen hovering about from one ifland to another; but the number of planters, who were properly the only the colonifts, was exceedingly limited. The government was fenfible how neceffary it was to multiply them; and the care of this difficult work was committed to a gentleman of Anjou, name Bertrand Dogeron.

The court of Verfailles acknowledged thefe enterprifing men, when they had acquired fome ftability, and gave them a governor.
This man, whom nature had formed to be great in himfelf, independent of the fmiles or frowns of fortune, had ferved fifteen years in the marines, when he went over to America in 1656. With the beft contrived plans, he failed in his firft attempts; but the fortitude he fhowed in his misfortunes, made his virtues the more confpicuous; and the expedients he found out to extricate himfelf, heightened the opinion already entertained of his genius. The efteem

and attachment he had infpired the French with at B O O K
St. Domingo and Tortuga, induced the government XIII.
to intruft him with the care of directing, or rather of
fettling, that colony.

The execution of this project was full of difficulties. It was neceffary to eftablifh the regularity of
fociety upon the ruins of a ferocious anarchy ; to fubject the uncontrouled fpirit of plunder to the facred
and fevere authority of the laws ; to revive fentiments
of humanity in men hardened by the habit of crimes;
to fubftitute the innocent inftruments of agriculture
to the deftructive weapons of murder ; to incite to a
laborious life, barbarians accuftomed to idlenefs, which
is the general attendant upon rapine ; to infpire violent men with patience ; to induce them to prefer
the tardy fruits of obftinate labour to rapid enjoyments, acquired by fudden exertions ; to fubftitute
a propenfity for peace to the thirft of blood ; to inftil
the fear of danger in the mind of him who delighted
to expofe himfelf to it, and the love of life in him who
defpifed it ; it was neceffary, in a word, that men
who had never refpected any thing, and who had always traded freely with all nations, fhould be prevailed upon to refpect the privileges of an exclufive
company formed, in 1664, for all the French fettlements. When all this was effected, it then became
neceffary to allure, by the fweets of a well regulated
government, new inhabitants into a country which
had been traduced as a bad climate, and which was
not yet known to be fo fertile as it really was.

Dogeron, contrary to the general opinion, was in
hopes he fhould fucceed. A long intercourfe with
men he was to govern, had taught him how they
were to be dealt with ; and his fagacity could fuggeft,
or his honeft foul adopt, no method of engaging them,
but what was noble and juft. The freebooters were
determined to go in fearch of more advantageous latitudes ; he detained them by relinquifhing to them
that fhare of the booty which his poft entitled him
to, and by obtaining for them from Portugal com-

B O O K miffions for attacking the Spaniards, even after they
   XIII.   had made peace with France. This was the only
method to make thefe men friends to their country,
who otherwife would have turned enemies, rather
than have renounced the hopes of plunder. The buccaneers, or huntfmen, who only wifhed to raife a fufficiency to erect habitations, found him ready to advance them money without intereft, or to procure
them fome by his credit. As for the planters, whom
he preferred to all the other colonifts, he gave them
every poffible encouragement within the power of his
induftrious activity.

Thefe happy alterations required only to be made
permanent. The governor wifely confidered, that
women could alone perpetuate the happinefs of the
men, and the welfare of the colony, by promoting
population. This was a natural one ; but it was neceffary to confider what kind of women they muft
have been, from whom fuch pleafing effects could
have been expected. Women born of honeft parents,
and well educated ; prudent and induftrious women,
who would one day become good wives and affectionate mothers. The total want of one fex in the new
fettlement, condemned the other to celibacy. Dogeron thought of remedying this kind of indigence,
which is the moft difficult of any to bear, and which
plunges a man into a ftate of melancholy, and infpires him with a difguft for life, deprived, for him,
of its moft powerful attraction. Fifty young women
were fent over to him from France, and were foon
difpofed of at a very high price. Soon after, a like
number arrived, and were obtained on ftill higher
terms. They were fold as fo many flaves, and bought
as any common merhcandife. It was money, and
not the choice of their heart, that decided their lot.
What expectations could be formed from alliances
thus contracted ? And yet this was the only way to
gratify the moft impetuous of all paffions without
quarrels, and to propagate the human race without
bloodfhed. All the inhabitants expected to have fe-

male companions from their own country, to alleviate and to fhare their fate. But they were difappointed; none were afterwards fent over, except abandoned women, vile and defpicable wretches, who embarked with all the vices of the mind, and the difeafes of the body, that are attached to an abject condition, which they were far from being afhamed of, fince they fhowed not the leaft reluctance to engage themfelves for three years in the fervice of the men. This method of loading the colony with the refufe of the mother-country, introduced fuch a profligacy of manners, that it became neceffary to put a ftop to fo dangerous an expedient, but without fubftituting a better. By this neglect, St. Domingo loft a great many brave men, who could not live happy there, and was deprived of an increafe of population which might have proceeded from the colonifts who ftill preferved their attachment to the ifland. The colony has long felt, and perhaps feels to this day, the effects of fo capital an error.

Notwithftanding this error, Dogeron found means to increafe the number of planters to fifteen hundred in four years time, when there were only four hundred at his firft coming. His fucceffes were daily increafing; when they were fuddenly ftopped, in 1670, by an infurrection, which put the whole colony in a ferment. He did not incur the leaft cenfure for this unfortunate accident, in which he certainly had no fhare.

When this worthy man was appointed by the court of France to the government of Tortuga and St. Domingo, he could only prevail upon the inhabitants to acknowledge his authority, by giving them hopes that the ports under his jurifdiction fhould be open to foreigners. Yet fuch was the afcendant he gained over their minds, that by degrees he eftablifhed in the colony the exclufive privilege of the company; which, in time, engroffed the whole trade. But this company became fo elated with profperity, as to be guilty of the injuftice of felling their goods for two thirds more than had till then been paid to the Dutch. So deſtructive a monopoly revolted the inhabitants. They took up arms ; and it was but a year after, that they laid them down, upon condition that all French ſhips ſhould be free to trade with them, paying five per cent. to the company at coming and going out. Dogeron, who brought about this accommodation, availed himſelf of that circumſtance to procure ſhips, ſeemingly deſtined to convey his crops into Europe, but which in fact were more the property of his coloniſts than his own. Every one ſhipped his own commodities on board, allowing a moderate freight. On the return of the veſſel, the generous governor cauſed the cargo to be expoſed to public view, and every one took what he wanted, not only at prime coſt, but upon truſt, without intereſt, and even without notes of hand. Dogeron had imagined he ſhould inſpire them with ſentiments of probity and greatneſs of ſoul, by taking no other ſecurity than their word. By this conduct, he exemplified how well he was acquainted with the human heart. The man whom we have degraded in his ſelf-eſtimation, by miſtruſting him, having nothing to loſe in our minds, will not ſcruple to ſhow himſelf occaſionally a rogue, a baſe villain, a traitor, an impoſtor, ſuch as he really is, or even perhaps ſuch as he is not, but ſuch as he knows you think him to be ; while the man, for whom we ſhall have ſhown ſome ſhare of eſteem, will not debaſe himſelf if he ſhould have deſerved it, and will pique himſelf upon his honour, if he ſhould not. To impute virtues or vices to men, is frequently the way to inſpire them with either. In the midſt of theſe parental offices Dogeron was cut off by death in 1675.

Miniſters and depoſitaries of the royal authority, inſtead of thoſe long and uſeleſs inſtructions drawn by clerks, as ignorant as they are rapacious, and ſent to the perſons whom you intend for the government of the colonies, who receive them with the utmoſt contempt ; get the life of Dogeron written for their

ufe, and let it be concluded with thefe words : POSSESS
THE VIRTUES OF THIS MAN, AND LET YOUR CONDUCT
CONFORM ITSELF TO HIS.

O Dogeron! thy neglected remains repofe, perhaps,
in fome unknown part of St. Domingo, or of Tortuga.
But if thy memory be extinct in thofe countries, if
thy name, tranfmitted from fathers to children, be
not pronounced with emotion ; the defcendants of
thofe colonifts, whofe felicity you infured by your
talents, by your difintereftednefs, by your courage,
by your patience, and by your labours, are ungrateful people, who do not deferve better governors than
moft of thofe who are fent to them.

Dogeron left no other inheritance than an example
of patriotifm, and of every humane and focial virtue.
Pouancey fucceeded him. With the fame qualifications as his uncle, he was not fo great a man ; becaufe he followed his fteps more from imitation, than
from natural difpofition. Yet the undifcerning multitude placed an equal confidence in both ; and both
had the honour and happinefs to eftablifh the colony
upon a firm footing, without laws and without foldiers. Their natural good fenfe, and their known in-
tegrity, determined all differences to the fatisfaction
of both parties ; and public order was maintained by
that authority which is the natural confequence of
perfonal merit.

So wife a conftitution could not be lafting ; it required too much virtue to make it fo. In 1684 there
was fo vifible an alteration, that, in order to eftablifh
a due fubordination at St. Domingo, two adminftrators
were called in from Martinico, where good policy was
already in a great meafure fettled. Thefe legiflators
appointed courts of judicature in the feveral diftricts,
accountable to a fuperior council at Little Guave. In
procefs of time, this jurifdiction growing too extenfive, a like tribunal was erected in 1701, at Cape St.
Francis, for the northern diftricts.

All thefe innovations could hardly be introduced
without fome oppofition. It was to be feared that

BOOK the hunters and pirates, who compofed the bulk of
XIII. the people, averfe from the reftraints that were going
to be laid upon them, would go over to the Spaniards and to Jamaica, allured by the profpect of
great advantages. The planters themfelves were under fome temptation of this kind, as their trade was
clogged with fo many reftrictions, that they were
forced to fell their commodities at a very low price.
The former were gained by perfuafions ; the latter
by the profpect of a change in their fituation, which
was truly defperate.

Skins had been the firft article of exportation from
St. Domingo, as being the only things the Buccaneers
brought home. Tobacco was afterwards added by
culture ; and it was fold to great advantage to all nations. This trade was foon confined by an exclufive
company ; which, indeed, was in a fhort time abolifhed, but with no advantage for the fale of tobacco,
fince that was farmed out. The inhabitants, hoping
to meet with fome indulgence from government, as a
reward for their fubmiffion, offered to give the king
a fourth part of all the tobacco they fhould fend into
the kingdom, free of all charge, even of freight, upon
condition they fhould have the entire difpofal of the
other three-fourths. They made it appear, that this
method would bring in a clearer profit to the revenue than the forty fols [1s. 8d.] per cent. which
were paid by the farmer. Private interefts oppofed
fo reafonable a propofal.

In circumftances fuch as thefe, I am always aftonifhed at the patience of the oppreffed people. I fay
to myfelf, why do they not all affemble together at
the houfe of the member of adminiftration appointed
to govern them, and addrefs him in the following
terms ? " We are weary of an authority which vexes
" us. Retire from our country, and tell the perfon
" whofe reprefentative you are, that we are no rebels,
" becaufe no rebellion can exift unlefs it be againft a
" good king, and that he is only a tyrant againft
" whom we have a right to revolt. You may add,

" that if he fhould be defirous of poffeffing a defert B o o k
" country he will foon be fatisfied ; for that we are XIII.
" all determined to perifh, rather than live any long-
" er miferable under an unjuft government." The
colonifts did not give way to the fuggeftions of defpair, but in their refentment they turned their induftry with fuccefs to the culture of indigo and cocoa. Cotton was a very promifing article, becaufe it
had in former times greatly enriched the Spaniards ;
but they foon gave it up, for what reafon is not
known ; and in a few years not a fingle cotton plant
was to be feen.

Till then the labours had all been performed by
hirelings, and by the pooreft of the inhabitants. Some
fuccefsful expeditions againft the Spaniards procured
them a few Negroes. The number was increafed by
two or three French fhips, and much more by prizes
taken from the Englifh during the war of 1688 ; by
an invafion of Jamaica, from whence the French
brought away three thoufand blacks, in 1694. Without flaves, the culture of fugar could not be undertaken, but they alone were not fufficient. Money
was wanting to erect buildings, and to purchafe utenfils. The profit fome inhabitants made with the freebooters, who were always fuccefsful in their expeditions, enabled them to employ the flaves. They
therefore undertook the planting of the canes, which
convey the gold of Mexico to thofe nations whofe
only mines are fruitful lands.

But the colony, which, though it had loft fome of A company
its Europeans, had ftill made a progrefs to the north is eftablifh-
and weft, amidft the devaftations that preceded the fouthern
peace of Ryfwick, was yet but little advanced to part of St.
the fouth. This part did not reckon a hundred inhabitants, all living in huts, and all extremely wretched. The government could fix upon no better expedient, to make fome advantage of fo extenfive and
fo fine a country, than to grant, in 1698, for the
fpace of half a century, the property of it to a company, which took the name of *St. Louis.*

This company engaged, under the penalty of for-
feiting their charter, to form a capital of 1,200,000
livres [50,000l.]. and to convey, in the courfe of the
five firft years, upon the lands granted to them, fifteen hundred white people, and two thoufand five
hundred Negroes, with one hundred of the former
and two hundred of the latter each of the following
years : they were to diftribute lands to whoever
fhould be defirous of them. Each perfon, according
to his wants and abilities, obtained flaves that were
to be paid for in three years; the men at the rate of
fix hundred livres [25l.], and the women at the rate
of four hundred and fifty livres [18l. 15s.]. The
fame credit was allowed for merchandife.

Upon thefe conditions, the charter enfured to the
new fociety the exclufive right of buying and felling
throughout the whole territory affigned to them, but
at the prices only that were fettled in the other parts
of the ifland. Even this dependence, oppreffive to
the colonift, was ftill alleviated, by allowing him to
take, where he thought proper, whatever he was left
in want of, and to pay out of his provifions, whatever he might have occafion to buy.

Monopoly, as a torrent that is loft in the abyfs itfelf
has made, works its own ruin by its rapacioufnefs.
The company of St. Louis affords an inftance, among
many others, of the defects and abufes of exclufive
affociations. It was ruined by the knavery and ex-
travagance of its agents; nor was the territory committed to its care the better for all thefe loffes. The
plantations and people that were found there, when
the company gave up her rights to the government
in 1720, were chiefly owing to the contraband traders.

The colony
of St. Do-
mingo be-
comes the
moft flou-
rifhing fet-
tlement in
the New
World, It was during the long and bloody war begun on
account of the Spanifh fucceffion, that this attempt
had been made towards the improvement of the colony. It might have been expected to have made a
fpeedy progrefs, when tranquillity was reftored to both
nations by the peace of Utrecht. Thefe happy pro-

fpects were blafted by one of thofe calamities which
it is not in the power of man to forefee. All the cocoa trees upon the colony died in 1715. Dogeron
had planted the firft in 1665. In procefs of time
they had increafed ; efpecially in the narrow valleys
to the weftward. There were no lefs than twenty
thoufand upon fome plantations ; fo that, though cocoa fold for no more than five fols [two pence half-
penny] a pound, it was become a plentiful fource of
wealth.

B O O K
XIII.

notwith-
ftanding
the calami-
ties it expe-
riences.

Cultivations of greater importance amply compen-
fated this lofs, when a circumftance of the moft diftreffing nature threw the whole colony into confternation. A confiderable number of its inhabitants,
who had devoted twenty years labour in a burning
climate, to lay up a competency to fpend a comfortable old age in their native country, were returned
to it, with a fufficient fortune to enable them to difcharge their debts and purchafe eftates. Their commodities were paid them in bank notes, which proved
ufelefs to them. This fatal calamity obliged them
to return poor into an ifland from whence they had
departed rich ; and reduced them, in their old age,
to folicit employment from the very people who had
formerly been their fervants. The fight of fo many
unfortunate perfons infpired a general deteftation for
the India Company, which was confidered as accountable for thefe calamities. This averfion, raifed by
mere compaffion, was foon changed into a profound
hatred, and not without fufficient reafon.

The French colonies, fince their eftablifhment, received their flaves from the hands of the monopoly,
and confequently received but few, and at an exorbitant price. Being reduced in 1713 to the impoffibility of continuing their languid operations, the company themfelves made the private merchants part-
ners in their trade, upon condition that they fhould
pay 15 livres [12s. 6d.] for every Negro they fhould
carry to the Windward Iflands, and 30 livres [1l. 5s.] for
thofe whom they fhould introduce into St. Domingo.

BOOK
XIII.

This new arrangement was followed by fo great a degree of activity, that the government were at length induced to give up exclufive privileges, by granting in 1716 the Guinea trade to the ports of Rouen, of Bourdeaux, of Nantz, and of La Rochelle. It was to coft them two piftoles [16s. 8d.] for every flave who fhould arrive in America ; but the commodities which were to be acquired by the fale of thefe unfortunate people, were exonerated from one half of the duties to which the other productions were fubject. The inhabitants were juft beginning to feel the good effects of this liberty, imperfect as it was, fince it was confined to four ports, when St. Domingo was condemned again to receive its planters from the India Company, who were not even obliged to furnifh them with more than two thoufand every year. We cannot, indeed, determine which is the moft aftonifhing circumftance in the courfe of the events relative to the New World, either the rage of the firft conquerors who laid it wafte, or the ftupidity of the governments, which by a feries of abfurd regulations, feem to have propofed to themfelves either to perpetuate the mifery of the inhabitants, or to plunge them again into that ftate, whenever they entertained hopes of emerging from it.

In 1722, the agents of this odious company arrived in the colony. The buildings where they tranfacted their bufinefs were burnt to the ground. The fhips that came to them from Africa were either denied admittance into the harbour, or not fuffered to difpofe of their cargoes. The chief governor, who endeavoured to oppofe thefe difturbances, faw his authority defpifed, and his orders difobeyed, as they were not enforced by any compulfive power : he was even put under arreft. Every part of the ifland refounded with the clamours of fedition and the noife of arms. It is difficult to fay how far thefe exceffes would have been carried, had not government had the prudence to make conceffions. In this one inftance, the people did not fuffer for the folly of their rulers ; and the duke of Orleans convinced mankind, upon this occasion, that he was above the ordinary stamp of men, by avowing himself the author of a rebellion which he had excited by a defective institution, and which, under a ruler less enlightened or less moderate, would have been severely punished. After two years of trouble and confusion, the inconveniencies resulting from anarchy disposed the minds of all parties to peace, and tranquillity was restored without having recourse to violent measures.

From that period, no colony ever so much improved its time as that of St. Domingo. It advanced with the utmost rapidity to a prosperous state. The two unfortunate wars which annoyed its seas, have only served to compress its strength, which has increased the more since the cessation of hostilities. A wound is soon healed when the constitution is found. Diseases themselves, in the state, as well as in the body, are a kind of remedies, which, by the expulsion of the vitiated humours, add new vigour to a robust habit of body. Those disorders that are fatal to either the one or the other, are such as, being slow in their progress, keep them in a state of perpetual indisposition, and lead them imperceptibly to the grave. But after diseases that are acute have brought on a violent crisis, the delirium ceases, and the debility goes off; and as the strength is restored a more regular and uniform motion is established, which promises a lasting duration to the machine. So war seems to strengthen and support national spirit in many states of Europe, which might be enervated and corrupted by the prosperity of commerce and the enjoyments of luxury. The immense losses which almost equally attend victory and defeat, excite industry and quicken labour. Nations will recover their former splendour, provided their rulers will let them follow their own bent, and not pretend to direct their steps. This principle is peculiarly applicable to France, where nothing more is requisite to prosperity than to give a free course to the activity of the inhabitants. Whereever nature leaves them at full liberty, they fucceed in giving her powers their full fcope. St. Domingo affords a ftriking inftance of what may be expected from a good foil, and an advantageous fituation in the hands of Frenchmen.

Settlements formed in the fouthern part of St. Domingo.
The fouthern part, which is occupied by France, extends from Pitre Point to Cape Tiburon. At the period of their conquefts in the New World, the Spaniards had built upon this coaft two large villages, which they forfook in lefs profperous times. The vacated places were not immediately occupied by the French, who muft be apprehenfive of the vicinity of St. Domingo, where the chief force of that power, upon whofe ruin they were rifing, was concentrated. Their privateers, who commonly affembled at the little ifland called Vache Ifland, to cruize upon the Caftilians, and divide their fpoils, encouraged fome planters to begin a fmall fettlement upon the continent in 1673. It was foon deftroyed, nor was it refumed till a confiderable time after. The company appointed to fettle and extend this colony did not fulfil their obligations. Its progrefs was owing to the Englifh of Jamaica, and to the Dutch of Curaffou, who having refolved to carry flaves to this place, bought up the produce of a land, which they themfelves alone contributed to improve. It was not till 1740, that the merchants of the mother-country began to attend to this fettlement. From this period they frequented this part of the colony a little, notwithftanding the winds, which often render the failing out of this road tedious and difficult.

The part which is to the eaft of all the reft is called Jaquemel. It confifts of three parifhes, which occupy thirty-fix leagues of the coaft, and run into a moderate and very unequal degree of depth. This vaft fpace is filled up with fixty plantations of coffee, fixty-two of indigo, and fixty of cotton. Moft of their planters are poor, and can never grow very rich. A foil, which is in general full of hills, ftony, and expofed to droughts, prevents them from afpiring

to wealth. This can only be done by thofe who divide the plain of Jaquemel. There are twenty very
fpacious habitations, of which ten only are watered,
though they be all fufceptible of this advantage. It
is there, that in an exhaufted foil, indigo, which
would require a virgin foil, is cultivated. When
hands, and other means for carrying on an extenfive
culture, fhall no longer be wanting, fugar will be
fubftituted to it, which fucceeds as well as can be
defired, in the only plantation where the colonifts
have begun to cultivate it.

Aquin hath an extent of fifteen leagues along the
borders of the fea, and of three, four, and fometimes
fix leagues in the inland parts. This fettlement reckons forty plantations of indigo, twenty of coffee,
and nine of cotton. Its mountains, lefs elevated
than thofe which are contiguous to them, on that account enjoy only the benefit of a few fprings, and
a fmall quantity of rain, and promife nothing but
great abundance of cotton, which will undoubtedly
be one day required of them. With regard to its
plains, they were formerly in a flourifhing ftate ; but
the droughts, which have gradually increafed in proportion as the country hath been cleared, have diminifhed more and more the quality of the indigo,
which conftituted all the riches of the colony. This
plant, which leaves the ground almoft habitually expofed to the heat of a burning fun, fhould be replaced by fugar, which would keep the earth covered for eighteen months together, and will preferve
in it for a long time the fmalleft degree of moifture.
Four of the moft wealthy inhabitants have already
made this change in their plantations. The nature
of the foil will allow twenty-five colonifts to follow
their example ; and they will no doubt refolve upon
it, when they fhall have acquired the means fufficient
for that purpofe, and when the waters of the river
Serpente fhall have been prudently diftributed. In
the prefent ftate of things, all the productions of that
diftrict are collected in one town only, which is far

BOOK
XIII.

advanced in the inland parts. The impoffibility of
conveying them to the coaft in the rainy feafons, and
the unavoidable expences of the carriage, even in
the moft favourable times, had fuggefted the idea of
forming this ftaple upon the borders of a deep bay,
where the commodities are fhipped : but this fituation doth not afford one acre of ground fit for cultivation ; there is no fweet water to be found in it,
and the ftagnating waters of the fea corrupt the air.
Thefe reafons have caufed this project to be laid afide,
for its inconveniencies would be greater than the advantages derived from it.

St. Lewis is a kind of town, which, though built
at the beginning of the century, hath no more than
fifty houfes. The forming of this fettlement was
determined upon, on account of an exceeding good
harbour, even for fhips of the line. Confiderable
fortifications were erected upon a fmall ifland, fituated at the entrance of the harbour, which were
deftroyed by the Englifh in 1748, and have never
fince been reftored. The territory of this diftrict extends five or fix leagues along the coaft. Its mountains covered with acacia wood, are moft of them
fufceptible of culture. Its plain, which is uneven,
hath fome fertile fpots upon it, and its numerous
moraffes might be dried up. There are no more than
twenty plantations of coffee, fifteen of indigo, fix
of cotton, and two of fugar here. This laft production would fucceed in ten or twelve plantations, e-
fpecially if they were watered by the river St. Lewis,
which, it is thought, they might eafily be.

Cavaillon doth not occupy more than three leagues
upon the borders of the ocean. This is a long neck
of land, which extends eight or nine leagues up the
country. It is divided by a large river, which, in
times of heavy rains, unfortunately overflows to a
confiderable diftance, and occafions great ravages.
At the diftance of two leagues from its mouth is a
fmall town, where the veffels arrive, and where they
take in the productions, which are furnifhed by twen-

ty plantations of coffee, ten of indigo, fix of cotton, and feventeen of fugar. The number of the laft might be. doubled, with facility, in a plain which hath five or fix thoufand fquares in extent ; but the three moft flourifhing of thofe which exift, have fcarce yielded half of what they might produce, and the others only yield a trifling produce, and of a bad quality. The mountains, though covered with an excellent foil, do not compenfate for this deficiency. The diftriɗs granted by government will remain un- cultivated, till roads fhall have been made for the conveyance of the produɗions. This undertaking, which is beyond the means of the inhabitants, ought to be executed by the troops. Idlenefs, and infeɗious moraffes, have hitherto deprived the foldiers of their induftry, and have made them perifh upon the banks of the fea. The frefhnefs of elevated places, the wholefome air which is breathed there, a moderate fhare of labour, and the eafy circumftances which it would be proper they fhould enjoy ; in a word, all thefe concurring caufes, would they not maintain them in their natural ftrength ? would they not en- fure their prefervation ?

The plain at the bottom of Vache Ifland contains twenty-five thoufand fquares, of a foil which is ex- cellent every where, except in fome parts that have been covered with gravel by the torrents, and a few moraffes, which might be eafily dried up. There have been fucceffively formed here eighty-three fu- gar plantations, and there might ftill be fifty more eftablifhed. Thofe which exift have fcarce more than one third of their territory cultivated, and yet they yield an immenfe quantity of raw fugar. From this we may judge how much the whole of the grounds would furnifh, if they were properly cultivated. One might depend upon a produce fo much the more re- gular, as the rains do not fail fo often in this diftriɗ as in the others, and as there are three rivers running through it, which offer themfelves, as it were, for the watering of all the plantations.

The fugar and the indigo which grow in the plain, the coffee and the cotton, which defcend from the mountains, are all carried to the town of Cayes, formed by near four hundred houfes, which are all built in a marfhy territory, and are moft of them furrounded with ftagnant waters. The air which is breathed in that place is equally deficient in elafticity as in falubrity.

This ftaple feems to have been placed, as it were, fortuitoufly, in the bottom of a fhallow bay, which grows more and more fo, and has but three channels. The anchorage is fo confined, and fo dangerous during the equinox, that fhips which happen to be there at that feafon are frequently loft. The great quantity of mud brought thither by the waters of a torrent on the fouth fide, has increafed to fuch a degree, that in twenty years time there will be no entrance. The canal, formed by the vicinity of Vache Ifland, is of no ufe, and only obftructs the navigation. The creeks in this place are the refort of the privateers of Jamaica. As they cruize there without fails, and can obferve without being feen, they always have the advantage of the wind over fuch veffels as are hindered, by the violence and conftant ftruggle of the winds, from paffing above the ifland. If it were poffible that any men of war could put into this bad harbour, the impoffibility of furmounting this obftacle and that of the currents, in order to get to windward of the ifland, would oblige them to follow the track of merchant-fhips. Doubling, therefore, one after another, the point of Labacou, on account of the fhoals, thefe fhips would get between the land and the enemy's fire, with the difadvantage of the wind, and would infallibly be deftroyed by an inferior fquadron.

The town of Cayes is not better than its harbour. It contains 280 houfes, all funk into fwampy ground, and moft of them furrounded with ftagnant water. The air of this fpot is foul and unwholefome; and on this account, as well as the badnefs of the harbour, it has often been wifhed by the court of Verfailles, that the trade with the mother-country could be transferred to St. Lewis. But the efforts that have been made to effect this, have hitherto been unsuccefsful; and will for ever be fo; becaufe it is reasonable to fuppofe, that exchanges will always be eftablifhed on that fpot where the productions are moft plentiful, and where the confumption is greateft. To pretend to thwart this order of things prefcribed by nature, would be to retard to no purpofe the progrefs of a good fettlement. Even the caprices of induftry fhould be indulged by government. The leaft uneafinefs in the trader creates diftruft. Political and military reafonings will never prevail againft thofe of intereft. Trade only flourifhes in a foil of its own choofing. It is alarmed at every kind of reftraint.

All that the French miniftry could reafonably propofe, would be to withdraw the tribunals from St. Lewis, which neither is, nor ever will be of any confequence, in order to transfer them to Cayes, where the population and the productions, which are already confiderable, muft increafe greatly; to dig a bed for a torrent, the violent overflowings of which frequently occafion inexpreffible ravages; and to fortify, and render the town more wholefome. Both might be effected, by digging a ditch all round the town, and the rubbifh would ferve to fill up the marfhes within. The ground, being raifed higher by this contrivance, would confequently grow drier; the water, which would be brought down by a gentle defcent from the river into this deep ditch, would, by the affiftance of fome fortifications, fecure the town from the attacks of the privateers; and would even afford a temporary defence, and allow time to capitulate with a fmall fquadron.

Greater improvements might and ought to be made. Why not allow a factitious harbour to an important mart, which will foon be ftopped? The merchant-fhips that feek fhelter in what is called the Flemifh Bay, two leagues to windward of Cayes, feem to point out this fpot as the harbour that this town ftands in need of. It would contain a con-fiderable number of men of war, fafe from all winds ; would afford them feveral careening places ; would admit of their doubling the Vache Ifland to wind-ward, and enable them to carry on with the town, along-fide the coaft, an intercourfe, which, being pro-tected by batteries properly difpofed, would keep the privateers in awe. The only inconvenience is, that the fhip-worm is more apt to injure the veffel in this place than in other parts, on account of the nature of the bottom and the calmnefs of the fea.

Abacou is a peninfula, which was formerly in a flourifhing ftate, on account of the abundance and the quality of its indigo. But fince this voracious plant hath deftroyed every principle of vegetation upon the numerous little hillocks of that place, it is nowhere cultivated with any fuccefs but upon the borders of the fea, which are enriched with the fpoils of the upper grounds. This decreafe hath determin-ed a certain number of colonifts to transfer their in-duftry to other parts. Thofe who, either from habit or reafon, have perfevered in remaining on their plan-tations, have enlarged them as much as they have found it convenient. They ftill maintain themfelves by fuffering part of their grounds to lie fallow, while the other part is cultivated. But this refource is not equal to what it would be in Europe. This is the opinion of the inhabitants themfelves, who direct their induftry towards the culture of fugar, as much as their fortune and their credit will allow them.

It is upon the cultivated and exhaufted heights of this quarter, that it would be proper to breed cattle. Government were in an error, when they ceded the mountains, upon condition that they fhould be co-vered with horned cattle. Befides that a virgin foil could not be reafonably employed in pafture ground, as it might be rendered more productive to the ftate ; it was impoffible to expect that enterprifing men

would make themfelves fhepherds, when they could
derive greater advantages from their grounds, in
whatever culture they might employ them. It may
even be affirmed, that the cattle will always be infinitely fcarce at San Domingo, even in thefe places
which cannot be employed for any other purpofe, as
long as the monopoly of flaughter-houfes fhall fubfift
in the colony.

Coteaux occupies about ten leagues of the fhore,
and is from two to five leagues in depth. Small
creeks are every where found, where it is eafy to
land ; but none of them offer a fecure fhelter in
rough weather. This quarter contains twenty-four
plantations of coffee, three of cotton, and fixty-fix of
indigo. This laft production hath lefs decreafed in
quantity, and lefs degenerated in quality, at this
place, than any where elfe ; advantages which muft
be attributed to the nature and to the difpofition of
the territory. The time, however, doth not feem far
diftant, when the borders of the fea will difplay fourteen or fifteen fugar plantations formed upon the
ruins of the ancient cultures. Habit, and the facility
of obtaining flaves by contraband connections, will
facilitate this revolution.

Tiburon, which hath ten leagues of extent upon
the borders of the fea, and two, three, or four in the
inland parts, terminates this coaft. The road of this
cape doth not offer a fufficient fhelter againft ftorms ;
but well-difpofed batteries may render it a place of
retreat for the French veffels, which are purfued in
time of war in thefe latitudes. This fettlement hath
four habitations for cotton, thirty for indigo, and
thirty-feven for coffee. Four fugar plantations have
been eftablifhed there fince the peace, and their
number may be increafed to fixteen.

All the fettlements which we have juft taken a re-
view of, languifh in a ftate of greater or lefs mifery.
Accordingly, the fales and the purchafes are not
made there with metals, as in the northern or eaftern
part of the colony. On the fouthern, the merchan-

Means by
which the
cultures of
the fouth-
ern part of
the colony
might be
improved.

B O O K dife of Europe is exchanged for the productions of
XIII.   America. This favage practice occafions eternal difcuffions, innumerable frauds, and ruinous delays,
which keep off the navigators, thofe efpecially who
carry on the flave-trade.

It is a fact, which is but too well proved, that the
annual lofs of Negroes amounts naturally to one twentieth part of them, and that accidents carry off a fifteenth part. From this circumftance it follows, that
the country we are fpeaking of, and in which upwards of forty thoufand flaves are collected, muft
have feen five and twenty thoufand of them die in
ten years time. Eight thoufand one hundred and
thirty-four Africans, who have been introduced by
French privateers from 1763 to 1773, have not certainly been able to fill up this great void. What
would then have been the fate of thofe fettlements
if the fmuggling trade had not fupplied the deficiency? But this is not the whole.

The fouthern part of St. Domingo hath a great
difadvantage. The mountains that command it, deprive it, as well as the weftern coaft, during the fpace
of about fix months, of the rains of the north and the
north-eaft, which fertilize the northern parts of the
country. It will then remain untilled or be ill cultivated, till the waters of the rivers fhall have fupplied
the place of thofe from the fky. This operation,
which would increafe the productions by two-thirds,
requires a vaft capital and a great number of flaves.
The trade of France, whether from inability or miftruft, doth not furnifh them.

What meafures ought government to purfue? They
fhould lay open that part of the colony for the fpace
of ten or fifteen years, freely to all foreigners. The
Englifh would carry Negroes to it, and the Dutch
would advance money at an intereft, which might
very well be fuftained by the cultures of the New
World. The fuccefs of this ftep would be infallible,
if laws were made which fhould give a proper degree
of validity to the credit of the two nations.

The western part of the colony differs greatly from
the southern. The first settlement of any confequence, which is found there, is that of Jeremiah,
or the Great Bay. It occupies twenty leagues of
coast, from Cape Tiburon to Petit-Trou, and extends
from four to six leagues in the inland parts. As this
district is still an infant settlement, the borders of the
sea only are inhabited, and these even very little.
All the productions, however, which enrich the rest
of the island are cultivated here. There is also one
production which is peculiar to it, and this is cacao,
which could not succeed in more open places ; and
one hundred thousand pounds weight are annually
gathered. The staple is a small town agreeably built
and situated upon an eminence, where the air is exceedingly wholesome It must in time become a considerable mart. Unfortunately it hath got a bad harbour ; whenever the north winds blow with any degree of violence, the ships are obliged either to take
refuge at Cape *Dame Marie*, where no measures have
been taken to protect them, or to seek for the island
of Caymites, which is exposed to the inroads of the
pirates.

The Little Guave was formerly in great reputation,
which was owing to its harbour, where ships of all
sizes found an excellent anchorage, conveniencies for
refitting, and a shelter from all winds. It was an
asylum the most convenient for adventurers, whose
only design was to appropriate to themselves the spoils
of the Spanish navigators. This place hath lost much
of its celebrity since cultures have succeeded to piracy ; it owes the small degree of consideration it still
retains to the richness of its territorial. productions,
which are limited to fifteen plantations of sugar, twenty of coffee, and twelve of indigo or cotton ; and still
more to the produce of twenty-four plantations of sugar, fifty of indigo, sixty-seven of coffee, and thirty-
four of cotton, which are poured into its staple from
the parishes of Petit-Trou, Lance-à-Veaux, St. Mi-
chael, and the Great Guave. It is unhealthy, and

B O O K
XIII.

Settlements
formed to
the west of
St. Domin-
go.

will always be fo, till a flope hath been made for the
river Abaret, the ftagnant waters of which form infectious moraffes.

The dependencies of Leogane have fome degree
of extent : twenty habitations are reckoned among
them deftined for indigo, forty for coffee, ten for
cotton, and fifty-two for fugar. Before the earthquake of 1770, which deftroyed every thing, the
town had fifteen regular built ftreets, and four hundred houfes of ftone, which are at prefent only built
of wood. Its pofition, which is upon a narrow, fertile, and well-watered plain, would be excellent, if
a navigable canal were made to open an eafy communication with its harbour, which is no more than
a mile diftant.

If it were advifable to have a fortified town on the
weftern coaft, undoubtedly Leogane would claim the
preference. It ftands upon plain ground, is not commanded by any eminence, nor can it be annoyed by
any fhips. But to fecure it from being furprifed, it
fhould at leaft have been furrounded with a deep
ditch, which might eafily be filled with water without the leaft expence. This might have been effected at a much more reafonable rate than the works
which have been begun at Port-au-Prince.

The weftern part of the ifland was the firft that
was cultivated by the French, that being at the greateft diftance from the Spanifh forces, which they had
then reafon to fear. This being in the centre of the
coafts that belonged to them, the feat of government
was fixed there. It was firft fettled at the Little Guave, hath been fince transferred to Leogane, and hath
at laft been fixed at Port-au-Prince in 1750.

The territory of this diftrict contains forty plantations of fugar, fifty of coffee, and fifteen of cotton. This
produce is increafed by feveral ftill more confiderable, which arife from the rich plains of the Cul-de-
Sac, of the Arcahaye, and of the mountains of Mirbalais. In this point of view, Port-au-Prince is an
important ftaple, to which a protection ought to be

granted fufficient to prevent any furprife, and to fe- cure the retreat of the citizens. But let us confider whether it was proper to concentrate in this fpot the civil and military authority, the tribunals, the troops, the ammunition, the provifions, and the arfenals; every thing, in a word, which contributes to the fupport of a great colony.

The place that was made choice of for the intended capital, is an opening of about 1400 toifes long in a direct line, and commanded on both fides. Two harbours, formed by fome iflets, have afforded a pretence for this injudicious choice. The harbour intended for trading veffels being now almoft filled up, can no longer admit men of war with fafety; and the great harbour defigned for thefe, being as unwholefome as the other, from the exhalations of the fmall iflands, neither is nor can be defended by any thing againft a fuperior enemy.

A fmall fquadron might even block up a ftronger one in fo unfavourable a pofition. Gonave, which divides the bay in two, would leave a free and fafe paffage for the fmaller fquadron; the fea winds would prevent the other fquadron from getting up to it; the land winds, by facilitating the exit of the enemy's fhips from the harbour, would leave them the choice of retreating through either of the outlets of St. Mark and Leogane; and all other circumftances being equal, they would always have the advantage of keeping Gonave between them and the French fquadron.

But what would be the confequence, if the French fquadron fhould prove the weakeft? Difabled and purfued, it could never gain a fhelter that runs fo deep into land as Port-au-Prince, before the conqueror had taken advantage of its defeat. If the difabled fhips fhould reach the place, nothing could hinder the enemy from purfuing them almoft in a line, and even from entering the king's harbour, where they would take refuge.

The beft of all ftations for a cruife is that where

one may choofe whether one will accept or decline the fight, where there is but a fmall fpace to guard, where the whole may be viewed from one central point, where a fafe anchorage may be found at every tack, where one may be concealed without going far, procure wood and water at pleafure, and fail in open feas, in which there is nothing to fear but from fqualls. Thefe are the advantages that an enemy's fquadron will always have over the French fhips at anchor in Port-au-Prince. A fingle frigate might fafely come and bid them defiance, and be fufficient to intercept any trading fhips that fhould attempt to go in or out without a convoy.

Neverthelefs, a harbour fo unfavourable as this, hath determined the building of the town. It extends along the fea-fhore the fpace of 1200 toifes, that is, nearly along the opening which the fea has made in the centre of the weftern coaft. In this great extent, which runs in to the depth of 550 toifes, are, as it were, loft, 558 houfes or dwelling-places, difperfed in 29 ftreets. The drainings of the torrents that fall from the hills, render this place always damp, without fupplying it with good water. Add to all this, the little fecurity there is in a place commanded on the land fide, and on the fea fide eafy of accefs in all parts. Even the fmall iflands which divide the harbours would be fo far from defending the town from an invafion, that they would only ferve to cover the landing.

Such is the fpot, which on account of private interefts, hath been unfortunately chofen to build the capital of St. Domingo upon. It hath been entirely deftroyed by an earthquake which happened in 1770. This was the time to have brought about an alteration, and there was the more reafon to expect it, as there is the greateft probability that the new town is built upon the cavern of the volcano. But thefe hopes were fruftrated; the private houfes and the public edifices have all been rebuilt.

Sleep on then, thou fenfelefs inhabitant of St. Do-

mingo, fince thou art fo intrepid; fleep on, upon B O O K
the flight and thin layer of earth which parts thee XIII.
from the gulf of fire that burns under thy pillow.
Remain ignorant of the danger with which thou art
threatened, fince thy apprehenfions would tend only
to embitter every inftant of thy life, without preferving thee from it.—Confider not how much thine
exiftence is precarious. Be not informed, that it depends upon the cafual fall of a ftream, or upon the
infiltration, already perhaps far advanced, of the
fmall quantity of waters by which thou art furrounded in the fubterranean cauldron, which thy habitation hath been doomed to cover. If thou fhouldft
emerge from thy ftupidity only for an inftant, what
would become of thee ! Thou wouldft behold death
moving under thy feet. The hollow found of the
torrents of fulphur expanded, would continually af-
fail thine ears. Thou wouldft feel the ofcillation of
the layer of earth that fupports thee. Thou wouldft
hear it open with tumultuous noife. Thou wouldft fly
from thy houfe, and run diftractedly about the ftreets.
Thou wouldft think that the walls of thy dwelling, and
all the edifices, were fhaking, and that thou wert going
to defcend in the midft of their ruins into the gulf which
is prepared, if not for thee, at leaft for thy unfortunate
pofterity. The completion of the difafter that awaits
them will be fhorter than my account of it. But if
there exift a juftice to avenge great crimes ; if there
be an infernal region, it is there, I truft, that the villains, who, blinded by views of felf-intereft, have impofed upon the throne, and whofe fatal councils have
raifed this monument of ignorance and ftupidity upon
which thou dwelleft, and which hath perhaps but an
inftant of duration ; it is there that they will go, and
groan perpetually in unextinguifhable flames.

St. Marc, which hath only two hundred houfes,
but pleafantly built, is fituated at the bottom of a
bay, which is crowned with a crefcent of little hills
filled with freeftone. Two rivulets run through the
town, and it's air is pure. There are to be found

upon its territory no more than ten plantations of sugar, thirty-two of indigo, one hundred of coffee, and seventy-two of cotton. Its harbour, however, though a bad one, attracts a great number of navigators, and it is indebted for this advantage to the riches of the Artibonite.

This is an exceeding good plain, fifteen leagues in length, and of unequal breadth, from four to nine leagues; it is divided into two parts by the river from which it takes its name, and which flows with rapidity along the higheſt part of the plain, after having run through ſome of the Spaniſh poſſeſſions and the country of Mirbalais. The elevation of theſe waters hath ſuggeſted the idea of dividing them, the poſſibility of doing which hath been geometrically demonſtrated. So great is the power of enlightened nations over nature itſelf; but a project founded on the baſis of mathematical knowledge, requires the utmoſt caution in the execution.

In the preſent ſtate of things, the plantations formed upon the right ſhore are expoſed to frequent droughts, which often diſappoint the beſt grounded expectations. Thoſe of the left ſhore, which are evidently placed much lower, are well watered, and have riſen by this advantage to the higheſt perfection in their cultures. The proprietors of the former haſten the ſpreading of the waters, which is guarded againſt by the latter, who are apprehenſive of ſeeing their grounds overflowed.

If, as it is generally underſtood, theſe are effectual methods to render one part fertile, without reducing the other part to barrenneſs, why ſhould this operation be poſtponed, by which an increaſe of ten or twelve millions weight of ſugar might be obtained? This increaſe would be ſtill more conſiderable, if a method could be deviſed to drain that part of the coaſt which is overflowed by the waters of the Artibonite. Thus it is, that the civilized man, by changing the courſe of rivers, makes the earth ſubſervient to his uſe. The fertility he imparts to the lands can only juftify his conquefts ; if indeed art and labour, B O O K laws and virtues, may be allowed in procefs of time XIII. to atone for the injuftice of invafion.

The territory of the Gonaves is flat, tolerably even, and very dry ; it hath two plantations of fugar, ten of coffee, fix of indigo, and thirty of cotton ; this laft production might be eafily multiplied, upon a great extent of fand, which at prefent doth not appear proper for any other kind of culture. But fhould the waters of the Artibonite be ever prudently diftributed, a confiderable part of this large diftrict would be covered with fugar canes. It would then be perceived, that the feat of government ought to have been placed in its port, which is excellent, and might be eafily fortified. Another advantage which muft neceffarily add to the value of this country, is, that mineral waters are to be found there. They were neglected for a long while, in a colony which is always full of fick perfons or convalefcents ; but at length in 1772, baths and fountains, commodious habitations, and an hofpital for foldiers and failors, were built there.

The colonies prefent us with fome contradictory phenomena which it is impoffible to deny, and which it is difficult to conciliate.

Reflections upon the little concern which the mother country and the colonies have for each other.

There can fcarce be a doubt, but that we hold the productions of the colonies in high eftimation. Why therefore do we concern ourfelves fo little about the profperity and the prefervation of the colonifts ? If the violence of a hurricane fhall have buried thoufands of unfortunate people under the ruins of their dwellings, and fhall have laid wafte their poffeffions ; this is an event which takes up our attention lefs than a duel fought, or an affaffination committed, at home. Should a vaft country of the diftant continent continue to be ravaged by fome epidemical difeafe, we talk of the matter at home with more coolnefs, than of the uncertain return of the fmall-pox after inoculation. If the horrors of famine fhould reduce the inhabitants of St. Domingo, or of Martinico, to feek

for their food in the country, or to devour one another, we are lefs concerned at fuch a cataftrophe
than at the calamity of a hail-ftorm, that fhould
have deftroyed the harveft in fome one of our villages.
It is natural enough to think, that this indifference
is the effect of diftance, and that the colonifts are not
more affected with our misfortunes than we are with
theirs.

But it will be faid, that our towns are contiguous
to our country places, and that we have the mifery
of their inhabitants inceffantly in our view. We are
not the lefs defirous of plentiful harvefts of all kinds
from them, and yet it is fcarce poffible, that there
fhould be a greater neglect fhown for the encouragement, the multiplication, and the prefervation of the
hufbandmen. From whence can this furprifing contradiction arife? It muft be, that we are mad refpecting the manner in which we treat our colonifts, and
both inhuman and mad in our conduct with our
farmers, fince both at home and at a diftance we require the fame things ; and that yet we will not adopt
the means of procuring them in either of thofe places.

But how doth it happen, that this inconfiftency of
the people fhould likewife extend to the government?
It is becaufe there is, according to all appearances,
a greater fpirit of jealoufy than of true intereft, either
in the acquifition or the prefervation of this fpecies
of diftant property ; it is becaufe the fovereigns fcarce
reckon the colonifts as among the number of their fubjects. I fhall not fcruple to declare, fince it is my
opinion, that an irruption of the fea, which fhould
fwallow up this portion of their domain, would affect
them lefs than the lofs of it from the invafion of a
rival power. They care very little whether thefe
men live or die, provided they do not belong to any
one elfe.

I fhall therefore firft addrefs myfelf to the fovereigns, and I fhall tell them : either leave thefe men
to their fate, or affift them. I fhall then addrefs
myfelf to the colonifts, and I fhall fay : implore the

affiftance of the mother-country, to which you are
fubject; and if you fhould experience a denial, break
off your connections with it. It is too much to be
obliged to fupport at once mifery, indifference, and
flavery.

But wherefore are the colonies worfe regulated,
and more unhappy ftill, under thofe powers to whofe
ftrength and fplendour they are the moft neceffary?
It is becaufe thofe powers are ftill more abfurd than
we are ; and being commercial ftates, the fpirit of
their adminiftration is ftill more cruel. It is becaufe,
in imitation of the farmer, who is not certain of enjoying a new leafe, they exhauft a land, which from
one year to another may pafs into the hands of a
new poffeffor. When the provinces of a ftate are
contiguous, thofe that are neareft the frontiers are
treated with moft management. It is directly contrary with the colonies. They are oppreffed, from
the fole apprehenfion, that in circumftances of a perilous nature the care that might have been beftowed
upon them fhould be entirely thrown away.

The weftern part of the colony is feparated from
the northern part by the Mole of St. Nicholas, which
lies on both coafts. At the head of the Cape is a
good, fafe, and commodious harbour. It ftands directly oppofite to Point Maizi, in the ifland of Cuba,
and feems naturally deftined, by this pofition, to become the moft important poft in all America for the
convenience of navigation. The opening of the bay
is 1450 toifes broad. The road leads to the harbour,
and the harbour to the bafon. All this great recefs
is wholefome, though the waters of the fea are almoft
in a ftate of ftagnation there. The bafon, which
feems as if made for the purpofe of careening, has
not the inconvenience of clofe harbours ; it is open
to the Weft and North winds ; and yet, if they blow
ever fo hard, they can never interrupt or retard any
work that is done in the port. The peninfula, where
the harbour is fituated, rifes gradually to the plains,
which ftand upon a very large bafis ; it feems, as it

BOOK
XIII.

Settlements
formed to
the north
of St. Do-
mingo.

B O O K were, a fingle mountain, with a broad and flat top,
XIII.   defcending with a gentle flope to unite with the reft
of the ifland.

The Mole of St. Nicholas was long neglected by
the inhabitants of St. Domingo. The bare hills and
flat rocks it abounded with, afforded nothing worth
their notice. The ufe which the Englifh made of it
during the laft war, has rendered it of fome kind of
confequence. The French miniftry, enlightened even
by their enemies, fettled in 1767 a ftaple there, where
foreign navigators might freely barter the wood and
cattle, of which the colony was in want, for its molaffes and brandy, which were rejected by the mother-country. This communication, which, by a reafonable toleration, and induftrious fmuggling, hath
,been extended to feveral other objects, gave birth to
a town, which at prefent confifts of three hundred
wooden houfes, brought ready built from New England.

At fome diftance from the port, but ftill within the
diftrict of the mole, is the town of Bombardopolis.
The Acadians and Germans, who had been carried
there in 1763, perifhed at firft with aftonifhing rapidity. This is conftantly the fate that attends all
new fettlements between the tropics. The few of
thefe unfortunate people that· have outlived the fatal
effects of the climate, and thofe of difappointment
and poverty, were wifhing only to quit this barren
foil, when the tranfactions carried on in their neighbourhood, revived, in fome meafure, their hopes. They
cultivate provifions, fruits, and vegetables ; which they
fell to the fhips, or to the inhabitants of the port, and
even a fmall quantity of coffee and cotton for Europe.

The next fettlement on the North coaft, after the
Mole of St. Nicholas, is called Port Paix. It owed
its origin to the neighbourhood of Tortuga, whofe inhabitants took refuge there when they forfook that
ifland. The grounds were cleared fo early, that this
is one of the healthieft fpots in St. Domingo, and has

long fince attained the utmoft degree of riches and population it is capable of; but thefe are not very confiderable, though induftry has been carried fo far as even to pierce through mountains for the conveyance of water to moiften the grounds. Port Paix is on all fides fo difficult of accefs, that it is in a manner cut off from the reft of the colony.

The little Saint Louis, the Borgne, Port Margot, Limbé, and Lacul, have likewife no communication with each other. Thefe places are divided by rivers, which overflow and ravage the beft lands. Accordingly, they are in general too cold for fugar-canes to thrive in them. The waters of thefe torrents ought to be confined in large and deep beds. After thefe labours are finifhed, it would be an eafy matter to conftruct bridges, which would draw the inhabitants nearer together, would enable them to communicate their improvements to each other, and would make them enjoy the advantages of a better regulated fociety. The plantations of indigo would then be improved, and thofe of fugar would be multiplied, while the coffee would not be forfaken; this plant is confidered as the beft of the kind in the colony. Limbé alone collects two millions weight of it, as good as that of Martinico.

This is very little, if indeed it be any thing, in comparifon of the productions of the plain of the Cape, which is twenty leagues in length, and about four in breadth. Few lands are better watered; but there is not a river where a floop can go up above three miles. All this great fpace is interfected with ftraight roads forty feet wide, and planted on both fides with hedges of citron trees. Thefe roads would have been perfect in their kind, had they been ornamented with tall trees, which woud have afforded a delightful fhade for travellers, and prevented that fcarcity of wood which this diftrict already begins to feel. This is the country of America which produces the greateft quantity of fugar, and of the beft fort. The plain is terminated by a ridge of moun-

(margin: BOOK XIII.)

(margin: Great importance of the town of Cape St. Francis fituated upon the northern coaft of St. Domingo.)

B O O K tains, which varies in depth from four to eight leagues.
  XIII. Few of them are very high ; several of them may be
cultivated to the very summit, and they are all interfected at intervals with an infinite number of plantations of coffee, and some exceeding fine plantations
of indigo.

Although the French had been early acquainted
with the value of a territory, the fertility of which
furpaffes all that can be faid of it, yet they did not
begin to cultivate it till 1670, the time when their
apprehenfions of the Spaniards, who till then had remained in force in the neighbourhood, were diffipated. A Calvinift, named Gobin, one of thofe whom
the fpirit of intoleration in religious matters began to
drive out from their native country, went and reared
the firft habitation at this Cape. More houfes were
built as the grounds were cleared. This fettlement
had already made fuch progrefs in the fpace of twenty years, as to excite the jealoufy of the Englifh.
They joined their forces with thofe of Spain, and, attacking it both by land and fea, in 1695, they took,
plundered, and reduced it to afhes.

A great advantage might have been made of this
misfortune. Intereft, which is the primary founder
of all colonies, had induced the inhabitants to choofe,
in a harbour that is three leagues in circumference,
the foot of a hill for the portion of the Cape, becaufe
it was the place that lay moft convenient for the anchorage. A fituation more wholefome, more convenient, and more fpacious, might have been chofen.
This was not attended to ; but the town was rebuilt,
where it ought never to have been built, in a bottom, where the rays of the fun are rendered more
fcorching by the reflection of the mountains ; and
which never can be refrefhed by the coolnefs of the
land breezes. Yet fuch is the richnefs of the adjacent country, that this fettlement hath continually
increafed.

The Cape is now cut by twenty-nine ftraight
ftreets, into 225 clufters of houfes, which amount to

900 ; but thefe ftreets are too narrow, and having no flope, though the foil itfelf be prominent in the centre, are always dirty ; for, as they are paved only in the middle, the kennels, which are not even on each fide, gather into puddles and common fewers, inftead of draining off the waters.

The old fquare of Nòtre-Dame, and the church built with ftones brought from Europe that terminates it ; the new fquare of Clugny, where the market hath been fixed ; the fountains that embellifh both of thefe monuments ; the governor's houfe, the barracks, the theatre ; none of thefe public edifices, in a word, would attract the notice of the curious traveller, who fhould have any idea of the principles of architecture. But if nature had endowed him with fenfibility, his heart would expand at the bare mention of the houfe called *La Providence*.

Moft of the adventurers who firft come into the colony, are deftitute of refources and talents, and before they have acquired induftry to procure fubfiftence, become fubject to diforders that are often fatal. A humane and generous citizen founded at the Cape two habitations for thefe helplefs and diftreffed perfons, where the men and the women are feverally provided with every thing they want. This fine inftitution, the only one of the kind in the New World, and which would never have been fufficiently fupported by authority, nor fufficiently enriched by the gifts of the citizens, had feen its revenues gradually decreafe by the difhonefty of thofe who adminiftered them, and by the neglect of government.

Is it then impoffible, that any good inftitution fhould fubfift among mankind ? Will the rich ftill continue to attack the poor, even in their afylum, if the prefence of the gallows doth not reftrain them ? Infamous wretches ! ye know not all the atrocioufnefs of your conduct ; if one of your fellow-creatures were brought before you, convicted of having feized upon a paffenger in the night time, and of having prefented a piftol to his breaft in order to get his

purfe, to what kind of punifhment would you fen-
tence him? Be it what it may, you deferve ftill a
greater one. You unite bafenefs, inhumanity, and
prevarication, to the theft; and to what fpecies of
theft; you take from him who is dying with hunger,
the bread that has been intrufted to you for his ufe;
You ftrip mifery itfelf abandoned to your care, and
you do it clandeftinely and without rifk. The im-
precation which I am going to thunder out againft
you, I extend it to all the difhoneft directors of hofpitals, of whatfoever countries they may be, even of
my own; I extend it to all negligent minifters, from
whom they fhall conceal the knowledge of their
crimes, or who fhall overlook them. May the ignominy, may the punifhments referved for the vileft
malefactors, fall upon the profcribed head of villians,
who are capable of fo enormous a crime againft humanity, and of a flagitious act fo contrary to good
policy; and if it fhould happen, that they fhould e-
fcape from infamy and from punifhment, may the
miniftry, who have been ignorant of fuch an excefs of corruption, or who have tolerated it, become
an object of execration among all nations and in all
ages.

Notwithftanding the confufion into which the houfes
of Providence, fo famous for the prefervation of the
human fpecies, are fallen, there are ftill proportionally
a lefs number of people who die at the Cape than in
any other of the maritime towns of the colony. This
advantage muft be attributed to the circumftance of
the whole territory being cultivated, to the filling up
of the neighbouring floughs, to diffipation, to the
conveniences of life, to induftry, and to fuccours of
all kinds, which are found united in a numerous and
active fociety. The air will acquire all the falubrity
which the nature of things will allow, when the moraffes of the little bay fhall have been dried, which
diffufe, in very dry feafons, an infectious odour.

The harbour is worthy of the town; and it is admirably well adapted to admit the fhips that come

from Europe, which may anchor here with conve- B O O K
nience and fafety, of whatever fize they may be. It XIII.
lies open to none but the north-eaft wind, and cannot
even be hurt by this, the entrance being full of reefs,
which break the violence of the waves.

It is into this famous ftaple that more than one half
of the productions of the colony are conveyed. They
are brought from the mountains and from the valleys,
but principally from the plains. The parifhes which
furnifh the moft important of them are known by the
names of the North Plain, the Little Bay, the Great
River, the Morin, the Lemonade, the Terrier Rouge,
Fort Dauphin, and Ouanaminthe, which terminates
at the river Maffacre. The diftrict Morin, and the
Iflet of Lemonade, are much fuperior to the other
fettlements, both in the quantity and quality of their
fugars.

All the productions of St. Domingo amounted, in Nature and
1720, to no more than one million four hundred thou- quantity of
fand weight of raw fugar, to one million four hundred tions,which
thoufand pounds of earthed fugar, and to one million France an-
two hundred thoufand pounds of indigo. Thefe pro- ceives from
ductions have had a prodigious and rapid increafe. To- its colony
of St. Do-
wards 1737, cotton and coffee were added to them. mingo.
Even the culture of cacao hath been revived, though
fomewhat later.

In 1775, France received from this colony, upon
three hundred and fifty-three fhips, one million two
hundred and thirty thoufand fix hundred and feventy-three quintals feventy pounds of fugar, which
were worth 44,738,139 livres 2 fols 2 deniers [about
1,864,089l. 2s. 7d.] ; four hundred and fifty-nine
thoufand three hundred and thirty-nine quintals forty-one pounds of coffee, which were worth 21,818,621
livres 19 fols 6 deniers [909,109l. 4s. 11¾d.] ; eighteen thoufand eighty quintals twenty-nine pounds of
indigo, which were worth 15,373,346 livres 10 fols
[640,556l. 2s. 1d.] ; five thoufand feven hundred
eighty-feven quintals fixty-four pounds of cacao,
which were worth 405,134 livres 16 fols [16,880l.

BOOK 12s. 4d.]; five hundred and eighteen quintals sixty-
XIII. one pounds of arnotto, which were worth 32,663
livres 2 fols 6 deniers [1360l. 19s. 3¾d.], twenty-fix
thoufand eight hundred and ninety-two quintals eighty-two pounds of cotton, which were worth 6,723,205
livres [280,133l. 10s. 10d.]; fourteen thoufand
one hundred and twenty-four hides, which were
worth 164,657 livres [6860l. 14s. 2d.]; forty-three
quintals forty-fix pounds of rope-yarn, which were
worth 43,460 livres [1810l. 16s. 8d.]; ninety quintals nineteen pounds of black caffia, which were
worth 2435 livres 11 deniers [about 101l. 9s. 2½d.];
ninety-two thoufand feven hundred and forty-fix
quintals ninety-two pounds of wood, which were
worth 908,368 livres 3 fols 8 deniers [about 37,848l.
13s. 5¾d.]; and in fmall productions, fome of which
belonged to the other colonies, 1,352,148 livres
[56,339l. 10s.], and in money, 2,600,000 livres
[108,333l. 6s. 8d.]. The total of all thefe fums produces an income of 94,162,178 livres 16 fols 9 deniers [3,923.424l. 2s. 4¾d.].

If to the 94,162,178 livres 16 fols 9 deniers
[3,923,424l. 2s. 4¾d.], the produce of San Domingo,
be added the 488,598 livres 3 fols 3 deniers [about
20,354l. 3s. 5½d.], produced by Cayenne; the
18,975,974 livres 1 fol 10 deniers [790,664l. 9s. 3d.],
produced by Martinico; and the 12,751,404 livres
16 fols 10 deniers [about $31,307l. 10s. 9d.], produ-
ced by Guadalupe, it will be found, that in 1775,
France received from her poffeffions in the New Hemifphere, upon five hundred and fixty-two fhips,
126,378,155 livres 18 fols 8 deniers [about 5,265,757l.
6s. 3½d.].

The kingdom confumed of thefe productions only
to the amount of 52,763,763 livres 5 fols 8 deniers.
[about 2,199,740l. 1s. 8¼d.]. The remainder, which
amounted to 73,584,392 livres 13 fols [3,066,016l.
17s. 2½d.], was confequently fold to foreigners.

This great exportation was formed by one million
forty thoufand nine hundred and ninety-eight quin-

tals fixty-fix pounds of fugar, which produced 38,703,463 livres [1,612,644l. 5s. 10d.]; by five hundred thoufand five hundred and eighty-two quintals forty-fix pounds of coffee, which produced 23,727,608 livres 13 fols [988,650l. 7s. 2½d.]; by eleven thoufand three hundred and fix quintals thirty-eight pounds of indigo, which produced 9,610,423 livres [400,434l. 5s. 10d.]; by feven thoufand nine hundred and twenty-two quintals feventy-five pounds of cacao, which produced 554,592 livres 10 fols [23,108l. 5d.]; by fifteen hundred and thirty-one quintals feventy-eight pounds of arnotto, which produced 95,838 livres [3993l. 5s. 10d.]; by one thoufand and twenty quintals eleven pounds of cotton, which produced 255,027 livres 10 fols [10,626l. 2s. 11d.]; by twelve hundred and feven quintals fifty-nine pounds of black caffia, which produced 32,605 livres [1358l. 10s. 10d.]; by forty-one thoufand eight hundred and eight quintals twenty pounds of wood, which produced 598,723 livres [24,947l. 5s. 10d.]; by five hundred and fixty-eight hides, which produced 5112 livres [213l.]; and by one hundred pounds weight of rope-yarn, which produced 1000 livres [41l. 13s. 4d.].

To return to St. Domingo; its aftonifhing wealth was produced by three hundred and eighty-five fugar houfes for raw fugars, and two hundred and fixty three for earthed fugars; by two thoufand five hundred and eighty-feven plantations of indigo; by fourteen millions eighteen thoufand three hundred and thirty-fix cotton plants; by ninety-two millions eight hundred and ninety-three thoufand four hundred and five coffee trees; and by feven hundred and fifty-feven thoufand fix hundred and ninety-one cacao trees.

At the fame period, the cattle of the colony amounted to feventy-five thoufand nine hundred and fiftyeight horfes or mules, and feventy-feven thoufand nine hundred and four head of horned cattle. Its provifions confifted of feven million feven hundred and fifty-fix thoufand two hundred and twenty-five banana trees; one million one hundred and seventy-eight thoufand two hundred and twenty-nine trenches of manioc; twelve thoufand feven hundred and thirty-four plots of maize; eighteen thoufand feven hundred and thirty-eight plots of potatoes; eleven thoufand eight hundred and twenty-five plots of yams; and feven thoufand forty-fix plots of fmall millet.

The labours occupied thirty-two thoufand and fifty white perfons, of all ages, and of both fexes; fix thoufand and thirty-fix Negroes, or free Mulattoes, and about three hundred thoufand flaves. The annual calculation did not indeed reckon the number of thefe unfortunate captives at more than two hundred forty thoufand and ninety-five; but it is well known, that at that time every planter concealed as many as he could from the refearches of the treafury, in order to avoid the rigour of the impofts.

Thefe cultures, and thefe inhabitants, are diftributed over forty-fix parifhes, fome of which are twenty leagues in circumference. The limits of a great number of them are not yet fixed, and moft of them have nothing but huts or ruins for their churches. Divine fervice is fcarce performed in any of them with proper decency. The churches of the fouth and of the weftern parts are under the direction of Dominican friars, and thofe of the north under Capuchins, who have fucceeded the Jefuits. They have all a large village or a town belonging to them.

The large villages are formed by the fhops of fome merchants, and by the manufactories of fome artificers, all of them conftructed round the prefbytery. On feftival days a kind of market is eftablifhed, to which the flaves refort, in order to barter the fruits, the poultry, and other trifling provifions which belong to them, for furniture, clothes, and ornaments, which, though of fmall value, procure them fome kind of convenience, and diftinguifh them from their fellow-creatures, who are not in poffeffion of fimilar enjoyments. We cannot fufficiently exprefs our indignation, that tyranny fhould ftill purfue them while they are employed in thefe trifling exchanges, and that the vile fatellites of juftice, intrufted with the regulation of the police of thefe affemblies, fhould make thefe unfortunate people fenfible of the hard-fhips of their fituation, even during the fhort refpite which is granted them by their barbarous mafters.

Here we may perceive two very odious characters; the bailiff who torments the flave, and the director who doth not exercife his authority againft the bailiff. But the bailiff is a man devoid of compaffion, whofe daily functions have perhaps hardened him to fuch a pitch, that he grows weary when the exercife of them is fufpended, and when he has no opportunity of making any one fuffer. The director, on the con-trary, is a magiftrate, whofe breaft doth not harbour the fame degree of ferocioufnefs, whofe habitual bu-finefs it is to difplay a kind of dignity, and in whom juftice ought always to be tempered with compaffion. How doth it happen, that two fuch different beings feem to concur in adding to the misfortune of the flaves? Is it owing to a barbarous contempt of thefe miferable people, who are almoft expunged from the race of mankind? Or are they fo completely doomed to grief and pain, that their cries and their tears fhall not make any further impreffion?

The towns of the colony, and in general all thofe of the American iflands, exhibit a picture very dif-ferent from that which the European towns difplay. In Europe, our cities are peopled with men of every clafs, of all profeffions, and of all ages; fome of them rich and idle, others poor and laborious; all of them purfuing, amidft the tumult and amidft the multi-tude, the object which they have in view; fome fol-lowing pleafure, others fortune; fome reputation, or momentary fame, which is often miftaken for it, and others feeking their fubfiftence. In thefe great vor-tices, the collifion and variety of paffions, of interefts, and of wants, neceffarily produce great agitations, unexpected contrafts, fome virtues, and many vices or crimes. Thefe are moving pictures, more or lefs

B O O K animated in proportion to the number of actors, and
   XIII.   confequently of fcenes that are exhibited there.   At
St. Domingo, and in the reft of the American Archipelago, the fpectacle prefented by the towns is
uniform, and exactly the fame. They have neither
nobles, tradefmen, nor annuitants. They prefent
nothing but magazines appropriated to the productions of the foil, and to the different labours they require. They have none but agents, inn-keepers,
and adventurers, exerting themfelves to obtain a poft
by which they may fubfift, and accepting the firft
that offers. Every man is in hafte to get rich, in order to quit a fituation where there are no diftinctions,
no honours, no pleafures to be found, and which fupplies no other ftimulus befide that of intereft. No
man refides there with an intention of living and dying upon the fpot. The views of all men are fixed
upon Europe ; and the principal idea that tends to
the increafe of riches, confifts in the expectation, more
or lefs diftant, of bringing them back into our hemifphere, among our own relations.

Connec-   Befide the immenfe productions which the colony
tions of St. fends to the mother-country, and which may at leaft
Domingo
with fo-   be increafed by one third, a fmall portion of them
reign na-   are delivered to its indolent neighbour. It is with
tions.   fugar, rum, and efpecially with liquors and the manufactures of Europe, that the colony pays what the
Spanifh part of St. Domingo furnifhes in pork and
hung beef, in wood, hides, horfes, and horned cattle, for its manufactures, and for its fhambles ; and
that it appropriates to itfelf all the filver fent from
the mines of Mexico to this ancient fettlement. The
court of Madrid have endeavoured to diminifh the
activity of this intercourfe, by prohibiting the foreign
merchandife from being brought into its poffeffions,
and by loading the cattle which might be exported,
with heavy duties. This faulty regulation hath had
no other effect than to put a reftraint upon thofe exchanges which ought to have continued perfectly
free. It is particularly in this part of the world,

that mutual wants prevail over natural antipathy, B O O K XIII. and that the uniformity of climate ftifles this fource of difcord.

The Dutch of Curaffou engrofs a great part of the trade of the French colony, during the wars in which they are not engaged ; and they likewife carry off fome commodities in peace time. It is with the pro-ductions in the Eaft Indies, and with bills of exchange, that they keep up this trifling intercourfe.

The connections between the people of Jamaica and thofe of St. Domingo, are much more confider-able. The twelve or thirteen thoufand flaves which are annually carried to the colony by the French na-vigators, do not prevent its receiving four or five thoufand from the Englifh. The latter coft one fixth lefs than the other, and are paid with cotton, and efpecially with indigo, which is accepted at a higher price than is given by the national trade. Thefe fmugglers carry it into their own country, as a pro-duction of the Britifh iflands, and receive a gratifica-tion of twelve fols [6d.] per pound.

It is with North America, however, that St. Do-mingo keeps up a more regular and more ufeful in-tercourfe. In times of urgent calamities, the veffels of that vaft region of the New World are admitted in all the harbours, but at ordinary times only in the mole of St. Nicholas. In common times, their car-goes confift of wood for fhip-building, vegetables, cattle, flour, and falt fifh. They carry off publicly five and twenty or thirty thoufand hogfheads of mo-laffes, and fraudulently, all the provifions which the colonifts can deliver to them, or choofe to do it.

Such is, in time of peace, the divifion which is made of the territorial riches of St. Domingo. War opens a new fcene. As foon as the fignal for hoftili-ties is given, the Englifh take poffeffion of all the la-titudes about the colony. They reftrain its exports and its imports. Every article, either entering or going out, falls into their hands ; and the fmall quan-tity which might have efcaped in the New Hemi-

The con-nections of France with St. Domingo become dangerous during times of war. Rea-fon of this.

fphere, is intercepted upon the coafts of the Old,
where the enemy are equally ftrong. The merchants
of the mother-country are then obliged to poftpone
their expeditions, and the inhabitants of the ifland
neglect their labours. Languor and defpair fucceed
to important and rapid communications, and laft as
long as the divifions fubfift between the belligerent
powers.

This would have been otherwife, had the French,
who firft appeared at St. Domingo, thought of eftablifhing cultures. They would have occupied, as they
might have done, that part of the ifland which lies
to the Eaft. The plains on this fide are fpacious and
fertile ; and the coafts are fafe ; a fhip enters the harbours upon the day they are difcovered, and lofes
fight of them the very day it fails out. Such is the
nature of the road, that the enemy cannot lay any
ambufcade there. The coaft is unfit for cruifing.
Thefe latitudes are convenient for the Europeans,
and the paffage expeditious; but as the fcheme of
thefe adventurers was to attack the Spanifh fhips,
and to infeft the Gulph of Mexico with their piracies,
the poffeffions they occupied upon a winding coaft,
were furrounded by Cuba, Jamaica, the Turks, Tortuga, the Caicos, Gonava, and Lucayos iflands. They
are alfo furrounded by a multitude of fand-banks and
rocks, which make the progrefs of a fhip flow and
uncertain ; and by narrow feas, which muft give a
great advantage to the enemy, either for landing, for
blocking up, or for cruifing.

The court of Verfailles will never be able to maintain a regular intercourfe with its colony during time
of war, unlefs by the means of fome fhips of the line
to the South and the Weft, and a good fquadron to
the North. Nature hath formed, at Fort Dauphin,
a vaft, commodious and fafe harbour, which can be
defended with facility. From this harbour, fituated
to the windward of the other fettlements, it would
be eafy to protect the feveral latitudes ; but the works
of the place ought to be repaired and extended, and

particularly a proper naval arfenal ought to be form- B O O K
ed. If this were done, the French admirals, being XIII.
fecure of an afylum, and of all the necefſary affiſt-
ances, after either a fuccefsful or an unfuccefsful engagement, would be no longer fearful of engaging
the enemies of their country.

The meafures which would be proper to be taken The part of
to prevent the ravages which the Spaniards might St Domin-
commit in the inland part of St. Domingo, deferve occupied by
likewife fome attention.

Caſtile, which is ſtill in poffeffion of two thirds of tacked by
the ifland, formerly had the whole of it, when, a the Spa-
little before the middle of the laſt century, a few are in pof-
bold and enterprifing Frenchmen went there to feek the other
a refuge from the laws, or from mifery. The Spa- part.
niards endeavoured to repulfe them ; but, though
without any other fupport than their courage, they
were not afraid of fuſtaining war with a people armed
under a regular authority. Thefe men were acknowledged by their nation as foon as they were thought
ſtrong enough to maintain themfelves in their ufurpations. A commander was fent to them. The
brave man, who was firſt appointed to command thofe
intrepid adventurers, caught their fpirit to fuch a
degree, as to propofe to his court the conqueſt of the
whole ifland. He pledged his life for the fuccefs of
the undertaking, provided they wou'd fend him a
fquadron ſtrong enough to block up the harbour of
the capital.

The miniſtry of Verfailles, neglecting a project which
was in reality more practicable than it appeared to
them at a diſtance, left the French expofed to continual hoſtilities. Notwithſtanding this, they always repulfed them fuccefsfully, and even carried devaſtation
into the enemy's country ; but thofe animofities kept
up in their minds a fpirit of robbery and plunder,
indifpofed them for ufeful labours, and ſtopped the
progrefs of agriculture, which fhould be the ultimate
end of every well-regulated fociety.

The error which France had fallen into, in not

BOOK
XIII.
seconding the ardour of the new colonists for the conquest of the whole island, had nearly occasioned her
the loss of that part of which she was already in pof-
seffion. While the French were engaged in carrying
on the war of 1688 against all Europe, the Spaniards
and the English, who both dreaded seeing them firmly established at St. Domingo, united their forces to
expel them. Their first attempts gave them reason
to expect an entire success; when they quarrelled
with each other, and from that time became irrecon-
cileable enemies. Ducasse, who managed the colony
with much sagacity and great reputation, took advantage of their divisions to attack them succeffively.
He first invaded Jamaica, where he destroyed every
thing with fire and sword. From thence he was preparing to turn his arms against St. Domingo; and
would infallibly have reduced the whole island, had
he not been stopped in this expedition by orders from
his court.

The house of Bourbon ascended the throne of
Spain, and the French nation lost all hopes of conquering St. Domingo. Hostilities, which had not
even been suspended there by the treaties of Aix-la-
Chapelle, Nimeguen, and Ryswick, ceased at last
between people who could never be true friends to
each other. Those who had established cultures derived some advantage from this reconciliation. For
some time past their slaves, availing themselves of the
national divisions, had shaken off their chains, and
removed into a district where they found freedom and
no labour. This defertion was abated, by the Spaniards entering into a contract to bring home the fugitives to their neighbours, for the sum of 250 livres
[10l. 8s. 4d.] a head. Although this agreement was
not very scrupulously observed, it proved a powerful
check, till the diffensions that divided the two nations
in 1718. At this period the Negroes deserted their
works in multitudes. This loss induced the French
to think of reviving their old project of expelling
totally from the island such neighbours, who were

equally dangerous from their indolence, as others would be from their turbulent fpirit. The war did not laft long enough to bring about this revolution. At the conclufion of the peace, Philip V. gave orders for the reftitution of all the fugitives that could be found. They were juft embarked, to be fent to their old mafters, when the people rofe and refcued them ; an act which we could hardly difapprove, had they been prompted to it by humanity, rather than by national hatred. It will always be pleafing to fee people excited to rebellion on account of the flavery of the Negroes. Thofe who were refcued on this occafion, fled into inacceffible mountains, where they have fince multiplied to fuch a degree, as to be able to afford a fafe retreat to all the flaves that can find means to join them. There, in confequence of the cruelty of civilized nations, they become as free and as favage as tigers ; in expectation, perhaps, of a chief and a conqueror, who may reftore the violated rights of mankind, by feizing upon an ifland which feems to have been intended for the flaves who till the ground, and not for the tyrants who water it with the blood of thofe victims.

The prefent fyftem of politics will not allow France and Spain to be at war with each other. Should any event occafion a rupture between the two nations, notwithftanding the compact between the two crowns, it would probably be but a tranfient quarrel, that would not allow time for projecting conquefts which muft foon be reftored. The enterprifes on both fides would, therefore, be confined to the ravaging of the country ; and in this cafe the nation that does not cultivate, at leaft at St. Domingo, would prove formidable, by its very poverty, to that which has already made fome progrefs in the culture of its lands. A Caftilian governor was fo fenfible of this, that he once wrote to the French 'commandant, that, if he forced him to an invafion, he would deftroy more in the compafs of one league, than the French could,

B O O K if they were to lay wafte all the country he com-
XIII. manded.

Hence it is demonftrable, that, if a war fhould
break out in Europe between thefe two powers, the
moft active of them ought to fue for a neutrality in
favour of this ifland. It ought even, as it hath often
been faid, to folicit the abfolute ceffion of a poffeffion
which is ufelefs, or burdenfome, to its poffeffor. We
know not whether the court of Verfailles have ever
entertained this ambitious idea. But how much muft
we fuppofe that the Spanifh miniftry would have been
averfe from this ceffion, when they have ftated fo
many difficulties refpecting the fixing of the confufed and uncertain limits of the two nations ! This
treaty, ardently defired, projected for a long time,
and even begun at feveral intervals, hath been at
length concluded in 1776.

Have the
limits be-
tween
France and
Spain, been
judicioufly
fettled at
St. Do-
mingo?

The only equitable and reafonable bafis of thefe
negotiations, fhould have been the ftate of thefe poffeffions in 1700.

At this period both nations, being upon friendly
terms, remained the juft owners of the lands they
then poffeffed. The encroachments made during the
courfe of this century, by the fubjects of one of the
crowns, are the encroachments of individuals upon
each other ; they are not become lawful poffeffors by
being tolerated ; and the rights of both powers are
ftill the fame, fince they have not been abrogated,
directly or indirectly, by any convention.

But it is certain, from inconteftible facts, that in
the beginning of this century, the French poffeffions,
which are now bounded on the northern coaft by the
river of Maffacre, extended then to the river Rebone.
Thofe of the fouthern coaft, which had been carried
on as far as the river of Neybe, have been at prefent
ftopped at the inlet of Pitre. This furprifing revolution is the natural confêquence of the economical
fyftem of the two neighbouring nations. The one
which has applied itfelf chiefly to agriculture, has
collected all its poffeffions towards the moft frequent-

ed ports, where the produce might be moſt certainly and advantageouſly diſpoſed of. The other, whoſe ſubjects have always continued ſhepherds, took poſſeſſion of all the lands that were abandoned, for the breeding of more cattle. The paſtures have naturally been enlarged, and the fields contracted, or at leaſt brought cloſer together.

A negotiation properly conducted, would have reſtored France to that ſituation in which it was when it gave a king to the Spaniards. This was the wiſh of equity and of reaſon ; which were not deſirous that active coloniſts, who render the land which they fertilize uſeful, ſhould be ſacrificed to a ſmall number of vagabonds, who conſume, without aſſiſting in theſe productions. Nevertheleſs, from motives of policy, the ſprings of which are unknown to us, the court of Verſailles have given up what they formerly poſſeſſed, and confined themſelves to what they were in actual poſſeſſion of, upon the borders of the ſea, at the time of the convention. But hath this power at leaſt regained in the inland parts what it hath ſacrificed upon the coaſt ? We are under the neceſſity of declaring, that it hath not received the ſmalleſt indemnity.

Before the treaty, the French colony formed a kind of creſcent, the convexity of which produced, around the mountains, an extent of two hundred and fifty leagues of coaſt to the North, to the Weſt, and to the South of the iſland. The ſame arrangement ſubſiſts ſince the limits have been ſettled ; ſooner or later it muſt be changed, for a reaſon which muſt prevail over all other conſiderations.

The French ſettlements, to the Weſt and the South, are divided from thoſe to the North by the Spaniſh territory. The impoſſibility of ſuccouring each other, expoſes them ſeparately to the invaſion of a power which is equally an enemy to both nations. Common intereſt will determine the court of Madrid to fix the limits in ſuch a manner, that her ally may meet with the aſſiſtance that may be want-

ed for her defence.   But this can never be, unlefs a
line be drawn from the two fixed points upon the
banks of the ocean, which fhall determine the property of the two people.   In vain would Spain perpetually grant to its neighbour the liberty of paffing
through its ftates, as it did in 1748, for a time ; this
complaifance would be of no ufe.   That fpace, of
fifteen or twenty leagues, is interfected with mountains fo fteep, forefts fo thick, ravins fo deep, and rivers fo irregular in their courfe, as to render it impracticable for an army to pafs through it in its prefent fituation.   Immenfe labours would be requifite
to render it ufeful, and thofe will never be executed,
unlefs by orders of the crown to which the domain
belongs.   The court of Madrid will the more readily
determine to cede this communication, fo neceffary
to a nation whofe interefts are the fame as their own, as
the intermediate territory is of little value.   It is rugged,
not very fertile, and at a great diftance from the fea.
A few fcattered flocks only are feen upon it.   The
proprietors of thefe uncultivated lands would be in-
demnified by France, with a generofity which would
leave them no room to regret what they had loft.

Means
which the
French part
of St. Do-
mingo hath
to protect
itfelf from
foreign in-
vafions.
When the poffeffions of the colony are thus connected and fupported internally, by an uninterrupted
chain of communication, the enemy will be more
eafily repulfed.   If the Englifh mean to attack St.
Domingo by the Weft or South, they will collect
their forces at Jamaica ; if by the North, they will
make their preparations at the Windward Iflands,
and moft probably at Antigua, which is the magazine
of their naval ftores.

The Weft and South are incapable of being defended.   The immenfe extent of the tract renders it
impoffible to maintain any connection or regularity
in the motion of the troops.   If they fhould be difperfed, they would become ufelefs by being thus divided ; if they fhould be collected for the defence of
fuch pofts as are moft liable to be attacked, from the
natural weaknefs of their pofition, they would be in

danger of being all loft together. Large battalions
would only be burdenfome to fuch extenfive coafts,
which prefent too much flank and too much front to
the enemy. It will only be neceffary to erect, or
keep up, batteries to protect the roads, the merchant-
fhips, and the coafting-trade ; to keep off privateers,
and even to prevent the landing of a man of war or
two, that might come to ravage the coaft, and levy
contributions. The light troops, which are fufficient
to fupport thefe batteries, will give ground in proportion to the advances of the enemy, and only take
care to avoid furrendering till they are in danger.

But it is not neceffary to relinquifh every kind of
defence. At the back of each coaft, there fhould be
a place for fhelter and for reinforcements ; always
open for retreat, out of the enemy's reach, fafe from
infults, and able to refift their attack. This fhould
be a narrow pafs, capable of being intrenched, and
of defending the troops to advantage. From thefe
impregnable retreats, the conqueror might continually
be haraffed ; who, having no ftrong hold, will be perpetually expofed to a furprife, and will fooner or
later be obliged to reimbark.

The northern coaft, richer, more populous, and lefs
extenfive than the other two, is more adapted to fupport a land war, and to make a regular defence.

The fea-fide, which is more or lefs full of reefs, affords in many places a fwampy ground ; and the
mangroves which cover thefe marfhes, make them
quite impenetrable. This natural defence is not fo
common as it was, fince many of thefe coppices have
been cut away. But the landing-places, which are
commonly no better than gaps, flanked by thefe
woods overflowed with water, require but a moderate
front to ftop them up. Magazines, and other ftone
buildings, are common there ; they furnifh pofts for
the erection of battlements, and fecure the placing of
fome mafked batteries,

This firft line of the fhore feems to promife, that a
coaft of eighteen leagues, fo well defended by nature,

B O O K would, when feconded by the valour of the French,
XIII. put the enemy in danger of being beaten the moment they fhould land. If their fchemes were difcovered, or if the difpofitions they were making at
fea fhould, from a diftance, point out the place of
their landing, the forces might repair thither and
prevent it. But experience fhows the infallible advantage of fquadrons at anchor.

It is not only by the firing of broadfides from the
fhips to cover the approach of boats, it is by the impoffibility there is of guarding every part of the coaft,
that a fquadron at anchor can eafily effect landing, as
it is a conftant check to fo many places at once.
Land forces move very flowly about the windings of
the coaft, while the boats and floops arrive fpeedily
by a fhorter way. The affailant follows the ftring,
while the other muft go all along the bow. Difappointed and wearied out with a variety of motions,
the latter is not lefs apprehenfive of thofe he fees in
the day-time, than of the manœuvres of the night
which he cannot fee.

In order to be able to oppofe a defcent, the firft
thing to be done is to fuppofe it actually accomplifhed ; all our courage and ftrength is then exerted in
taking advantage of the delays or miftakes of the
enemy. As foon as they are obferved at fea, they
may immediately be expected on land. A large fhore,
on which a landing may be effected, will always leave
the plain of the Cape open to invafion ; fo that the
chief attention muft be directed, not to the fea-fhore,
but to the inland parts.

The inland parts are in general covered with fugar-canes, which being more or lefs high, according
to their degree of maturity fucceffively make the
fields appear fo many thickets. Thefe are occafionally fet on fire, either to cover a march, or to retard
the enemy's purfuit, to deceive or aftonifh him. In
two hours time, inftead of fields covered with crops,
nothing is to be feen but an immenfe wafte, covered
with ftubble.

The partitions of the cane grounds, the favannahs, and the ftorehoufes for provifions, do not obftruct the motions of an army more than our meadows. Inftead of our villages, they have their habitations, which are not fo full of people, but are more numerous. The thick and ftraight hedges of citron-trees are clofer and more impenetrable than the fences that enclofe our fields. This is what conftitutes the greateft difference in the view of the fields of America and thofe of Europe.

A fmall number of rivers, fome hollow ways, very low hillocks, a foil generally even, fome dikes conftructed againft inundations, few ditches, if any, one or two forefts, not very thick fet with trees, a fmall number of moraffes, a ground that is overflowed in a ftorm, and grows dufty again with twelve hours funfhine, rivers that are full one day, and dried up the next; thefe are the general appearances of the plain of the Cape. This diverfity muft afford advantageous encampments, and it muft ever be remembered, that in a defenfive war, the poft one removes to, cannot be too near the one that is quitted.

It is not the province of a writer to prefcribe rules to military men. Cæfar himfelf has told us what he has done, not what we are to do. Topographical defcriptions, determining the goodnefs of fuch or fuch a poft, the combination of marches, the art of encampments and retreats, the moft learned theory; all thefe muft be fubmitted to the eye of the general, who, with the principles in his mind, and the materials in his hand, applies both to the circumftances of time and place, as they chance to occur. The military genius, though mathematical, is dependent on fortune, which fuits the order of the operations to the diverfity of appearances. Rules are liable to numberlefs exceptions, which muft be difcovered in the inftant. The very execution almoft always alters the plan, and difcompofes the fyftem of an action. The courage or timidity of the troops, the rafhnefs of the enemy, the cafual fuccefs of his meafures, an

accidental combat, an unforeseen event, a storm that
swells a torrent, a high wind that conceals a snare or
an ambuscade under clouds of dust, thunder that
frightens the horses, or is confounded with the report
of the cannon, the temperature of the air, which
constantly influences the spirits of the commander
and the blood of the soldiers : all these are so many
natural or moral causes, which, by their uncertainty,
may overturn the best-concerted projects.

Whatever place is made choice of for a descent at
St. Domingo, the town of the Cape will always be
the object of it. The landing will be somewhere in
the bay of the Cape, where the ships will be ready
to augment the land-forces with two-thirds of their
crews, and to furnish them with artillery, ammunition,
and whatever they may want for the siege of that
opulent fortress. It is towards this bulwark of the
colony that all endeavours to keep off the assailer
must be directed. The choice of advantageous po-
sitions will, in some measure, compensate for the ine-
quality of numbers. At the moment of landing, the
ground must be disputed by supporting a kind of false
attack, without engaging the whole of the troops.
These must be posted in such a manner as to secure
two retreats, the one towards the Cape, to form the
garrison of that place, the other in the narrow passes
of the mountains, where they will keep an intrenched camp, from whence they may annoy the besiegers,
and retard the taking of the place. Should the place
surrender, as it would be an easy matter to favour
the evasion of the troops when they evacuate it, the
conquest would not yet be completed. The mountains in which they would take refuge, inaccessible
to an army, surround the plain with a double or treble chain, and guard the inhabited parts, by very
narrow passes, which may be easily defended. The
principal of these is the defile of the great river,
where the enemy would find two or three passes of
the river, that reach from one mountain to the other.
In this place four or five hundred men would stop

the moſt numerous army, by only ſinking the bed of the waters. This reſiſtance might be ſeconded by 25,000 inhabitants, both white and black, who are ſettled in theſe valleys. As the white men are more numerous here than upon the richer lands, and their crops are ſmaller, they cannot afford to conſume any great quantity of the produce of Europe, ſo that what they cultivate is chiefly for their own ſubſiſt-ence ; from this they might eaſily ſupply the troops that ſhould defend their country. Any deficiency in the article of freſh meat could be made up by the Spaniards, who breed vaſt quantities of cattle on the backs of theſe mountains.

After all, it may happen that the firmneſs of the troops may be ſunk under the want of proviſions or warlike ſtores, and they may be either forced or turn-ed back. This ſuggeſted the idea ſome years ago at Verſailles, of building a fortified town in the centre of the mountains. Marſhal Noailles was a warm ad-vocate for this ſcheme. It was then imagined, that by means of ſome redoubts of earth ſcattered upon different parts of the coaſt, the enemy might be en-ticed by regular attacks, and inſenſibly exhauſted by the loſs of a great number of men, in a climate where ſickneſs ſuddenly proves more deſtructive than the ſword. It was ſuggeſted that no more ſtrong-holds ſhould be erected on the frontiers, where they lie ex-poſed to the invaſion of the maſters of the ſea ; be-cauſe, while they are unable to defend their own habitations, they become ſo many bulwarks for the conquerors, who can eaſily take and guard them with their ſhips, and depoſe or draw from thence arms and men to intimidate the vanquiſhed. An entirely open country was better, in their opinion, for a power that has no maritime ſtrength, than forces diſ-perſed and forſaken upon ſhores, waſted and depo-pulated by the inclemency of the climate.

It was in the centre of the iſland that the ſtrongeſt place of defence was expected to be made. A road of twenty or thirty leagues, full of obſtacles, where

B O O K every march muft be attended with feveral engage-
XIII. ments, in which the advantage of the pofts would
render a detachment formidable to a whole army;
where the removing of the artillery would be tedious
and laborious; where the difficulty of convoys, and
the diftance of cummunication with the ocean; where
every thing, in fhort, would confpire to deftroy the
enemy: fuch was to be, as it were, the glacis of the
intended fortification. This capital was to ftand upon
high ground, where the air is more pure and temperate than in the plains beneath; in the midft of a
country which would fupply the town with neceffaries; furrounded with flocks and herds, which, feeding upon a foil moft favourable to their increafe,
would be referved for times of want; provided with
ftorehoufes proportioned to the town and garrifon;
fuch a city would have changed the colony into a
kingdom, able to fupport itfelf for a long time;
whereas its prefent opulence does but weaken it,
and having fuperfluities without neceffaries, it en-
riches a few proprietors, without affording them fuf-
tenance.

If the enemy had made themfelves mafters of the
fea-coaft, which would not be difputed with them,
and were defirous of collecting the produce of the
lands, they would ftand in need of whole armies to
keep merely upon the defenfive; for the continual
excurfions from the centre would not permit them to
do more than this. The troops in the inland parts
of the ifland, always fure of a refpectable retreat,
might eafily be relieved by recruits from Europe,
which would find no difficulty in penetrating to the
centre of a circle of fo immenfe a circumference;
whereas all the Englifh fleets would not be fufficient
to fill up the vacancies which the climate would be
continually making in their garrifons.

Notwithftanding the evidence of thefe advantages,
the project of a fortification in the mountains has
been dropt, and a fyftem purfued, which would confine the whole defence of the ifland to the Mole of

St. Nicholas. This new plan could not fail of being applauded by the planters, who were not fond of citadels and garrifons near their plantations, as they are more injurious than they can poffibly be beneficial to them. They are fenfible, that the whole force being directed to one point, they fhould have none but light troops left in their neighbourhood, on the three coafts, which are fufficient to drive away the privateers by the affiftance of their batteries; and are, befides, very convenient defenders, ever ready to yield without refiftance, and to difperfe or capitulate on the leaft intimation of an invafion.

This plan, fo favourable to private intereft, has alfo met with the approbation of fome perfons well verfed in military affairs. They were of opinion, that the few troops which the colony will admit of, being in a manner loft in fo large an ifland as St. Domingo, would make an appearance at the Mole. Bombardopolis is the place that has been chofen, as the moft refpectable poft. This new city ftands on the margin of a plain, which is fufficiently elevated to render it cool and temperate. Its territory is covered with a natural favannah, and adorned with groves of palm trees of various kinds. It is not commanded; which is an uncommon circumftance at St. Domingo. It might be made a regular fortification, and of any degree of ftrength. If it did not prevent an invafion, it would, at leaft, prevent the conquerors from getting a firm eftablifhment upon the coafts.

It were to be wifhed, fay the partizans of this new fyftem, that from the firft moment the works had been begun at the Mole, it had at the fame time been fortified to the degree that fo advantageous a fituation would admit of. It is a treafure, the poffeffion of which fhould have been fecured as foon as it was difcovered. Should this valuable key of St. Domingo, and, indeed, of all America, fall into the hands of the Englifh, this Gibralter of America would be_more fatal to France and Spain than even that of Europe.

It is no wonder, if all the precautions which have been taken hitherto for the defence of St. Domingo, have been conducted with so little judgment. As long as forecast and protection shall be confined to secondary means, which can only protract, not prevent, the conquest of this island, no invariable plan can be pursued. Fixed principles are the exclusive privilege of such powers as can depend upon their naval force, to prevent the loss, or secure the recovery, of their colonies. Those of France have not hitherto been guarded by those floating arsenals, which can at the same time attack and defend; but this power hath at length been roused, and its navy is becoming formidable. But does she govern her possessions abroad by the maxims of sound policy and good order? This is what we shall next inquire into.

The British government, ever actuated by the national spirit, which seldom deviates from the true interests of the state, has carried into the New World that right of property which is the ground-work of her legislation. From a conviction, that man never thinks he has the entire possession of any thing but what he has lawfully acquired, they have, indeed, sold the lands in the islands, but at a very moderate price, to such as were willing to clear them. This hath appeared the surest way to hasten the cultivation of them; and to prevent partialities and jealousies, the necessary consequences of a distribution guided by caprice or favour.

Is the right of property well established in the French Islands? France has taken a method seemingly more generous, but not so prudent, that of granting lands to all who applied for them. In the infant state of these colonies, a vagabond went into the midst of the forests and marked out the space of greater or less extent which he chose to occupy, and fixed its limits by cutting down trees all around it.

This confusion could not last long, and yet authority did not choose to strip those who had thus settled their own rights. It was ordained only, that for the future there fhould be no legitimate property but that which was granted by the adminiftrators. Protection became then the only rule of the diftributions, without any regard to talents or to means. Indeed it was ftipulated, that they fhould begin their fettlements within a year after the grant, and not difcontinue the clearing of the ground, upon pain of forfeiture. But, befide the hardfhip of requiring thofe men to be at the expence of clearing the land, who could not afford to purchafe, the penalty fell upon thofe only, who, not having the advantage of family and fortune, could not make intereft with the great; or upon minors, who being left deftitute by the death of their parents, ought rather to have been affifted by the public; whereas every proprietor who was well recommended or fupported, was not called to account, though he let his grounds lie fallow.

To this partiality, which evidently retarded the progrefs of the colonies, we may add a number of illjudged regulations relative to cultivation. Firft, it was required of every perfon who obtained a grant of land, to plant 500 trenches of manioc for every flave he had upon his plantation. This order was equally detrimental both to private and public intereft, as it compelled the planter to encumber his ground with this ordinary production, when it was able to yield richer crops; and rendered the poor grounds, which were only fit for this kind of culture, ufelefs. This double error could not but leffen the growth of all kinds of commodities; and indeed, this law, which laid a reftraint upon the difpofal of property, has never been ftrictly put in execution; but as it has alfo never been repealed, it ftill remains a fcourge in the hand of an ignorant, capricious, or violent minifter, who may choofe to make ufe of it againft the inhabitants. This evil, great as it is, is, however, the leaft of thofe they have to complain of from adminiftration. The reftraint of the agrarian law is ftill increafed by the burden of labours impofed upon the vaffals.

There was a time in Europe, that of the feudal government, when gold and filver were little regarded
in public or private tranfactions. The nobles ferved
the ftate, not with their purfes, but with their perfons; and thofe of their vaffals, who were their property by right of conqueft, paid them a kind of quit-
rent or homage, either in the fruits of the earth, or
in fo much labour. Thefe cuftoms, fo deftructive to
men and lands, tended to perpetuate that barbarity
to which they owed their rife. But at length they
were gradually laid afide, as the authority of kings
prevailed in overthrowing the independence and tyranny of the great, by reftoring freedom to the people. The prince, now become the fole mafter, abolifhed, as a magiftrate, fome abufes arifing from the
right of war, which deftroys every other right. But
feveral of thefe ufurpations, which time had confecrated, were ftill retained. That of the average, or
a certain proportion of labour required of the vaffals,
has been kept up in fome ftates, where the nobles
have loft almoft every advantage, though the people
have not acquired any. The liberty of France is at
this day infringed by this public bondage; and this
injuftice has been reduced into a fyftem, as if to give
it a colour of juftice.

Who would imagine that in the moft enlightened
age of the nation, at a time when the rights of man
have been moft rigidly difcuffed, when the principles
of natural morality have no longer been contradicted,
under the reign of a beneficent king, under humane
minifters, and under upright magiftrates; who would
imagine, that it fhould have been pretended to be
confiftent with the order of juftice and agreeable to
the conftitution of the ftate, that a fet of unhappy
people who have no property fhould be dragged from
their huts, taken from their repofe, or from their labours, they, their wives, their children, and their
cattle, in order to go and exhauft themfelves after
long fatigues in labours of a new kind : in the con-

ftruction of roads more pompous than they are ufe- **BOOK** ful, for the benefit of thofe who poffefs every thing, **XIII.** and this without pay and without food ?

O men! whofe hearts are of fteel, go one ftep further, and you will foon perfuade yourfelves that you are allowed!... But here, let me hold : indignation would carry me too far. It is, however, proper to warn government, that the dreadful fyftem of vaffalage is ftill more fatal the colonies.

The culture of thefe lands, from the nature of the climate and of the productions, requiring expedition, cannot eafily fpare a number of hands to be fent to a great diftance, and employed in public works, which are often ufelefs, and fhould never be carried on but by idle perfons. If the mother-country, with all the various means fhe can employ, has never yet been able to correct or mitigate the hardfhips of vaffalage, fhe ought to confider what evils muft refult from them beyond the feas, where the direction of thefe works is committed to two overfeers, who can neither be directed, cenfured nor controlled, in the arbitrary exercife of abfolute power. But the burden of thefe fervices is light, when compared with that of the taxes.

A tax may be defined to be a contribution towards *Are the* public expence, neceffary for the prefervation of pri- *taxes properly levied* vate property. The peaceable enjoyment of lands *in the* and revenues requires a proper force to defend them *French* from invafion, and a police that fecures the liberty *iflands?* of cultivating them. Whatever is paid towards the maintenance of public order, is right and juft ; whatever is levied beyond this, is extortion. Now, all the government expences which the mother-country is at for the colonies, are repaid her by the reftraint laid upon them, to cultivate for her alone, and in fuch a manner as is beft adapted to her wants. This fubjection is the moft burdenfome of all tributes, and ought to exempt them from all other taxes.

Any one muft be convinced of this truth, who re-

BOOK XIII. flects on the difference of fituation between the Old World and the New. In Europe, fubfiftence and home confumption are the principal object of culture and of manufactures ; exportation only carries off the overplus. In the iflands, the whole is to be exported. There life and property are equally precarious.

In Europe, war only deprives the manufacturer and the hufbandman of the trade to foreign countries; they ftill have their refource in that which circulates in the internal part of the kingdom. In the iflands, hoftilities annihilate every thing ; there are no more fales, no more purchafes, no more circulation; the planter hardly recovers his cofts.

In Europe, the owner of a fmall eftate, who is able to make only a few expences, improves his land as much in proportion as he who hath a wide domain and immenfe treafures. In the iflands, the improvement of the fmalleft plantation requires a tolerable ftock to begin with.

In Europe, it is commonly one citizen that is indebted to another ; and the ftate is not impoverifhed by thefe private debts. Thofe of the iflands are of a different nature. Many planters, in order to carry on the labour of clearing their grounds, and to repair the loffes incurred by the misfortunes of war, which had put a ftop to their exports, have been obliged to borrow fuch large fums, that they may be confidered rather as farming the trade, than as proprietors of the plantations.

Whether thefe reflections have not occurred to the French miniftry, or whether particular circumftances have obliged them to depart from their plan ; certain it is, they have added frefh taxes to the obligation already laid on the colonies to draw all their neceffaries from France, and to fend thither all their own commodities. Every Negro has been taxed. In fome fettlements this poll-tax has been confined to the working blacks ; in others it was laid on all the flaves without diftinction. Both thefe arrangements

have been oppofed by the colony affembled at St. B O O K
Domingo. Let us now judge of the force of their ar- XIII.
guments.

Children, old and infirm men, make up about one
third of the flaves. Far from being ufeful to the
planter, fome of them are only a burden, which humanity alone can prompt him to fupport, while the
reft can afford him but diftant and uncertain hopes.
It is difficult to conceive how the treafury fhould
have thought of taxing an object that is already
chargeable to the owner.

The poll-tax upon blacks extends beyond the
grave; that is to fay, it is fixed upon a perfon who
exifts no more. If a flave fhould die after the affeff-
ment has been made, the planter, who is already
unhappy on account of the diminution in his income
and of his capital, is ftill obliged to pay a tax, which
reminds him of his loffes, and makes him feel them
more fenfibly.

Even the working flaves are not an exact tariff of
the appraifement of a planter's income. With a few
Negroes, a good foil will yield more than a poor one
with a great number. The commodities are not all
of the fame value, though they are all procured by
the labour of thofe perfons upon whom the tax is
equally laid. The changing from one kind of culture to another, which the ground requires, fufpends
for a while the produce of labour. Droughts, inundations, fires, devouring infects, often deftroy the
fruits of labour. Suppofe all things alike, a lefs number of hands makes in proportion a lefs quantity of
fugar ; either becaufe the whole of the wants muft
be taken into confideration, or becaufe labour is truly
advantageous fo far only as the moft favourable opportunities can be improved.

The poll-tax upon blacks becomes ftill more oppreffive in time of war. A planter who cannot then
difpofe of his commodities, and muft run in debt to
fupport himfelf and to keep up his land, is further

obliged to pay a tax for flaves, whofe labour will hardly be equivalent to their maintenance. Nay, he is often conftrained to fend them at a diftance from his plantation for the imaginary wants of the colony, to fupport them there at his own expence, and to fee them perifh without any reafon, while he is under the fevere neceffity of replacing them one time or other, if ever he means to retrieve his wafted and almoft ruined lands.

The burden of the poll-tax was ftill heavier upon fuch of the proprietors as were abfent from the colony, for thefe were condemned to pay the tax treble; which was the more unjuft, as it was matter of indifference to France whether her commodities were confumed at home or in the iflands. Could it be her intention to hinder the emigration of the colonifts? But it is only by the mildnefs of the government that citizens can be induced to fix in a country, not by prohibitions and penalties. Befides, men who by hazardous labours carried on in a fultry climate, had contributed to the public profperity, ought to have been indulged in the liberty of ending their days in the temperate regions of the mother-country. Nothing could more effectually roufe the ambition and activity of numbers of idle people, than to be fpectators of their fortune; and the ftate might thus be relieved of the load of thefe ufelefs men, to the profit of induftry and commerce.

Nothing can be more detrimental to both than this taxing of the blacks, as the neceffity of felling obliges the planter to lower the price of his commodities. A moderate price may be an advantageous circumftance, when it is the refult of great plenty, and of a very quick circulation. But it is ruinous to be obliged to lofe conftantly upon one's merchandife, in order to pay taxes. Finance is like a foul ulcer, in which the mortified flefh deftroys the live flefh. In proportion as the blood is conveyed into the wound by the circulation, it becomes corrupted there while it fupplies it. The profits of trade are all abforbed B O O K by the treafury, which is continually receiving, with- XIII. out making any returns.

Laftly, it is a very difficult matter to levy this tax. Every proprietor muft give in an annual account of the number of his flaves. To prevent falfe entries, they muft be verified by clerks or excifemen. Every Negro that is not entered muft be forfeited ; which is a very abfurd practice, becaufe every labouring Negro is fo much ftock, and by the forfeiture of him the culture is diminifhed, and the very object for which the duty was laid is annihilated. Thus it happens, that in the colonies, where the fuccefs of every thing depends upon the tranquillity which is enjoyed, a deftructive war is carried on between the financier and the planter. Law-fuits are numerous, removals frequent, rigorous meafures become necef-fary, and the cofts are great and ruinous.

If the Negro-tax be unjuft in its extent, unequal in its repartition, and complicate in the mode of levying it, the tax laid upon the commodities that are carried out of the colonies is nearly as injudicious. The government have ventured to impofe this duty, from a perfuafion that it would fall entirely upon the confumer and the merchant ; but there cannot be a more dangerous error in political economy than this is.

The act of confuming does not fupply money to buy what is confumed ; this muft be gained by la-bour ; and all labour, if things are traced up to their origin, is, in fact, paid by the firft proprietor out of the produce of the earth. This being the cafe, no one article can be always growing dearer, but all the reft muft rife in proportion. In this fituation, there is no profit to be made upon any of them. If this equilibrium between the articles of commerce be re-moved, the confumption of the advanced article will decreafe ; and, if it decreafe, the price will fall of courfe, and the dearnefs will have been only tran-fient.

The merchant can no more take the duty upon

BOOK him than the confumer. He may, indeed, advance
XIII. it once or twice ; but if he cannot make a natural
and neceffary profit upon the commodities fo taxed,
he will foon difcontinue that branch of trade. To
hope that competition will force him to take the payment of the duty out of his profits, is to fuppofe that
they were exorbitant ; and that the competition,
which was then infufficient, will become more confiderable when the profits are lefs. If, on the other
hand, things were as they ought to be, and the profits no more than neceffary, it is fuppofing that the
competition will fubfift, though the profits that gave
rife to it fubfift no longer. We muft admit all thefe
abfurdities, or allow that it is the planter in the
iflands who pays the duty, whether it be levied from
the firft, fecond, or hundredth hand.

Far from thus burdening the cultivation of the colonies with taxes, it ought to be encouraged by liberalities ; fince by the ftate of reftraint in which
trade is kept, thefe liberalities, with all the advantages arifing from them, muft neceffarily return to
the mother-country.

If the fituation of a ftate, that is in arrears on account of loffes or mifmanagement, will not admit of
liberalities, or eafing the fubjects of their burdens,
the payment of the taxes in the colonies themfelves
might, at leaft, be fuppreffed, and the produce of
them levied at home. This would be the next beft
fyftem that could be purfued, and would be equally
agreeable to the Old and New World.

Nothing is fo pleafing to an American, as to remove from his fight every thing that denotes his dependence. Wearied with the importunities of col-
lectors, he abhors ftanding taxes, and dreads the increafe of them. He in vain feeks for that liberty
which he thought to have found at the diftance of
two thoufand leagues from Europe. He difdains a
yoke which purfues him acrofs the ftorms of the
ocean. Difcontented, and inwardly repining at the
reftraint he ftill feels, he thinks with indignation on

his native country; which, under the name of mo- ther, calls for his blood, inftead of feeding him. Remove the image of his chains from his fight; let his riches pay their tribute to the mother-country only at landing there, and he will fancy himfelf free and privileged; though at the fame time, by lowering the value of his own commodities, and enhancing the price of thofe that come from Europe, he, in fact, ultimately bears the load of a tax of which he is ignorant.

Navigators will alfo find an advantage in paying duties only upon goods that have reached the place of their deftination in their full value, and without any rifk, and will reftore the capital of their ftock along with the profits. They will not then have the mortification of having purchafed of the prince the very hazards of fhipwreck, and of lofing a cargo for which they had paid duty at embarking. Their fhips, on the contrary, will bring back, in merchandife, the amount of the duty; and the productions being advanced in value by exportation, the duty will hardly be felt.

Laftly, the confumer himfelf will be a gainer by it; becaufe the colonift and the merchant cannot benefit by any regulation, of which in time the confumer will not experience the good effects. All the taxes will no fooner be reduced to a fingle one, but trade will be clogged with fewer formalities, fewer delays, fewer charges, and confequently the commodities can be fold at a more reafonable rate.

This fyftem of moderation, which every thing feems to point out as the fitteft, will be eafily introduced. All the productions of the iflands are fubject, at their entry into the kindom, to a duty known by the name of *Domaine d'Occident*, or Weftern Domain, which is fixed at three and a half per cent. with eight fols [4d.] per pound. The value of thefe productions, which is the rule for the payment of the duty, is determined in the months of January and July. It is fixed at twenty, or five and twenty per cent. below the real price. The western office allows, besides, a more considerable tare than the seller in trade does. Add to this duty that which the commodities pay at the custom-houses of the colonies, which produces nearly the same, and those that are paid in the inland parts of the islands ; and we shall have the whole of the revenue which the government draws from the settlements in America.

If this fund were confounded with the other revenues of the state, we might be apprehensive that it was not applied to its destination, which should be solely the protection of the islands. The unforeseen exigencies of the royal treasury would infallibly divert it into another channel. There are some moments when the critical state of the disease will not admit of calculating the inconveniencies of the remedy. The most urgent necessity engrosses all the attention. Nothing then is secured from the hand of of arbitrary power, urged by the wants of the present moment. The ministry is continually drawing out of the treasury, under the delusive hopes of replacing in a short time what they have received ; but the execution of this design is perpetually retarded by fresh demands.

Hence it appears, that it would be highly necessary that the treasury, destined for the duties on the productions of the colonies, should be kept wholly separate from that destined to receive the revenues of the kingdom. The sums deposited there, as in trust, would always be ready to answer the demands of those settlements. The colonist who always has stock to send over to Europe, would gladly give it for bills of exchange, when he was once assured that they would meet with no delays or difficulties in the payment of them. This kind of bank would soon create another means of communication betwen the mother-country and the islands ; the court would be better acquainted with the state of their affairs in these distant countries, and would recover the credit they have long since lost ; but which is of the utmost confequence, efpecially in time of war. We fhall now put an end to our difcuffions on taxes, and confider the regulations refpecting the militia.

The French iflands, like thofe of other nations, had no regular troops at firft. The adventurers, who had conquered them, looked upon the right of defending themfelves as a privilege ; and the defcendants of thofe intrepid men thought themfelves fufficiently ftrong to guard their own poffeffions. They had nothing, indeed, to do but to repulfe a few veffels, which landed fome failors and foldiers, as undifciplined as themfelves.

Is the militia well regulated in the French iflands?

The fituation of affairs has, indeed, undergone an alteration. As thefe fettlements became more confiderable, it was to be expected that they would fooner or later be attacked by numerous European fleets and armies ; and this made it neceffary to fend them other defenders. The event has fhown the infufficiency of a few fcattered battalions, to oppofe the land and fea forces of England. The colonifts themfelves have been convinced that their own efforts could never prevent a revolution ; and fearing that a fruitlefs refiftance would only exafperate a victorious enemy, they were more inclined to capitulate than to fight. Having become political calculators, their weaknefs made them fenfible that they were unfit for military operations, and they have contributed their money in order to be difcharged from a fervice, which, though glorious in its principle, had degenerated into a burdenfome fervitude. The militia was fuppreffed in 1763.

This act of compliance has been applauded by thofe who only confidered this inftitution as the means of preferving the colonies from all foreign invafions. They very fenfibly imagined, that it was unreafonable to require that men, who were grown old under the hardfhips of a fcorching climate, in order to raife a large fortune, fhould expofe themfelves to the fame dangers as thofe poor victims of our ambition, who are perpetually hazarding their lives for a pay which

BOOK is not fufficient for their fubfiftence. Such a facri-
XIII.
fice hath appeared to them too unreafonable to expect it fhould be complied with; and the miniftry,
who faw the impropriety of keeping up fuch a vain
and burdenfome fervice, have therefore difcontinued
it, and been commended.

Thofe who are better acquainted with the American fettlements, have not judged fo favourably of
this innovation. The militia, fay they, is neceffary
to preferve the interior police of the iflands; to prevent the revolt of the flaves; to check the incurfions
of the fugitive Negroes; to hinder the banditti from
affembling in troops; to protect the navigation along
the coafts, and to keep off the privateers. If the inhabitants be not embodied; if they have neither
commanders nor ftandards, how can they avert fo
many dangers? How will it be poffible to diffipate
thefe deftructive calamities, when they have not been
able to check them before they broke out? From
whence will arife that harmony and uniformity of
action, without which nothing can be carried on with
propriety?

Thefe reflections, which, though ftriking and natural, had at firft efcaped the court of Verfailles, foon
produced an alteration in their conduct. They became convinced of the neceffity of reftoring the militia, but without giving up the taxes which were
agreed to for the fupport of the regular troops. It
was a difficult matter to difpofe the people to confent
to this arrangement. The miniftry negotiated, bribed,
and threatened. Guadalupe and Martinico, though
difpleafed with the abufes committed by an inconftant and precipitate authority, fubmitted at length,
in 1767, to the wifhes of adminiftration; but this
example did not make the impreffion upon St. Domingo that was defired, and perhaps expected. The
year following it became neceffary to carry on a war
againft this rich colony, and it was not till after the
magiftrates of the weft and fouth of the ifland had
been thrown into prifon, and till the earth was ftrew-

ed with dead bodies, that it was poffible to reduce to fubmiffion the planters, exafperated by the vexations of a rapacious government.

Since this period, unfortunately ftamped with cha-racters of blood, all the inhabitants of the other he-mifphere are again embodied. The obligations that are impofed by this kind of regiftering are various, and are not yet properly explained. This obfcurity, which is always dangerous in the hands of rulers, who are perpetually intent upon the extending of their jurifdiction, keeps the citizens in continual alarms for their liberty, which they are more jealous of in the colonies than we are in Europe; it expofes them to numberlefs vexations. The evils it has occafioned have excited a deteftation for this kind of fervitude, which none but tyrants or flaves can be furprifed at. It is neceffary, if poffible, to eradicate the impreffions of the paft, and remove all miftruft for the future. The legiflature will fucceed in this by making all thofe alterations in the form of the militia, which are confiftent with its object; which is, to maintain pub-lic order and fafety. The welfare of the people is the great end of all authority. If the actions of the fovereign do not tend to this end, his exiftence will be fupported only by the affiftance of money, or the fanction of old records, which time will deftroy or pofterity defpife. In vain does flattery raife number-lefs and magnificent monuments to princes; the hand of man erects them, but it is the heart that confe-crates them, and affection that renders them immor-tal. Without this, public trophies are only a proof of the meannefs of the people, not of the greatnefs of the ruler. There is one ftatue in Paris, the fight of which makes every heart exult with fentiments of affection. Every eye is turned with complacency towards this image of paternal and popular goodnefs. The tears of the diftreffed filently call upon it under the hardfhips of oppreffion. Men fecretly blefs the hero it immortalifes. All voices unite to celebrate his memory after two centuries are elapfed. His

B O O K name is in veneration to the uttermoft parts of Ame-
XIII. rica. In every heart he protefts againft the abufes of
authority ; he declares againft the ufurpations of the
rights of the people ; he promifes the fubjects the
redrefs of their grievances, and an increafe of profperity ; and demands both of the miniftry.

Is the re-   Among the circumftances which require reforma-
gulation of
inheritance tion, we ought to reckon a cuftom eftablifhed in the
properly
fettled in French poffeffions in the New World, of dividing
the French equally the paternal inheritance among all the chil-
iflands ?
dren, and the inheritance of a relation among all the
coheirs.

We hold in abhorrence, with all reafonable men,
whom pride or prejudice have not corrupted, the abfurd right of primogeniture, which transfers the entire patrimony of a family to the eldeft fon, whofe
morals are corrupted by it ; which reduces his bro-
thers and fifters to a ftate of indigence, and punifhes
them as it were, for the cafual fault of having
been born a few yers too late. Are they the lefs legitimate on that account ? and is the perfon who hath
given them exiftence the lefs refponfible for their
happinefs ? A chief of a family is nothing more than
a depofitary ; and is a depofitary ever allowed to
make an unequal divifion of his truft between perfons
who have an equal claim ? If a favage fhould be in
poffeffion, at his death, of two bows, and fhould have
two children ; and if he fhould be afked, what was
to be done with the two bows ; would he not anfwer,
that one fhould be given to each of his children?
And if he were to bequeath them both to one, would
it not be underftood that he had confidered the excluded child as not being his own offspring ? In the
countries where this monftrous cuftom of difinherit-
ing is authorifed, the father is the leaft refpected by
all ; by the eldeft, becaufe he can take nothing away
from him ; and by the youngeft children, becaufe he
can give them nothing. To filial affection, which is
extinguifhed, fucceeds a meannefs of fentiment, which
accuftoms three or four children, almoft as foon as they

are born, to cringe to one alone, who from this cir- cumftance conceives a degree of perfonal importance, which feldom fails to render him infolent. Refpectable parents are apprehenfive of multiplying around them a number of indigent perfons who are to be condemned to celibacy. The whole inheritance is placed in the hands of a madman, whofe diffipations can only be put a ftop to by fubftitution, which is another evil. Calamities of fo great magnitude muft neceffarily fuggeft the idea, that the right of primogeniture, which was not originally confecrated by fuperftition, and which defpotifm hath no intereft in perpetuating, will, fooner or later, be abolifhed. It is the remains of feudal barbarifm, which our defcendants will one day be afhamed of.

The law of equality, however, which feems dictated by nature; which occurs inftantly to every juft and good man; which leaves no doubt in the mind as to its rectitude and utility; this law may fometimes, perhaps, be prejudicial to the prefervation of fociety. We have an inftance of this in the French iflands, which it diverts from the end of their deftination, and gradually paves the way for their ruin.

This divifion was neceffary at the firft formation of colonies. Immenfe tracts of lands were to be cleared. This could not be done without people; nor could men, who had quitted their own country for want, be any otherwife fixed in thofe diftant and defert regions, than by affigning them a property. Had the government refufed to grant them lands, they would have wandered about from one place to another; they would have begun to eftablifh various fettlements, and have had the difappointment to find, that none of them would attain to that degree of profperity as to become ufeful to the mother-country.

But fince inheritances, too extenfive at firft, have in procefs of time been reduced by a feries of fucceffions, and by the fubdivifions of fhares, to fuch a compafs as renders them fit to facilitate cultivation; fince they have been fo limited as not to lie fallow

BOOK for want of hands, proportionable to their extent,
XIII. a further division of lands would again reduce them
to nothing. In Europe, an obscure man, who has
but a few acres of land, will make that little estate
more advantageous to him in proportion, than an
opulent man will the immense property he is possessed of, either by inheritance or chance. In America,
the nature of the productions, which are very valuable ; the uncertainty of the crops, which are but
few in their kind ; the quantity of slaves, of cattle,
of utensils necessary for a plantation ; all this requires
a large stock, which they have not in some, and will
soon want in all the colonies, if the lands be parcelled out and divided more and more by hereditary
successions.

If a father leave an estate of 30,000 livres [1250l.]
a year, and this estate be equally divided between
three children, they will all be ruined if they make
three distinct plantations; the one, because he has
been made to pay too much for the buildings, and
because he has too few Negroes, and too little land
in proportion ; the other two, because they must
build before they can begin upon the culture of their
land. They will all be equally ruined, if the whole
plantation should remain in the hands of one of the
three. In a country where a creditor is in a worse
state than any other man, estates have risen to an immoderate value. The possessor of the whole will be
very fortunate if he is obliged to pay no more for interest than the net produce of the plantation. Now,
as the primary law of nature is the procuring of subsistence, he will begin with procuring that without
paying his debts. These will accumulate, and he
will soon become insolvent, and the confusion conse-
quent upon such a situation will end in the ruin of
the whole family.

The only way to remedy these disorders, is to abo-
lish the equality of the division of land. In this enlightened age, government should see the necessity
of letting the colonies be more stocked with things

than with men. The wifdom of the legiflature will,
doubtlefs, find out fome compenfation for thofe it has injured, and in fome meafure facrificed to the welfare of the community. They ought to be placed upon frefh lands, and to fubfift by their own labour. This is the only way to maintain this fort of men; and their induftry would open a frefh fource of wealth to the ftate.

At the conclufion of the peace, a favourable opportunity offered itfelf for making the propofed alteration in St. Lucia and Guiana. The French ought not to have neglected this opportunity, perhaps the only one that will offer, to repeal the law relating to the divifions of eftates, by diftributing to thofe, whofe expectations they had fruftrated, fuch lands as they intended to cultivate; and by giving them thofe confiderable fums that have been expended to no purpofe, as the neceffary advance for carrying on the cultivation. Men inured to the climate, acquainted with the only kind of culture that could poffibly be thought of, encouraged by the example, affiftance, and advice of their own families, and aided by the flaves with which government would have fupplied them, were much fitter for this purpofe than a fet of profligate men, collected from the refufe of Europe, and were not much more likely to raife new colonies to that pitch of wealth and profperity which might be expected. Unfortunately, it was not forefeen, that the firft colonies in America muft have increafed by flow degrees and of themfelves, with the lofs of a great many men, or by extraordinary exertions of bravery and patience, becaufe they had no competition to fupport; but that the fucceeding fettlements could only be formed by the natural means of population, as an old fwarm begets a new one. The overflowings of population in one ifland muft fpread into another; and the fuperfluities of a rich colony furnifh neceffaries to an infant fettlement. This is the natural order which good policy points out to maritime and commercial powers. All other methods

B O O K are irrational and deftructive. Though the court of
XIII. Verfailles have overlooked this plain principle, productive of fo much good, this is no reafon why they
fhould reject the propofal of putting a ftop to the
further divifion of lands. If the neceffity of fuch a
law be evident, it muft be enacted, though the prefent time be lefs favourable than that which has been
neglected. When the plantations are reftored to
their ftate of profperity, by the fuppreffion of that
divifion of land, which precludes every means of
improvement, the planters may then be compelled
to clear themfelves of the debts with which their
plantations are now oppreffed.

Has the   Part of thefe debts originated from the claims that
payment of
the debts   were allowed, by an injudicious law, to the feveral
contracted   coheirs. This diftreffed fituation hath increafed in
by the
French   proportion as the colonies have acquired more wealth.
iflands been When they had increafed fo far, as that the number
wifely pro- of inhabitants became fuperior to the plantations, the
vided for?   fuperabundant part of the population remained idle
creditors of the lands they did not occupy, and confequently ufelefs, and even burdenfome, to the culture.

There are other credits proceeding from the fale
which the colonifts have reciprocally made of their
habitations. We feldom go to America, without the
profpect of enjoying in Europe thofe riches, which
are commonly acquired by obftinate labour, or by
fortunate events. Thofe who do not lofe fight of
this aim, live with more or lefs economy, and fend to
their own country all that they have been able to
fave out of their income. As foon as they have acquired that degree of fortune to which they afpired,
they endeavour to difpofe of their plantations. In a
country where the fpecie is deficient, it is neceffary
to fell them upon credit, or to keep them ; and moft
of the proprietors rather choofe to give up their poffeffions to purchafers who fometimes fail in their engagements, than to truft them in the hands of ftew-
ards who are feldom faithful.

Laftly, the advances made to the colonifts have

been the occafion of much credit being given. The lands of the French iflands, as well as of the other iflands in America, did not originally yield any production fit for exportation. Funds were neceflary to clear them, and the firft Europeans who occupied them had no property. Trade came to their affiftance; it furnifhed them with utenfils, provifions, and flaves, neceffary to form productions. This affociation between monied and induftrious people gave birth to a great number of debts, which have multiplied in proportion asthe plantations have increafed.

The debtors have but too often failed in fulfilling the obligations they had contracted. An inordinate luxury, which cannot be excufed in men who are born in mifery, hath compelled feveral of them to this breach of faith. Others have been drawn into it by an indolence, inconceivable in eager minds, that had gone beyond the feas to feek an end to their indigence. The moft abundant means have been loft in the hands of fome people, who were deftitute of the fkill neceffary to improve them. There have been likewife fome planters devoid of fhame, and without principle, who, though capable of fettling with their creditors, have daringly withholden the property of others. Other caufes have likewife occurred in leffening the force of engagements.

Hurricanes, the violence of which cannot be eafily defcribed, fubverted the country and deftroyed the crops. The moft expenfive and the moft neceffary buildings have been fwallowed up by earthquakes. Infects, which could not be deftroyed, have devoured, during a long feries of years, all the produce that might have been expected from a fertile and well-cultivated foil. Some commodities, the produce of which hath exceeded their confumption, have loft their value, and have fallen into the utmoft contempt. Long and cruel wars, by oppofing infurmountable obftacles to the exportation of the productions, have rendered ufelefs the moft conftant and moft obftinate labours.

Thefe calamities which have fometimes happened

B O O K at the fame time, or which have at leaft fucceeded
XIII. each other too rapidly, have given rife to a fyftem of
jurifprudence favourable to the debtors. The legiflature have encumbered the feizure of lands and flaves
with fo many formalities, that it fhould feem as if
their defign had been to render it impracticable.
The public opinion hath branded the fmall number
of creditors who have undertaken to overcome thefe
difficulties; and the tribunals themfelves did not accede, without extreme reluctance, to the rigorous
meafures they were defirous of purfuing.

This fyftem, which hath appeared for a long time
the beft that could be followed, hath ftill its parti-
fans. What is it to the ftate, fay thefe political calculators, whether the riches be in the hands of the
creditor or of the debtor, provided public profperity
be increafed? But can public profperity increafe
when juftice is trampled upon; when adminiftration
encourages a breach of faith, by offering it an afylum
under the protection of the laws, for if the laws
do not profecute they protect; when the feeds
of miftruft are encouraged among citizens, which
muft in time render them fo many rogues, and enemies to each other; when loans, without any kind
of fecurity, fhall have become impoffible, or ruinous;
when the rapacioufnefs of ufury fhall be exercifed
without reftraint; when credit fhall no longer exift
either in or out of the ftate; and when the whole
nation fhall be confidered as a fet of men devoid of
principles and of morality. General felicity can have
no folid foundation, without the validity of engagements from whence it arifes. Even the government
ought only to free itfelf from its encumbrances according to the rules of juftice. A bankruptcy of the
ftate is infamous, and ftill more prejudicial to the morality of fociety than to the fortunes of individuals.
A time will come, when all thefe iniquities fhall be
fummoned to the tribunal of nations, and when the
power which hath committed them fhall be judged
by its victims.

Other fpeculators, not fo loofe in their principles, have afferted, that an enlightened legiflation would annul the debts anterior to a period which ought to be fixed. We will not examine whether this practice of fome ancient republics hath ever been falutary; but we will affirm, without any fear of miftaking, that fuch a breach of the public faith, if it were common, would again plunge Europe, now become commercial, into that ftate of inaction and mifery in which it was three or four centuries ago. Fortunately, this deftructive revolution is not to be apprehended. The refpect for property increafes daily even among the leaft enlightened nations. In procefs of time, it will be eftablifhed in the French iflands, as well as elfewhere, when government fhall at length compel the colonifts to give fome kind of fatisfaction to their creditors. The beft method of bringing about this act of juftice is not yet agreed upon.

Some perfons are defirous of fumptuary laws, which, by reftraining the expences of the inhabitants, would enable them to fulfil their engagements. How could fuch an idea ever enter into the minds of men, to eftablifh this fyftem of privation as a maxim in the colonies? The value of their productions being entirely owing to exchanges, would not the annihilation of thefe compel the Americans either to raife few commodities, or to fell them for a trifle? Should the mother-country be willing to make up in money the deficiencies in the fale of their merchandife, then all the gold that is drawn from one part of America would return into the other. After fifteen or twenty years of fuch a trade, the powers that are enemies to France would have an additional motive for attacking poffeffions, the fertility of which excites in them fo much furprife and jealoufy.

Others have imagined, that all kind of credit fhould henceforward be prohibited. But would not the cultures already eftablifhed fuffer from fo abfurd a fyftem? Would not the cultivation of the virgin lands, which are generally moft productive, be impeded?

BOOK XIII.

Would not the operations of the merchants in the mother-country become daily more languid?

It is well known how reluctantly they see the rich planter accustom himself to send his own productions to Europe, to draw the articles of his own consumption from thence, and reduce his correspondents to the bare profits of commission. If that dependence, which is a necessary consequence of debts, should cease, they would no longer be a few planters, but the whole colony, who would make their own purchases and sales in the mother-country ; they would all become traders, and even would soon have no competitors, because they alone would be acquainted with the measure of their own wants.

Several persons have wished that it should be permitted to seize and to sell the Negroes of debtors. Then the slaves who should cease to work upon one plantation, would be employed upon another, and the colony would not be injured. This is a mistake; the Negroes will never be made to pass, without mischief, from one plantation to another. These men, already too unhappy, would not contract the fresh habits required by a change of place, of master, of method, and of employment. They cannot live without their mistresses and their children, which are their dearest comforts, and the only thing that makes them endure life. Separated from this only consolation to men in affliction, they pine away, and sicken, and frequently desert, or at least they work but with reluctance and carelessness.

Moreover, by securing the payment of one creditor, several would infallibly be ruined. The most intelligent and the most active planters, deprived of part of the hands requisite for the labours of their plantations, would soon become insolvent, and would continue so for ever.

Honour hath appeared to some people a more effectual resource than any other. Stamp, say they, but a mark of infamy upon the fraudulent debtor, render him incapable of ever exercising any public

office, and we need not apprehend he will fport with B O O K
this prejudice. The moft rapacious of men, and XIII.
efpecially the American planters, facrifice a part of
their lives to hard labour, with no other view than
to enjoy their fortune. But there is no enjoyment
for a man who is branded with infamy. Obferve only how punctually all debts of honour are paid. It
is not an excefs of delicacy, it is not a love of juftice
that brings back the ruined gamefter, within four-
and-twenty hours, to the feet of his creditor, who,
perhaps, is no better than a fharper ; it is the fenfe
of honour ; it is the dread of being excluded from
fociety. But in what age, and what period, do
we here invoke the facred name of honour ? Should
not the government fet the example of that juftice,
the practice of which it means to inculcate ? Is
it poffible that public opinion fhould difgrace individuals for actions which the ftate openly commits ?
When infamy has infinuated itfelf into families, into
great houfes, into the higheft places, even into the
camp and the fanctuary, can there be any fenfe of
fhame remaining ? What man will henceforth be jealous of his honour, while thofe who are called men of
honour know of no other than that of being rich to
get places, or of getting places to grow rich ; when
a man muft cringe in order to rife ; pleafe the great
and the women to ferve the ftate ; and when the art
of being agreeable, implies at leaft an indifference
for every virtue ? Shall honour, which feems to be
banifhed from Europe, take refuge in America ?

The court of Verfailles, perpetually led aftray by
the adminiftrators of its colonies, have always appeared defirous that the payment of debts fhould depend
entirely upon their arbitrary decifion. They have
never comprehended that this was eftablifhing a fyftem of tyranny in the New World. Ignorant, capricious, interefted, or vindictive chiefs, may felect, at
pleafure, thofe debtors whom it may fuit them to
ruin. It is equally in their power to commit injuf-
tices towards the creditors. It will neither be the

BOOK
XIII.
oldeſt nor the moſt diſtreſſed, nor the moſt honeſt creditor whom they will cauſe to be paid ; but the moſt
powerful, the beſt protected, the moſt active, or the
moſt violent. Authority ought not to take place of
juſtice, nor probity or virtue of the law, in any part
of the world, or from any motive whatever ; becauſe
all authority is liable to corruption, and becauſe there
is no probity or virtue which may not be ſhaken.

Two centuries, waſted in attempts, experiments
and combinations, muſt have convinced the French
miniſtry, that the calamity which we here deplore,
can only be put a ſtop to by clear and plain regulations, eaſily carried into execution. When creditors ſhall be able, without delays, without expence,
and without reſtraining formalities, to take poſſeſſion
of all the property of their debtors ; then only will
order be eſtabliſhed. This ſevere act of juriſpru-
dence ſhould not have a retroactive effect. Humanity and policy will indicate the proper medium to be
adopted for the liquidation of old debts. But with reſpect to new engagements, nothing ſhould ſcreen them
from the rigour of the law that ſhould be enacted.

Very bitter remonſtrances will certainly be made
at firſt. Where ſhall we find, will it be ſaid, a planter ſo raſh as to attempt an undertaking of any conſequence, when he ſhall be certain of ruin, if his labours ſhould not be ſeconded by chance and by the
elements, upon the day appointed for him to fulfil
his engagements ? The dread of miſery and of ignominy will ſeize upon the minds of all men. Henceforward there will be no loans, no buſineſs, no circulation. Induſtry will degenerate into ſloth, and credit will be deſtroyed by the very ſyſtem adopted to
re-eſtabliſh it.

We have no doubt but that this would be the language of the coloniſts in the firſt inſtance ; but in the
end, and even in a ſhort time, this arrangement would
be moſt agreeable to thoſe who had been at firſt the
moſt violent againſt it. Informed by public knowledge and by experience, they would be ſenſible that

the facility of putting off payment had been burdensome to them, and that they had found credit only by purchasing it upon such terms as were sufficient to balance the risk of lending to them.

The indulgences which might have been proper in the early state of the colonies, would, in our days, become an inexcusable weakness. These settlements will never thrive as they ought to do, unless the means of cultivation be multiplied ; which they will not be, till the creditor be enabled to put an entire confidence in his debtor The system which is favourable to want of skill, to rash undertakings, and to dishonesty, must be overturned ; and the face of all things will soon be changed. The European merchant, who at present only advances trifling sums to the American planter, and that with great apprehensions, will not find a better way of employing his capital. With greater assistances, other plantations would be formed ; and the old ones will acquire a new value. The French islands will at length arrive to that degree of fortune, to which the richness of their soil hath in vain for so long a time invited them. If, notwithstanding the progress of knowledge, the court of Versailles should not be able to contrive a system of legislation, more wise and more perfect than that which is established in the English and in the Dutch possessions, they must not hesitate to adopt the same. Already have these three powers shown other marks of conformity in their principles. They have alike concentrated the connections of their American settlements in the mother-country.

All the colonies have not had the same origin. Some took their rise from the restless spirit of some tribes of barbarians, who, after having long wandered through desert countries, fixed themselves at last, from mere weariness, in any one where they might form a nation. Others, driven out of their own territory by some powerful enemy, or allured by chance to a better climate than their own, have removed thither, and shared the lands with the natives. An excess of

Has the mother-country, in compelling the islands to deliver their produce only to herself, sufficiently secured the exportation of them?

population, an abhorrence for tyranny, factions, and revolutions, have induced other citizens to quit their native country, and to go and build new cities in foreign climes. The spirit of conquest made some soldiers settle in the countries they had subdued, to secure the property of them to themselves. None of these colonies were first formed with a view to trade. Even those that were founded by Tyre, Carthage, and Marseilles, which were all commercial republics, were only meant for necessary retreats upon barbarous coasts, and for marts, where ships that were come from different ports, and tired with a long voyage, reciprocally made their exchanges.

The conquest of America gave the first idea of a new kind of settlement, the basis of which is agriculture. The governments that founded those colonies, chose that such of their subjects as they sent thither, should not have it in their power to consume any thing but what they drew from the mother-country, or to sell the produce of their lands to any other state. This double obligation has appeared to all nations to be consonant to the law of nature, independent of all conventions, and self-evident. They have not looked upon an exclusive intercourse with their own colonies as an immoderate compensation for the expences of settling and preserving them. This has constantly been the system of Europe relative to America.

France, like other nations, was always desirous that its settlements of the New World should send all their productions to the mother-country, and should receive all their provisions from thence. But, in the present state of things, this arrangement is impracticable.

The islands are in want of flour, wine, oil, linen, stuffs, household furniture, and every thing that contributes to the conveniences of life. They must receive all these things from the mother-country, which even supposing a system of indefinite liberty, would sell them exclusively, except flour, which North America might furnish at a cheaper rate.

But thefe poffeffions are likewife in want of Negroes to carry on the labours. The mother-country
hath hitherto fupplied this deficiency in a very imperfect manner only. It therefore becomes neceffary to have recourfe to the Englifh, who are alone
able to fill up the void. The only precaution which
would be proper to be taken, would be, to eftablifh,
perhaps, upon the fuccours received from thefe rivals,
a duty that would deprive them of the advantages
which particular circumftances give them over the
French merchants.

Laftly, in the prefent ftate of the colonies, cattle,
falt fifh, and foreign woods, are become abfolutely
neceffary for them. It muft be confidered as an impoffibility to convey them from Europe ; and it is
only from New England that they can obtain thefe
means which are effentially requifite for the culture
of their plantations.

Smuggling, more or lefs tolerated, hath been hitherto the only refource of the planters ; but this method,
befide being too expenfive, is difhoneft and infufficient. It is time that prohibitive laws fhould give
way to the imperious law of neceffity. Government
fhould point out the ports where foreign productions
may be received ; they fhould fettle the provifions
which fhould be allowed to be carried ; they fhould
form judicious inftitutions, which might give a degree of confiftency to this arrangement ; and advantages will be found to accrue from this new fyftem,
exempt from every inconvenience ; a trial was made
of it in 1765. If this fortunate plan was given up,
it was on account of that fatal inftability which hath
for a long time difgraced the naval operations of
France ; it will therefore be refumed, and at the
fame time the colonies will be fecure of a mart for
all their productions.

Thefe fettlements fend annually to the mother-
country, befides what they keep for their own confumption, a hundred thoufand hogfheads of molaffes ;
the value of which may be from nine to ten millions.

BOOK [from 375,000l. to 416,666l. 13s. 4d.]. From ill-
XIII. judged motives of intereft, perhaps, fhe hath deprived them and herfelf of this benefit; from an apprehenfion of injuring the fale of her own brandy. The
brandies drawn from fugar, always inferior to thofe
extracted from wine, can only be for the ufe of poor
nations, or of the lower clafs of people in the rich
ones. They will never be preferred to any but malt
fpirits, and thefe are not diftilled in France. There
will always be a demand for the French brandies,
even in the iflands, for the ufe of that clafs of men
who can afford to pay for them. The government,
therefore, can never too foon retract fo unjuft and fo
fatal an error, and ought to admit molaffes and rum
into its ports, to be confumed there, or wherever elfe
they may be wanted. Nothing would more extend
their confumption, than to authorife French navigators to carry them directly to the foreign markets.
This indulgence ought even to be extended to the
whole produce of the colonies. As an opinion that
clafhes with fo many interefts and fo many prejudices
may probably be contefted, it will be proper to eftablifh it on clear principles.

The French iflands furnifh the mother-country
with fugars, coffee, cotton, indigo, and other commodities, that are partly confumed at home, and
partly difpofed of in foreign countries, which return
in exchange either filver, or other articles that are
wanted. Thefe iflands receive from the mother-country clothes, provifions, and inftruments of hufbandry.
Such is the twofold deftination of the colonies. In
order to fulfil it, they muft be rich. In order to be
rich, they muft grow large crops, and be able to difpofe of them at the beft price: and, that this price
may be kept up, the fale of them muft be as general
as poffible. To obtain this, it muft be made entirely
free. In order to make it as free as poffible, it muft
be clogged with no formalities, no expences, no labours, no needlefs incumbrances. Thefe truths, which
may be proved from their clofe connection with each

other, muſt determine whether it be advantageous that the trade of the colonies ſhould be ſubjected to the delays and expence of a ſtaple in France.

Theſe intermediate expences muſt neceſſarily fall either upon the conſumer or upon the planter. If upon the former, he will conſume leſs, becauſe his means do not increaſe in proportion to his expences; if upon the latter, as his produce brings in leſs, he will be leſs able to make the neceſſary advances for the next crop, and of courſe his lands will yield leſs. The evident progreſs of theſe deſtructive conſequences is ſo little attended to, that every day we hear people confidently ſay, that merchandiſe, before it is conſumed, muſt paſs through many hands, and undergo many charges, both for handicraft and carriage; and that as theſe charges employ and maintain a number of perſons, they are conducive to the population and ſtrength of a ſtate. Men are ſo blinded by prejudice, as not to ſee, that if it be advantageous that commodities, before they are conſumed, ſhould undergo a twofold expence, this advantage will ſtill be increaſed, to the greater emolument of the nation, if this expence ſhould amount to four, eight, twelve, or thirty times more. Then, indeed, all nations might break up their highways, fill up their canals, prohibit the navigation of their rivers; they might even exclude animals from the labours of the field, and employ none but men in theſe works, in order to add to the expences that precede the conſumption of the produce. Yet ſuch are the abſurdities we muſt maintain, if we admit the falſe principle we are now oppoſing.

But political truths muſt be long canvaſſed before they are perceived. I ſhall advance, without fearing to be contradicted, that the tranſcendant parts of geometry have neither the depth nor the ſubtilty of this ſpecies of arithmetic. There is nothing poſſible in mathematics, which the genius of Newton, or of ſome of his ſucceſſors, might not have flattered itſelf to accompliſh. But I ſhall not ſay as much of

BOOK
XIII.
them, with refpect to the matters we are now treating of.   At firft fight we imagine that we had but
one difficulty to folve : but this difficulty foon brings
on another ; that again a third, and thus we proceed
ad infinitum ; and we perceive that we muft either
give up the work, or embrace at once the whole immenfe fyftem of focial order, without which we fhall
obtain only an incomplete and defective refult.   The
data and the calculations vary according to the nature of the place, its productions, its fpecie, its refources, its connections, its laws, its cuftoms, its tafte,
its commerce, and its manners.   Where fhall we find
the man fufficiently informed to embrace all thefe
elements ?   Where the mind fufficiently accurate to
appreciate them only at their proper value ?   All in-
formations concerning the different branches of fociety, are no more than the branches of that tree,
which conftitutes the fcience of the man engaged in
public life.   He muft be an ecclefiaftic, a military
man, a magiftrate, a financier, a merchant, and a
hufbandman.   He muft have weighed all the advantages and obftacles which he is to expect from paffion,
from rival pretenfions, and from private intereft.
With all the knowledge that may be acquired without genius, and with all the genius that may have
been beftowed upon him without knowledge, he is
inftantly led into miftakes.   It is not therefore furprifing, that fo many errors fhould have gained credit among the people, who never repeat any thing
but what they have heard ; that fo many fhould have
prevailed among fpeculators, who fuffer themfelves
to be led away by the fpirit of fyftem, and who fcruple not to conclude a general truth, from fome particular fuccefs ; that fo many miftakes fhould happen
among men of bufinefs, who are all of them more or
lefs enflaved to the routine of their predeceffors, and
more or lefs reftrained by the ruinous confequences
of attempting any thing contrary to cuftom ; in a
word, that fo many faults fhould be committed among
ftatefmen, who by their birth, or by favour, are

brought up to important places, to which they come with profound ignorance, that leaves them at the difcretion of corrupt fubalterns, who either deceive or miflead them. In every well-regulated fociety, there ought to be no matter upon which a freedom of difcuffion fhould not be allowed. The more weighty and the more difficult this matter is, the more neceffary doth this difcuffion become. Can we then have a more important, a more complicated fubject than that of government? Or could any court, that was fond of truth, do better than to encourage all men to exercife their thoughts upon it? And fhould we not be authorifed to think of that court, who fhould forbid this ftudy, that we muft either diftruft their operations, or conclude them to be bad? The true refult of a prohibitive edict upon this point, might very properly be contained in the following words? THE SOVEREIGN FORBIDS THAT IT SHOULD BE DEMON-STRATED TO HIM, THAT HIS MINISTER IS EITHER A FOOL OR A KNAVE, FOR IT IS HIS PLEASURE THAT HE SHOULD BE EITHER THE ONE OR THE OTHER, WITHOUT ANY NO-TICE BEING TAKEN OF IT. The council of Verfailles, long blinded by that darknefs in which they fuffered their nation to remain, had not yet acquired a fufficient degree of knowledge to difcover what kind of adminiftration was fitteft for the colonies; and they are ftill equally ignorant of the form of government beft calculated to make them profper.

The French colonies, fettled by profligate men, who fled from the reftraints or punifhments of the law, feemed at firft to ftand in need of nothing but a ftrict police; they were therefore committed to chiefs who had an unlimited authority. The fpirit of intrigue, natural to all courts, but more efpecially familiar to a nation where gallantry gives the women an univerfal afcendant, has at all times filled the higher pofts in America with worthlefs men, loaded with debts and vices. The miniftry, from fome fenfe of fhame, and the fear of raifing fuch men where their difgrace was known, have fent them beyond fea, to

Is the authority in the French iflands committed to thofe perfons who are moft proper to make them flourifh?

B O O K improve or retreive their fortunes, among people who
XIII.   were ignorant of their mifconduct. An ill-judged
compaſſion, and that miſtaken maxim of courtiers,
that villany is neceſſary, and villains are uſeful, made
them deliberately ſacrifice the peace of the planters,
the ſafety of the colonies, and the very intereſts of
the ſtate, to a ſet of infamous perſons only fit to be
impriſoned. Theſe rapacious and diſſolute men ſtifled
the ſeeds of all that was good and laudable, and checked the progreſs of that proſperity which was riſing
ſpontaneouſly.

Arbitrary power carries along with it ſo ſubtle a poiſon, that even thoſe men who went over with honeſt
intentions, were ſoon corrupted. If ambition, avarice, and pride, had not begun to infect them, they
would not have been proof againſt flattery, which
never fails to raiſe its meanneſs upon general ſlavery,
and to advance its own fortune by public calamities.

The few governors who eſcaped corruption, meeting with no ſupport in an arbitrary adminiſtration,
were continually committing miſtakes. Men are to
be governed by laws, and not by men. If the governors be deprived of this common rule, this ſtan-
dard of their judgments, all right, all ſafety, and all
civil liberty, will be extinct. Nothing will then be
ſeen but contradictory deciſions, tranſient and oppo-
ſite regulations and orders, which, for want of fundamental maxims, will have no connection with each
other. If the code of laws were cancelled, even in
the beſt conſtituted empire, it would ſoon appear
that juſtice alone was not ſufficient to govern it well.
The wiſeſt men would be inadequate to ſuch a taſk.
As they would not all be of the ſame mind, and as
each of them would not always be in the ſame diſpo-
ſition, the ſtate would ſoon be ſubverted. This kind
of confuſion was perpetual in the French colonies,
and the more ſo, as the governors made but a ſhort
ſtay in one place, and were recalled before they had
time to take cognizance of any thing. After they
had proceeded without a guide for three years, in a

new country, and upon unformed plans of police and laws, thefe rulers were replaced by others, who, in as fhort a fpace, had not time to form any connection with the people they were to govern, nor to ripen their projects into that juftice which, when tempered with mildnefs, can alone fecure the execution of them. This want of experience, and of precedents, fo much intimidated one of thefe abfolute magiftrates, that, out of delicacy, he would not venture to decide upon the common occurrences. Not but that he was aware of the inconveniencies of his irrefolution ; but, though an able man, he did not think himfelf qualified to be a legiflator, and therefore did not choofe to ufurp the authority of one.

Yet thefe diforders might eafily have been prevented, by fubftituting an equitable legiflation, firm, and independent of private will, to a military government, violent in itfelf, and adapted only to critical and perilous times. But this fcheme, which has often been propofed, was difapproved by the governors, jealous of abfolute power ; which, formidable in itfelf, is always odious in a fubject. Thefe flaves, efcaped from the fecret tyranny of the court, were remarkably attached to that form of juftice which prevails in Afiatic governments, by which they kept even their own dependents in awe. The reformation was rejected even by fome virtuous governors, who did not confider, that, by referving to themfelves the right of doing good, they left it in the power of their fucceffors to do ill with impunity. All exclaimed againft a plan of legiflation that tended to leffen the dependence of the people ; and the court was weak enough to give way to their infinuation and advice, from a confequence of that propenfity to arbitrary power natural to princes and their minifters. They thought they provided fufficiently for their colonies, by giving them an intendant to balance the power of the governor.

Thefe diftant fettlements, which, till then, had groaned under the yoke of one proprietor only, now

BOOK became a prey to two, equally dangerous by their
 XIII. divifion and their union. When they were at vari-
ance they divided the minds of the people, fowed
difcord among their adherents, and kindled a kind
of civil war. The rumour of their diffenfions was at
length brought to Europe, where each party had its
favourers, who were animated by pride or intereft to
fupport them in their pofts. When they agreed,
either becaufe their good or bad intentions happened
to be the fame, or becaufe the one had got an entire
afcendant over the other, the colonifts were in a worfe
condition than ever. Whatever oppreffion thefe victims laboured under, their complaints were never
heard in the mother-country, who looked upon the
harmony that fubfifted between her delegates, as the
moft certain proof of a faultlefs adminiftration.

The fate of the French colonies is not much improved. Their governors, befides having the difpofal of the regular troops, have a right to inlift the
inhabitants; to order them to what works they think
proper; to employ them as they think proper in
time of war, and even to make ufe of them for conqueft. Intrufted with abfolute authority, and defirous of exerting all the powers that can eftablifh or
extend it, they take upon themfelves the cognizance
of civil debts. The debtor is fummoned, thrown into prifon, or into a dungeon, and compelled to pay
without any other formality; and this is what they
call the fervice, or the military department. The
intendants have the fole management and difpofal of
the finances, and generally order the collecting of
them. They inquire into all caufes, both civil and
criminal; whether juftice·has not yet taken cognizance of them, or whether they have already been
brought before the fuperior tribunals; and this is
what they call adminiftration. The governors and
intendants jointly grant the lands that have not yet
been given away, and determined, a few years ago,
all differences that arofe refpecting the old poffeffions.
This arrangement placed the fortunes of all the co-

lonifts in their hands, or in thofe of their clerks and precarious, and occafioned the utmoft confufion.
dependents ; and confequently made all property
precarious, and occafioned the utmoft confufion.

In mechanics, the further the refifting powers are
removed from the centre, the more the moving force
muft be increafed ; in like manner, we are told, the
colonies cannot be fecured any otherwife than by a
harfh and abfolute government. If fo, Sir William
Petty was in the right to difapprove of thefe fort of
fettlements. It would be better that the earth fhould
remain unpeopled, or thinly inhabited, than that
fome powers fhould be extended to the misfortune of
the people. It is incumbent upon France to invalidate this fyftem of an Englifhman againft colonies,
by improving more and more in the method of governing them. That enlightened fpirit which diftinguifhes the prefent age, whatever may be the
affertion of thofe who attribute to the contempt of
certain prejudices the vices infeparable from luxury,
and to the freedom of thinking and writing, thofe
corrupt manners that arife from the paffions of the
great, and from the abufe of power : that enlightened fpirit, I fay, which ftill fupports and guides the
nation, while morality is little attended to, will reftore
the court of Verfailles to thofe judicious principles
which we have fo often pointed out to them. If any
perfon hath been offended by them, he need only be
queftioned, and it will be found that he is fome vile
adulator of the great, or fome inferior perfon attached
by his fituation or by intereft to the adminiftration of
which he is the panegyrift ; we may conclude, that
he hath not the leaft idea of the duty which a citizen
owes to his country. Shall I be confidered as the
accomplice of a villain, if I fhould not call out when
I fee him throwing a lighted torch into the houfe of
a fellow-citizen ; and fhall not my filence be deemed
culpable, when I fee the whole empire threatened
with a conflagration ? It is not the fubjeȼt who keeps
his fovereign in the dark refpecting the dangers of
his fituation, who can be called a faithful fubjeȼt ; it

B O O K is he who acquaints him of it with franknefs at the
XIII. rifk of incurring his difpleafure. But it is urged,
why do you not addrefs yourfelf to thofe who govern
the kingdom, rather than to the public? Can thofe
who govern it be approached? Would they liften to
you? Do they not think that all knowledge is cen-
tered in them? Do they judge for themfelves?
Would not the moft important fpeculations be fent
back to offices and fubmitted to the decifion of a
clerk, who would not fail to difapprove them, either
from ignorance, from vanity, or from fome other lefs
fecret and more vile motive. It is not certain that I
fhould be heard, even if my voice were affifted by a
multitude of other voices. Let me therefore be allowed to fpeak. Let me be allowed to tell my country what can raife her poffeffions in the New World,
to that degree of profperity and of happinefs of which
they are fufceptible.

Changes Few alterations will be found neceffary, with re-
which gard to what concerns public worfhip; it hath been
ought to be
made in the made fubordinate as much as poffible to civil autho-
adminiftra- rity. Its minifters are monks, whofe appearance of
tion of the
French gravity, and whofe fingular drefs, make more impref-
iflands. fion upon the ignorant and fuperftitious Negroes, than
could be expected from the moft fublime moral precepts
of religion. The allurement of novelty, fo powerful in
France, had a few years ago fuggefted a project of
fubftituting bifhops and a numerous clergy to thefe
convenient paftors. In vain had all men united in
rejecting a body of clergy, formidable by their ambition, their avarice, and their pretenfions. Had not
the turbulent and unfkilful minifter, who had formed
this deftructive plan, been difgraced, the French colonies would have been tormented by a calamity,
ftill greater than that which they have experienced
for fo long a time from legiflative authority.

Thefe great fettlements were founded by chance,
either fortunate or unfortunate, a little before the
middle of the laft century. There was at that time
no fixed idea refpecting the countries of the New

World. For this reafon the cuftoms adopted at Paris, and the criminal laws of the kingdom, were chofen for their regulation. Judicious men have fince that been well aware, that this kind of jurifprudence could not be fuitable to a country of flavery, to a climate, to morals, to cultures, and to poffeffions, which have no kind of refemblance to ours; but thefe reflections of fome individuals have had no influence upon the operations of government. Far from correcting the defects of thefe firft inftitutions, they have added to the abfurdity of the principles, embarraffments, confufion, and a multiplicity of forms, and confequently no juftice hath been rendered.

Things will remain in the fame ftate till a fyftem of legiflation peculiarly adapted to the iflands fhall render juridical decifions poffible and even eafy : but this important work cannot be done in France. Leave to the colonifts affembled the care of reprefenting their own wants, let them be fuffered to form themfelves fuch a code as they fhall think moft fuitable to their fituation. When this great labour fhall have been executed with mature deliberation, it fhould be fubmitted to the deepeft and moft rigorous difquifitions. The fanction of government ought not to be granted to it, till every doubt be removed with refpect to its utility and to its perfection. There will then be no fear of a want of good magiftrates. The laws will be fo precife, fo clear, and fo well adapted to bufinefs, that the tribunals will no longer be accufed of ignorance, of want of application, or of difhonefty.

From this new order of things an exact police would arife. This method of keeping the citizens in order is eafy in Europe. A father does the office of a cenfor in his own family; he watches over his wife, his children, and his domeftics. The proprietor, or the principal tenant, exerts the fame authority in his houfe; the manufacturer or the tradefman in his warehoufe, or in his workfhop. One neighbour is a kind of infpector over another. Affociations of men

B O O K jealous of their honour, keep a vigilant eye over the
XIII. conduct and actions of their members; no man of
bad character is received among them, and they expel thofe who have difgraced themfelves. A dangerous man is foon found out, and every door is fhut
againft him. There is a tribunal of honour, and another of fcandal. Morality exerts a kind of judicature which no one can avoid. Where is the man,
who is not more or lefs reftrained by the public opinion? All thefe fpecies of authority derogate from
the functions of government. America, full of infulated individuals, without country, and without relations, who are for ever changing place, and inceffantly renewed, and who are urged to the boldeft
enterprifes by their thirft after riches: America requires a more active, a more fteady, and a more cir-
cumftantial adminiftration.

Inftead of this, one officer, under the name of
King's Lieutenant, refiding in a port, or in a fmall
town, was for a long while folely intrufted with that
important office in the French iflands. This man
was a petty tyrant, who diftreffed the planters, who
extorted money from trade, and who preferred the
felling of a pardon to the prevention of mifdemea-
nors. For fome years paft the commanders of the
militia have in each diftrict been intrufted with the
care of maintaining public tranquillity, under the infpection of the chief of the colony. This new arrangement is not fo defective as the former, but it is
ftill too arbitrary. Let us indulge in the pleafing
expectation, that the fame code by which the fortune of each individual fhall be put under the protection of the laws, will alfo fecure his liberty.

At this period trade will be better regulated than
it hath yet been. The French merchants do not go
themfelves to the iflands, but they fend there cargoes
more or lefs valuable. Thofe which are not of much
value, are commonly diftributed by the captains of
the fhips for ready money. The moft important of
them, fuch as thofe which carry flaves, are moftly

delivered upon credit, and agents are fixed in thofe fettlements for the collecting of the money. The payments are feldom made at the appointed time; and this want of punctuality hath always occafioned difputes between the colonies and the mother-country. Adminiftration have for a long time been endeavouring to put an end to thefe eternal difcords. Might there not be a regifter kept in each jurifdiction, in which every debt fhould be noted in the fame order in which it had been contracted? When intelligent perfons fhould determine, that the debtor's eftate was mortgaged for more than half its value, every creditor fhould be allowed to put it up to fale.

This arrangement, though wife and neceffary, would certainly difpleafe the colonifts ; but they would foon be comforted, refpecting what they might at firft have confidered as an unfortunate circumftance, fhould that rigour be moderated by a better adminiftration of the finances. Government were cruel enough, even at the firft origin of the colonies, to exact a tribute from thofe unfortunate people who went to the New World to feek their fubfiftence. Stronger contributions were required of them, in proportion as their labours and the fruits of their induftry were multiplied ; and yet this enormous weight, with which their commodities, their confumptions, and their flaves were overloaded, fcarcely excites a feeble remonftrance. The complaints are generally founded upon the tyrannical manner in which the public revenue is collected, and upon the pernicious ufes to which it is applied. It is alleged, that their treafury thinks itfelf exhaufted by the expences which are required for the prefervation of the iflands. They themfelves offer to defray all thefe expences in the moft ample manner, provided that the taxes be regulated and difpofed of by the national affemblies. The troops will then be more regularly paid, and the fortifications kept in better order, under the infpection of government itfelf. Difencumbered from that multitude of officers, who, under the name of the ftaff, exhauſt them ; of thoſe legions of rapacious farmers of the revenue who oppreſs them inceſſantly and beyond meaſure, the colonies will attend to their improvement. Convenient roads will be opened on all ſides, the moraſſes will be dried up, a bed will be digged for the torrents, that of the rivers will be repaired, and bridges will be conſtructed to ſecure the communications. The young Creoles will receive upon their own ſoil a proper education, which they did not obtain even by croſſing the ſeas. In a word, there will be a body appointed, which ſhall be authoriſed to purſue, even to the foot of the throne, that deſpotic rage which ſo frequently ſeizes upon thoſe vain or corrupt men, who are choſen by intrigue or by ignorance to govern theſe diſtant regions.

Nothing appears to be more conſonant to the ends of ſound policy, than to allow theſe iſlanders the right of governing themſelves, provided it be in ſubordination to the mother-country ; nearly in the ſame manner as a boat follows all the directions of the ſhip it is faſtened to. It will, perhaps, be objected, that the people in thoſe remote iſlands being continually renewed by the fluctuation of commerce, this will naturally bring in a number of worthleſs men ; and that it will be long before we can expect to ſee thoſe manners and that ſagacity among them, which will be productive of public ſpirit, and of that dignity which is requiſite to ſupport the weight of affairs and the intereſts of a nation. This objection might have ſome foundation, if we attended merely to the character of thoſe Europeans who are driven to America by their wants or their vices ; who, by thus tranſporting themſelves, either by choice or from other motives, are ſtrangers every where ; commonly corrupted by the want of laws, ill-ſupplied by an arbitrary police ; by that depraved taſte for dominion, which reſults from the abuſe of ſlavery ; and by the dazzling luſtre of a great fortune, which makes them forget their former obſcurity. But this claſs of men ought to have no fhare in the adminiftration, which B O O K fhould be wholly committed to proprietors, moftly XIII. born in the colonies : for juftice is the natural confequence of property ; and none are more interefted in the good government of a country, than thofe who are entitled by their birth to the largeft poffeffions in it. Thefe Creoles, who have naturally a great fhare of penetration, a franknefs of character, an elevation of foul, and a certain love of juftice that arifes from thefe valuable difpofitions, would be fo fenfible of the marks of efteem and confidence which would be fhown them by the mother-country, in intrufting them with the interior management of their own, that they would grow fond of that fertile foil, take a pride in improving it, and be happy in introducing all the comforts of a civilized fociety. Inftead of that antipathy to France, which is a reflection upon her minifters, and upbraids them with their feverity, we fhould fee in the colonies that attachment which paternal kindnefs always infpires to children. Inftead of that fecret eagernefs which, in time of war, makes them readily fubmit to a foreign yoke, we fhould fee them uniting their efforts to prevent or repulfe an invafion. Fear will reftrain men under the immediate eye of a powerful and formidable mafter ; but affection alone can command them at a diftance. This is, perhaps, the only fpring that acts upon the frontier provinces of an extenfive kingdom ; while the indolent and rapacious inhabitants of the metropolis are kept in awe by authority. Attachment to the fovereign is a principle which cannot be too much encouraged or too much extended ; but if it be neither merited nor returned, he will not enjoy it long. No more joy will then appear in public feftivals, no tranfports of exultation, no involuntary acclamations will be heard at the fight of the beloved idol. Curiofity will bring a throng wherever there is a public fpectacle ; but contentment will not appear in any countenance. A fullen difcontent will arife, and fpread from one province to another ; and from the

B O O K mother-country to the colonies. When the fortunes
   XIII.
‿‿‿‿ of all men are injured or threatened at once, the
alarm and the commotion becomes general. Exertions of authority, multiplied by the imprudence of
thofe who firſt venture upon them, occaſion a general
alarm, and fall fucceſſively upon all bodies of men.
The avengers of crimes, and fupporters of the rights
of the coloniſts, are brought up even from America,
and confined like malefactors in the priſons of Europe. The weapons of government, which feemed
ufelefs againſt the enemy, are directed againſt thefe
valuable fubjects of the ſtate. Thofe people who
could not be defended in time of war, are alarmed
in time of peace. The French miniſtry have never
granted to their poſſeſſions in the New World the
fupport requiſite to preferve them from ravages or
from invaſion, and they will never fulfil this obligation, unleſs they increaſe in the Old World their
arfenals, their manufactures, and their ſlaves. Phi-
loſophers of all countries, friends of mankind, pardon
a French writer who endeavours to excite his country to raiſe a formidable navy. It is in order to fecure the tranquillity of the world that he wiſhes to
fee that fame equilibrium eſtabliſhed in all the feas,
which conſtitutes at prefent the fecurity of the continent.

Can France   If it ſhould be doubted whether France can afpire
acquire a
military   to that kind of power, we have only to confider its
navy? Doth poſition. Sufficiently extenſive to prevent it from be-
it fuit her :
to have   ing dependent upon any of the furrounding powers,
one? What   and yet fo fortunately limited as not to be weakened
meafures
muſt be ta- by its extent, this monarchy is fituated in the centre
ken for that of Europe, between the ocean and the Mediterra-
purpofe?
nean. It can tranfport all its productions from one
fea to another, without paſſing under the threatening
cannon of Gibraltar, or under the infulting flag of
the Barbary powers. Moſt of its provinces are watered by rivers, or interfected by canals, which fecure
the communication between its inland countries and
its ports, and between its ports and its inland coun-

tries. Its neighbours are, fortunately, not able to
furnifh their own fubfiftence, or carry on a trade that
is merely paffive. The temperature of its climate
procures to it the ineftimable advantage of fending
out and receiving its fhips at all feafons of the year.
The depth of its harbours enables it to give to its
fhips the form the moft proper for fwiftnefs and fecurity.

Can France be in need of objects and of materials
for exportation? Its productions, of the Old and of
the New World, are eagerly fought after by all nations : but it is more efpecially by its manufactures,
and by its fafhions, that it hath fubdued Europe, and
fome parts of the other hemifphere. The nations are
fafcinated, and will ever remain fo. The endeavours
which have every where been made to get rid of fo
ruinous a tribute, by imitations of this foreign induftry, have nowhere had the expected fuccefs. The
fertility of invention will ever be beforehand with
the quicknefs of imitation ; and the agility of a people, in whofe hands every thing affumes a youthful
appearance, and who have the art of making every
thing appear old among their neighbours, will deceive the jealoufy and the avidity of thofe who endeavour to enter into a competition with them by
imitation. How extenfive might the navigation of
an empire be, which furnifhes to the other ftates the
objects of their vanity, of their luxury, and of their
voluptuoufnefs?

Can the population of France be deemed inadequate to numerous armaments? It is well known at
prefent, that this power reckons twenty-two millions
of inhabitants. The reproach that is made them,
that they have more failors upon each of their fhips
than their rivals, is alone a fufficient proof that men
are not wanted for the naval art, but that they are
themfelves deficient in it. Yet no people have ever
received from nature more of that vivacity of genius,
fit to improve the building of fhips, or more of that
dexterity of body, fo well calculated to fpare the

BOOK time and expences of handicraft, by the simplicity
XIII. and celerity of the means employed.

Is it because France cannot furnish from itself all sorts
of naval stores, that it can be thought unable to have
a maritime force ? But are not her rivals likewise obliged to have recourse for these things to the north of
Europe, and even more than France herself ? Doth
their climate, their industry, and their colonies, furnish them with the same facility of completing their
exchanges in the Baltic ?

France hath therefore all the requisites necessary
to become a truly naval power : but doth it suit her
to entertain this ambitious idea ?

For a long time, the only method known to acquire
fortune and glory, was by numerous and well-disci-
plined armies. The East and the West Indies were
discovered ; and this unforeseen event occasioned an
astonishing revolution in the minds of all men. Perhaps a reasonable ambition would have been contented with obtaining, by the mode of exchange, the
riches and the productions of these two extensive parts
of the globe. The thirst of dominion, too common
among nations, occasioned the ruinous and destructive system of conquests to be generally preferred.
These immense regions were mostly subdued. Matters were carried still further. The people who inhabited these new climates were either too weak or
too indolent to serve as the instruments of the cupidity of an unjust invader. In several places, they
were all either exterminated, or expelled from the
countries that had given them birth, and Europeans,
or African slaves, were substituted to them, who multiplied the commodities, the germina of which they
found there, and who established other cultures, which
a new, fertile, and varied soil could easily supply.

It was necessary to give some stability to these settlements. The restlessness of the nations which had
divided these virgin regions, and the jealousy of those
which had not enjoyed that advantage, were equally
to be apprehended. A naval force alone could give

confiftence to the rifing colonies, and even to thofe
which were in the greateft forwardnefs. To preferve
them from invafion, fleets were conftructed and fitted
out. At this remarkable period, the fyftem of politics was entirely altered. The earth was in fome meafure fubjected to the fea, and the great political ftrokes
were ftricken on the ocean.

France, lefs accuftomed to ferve as a guide, than to
furpafs its mafters, beheld without emulation the rife
of a new fpecies of power. The navy did not even
form any part of the too extenfive projects of the ambitious Richelieu. It was referved to the monarch for
whofe grandeur he had paved the way, to make his
flag refpected in the two hemifpheres. But this glory
was of fmall duration. Lewis XIV. by his enterprifes,
irritated the whole continent, and, in order to refift
the leagues which were formed there againft him, was
obliged to maintain innumerable armies. His kingdom foon became nothing more than a camp; and
his frontiers were only a ftring of fortified places. The
fprings of the ftate were always kept in too high a degree of tenfion under this brilliant reign. One crifis
was fucceeded by another. At length the finances
were in diforder; and in the impoffibility of defraying
all the expences, the facrifice of the naval forces was
thought, perhaps improperly, to be indifpenfable.

Since the end of a century, in which the nation fuftained its difgraces, by the remembrance at leaft of its
fucceffes, and ftill kept Europe in awe by forty years
of glory, cherifhed a government by which it had been
honoured, and bade defiance to rivals whom it had
humbled: fince that period, France hath loft much of
its pride, notwithftanding the acquifitions with which
its territory hath been extended. A long peace would
not have enervated her, if her forces, too long lavifhed
in war, had been turned to the navy: but her naval
powers have acquired no confiftence. The avarice of
one minifter, the prodigality of another; the indolence
of feveral; falfe notions, trifling interefts, the intrigues
of the court, by which government is guided; a feries

B O O K of vices and of faults; a number of obſcure and deſpi-
XIII   cable cauſes: all theſe circumſtances have prevented
the nation from becoming as powerful upon ſea as it
had been on the continent; at leaſt from acquiring a
balance, if not a preponderance, of power. Even the
loſſes which France experienced in all parts of the
globe, during the hoſtilities begun in 1756; the hu-
miliations which ſhe was obliged to ſubmit to at the
peace of 1763, did not reſtore a ſpirit of wiſdom to
the council that governed the nation, and did not turn
their projects and their efforts towards the ſyſtem of
a formidable navy.

But what meaſures ſhould France purſue, in order
to create and maintain a naval force?

The firſt ſtep to be taken, without which the others
would become either uſeleſs or fatal, muſt be, to encourage the mercantile branch of the navy. It is that
alone which can form men, inured to the hardſhips of
climates, to the fatigues of labour, and to the dangers
of ſtorms. This truth being once eſtabliſhed, thoſe
innumerable ſhackles which have hitherto excluſively
enſured the exportation of the commodities of the
kingdom to foreign nations, and which have even too
often given up to them the coaſting trade, will be taken off. We will not affirm, that an act of navigation,
ſimilar to that which hath occaſioned the glory of
England, would be ſuitable to France: but that crown
ought at leaſt to eſtabliſh ſuch regulations as might
enable its ſubjects to ſhare thoſe benefits which the
Swedes, the Danes, and the Dutch, come and take
from them even in their own harbours.

This new order of things will never be eſtabliſhed,
till the naval trade ſhall emerge from that humiliating
ſtate into which it hath hitherto unfortunately been
plunged. The laws forbid any navigator from commanding a trading veſſel, till he ſhall have made three
voyages upon a king's ſhip: after this trial, he may
ſtill be compelled to remain in the king's ſervice during a time of war. The abject ſtate in which he is
kept in that ſervice muſt neceſſarily excite an averſion

for the fea in all men who have received any education, who enjoy fome kind of fortunes, or who have
fome degree of fpirit. Either thefe fhameful fetters
muft be broken, or the French muft give up the hopes
of feeing the ocean covered with their numerous and
rich armaments.

The ftate of oppreffion in which the failors are kept,
is another obftacle to the multiplication of expeditions.
Thefe men, who fo effentially contribute to the opulence and to the ftrength of the kingdom, are infcrib-
ed in regifters, and are inftantly obliged to embark on
board of men of war, upon receiving orders from the
miniftry, for whatever time they fhall choofe, and at
whatever ftipend it may be thought proper to give
them ; nor are thefe hard terms in the leaft alleviated
by any confideration either of talents or age. At the
time even when they are not employed in the public
fervice, they are not allowed to difpofe of their induftry and of their leifure, without the permiffion of an
agent of government. This flavery averts from this
neceffary profeffion moft of thofe whofe inclination
would otherwife have led them to it, if it were not
deftructive of all kind of liberty. If thefe inftitutions
were fuppreffed, or at leaft the feverity of them were
diminifhed, the harbours and the coafts of France
would then be filled with failors.

But who fhall lead them on to action, and to the
defence of their country? Seignelay decided that it
fhould be the nobility, and his opinion hath been
adopted ever fince. Hath nature then exclufively
granted to a nobleman a natural conftitution, which
cannot be affected by climate, by hunger, and by fatigue? Hath fhe exclufively granted to him the boldnefs that bids defiance to danger, and the coolnefs that
furmounts it? Hath fhe given to him exclufively that
genius which determines and enfures victory? It is
faid, that opinion and prejudice infpire men of this
rank with an ardour for glory, and an indifference for
wealth, which are not to be found among other claffes
of men! What! is it in the midft of a corrupt court.

BOOK XIII. is it among the rubbish of a ruined castle, that principles of elevation and of disinterestedness are to be pre-
ferably sought for? The son of a navigator, whose fortunate labours have been crowned with wealth, and
who can have no other ambition than that of rendering his name illustrious, is no less powerfully excited
to memorable actions and to great sacrifices, than that
young nobleman who is constantly sheltering himself
under the laurels of his ancestors. What period hath
ever shown, that a title which we are in possession of
is a more powerful stimulus than one to which we a-
spire? What was the first person who deserved nobility before he had obtained it? If some of his illustrious descendants had been in his place, his children
and his posterity would have remained in obscurity.
True nobility was in the blood and in the destiny of
man, before it existed upon parchment. To acquire
it, it is necessary to have good fortune and merit:
good fortune, which shall present occasions to us, and
merit, by which we may improve them. All who
have been ennobled in past ages, and all who shall be
ennobled in future, have proved, and will hereafter
prove, that this great road is open to a few men only;
and that it is as easy to find a great mind under a plain
dress, as a mean spirit under the decoration of a rib-
band. Courage, virtue, and genius, belong to all
ranks. But in order to ascertain this matter, let the
career be laid open indiscriminately to all persons who
shall have received a decent education. Let them be
embarked on board men of war; let them make a few
voyages under experienced commanders; let them be
subjected to all the labours, and to all the self-denials,
which this difficult profession requires. After these
trials, let those who have shown the greatest degree of
spirit, of skill, of courage, and of emulation, be admitted into the royal navy.

The excellence of an art, which enables us sometimes to subdue the elements; the advantages of a
profession, in which the opportunities of signalizing
one's self are more frequent, and in which glory is the

personal acquisition of every man, as soon as he hath B O O K
XIII.
obtained the command of the smallest vessel; all these
reasons will induce them to study, to reflect, and especially to be always manœuvring; for in this profession, the most learned theory must be constantly accompanied with practice. Either in action, or in simple navigation, resolutions must be so quick, that they
shall appear rather as the result of feeling than of reflection. The sea officer is more particularly in need
of those decisive thoughts, of those sudden illumina-
tions, as they have been so well described by a sublime orator, in his eulogium of a great captain : and
these strokes of instinct and talents, to speak in a less
elevated style, must be sooner acquired by practice
than by theory.

This idea of continual practice the French navy are
utterly strangers to. Loose armaments, voyages of a
day, in which the time of returning into port is known
at the time of going out of it : coasts which are visit-
ed with as little attention as those countries through
which a man travels post : colonies, of which we know
as little when we leave them as we did at our arrival :
expeditions, in which a speedy return is the only prevailing idea, and where the mind is constantly absorbed in attention to former habits : ships, which are considered as prisons, and which are quitted with trans-
port, without being acquainted either with their defects or perfections. O Frenchmen ! O my fellow-
citizens ! this is exactly a true picture ! such hath
been hitherto the deplorable employment of the naval
forces of our country.

To these successive armaments of a few solitary frigates, the transient expedition of which is of no real
utility, let us substitute permanent squadrons, that
shall remain three years, or more, in all the latitudes
of the Old and of the New World, where we have
any settlements, or where we carry on an extensive
trade. Let these instructive cruises constantly employ
one half of our inferior vessels, and some ships of the
line. Then the officers who remain in the profession

merely on account of the facility of fulfilling the duties of it, will retire ; and thofe who perfevere in this
perilous and honourable employment will then acquire
information, experience, and a fondnefs for that element, upon which they expect to obtain glory and fortune. Subalterns then growing emulous to pleafe fu-
periors deftined to command them for a length of
time, will learn fubordination. The crews, trained
up with care to the fervice, and inftructed in the manœuvres by the captains who are to reap the fruits of
all their trouble, will then fight with more refolution
and with better fkill. Europe hath appeared aftonifhed that the French, who were worthy rivals of the Englifh at the beginning of the laft wars, had loft in time
that honourable equality. Several caufes have occafioned this revolution : the principal of them, and
which hath not been attended to, is, that the French
have had frefh failors every campaign, and that their
rivals have always kept the fame till the termination
of hoftilities.

The eftablifhment of ftationary fquadrons fhould be
followed by other innovations of no lefs importance.
The corps of the navy, at prefent too numerous, and
burdened with ufelefs and idle members, ought to be
proportioned to the number of fhips and of armaments.
Thofe fatal departments, which excite jealoufy without emulation, and which, by hereditary hatred, often
occafion the mifcarriage of the beft contrived projects,
muft be abolifhed. Rank, which every where, and in
all ages, hath ftifled genius and talents, will ceafe to
prefide over the promotions and the rewards. Among
the too great number of ranks it is necefsary to pafs
through, feveral muft be fuppreffed, in order that it
may be poffible for a man to acquire a command before the time prefcribed by nature for quitting it. If
it be thought necefsary to preferve the different claffes
of officers, the direction of them will be altered and
better regulated. The admirals, whofe ftrength, courage, and activity, fhall be diminifhed, either by age,
by labour, or by the wounds they may have received,

muft form a tribunal, which fhall direct the choice, the B O O K preſervation, and the employment of the naval ſtores. XIII. It muſt be the buſineſs of this tribunal to regulate admiſſion into the navy, to determine the promotions, to beſtow the command, to ſettle the cruiſes, and direct as much as poſſible all the operations. Such will hereafter be the council of a miniſter, who, ignorant of his functions, ſituated at the diſtance of a hundred leagues from the ſea, devoted, either from inclination or neceſſity, to the intrigues of a tempeſtuous court, hath been conſtantly, to the preſent time, the ſport of a few obſcure, ignorant, and intereſted adventurers.

In proportion as theſe plans of reformation which we have been tracing ſhall be carried into execution, the ſhips, which were growing rotten in a ſtate of inaction, will be repaired, and others will be conſtructed. France will ſoon acquire numerous fleets. But where ſhall the reſources be found to put them in action?

Let thoſe two magnificent or uſeleſs edifices, the maintaining of which becomes ruinous, be demoliſhed: let there be a ſtop put to the diſhoneſty which hath but too commonly prevailed in the purchaſe of naval ſtores, and to the negligence with which they have been hitherto taken care of: let thoſe uſeleſs hands, which protection hath multiplied in our arſenals, be diſmiſſed: let the meaſures of adminiſtration be rendered more ſimple, by introducing juſtice and punctuality in our payments: let the crews of the ſhips, which all diſintereſted perſons acknowledge to be too numerous, be diminiſhed: let all thoſe officers, who are not employed at ſea in the ſervice of the ſtate, be reduced to half pay: let every ſpecies of luxury, delicacy, and voluptuouſneſs, which enervates our defenders and ruins our ſquadrons, be aboliſhed: let the refitting and repairing of our ſhips become leſs frequently neceſſary. After all theſe alterations, the funds at preſent ſet apart for the navy will be found ſufficient to put this eſſential branch of our power upon a reſpectable footing. There is even a very ſimple

method of raifing it ftill higher, without any additional expence, which I fhall now point out.

France hath formed colonies in the New World,
from which it annually receives to the amount of
130,000,000 of livres [5,416,666l. 13s. 4d.] in commodities. The lofs of fo confiderable a produce would
leave an immenfe vacancy in its fpecie, in its population, in its induftry, and in its public revenue. The
importance of preferving thefe rich fettlements hath
been underftood, and in order to accomplifh it, recourfe hath been had to battalions and fortreffes.
Experience hath proved the infufficiency of thefe
means. The defence of thefe colonies belongs, and
muft exclufively belong, to the navy. The iflands
muft therefore be put under its protection, and the
expences incurred for the infufficient protection of
them muft be turned into its treafury: then will the
ordinary funds of the navy of France be found fufficient for the purpofe of carrying on its operations
with dignity and advantage.

Such are the expectations of Europe. She will not
think her liberty fecured, till a flag fhall be feen difplayed upon the ocean that fhall not tremble before that of Great Britain. The wifhes of the nations
are now united in favour of that power which may be
able to defend them againft the pretenfions of one
fingle people to the univerfal monarchy of the feas;
and at this prefent period there is none but France
that can free them from this anxiety. The fyftem
of equilibrium requires, therefore, that the court of
Verfailles fhould increafe their navy, more efpecially
as they cannot do it without diminifhing their land
forces. Their influence being then divided between
the two elements, will no longer be formidable on either except to thofe who fhould be defirous of difturb-
ing the harmony.

Before I die, may this great revolution, already begun, be completed; together with other reformations
which I have pointed out. Then fhall I have obtained the true reward of my vigils. Then fhall I ex-

claim : It is not in vain that I have obferved, reflected, B O O K
and laboured. Then fhall I addrefs myfelf to Hea-   XIII.
ven, and fay : " Difpofe of me at prefent according to
" thy will, for mine eyes have feen the fplendour of
" my country, and the liberty of the feas reftored un-
" to all nations !"

END OF THE FOURTH VOLUME.